D0319807

7/2426572

THE TOP 500 SUMMITS

A LIFETIME OF HILLWALKING

Barry K. Smith

Mountain Safety

This book is not intended to be a guidebook and should not be used as one. The routes are my recollections and cannot be assumed to be accurate. A map, a compass and appropriate clothing should always be carried. Good navigation skills, equipment, and clothing all help to reduce the chances of an accident. Plenty of time should be allowed for any walk and a second person should be aware of the intended route and expected time of return.

Mobile phones can help but they do not work all over the mountains. They also rely on batteries and are easily damaged. Consequently, they cannot be relied upon.

There are many potential hazards in the mountains; such as, winter conditions, changes in weather, rivers in spate, poor underfoot conditions and little or no visibility. These need to be borne in mind on all walks and the ability of the walkers matched to the conditions.

ISBN 9780995673502

Every reasonable effort has been made by the author to trace copyright holders of material in this book. Any errors or omissions should be notified in writing to the author, who will endeavour to rectify the situation for any future reprints.

Designed and typeset by BakerTaylor Associates *(www.bakertaylor.co.uk)*.

Published by Where2walk.

Printed and bound in Great Britain by CPI Group (UK) Ltd, Croydon CR0 4YY.

Correspondence address:
Applecross
Church Street
Long Preston
Near Skipton
North Yorkshire BD23 4NJ

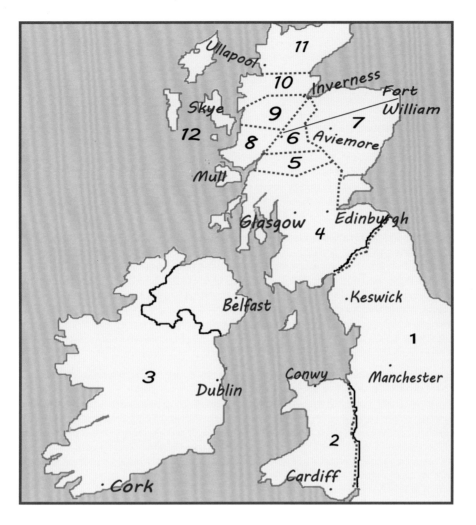

FOREWORD 4
INTRODUCTION 6
   1 ENGLAND 11
   2 WALES 33
   3 IRELAND 53
   4 SOUTH SCOTLAND 79
   5 RANNOCH TO GLENCOE 109
   6 CENTRAL HIGHLANDS 135
   7 EAST HIGHLANDS 165
   8 FAR WEST HIGHLANDS 195
   9 NORTH WEST GLENS 229
  10 NORTH HIGHLANDS 253
  11 FAR NORTH SCOTLAND 285
  12 SCOTTISH ISLANDS 303
TOP 500 LISTING 320
MUNROS NOT QUALIFYING 338
INDEX OF WALKING COMPANIONS 341
BIBLIOGRAPHY 342

FOREWORD

I HAVE KNOWN BARRY since primary school days, a period of more than 50 years, and we have shared many sporting and leisure-time interests, completed at varying degrees of skill and dedication. Barry received an early grounding in hillwalking as his father Tom was inspired by the opportunities offered by the Lakeland fells. For much of his childhood there were regular family trips to the Lakes which became even more frequent when the family bought a cottage in the north Lakeland village of Threlkeld.

His father was a stern task-master on the fells and Barry learnt to be relentless in the climb to the top of the chosen hill. He recounts one incident, at the age of seven, on an ascent up Great Gable, when the family paused for a break on top of a steep slope to take in the view and rest. Barry proceeded to unburden himself of his rucksack but didn't pay sufficient attention to securing it properly. Gravity intervened and took it a couple of hundred feet down the hillside. Tom was not one to condone incompetence and one small boy was despatched down the steep hillside to retrieve his sack. The subsequent 200 foot retracing of his footsteps left an indelible impression on Barry on the need for self-reliance.

Barry has displayed reasonable competence at ball sports, namely tennis, squash and golf, but while at boarding school at Sedbergh he found his own niche of cross-country running. His early fell walking in the Lakes was good preparation for his exploits running up the Howgill Fells. His high level of concentration and determination to succeed, which have served him well in many facets of his life, were honed on the fells of Cumbria and West Yorkshire. He has been driven by goals and targets, and what he may have lacked in natural flair, has always been compensated by sheer force of will. He demonstrated this tenacity by climbing the 500 summits that make up the listing in this book, a huge undertaking.

Those who have walked with Barry would not forgive me if I didn't refer to his rather unique walking style, which cannot be described as elegant. He does not initially strike you as someone who will cover the ground rapidly, rather he strikes you as someone who looks slightly weary, having just emerged from a long sleep. He has a laboured and loping gait, which is disarmingly effective, particularly on a long ascent, and he has the resolve and technique to cover long distances surprisingly quickly.

In the early 1970s foreign travel was out of reach so holidays were often taken in Scotland. Our progress around Scotland was hampered by the lack of a motor car and we relied upon a mixture of hitching lifts and various forms of public transport including ferries between the Scottish Islands. My memories of trips to Skye and the Western Highlands were that they were beset by inclement weather. Our first ascent into the Cuillins was also hampered by poor map reading. Although we did manage to scramble across heather and up scree slopes and make the ridge, we had most certainly lost the path and were nowhere near the top of Sgurr nan Gillean, which was our original aim.

In 1976 we managed to find our way to the tops of both Banachdich and Gillean. Indeed it was on the trip up Gillean that I realised I was always going to struggle with vertigo, as I found it impossible to walk normally up the final ascent of that airy peak and I shuffled my way on all fours to a point close to the peak. Barry had no such issues and would later take the Inaccessible Pinnacle and the Aonach Eagach ridge in his stride without a thought of falling off.

FOREWORD continued

Beinn Dearg and Beinn Enaiglair from Ullapool.

Ullapool is one of Barry's favourite places in Scotland, known for its stunning scenery, massive sea lochs and warm hospitality. The highlight of our first trip in 1975 was the ascent of Beinn Dearg via the Corbett of Beinn Enaiglair. The walk was undertaken in benign weather with a gentle breeze and a few whispy clouds near the top. We were rewarded at the top with stunning views across the whole of the Highlands with the spectre of the Atlantic and the Western Isles to the west, and Ben Wyvis and the Firth of Dornoch and ultimately the North Sea to the east.

Beinn Dearg certainly fired my imagination and I accompanied Barry on a trip to the Cullins on Skye the following year. Two years later we returned to Ullapool for a windy ascent of An Teallach, where the strength of the wind forced us into the lee of the ridge to avoid being blown away. We also managed an ascent of the small but beautifully formed Stac Pollaidh, and found ourselves ejected from the lower slopes of Ben Stack by a team of stalkers.

After these early experiences in Scotland and having read Hamish Brown's book, *A Mountain Walk*, Barry developed a passion to complete the Munros. In hindsight I have mused on the motivation behind this desire. Was it an antidote to the daily grind of practising as an accountant or an excuse for the occasional peaceful weekend away from home? Did he wish to challenge his endurance capacity against the elements and complete a project that comparatively few had undertaken, or was it simply because the mountains were there? During these years he maintained a map of Scotland in a spare bedroom, which was festooned with coloured pins representing those Munros he had climbed and those still to be scaled.

This book is an excellent means of dipping in and out of all the major hillwalking opportunities in Britain and Ireland. It gives an insight into many lesser climbed peaks. In my view it is an excellent book for anyone interested in hillwalking. I hope Barry's enthusiasm for the hills and mountains will encourage more people to explore the more remote parts of these wonderful islands.

Barry has also included a number of interesting and at times amusing stories written by those who accompanied him on his many trips to the mountains. I hope you find this book both an informative and stimulating read and it takes you to some places you had never previously considered visiting.

DONALD BAILEY

INTRODUCTION

Top 500 Summits

I love the mountains – the places, the challenge of reaching the summit and the satisfaction of a great day out. For a long time I thought that a comprehensive list of the highest mountains of Britain and Ireland would provide a great challenge. The **Top 500 Summits** seeks to be that list. It details the highest 500 mountains in the British Isles with a drop of at least 500 feet on all sides.

The highest mountain on the list is Ben Nevis in Scotland (4,411ft) and the lowest is Knockanaffrin in Ireland (2,477ft). The list includes most of the Munros (some have a drop of less than 500ft between them), all the Corbetts and the highest mountains in England, Wales and Ireland with a drop of 500ft. A full list of the Top 500 Summits is included at the back of the book.

It has taken me over 50 years, a lifetime, to climb them all but they could be completed considerably quicker. 20 of the mountains are in England, 21 in Wales, 29 in Ireland and 430 in Scotland. The most popular mountains include Ben Nevis, Snowdon and Scafell Pike, the highest mountains in Scotland, Wales and England, but there are many other household names on the list, for example Helvellyn, Ben Lomond and Pen y Fan.

Early Years

I was born in Newcastle in 1955, and have two younger brothers; Alistair born in 1958 and Jonathan in 1964. From an early age we were taken by our parents to the Lake District for holidays and introduced to walking the fells. My first recollection of the hills was being dragged up Latrigg by my mother at the age of three. Skiddaw Low Man and Dale Head followed at the age of four and eventually I reached the summit of Scafell Pike at the age of seven.

From the age of 13 I went to school at Sedbergh and started cross-country running. We used to roam the local fells in training. At university I was fortunate to meet up with a group of rock climbers and they helped me up a number of rock-climbing routes in England, Scotland and Wales, although I struggled to climb anything beyond 'severe'.

Climbing the Top 500 Summits

After leaving university in 1977, I did less walking and climbing but always had a yearning to climb the mountains of Scotland. In 1985 I decided to climb the Munros. For 30 years I have visited Scotland on a regular basis and could probably drive the M74 or the routes between Newcastle and Edinburgh blindfold. In 2004 I completed the Munros, finishing on the Saddle in the midst of a storm, a mere 33 years after climbing my first Munros, Stuc a' Chroin and Ben Vorlich whilst on a school camp.

After finishing the Munros I climbed the Corbetts and the mountains of Wales and Ireland. On 18 June 2016, I climbed my final Top 500 Summit, Monamenach, near Glenshee, with my two sons, Alex and James.

This book is my personal journey over the 500 summits that comprise **The Top 500 Summits in Britain and Ireland**. I believe this is an excellent challenge for anyone who loves the mountains, a challenge that can be put aside for many years and returned to as time allows. Anyone completing the challenge will also complete the Munros (with only a few days of additional walking) and the Corbetts.

INTRODUCTION continued

Mountain Companions

Three people became my regular walking companions. They were my brothers, Alistair and Jonathan and Jonathan's friend, Jonathan Pyman, described as JP in the book. We set ourselves the challenge of completing the Munros and kept score as to how many summits we had climbed. Eventually we all completed the Munros. Jonathan and JP completed them in 2003 on Sgor na h-Ulaidh and myself in 2004 on the Saddle. Finally Alistair completed them on Ben More on Mull on 28 May 2016. I believe Alistair's completion meant that we became the first **three siblings** to climb all the Munros.

Alistair came on many of the earliest visits to Scotland. In 1976 we visited Fort William and the Isle of Skye, climbing a few Munros in rather random fashion. In those days we did not know how many Munros there were or where they were all situated. Alistair missed many Munro trips in the late 1980s and early 1990s. He has also suffered from having to have a number of operations on his knees, which has slowed his progress and meant he had to use a knee brace for descending. All this made his completion of the Munros in 2016 a great achievement.

Jonathan is a very enthusiastic walker with a successful company called *Where2Walk*. The website details more than 500 walks in Yorkshire and the Lake District. He is a qualified mountain guide and arranges walking holidays for visitors to Yorkshire and the Lake District. He was the first of us to complete the Munros, going at about twice my pace to catch and overtake me on number of Munros completed. He finished in 2003, going on to complete the Munro Tops.

Jonathan Pyman (JP) is Jonathan's oldest friend. He completed the Munros in 2003 at the same time as Jonathan, having done a number of long walks across Scotland. When he was young and fit he completed the round of Mullardoch, normally a three day circuit in summer, in two days in November and has been 'dining out' on the experience ever since! He has written a number of personal views that describe some of his longer walks across Scotland. Living in Kent for the last 20 years has curtailed the number of trips he has made to the mountains.

Wisdom of the Hills

I have walked with many other friends and relatives, some of whom feature in the book. One of them asked what I had learnt in 50 years of hillwalking so here is a list:

» Children who say 'I am going to stay here until I die' halfway up a mountain will be left behind;

» Chocolate bars are bad for dogs so there is no need to part with any of them;

» Reaching the summit is only half the battle;

» Dreaming of long, sunny days in the Western Highlands of Scotland is a triumph of hope over experience;

» Most mountains have false tops, particularly when it is cold and wet;

» Two bars of chocolate are inadequate for two days on the mountains and a night in a bothy;

» Mountain streams can make you ill but sometimes you have to risk it;

» Planning walks after a few pints in the pub is unwise.

I also learnt how to use a compass, read a map and to be properly equipped when climbing. But most of all I learnt about the remote parts of Britain and Ireland – the valleys, ridges, mountains and coasts that stretch through large parts of the British Isles.

INTRODUCTION continued

The Top 500 Challenge

We climb Munros, Corbetts, Grahams, Wainwrights and mountains in many other lists but there is no combined listing of the highest mountains in Britain and Ireland. Many years ago I started to think about what a list would look like and thought the list should include all mountains over 2,500ft with a 500ft drop between them.

Why a 500 foot drop?

There seems to be a general acceptance in Britain and Ireland that, if the drop between any two mountains is 500ft or more, then both summits should be classified as separate mountains. There is no list that uses a bigger drop to classify a separate mountain. The Corbett list uses the 500ft criterion and the Marilyn list an approximate metric equivalent of 150 metres. Any mountain over 3,000ft not previously classified as a Munro but with a drop of 500ft or more was promoted to Munro status in 1997.

Why all mountains over 2,500 feet?

It seemed important to include all the mountains over 2,500ft with a 500ft drop, not only so that the full list of Scottish Corbetts was included, but also because there appears to be an acceptance in the British Isles that mountains over 2,500ft have a special status. I do not think it would give a fair representation of the mountains of England, Scotland, Wales and Ireland to include only those mountains over 3,000ft, and using any height between 2,500ft and 3,000ft was surely too arbitrary. Thus all mountains over 2,500ft with a 500ft drop between them had to be included.

Creating the List

In order to create the list I started with a full list of the Scottish Munros and Corbetts, and the mountains over 2,500ft in England, Wales and Ireland. I then deleted those mountains which did not have a 500ft drop on all sides. Mullach an Rathain (Liathach), in the North Highlands of Scotland, gave rise to some difficulty as no amount of research showed whether the drop was over or under 500ft. Eventually we climbed it with an altimeter and concluded that the drop was over 500ft.

500 Summits

Having completed the research, I found that 488 mountains satisfied the 500ft drop and 2,500ft height criteria. Therefore it was easy to add the next 12 summits just below 2,500ft to create the **Top 500 Summits of Britain and Ireland**. The addition of the extra 12 summits has meant a number of gems are included, such as Beinn Shiantaidh, the second highest Pap of Jura, and Y Llethr in the Rhinogs. In addition, there was a pleasing symmetry in creating a list of 500 summits with a 500ft drop criterion.

For me the attraction of the list is that it includes virtually all the great mountains of Britain and Ireland. Brandon Mountain in Ireland, Tryfan in Wales, Helvellyn in England and the Cobbler in Scotland are all included in one list. In reality most of these are mountains that I have been climbing all my life. However, the challenge of completing this list has taken me to places I might never have visited. It has been a delight to climb the mountains near Westport in Ireland, Mweelrea and the Sheeffry Hills, and the Welsh sub-3,000ft mountains, including the Arans and the Rhinogs. Certainly it is unlikely that I would have climbed Mickle Fell in England without the list to drive me on!

INTRODUCTION continued

Layout of the Book

I have divided the 500 mountains into 200 'walks' with the listing of the 500 mountains at the back of the book. In some cases I have grouped mountains together as a walk for convenience but these walks are best divided into two or more half day walks. Four of the walks took two days and therefore included an overnight stop in a bothy or a tent. The two day walks are Blair Atholl to the Linn of Dee over the Grampians, the round of Loch Mullardoch, the Ben Alder six, and Kinlochewe to Dundonnell across the Fisherfield Forest. I have given 70 of the walks two pages. These were my favourite walks but of course this is somewhat weather dependent as a walk always looks better on a sunny day.

Each walk contains the following information:

1. **A list of the summits** to be climbed and a comment on any other summits that could be included in the walk (e.g. Munros that do not qualify for the Top 500 list because there is not a 500ft drop).

2. **A Personal View** which gives my thoughts or the thoughts of my brothers or friends on the mountains and what it was like climbing them. This section has caused the greatest number of debates and hopefully includes some interesting anecdotes.

3. **My Route** is a summary of the route or routes by which I climbed the mountains. These routes are not intended, nor should they be used, as any form of guide. For most of the walks I have included a map to support the narrative under my route. My rough timings for the walks are included but these vary depending on weather, fitness, number of stops and the like. The timings are for the full walk including the descent.

4. **Key Details** show the approximate distance for the walk including the return journey and height climbed. A grid reference is included to show the start point.

5. I have also commented on **Points of Interest** where I visited notable sites, or the mountains had unusual features. Finally, **Places to stay, drink or eat** are included for some of the walks but these are purely based on our experiences.

One of the prime objectives for the book has been to provide a broad and interesting set of photographs. The majority of the photographs are my own taken over the last 50 years but I am grateful to Alistair for a number of Munro photographs and Jonathan who provided most of the English photographs. Friends have also provided some excellent photographs; particular thanks go to Heather Thomas-Smith, Chris Wood and Cornell Griffith. Where the photographs were not taken by me or one of my brothers I have named the photographer.

I have divided the book into 12 sections. There is one section each for England, Wales and Ireland and nine sections for Scotland. This reflects the fact that 430 out of the 500 summits are in Scotland and its islands.

At the end of the book there is a complete listing of the Top 500 Summits by height. There is also a listing of the Munros that are not included in the Top 500 because the drop between them and another Munro is under 500ft.

INTRODUCTION continued

Great Days on the Mountains

There have been many great days in the mountains which stand out in my memory. I have listed ten of the best below:

1. Our 13 hour crossing of the Fisherfield Forest in 1992 from the Carnmore bothy to Dundonnell. Most of all I remember the brew we had in a snow shower at the col between Beinn Tarsuinn and Mullach Coire Mhic Fhearchair. The tea was grey and luke-warm.

2. My first ascent of Ben Nevis in 1974 by an unknown route on the north face. The purple-looking sandwiches we ate at the summit are etched in my memory and I still blame them for making me sick that evening.

3. The round of Coire Lagan with a guide to take us up the Inaccessible Pinnacle in 1989. A truly idyllic trip along the Cuillin ridge in perfect weather. Abseiling off the Inaccessible Pinnacle we were watched by a crowd of 20 people sunbathing on the summit of Sgurr Dearg.

4. A fabulous day of warm sunshine on the Paps of Jura in 2008. After the walk we stood outside the pub at Craighouse enjoying a drink next to the sea.

5. My earliest recollections of Scafell Pike and Scafell in 1963. When climbing Lord's Rake at the age of seven, I can recall wondering whether all mountains were as difficult as this.

6. The walk from the Scafell Inn at the head of Wastwater to Honister Pass during the second day of our three-day Bob Graham round. Setting off at 6 a.m. on a beautiful June morning and climbing straight up the side of Yewbarrow was unforgettable.

7. My first traverse of the Snowdon Horseshoe in mist in 1976. We finished on the fine ridge of Y Lliwedd as the sun came out. Finally we saw the sharp ridge of Crib Goch.

8. A beautiful January day on Cadair Idris in 2013. It was warm enough to be looking out to sea wearing just a shirt and shorts on the summit, a glorious moment. I felt privileged to be there on a weekday in January, having spent the previous 35 years working on weekdays in January!

9. Climbing the Brandon Mountain in 1983 while staying at Dingle. On this occasion the mystique of Brandon Mountain was enhanced by mist which was virtually down to the valley floor.

10. A perfect summer day on the Mourne Mountains in 2013, two months after failing to climb Slieve Donard in a blizzard with snow up to the top of the wall. In particular I recall the great atmosphere on the summit of Slieve Donard, with many different nationalities gathered together.

Thank You

I would like to thank everyone who helped with the preparation of this book, including those who sent me notes of their experiences and provided photographs. This book would not have been possible without your help.

Most of all, I would like to thank all those who have walked with me or joined me on trips to the mountains over the last 50 years. I could not have done it without you.

Stockley bridge on the way to Scafell Pike.

ENGLAND

There are 20 Top 500 Summits in England. 17 are in the Lake District including the highest peak in England which is Scafell Pike (3,210ft). The mountains have been divided into 13 walks as follows:

WALKS 1 TO 13

	Walk	Feet	Pg.
1	Grasmoor	2,795	13
	Grisedale Pike	2,595	
2	Skiddaw	3,054	14
3	Blencathra	2,847	16
4	High Stile	2,648	18
5	High Raise	2,500	19
6	High Street	2,718	20
7	Red Screes	2,547	21
	Stony Cove Pike	2,502	
8	Helvellyn	3,116	22
	Fairfield	2,863	
	St Sunday Crag	2,760	
9	Great Gable	2,949	24
	Pillar	2,927	
	Kirk Fell	2,631	
10	Scafell Pike	3,210	26
11	Coniston Old Man	2,635	29
12	The Cheviot	2,674	30
13	Cross Fell	2,930	31
	Mickle Fell	2,585	

17 of the 20 summits in England included in the list are to be found in the Lake District. The Lake District lies in the north west corner of England and with its beautiful lakes and mountains has always been one of England's most popular tourist areas. The mountains are rugged with some fine ridges, particularly Sharp Edge on Blencathra and Striding Edge on Helvellyn. However, there are good paths up all the main hills and plenty of guidebooks, the best known being Wainwright's *A Pictorial Guide to the Lakeland Fells*. These were published in the 1950s and 1960s.

The three fells (mountains in northern England are normally described as fells) that lie outside the Lake District offer something of a challenge, mainly due to the more awkward access. Cross Fell involves a long walk in, The Cheviot is a long distance from any other mountains, whilst Mickle Fell is just difficult!

The 500 foot drop rule means that many familiar names are omitted, notably some of the Lake District summits including Scafell, Bowfell, Esk Pike, Crinkle Crags, Red Pike and many others. The Three Peaks of Yorkshire which include Pen-y-ghent, Whernside and Ingleborough are not included as the summits fall just short of the required height.

COLEDALE ROUND

GRASMOOR *(2,795ft)*
GRISEDALE PIKE *(2,595ft)*

» These two mountains create a good circular walk from Braithwaite near Keswick.

» The route below goes over five Lake District summits or 'Wainwrights'.

» The mountains are well seen from Millbeck across the valley.

My Route (6-7 hours)

We started near Coledale House on the west side of Braithwaite. A footpath ascended WSW along the ridge of Steel How and up Grisedale Pike. From here there was a good ridge to Hopegill Head. Then we descended to Coledale Hause. From Coledale Hause we took the right hand path and climbed SW to the summit plateau of Grasmoor. The top was marked by a shelter near the south face.

From Grasmoor we followed a path east to Eel Crags. The path carried on to Sail then down to Sail pass. We omitted Scar Crags and Causey Pike and walked NNE to the saddle of High Moss, then descended to Braithwaite.

Personal View

The Coledale Round is a pleasant and satisfying circuit over a number of Lake District peaks surrounding Coledale Beck. The complete round includes Grisedale Pike, Hopegill Head, Grasmoor, Eel Crags and Sail. There are some excellent pubs in Braithwaite which has always made this a popular round with friends.

The Coledale Round figured prominently during my early days on the mountains. My Grandmother lived in the Lake District from 1965 to 1971 in a house called 'Rowling End', so named because of the view across the valley to Causey Pike and its lower eastern ridge, Rowling End. This seemed to inspire my father to take us on regular walks up Causey Pike and eventually along the full ridge to Grasmoor, thus completing half the Coledale Round.

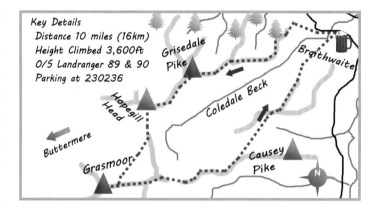

Key Details
Distance 10 miles (16km)
Height Climbed 3,600ft
O/S Landranger 89 & 90
Parking at 230236

POINTS OF INTEREST

Three miles from Braithwaite up the Coledale valley is Force Crag mine restored for the National Trust. Here you can see the buildings and machinery of the last working mine in the Lake District.

The Coledale Round from Barrow; the route follows the skyline from right to left.

PLACES TO STAY/DRINK
Braithwaite has several pubs offering food and drink as well as a campsite and bed and breakfasts. Keswick is only ten minutes away by car.

SKIDDAW

Skiddaw Low Man (which I first climbed at the age of four) from the slopes of Skiddaw early in the morning on the third day of our Bob Graham Round (2014).

SKIDDAW *(3,054ft)*

» **Skiddaw is an iconic peak overlooking Keswick and one of only four mountains over 3,000ft in England.**

» **One of the best known views in the Lake District is the view of Skiddaw from the shores of Derwentwater.**

» **The classic route up Skiddaw starts at a car park near Latrigg and goes up along the skyline ridge.**

» **Skiddaw is the first mountain on the Bob Graham Round.**

Personal View – Bob Graham Round (Jo)

On the third day the alarm went off at 5 a.m. for the longest day. I ate as much as I could, re-plastered my feet and with aching legs and feet departed the Skiddaw Hotel guided by the iPhone's satnav. The route across the river and up to the old railway line is not obvious and it was no time to get lost. The eight of us soon stretched out around Latrigg to the broad steep path up Jenkin Hill. Barry dropped back with Angie and Alastair, unsure as to whether he was capable of finishing.

Inevitably we were all slower than on the previous two days and from the cool morning air we eased our way into sunshine and past Skiddaw Low Man. We reached Skiddaw summit in one hour, considerably slower than the split time of 45 minutes but we presumed this peak is normally taken at speed as it would be the first on the twenty-four hour Bob Graham Round.

My comment. I was left behind at this stage and it took me one hour and ten minutes to reach the summit of Skiddaw. However, I climbed considerably faster than on my first attempt to climb Skiddaw when at the age of four my father took me up. We only reached Skiddaw Low Man as there was no time to carry on. Even then I was too slow!

My Route (3-4 hours)

My favourite route up Skiddaw is from Millbeck. My grandmother lived in Millbeck between 1965 and 1971. When staying there I was allowed to climb Carl Side or Skiddaw on my own. From the crossroads at Millbeck, I would walk a short way NW then a path led onto the hillside and climbed broadly north up Carl Side. From the summit of Carl Side it is an easy descent NE, then a steep climb of nearly 700ft to the summit ridge of Skiddaw. The summit is towards the north end of the ridge.

When climbing Skiddaw I would return by the same route or go left at the col between Carl Side and Skiddaw. From there a path goes south down the side of Slades Beck to return to Millbeck.

The classic route up Skiddaw starts from near Latrigg and follows a path which runs NNW past Lonscale Fell and Skiddaw Little Man. We took this route on the third day of our Bob Graham Round.

PLACES TO STAY/DRINK
Keswick has plenty of places to eat, drink and stay. On the Bob Graham Round we stayed at the Skiddaw Hotel in the centre of Keswick.

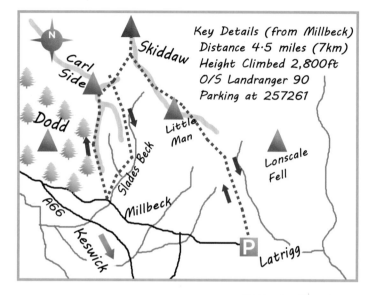

Key Details (from Millbeck)
Distance 4·5 miles (7km)
Height Climbed 2,800ft
O/S Landranger 90
Parking at 257261

Skiddaw from Derwentwater.

15

BLENCATHRA

Looking towards Derwentwater from near the summit of Blencathra *(Wayne Dentith)*.

BLENCATHRA *(2,847ft)*

» Blencathra is a popular mountain and is sometimes known as Saddleback. This is because of the distinctive saddle on the summit when seen from the Penrith to Keswick road.

» There are some great ridges on Blencathra including Sharp Edge and Halls Fell.

» The lands to the north of Blencathra are still quiet and largely undiscovered.

Personal View (Jonathan)

For well over forty years I have been climbing Blencathra (or Saddleback as it is wrongly known) and must have ascended and descended every conceivable route. My favourite is via Hall's Fell (described on the next page) which can be combined with a perfect afternoon descent over Blease Fell. Keswick, Derwentwater and the North Western Fells are all laid out in front of you; the path is good and the world just seems like a better place.

The summit is a surprise, particularly if you have arrived via one of the rocky southern ridges; a large expanse of near flat short grass, good enough for a game of cricket. Three times I have taken a sleeping bag and slept near the summit cairn and each time have been rewarded with a wonderful sunrise over Cross Fell and the Pennines.

To the north of the summit ridge is a large area of wilderness which offers some quiet approaches to Blencathra. JP and I took one of these to tick off surely the most pointless Wainwright summit, Mungrisdale Common. We found it and descended a full ten feet before climbing Blencathra. Such is the power of ticking that there are now paths approaching this small lump from four different directions.

Two of Our Routes

The first walk outlines Jonathan's favourite route up Hall's Fell whilst the second looks at the possibilities of climbing Sharp Edge.

JONATHAN'S ROUTE (3-4 hours)

I started at Threlkeld. The path led directly uphill past the school before passing through some woodland and reaching the open fellside. I turned right and skirted the distinctive shape of Knott Halloo then crossed a mountain stream. From here the path climbed steeply up Hall's Fell until it reached the ridge of Narrow Fell. Mild scrambling brought me out at the summit cairn of Blencathra.

I turned left (south west) at the summit and followed the ridge for a mile until it started to descend steeply down Blease Fell. The ridge was delightful, a wide expanse of easy walking with views towards Skiddaw and southern Scotland, and later over Keswick into the heart of Lakeland.

ALTERNATIVE OVER SHARP EDGE (4-5 hours)

An alternative route starts at Scales ascending Sharp Edge and descending Scales Fell. Scales lies two miles east of Threlkeld along the A66. Sharp Edge itself is a tricky scramble with an exposed section. It should only be taken on by confident walkers and avoided in wet or wintry conditions. However, the rewards are good for those prepared to try it.

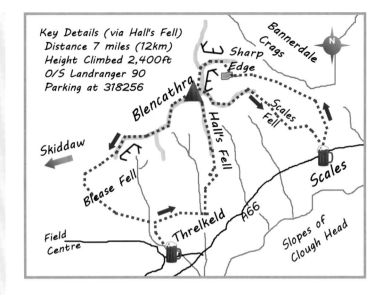

Key Details (via Hall's Fell)
Distance 7 miles (12km)
Height Climbed 2,400ft
O/S Landranger 90
Parking at 318256

PLACES TO STAY/DRINK

Threlkeld has two excellent pubs, the Horse and Farrier and the Salutation ('*The Sally*') both serving food and good beer whilst the White Horse at Scales is convenient for those tackling Sharp Edge.

Blease Fell from near our cottage in Threlkeld.

HIGH STILE

HIGH STILE *(2,648ft)*

» High Stile is the highest point of the ridge running along the west of Buttermere.

» This is an attractive ridge walk particularly if the weather is good.

» Buttermere tends to be a less visited part of the Lake District and it is not easy to access. The road from Keswick goes over a pass, Newlands Hause.

Personal View

High Stile is the highest point of the ridge west of Buttermere. However, it is best to climb the full ridge including High Crag, Red Pike (Buttermere) and Haystacks to fully appreciate these mountains.

My lasting recollection of High Stile dates back over forty years. When I was 15, I was on the ridge between High Stile and High Crag in thick mist with my uncle and cousins. I was convinced the route was one way but my uncle simply pointed to the compass and said I was wrong. Of course the compass was right and it is a lesson I have never forgotten.

My Route (4-5 hours)

On my last visit we started at Buttermere village and walked along the minor road which leads to the NW corner of the lake. We followed a path along the lake. Soon after passing the southern end of the lake, we went up the hillside to the right.

The path climbed steeply then flattened to pass High Wax Knott. We turned right up a steep path to reach the SE ridge of High Crag at 2,000ft and then went up this ridge to High Crag summit. An easy walk NW beside a line of fence posts led to High Stile. The summit is at point 807m, 250m to the east of the fence posts. We continued NW following the fence posts to Red Pike and descended in an easterly direction past Bleaberry Tarn to Buttermere village.

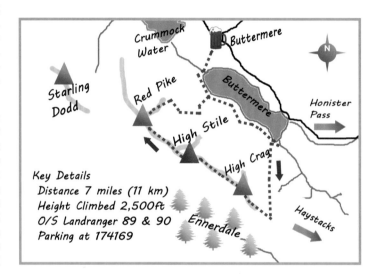

Key Details
Distance 7 miles (11 km)
Height Climbed 2,500ft
O/S Landranger 89 & 90
Parking at 174169

High Stile ridge and Buttermere.

POINTS OF INTEREST
Haystacks, Wainwright's favourite peak, can be added to this walk. His Ashes are spread on Innominate Tarn on Haystacks.

HIGH RAISE

The Langdale Pikes from the south, High Raise is far right, a small pimple at the back.

HIGH RAISE (2,500ft)

» High Raise is hidden by its well known neighbours, the Langdale Pikes.

» The Langdale Pikes, including Harrison Stickle and Pike o'Stickle, should be added to an ascent of High Raise.

» High Raise is regarded as the most central summit in the Lake District.

My Route (3-4 hours)

We started from The New Dungeon Ghyll and followed the path which went NNW to Stickle Tarn. The path traversed the right side of Stickle Tarn and continued NNE to the SE ridge of Sergeant Man. We continued in a NW direction over Sergeant Man to reach the Trig Point and stone shelter at the summit of High Raise.

From High Raise we followed a good path south towards the heart of the Langdale Pikes. The path went over Thunacar Knott and then led SSE to Harrison Stickle. From the summit of Harrison Stickle, the 'King of the Langdale Pikes' we descended to The New Dungeon Ghyll.

Personal View

Most people come to the Langdales to climb the rough peaks of Harrison Stickle, Pike o'Stickle and Pavey Ark leaving out High Raise with its flat profile even though it is the highest summit in the area. Personally I have only been to its summit twice, on the last occasion as part of the Bob Graham walk as it is one of the peaks on the round. However, there are many 'ticks' to be gained from this shy and retiring summit. It is a Wainwright, a Marilyn, and a Top 500 Summit.

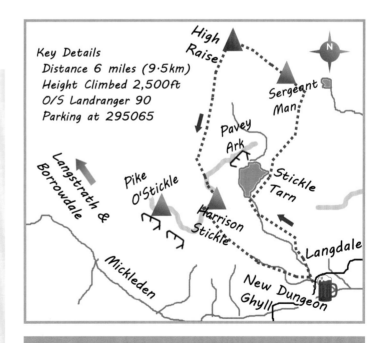

Key Details
Distance 6 miles (9·5km)
Height Climbed 2,500ft
O/S Landranger 90
Parking at 295065

PLACES TO STAY/DRINK

Both The New Dungeon Ghyll and The Old Dungeon Ghyll provide food, drink and accommodation.

HIGH STREET

HIGH STREET *(2,718ft)*

» High Street is a well known fell in the east of the Lake District.

My Route (4-5 hours)

My last visit to High Street was nearly twenty years ago when a group of us climbed the mountain from Haweswater. We followed the path around the head of the lake, then NE up the thin finger of the lake. Soon the path started to ascend onto the ridge leading up to Rough Crag.

After Rough Crag the path descended to a col, then climbed to the broad plateau of High Street. We walked SW and after a few hundred metres reached the summit of High Street. We continued south on a path next to a wall then went SE to Mardale III Bell, a minor top, and down to Nan Bield Pass. From the pass we descended past Small Water to return to the start.

Key Details

» Distance 6 miles (10km)
» Height climbed 2,000ft
» O/S Landranger 90
» Parking 469107.

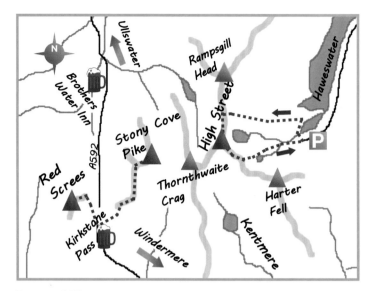

Personal View

My earliest and to this day lasting recollection of High Street was a school trip at the age of 15. We camped near Caudale Beck on a beautiful evening in early May. The setting was superb and we had no idea what was to follow the next day. We woke up to find rain battering the tents which got worse all day. Somehow we managed to find the correct route and trudged up High Street in high winds and driving rain.

We went over the summit and headed east towards Ullswater. Most of the groups abandoned the trip. We slogged on down to the road near Hartsop with the tents and sleeping bags, then sheltered at a bus stop for an hour until the transport back to school arrived.

POINTS OF INTEREST

High Street used to be a Roman road (hence the name) linking the forts at Ambleside and Brougham. Later, horse races used to take place there.

Hayes Water from High Street.

KIRKSTONE PASS

RED SCREES *(2,547ft)*
STONY COVE PIKE *(2,502ft)*

» Two less 'fashionable' Lake District summits climbed from the top of Kirkstone Pass.

» Red Screes is the first peak on a classic walk from Kirkstone Pass over Helvellyn to Threlkeld.

My Routes

These two mountains can be climbed as a circuit or by starting and returning to Kirkstone Pass both times. I followed the less interesting option returning to Kirkstone Pass after each ascent. For reference, see the map opposite, page 20.

RED SCREES *(1-2 hours)*

Starting from the car park at Kirkstone Pass I followed a path which led NW up Red Screes to the dramatic summit above Kirkstone Pass. The distance was short and I returned the same way to Kirkstone Pass summit.

STONY COVE PIKE *(2-3 hours)*

From the top of Kirkstone Pass I followed a path which climbed 500ft east to St Raven's Edge. I continued north and NNE along a path which climbed gradually for just over 2km. Eventually the path turned east and after a few hundred metres I reached the summit of Stony Cove Pike.

Key Details

» Distance 7.5 miles (12km)
» Height climbed 3,100ft
» O/S Landranger 90
» Parking at Kirkstone Pass, 402081.

Personal View

Such is the unfashionable nature of these summits that, when I decided to complete the Top 500 Summits in the British Isles, I wasn't sure if I had climbed them despite numerous visits to the Lake District.

Thus it was an excuse to return to the Lake District and one Sunday I drove from Loughborough to the top of Kirkstone Pass. From Kirkstone Pass I climbed Stony Cove Pike (sometimes known as Caudale Moor) and then Red Screes. Both were relatively short climbs from the top of the pass.

Summit of Stony Cove Pike in winter looking east over Thornthwaite Crag and High Street.

POINTS OF INTEREST
Kirkstone Pass at 1,500ft is the highest pass in the Lake District. There is a pub at the top of the pass, the Kirkstone Pass Inn.

HELVELLYN ROUND

Striding Edge from near the summit of Helvellyn.

HELVELLYN *(3,116ft)*
FAIRFIELD *(2,863ft)*
ST SUNDAY CRAG *(2,760ft)*

» Helvellyn is the most popular mountain in England and on summer weekends it is common to see over one hundred people on the summit.

» The route from Patterdale to the summit of Helvellyn passes over Striding Edge and should be avoided in winter.

» Fairfield and St Sunday Crag are fine mountains sitting to the south of Helvellyn.

Personal View (Jonathan)

A scramble up Striding Edge is one of the great walking challenges for anyone in the Lake District. Whether sticking to the crest or taking the path which skirts the knife edge ridge it is a fine crossing which will live long in the memory. However, great care should be taken. In winter it is best to leave Striding Edge to those experienced in winter conditions.

In complete contrast to the serrated edges and deep corries to the east of Helvellyn the summit area is flat and expansive, so flat that a small plane has landed on it recently. Although the western slopes are dull the views on the walk south to Grisedale Tarn are magnificent. There is nothing better than walking on the broad, grassy ridge to Dollywaggon Pike on a fine day. The walk over all three Top 500 Summits is challenging and St Sunday Crag (surely one of the finest names of any British mountain) offers a fitting final summit. The final leisurely descent offers some wonderful views of Ullswater with the pubs of Glenridding beckoning.

My Route (6-8 hours)

I have climbed these mountains many times but only once completed the circuit of all three summits. My route is set out below:

We followed the road which led out of Patterdale SW from Grisedale Bridge. After 1km we turned right, crossed a bridge and followed the path which led up the hillside towards Striding Edge. The path went west then SW up the hillside to the 'hole in the wall'. We carried on in the same direction to Striding Edge.

To traverse Striding Edge we followed a path which ran below the crest of the ridge, then climbed the steep stony slopes to the summit. From the summit we walked south along a gently undulating ridge over Nethermost Pike and Dollywaggon Pike, then descended to Grisedale Tarn.

We walked round to the south side of Grisedale Tarn and to the top of Grisedale Hause. A steep climb led to the summit of Fairfield. From there the route took us north over Cofa Pike, then down to Deepdale Hause. The path went NE over easier ground climbing to the summit of St Sunday Crag. The descent was NE from the summit to return to Patterdale.

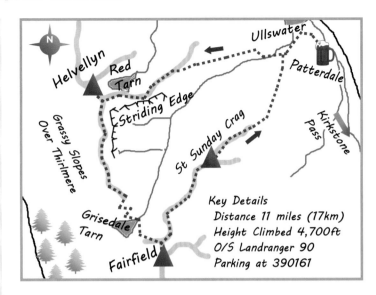

Key Details
Distance 11 miles (17km)
Height Climbed 4,700ft
O/S Landranger 90
Parking at 390161

St Sunday Crag (left) and Fairfield from Seat Sandal on a summer evening (2014).

POINTS OF INTEREST

The Lake District National Park Authority employs two fell top assessors during the winter months. Working alternate weeks one of these walks up Helvellyn each day during that period to check the weather, snow and walking conditions.

GABLE AND PILLAR

Steeple from Scoat Fell (2014).

GREAT GABLE *(2,949ft)*
PILLAR *(2,927ft)*
KIRK FELL *(2,631ft)*

» Three great Lake District peaks in a classic round from Wasdale Head.

» Great Gable is seen at its best from Wastwater from where it is often painted and photographed.

» Pillar and its beautifully sharp neighbour Steeple are also great mountains standing above Ennerdale Water.

Personal View – Bob Graham Round (Jo)

The great whaleback of Pillar shone ahead while Kirk Fell and Great Gable were silhouetted against the morning sun. Three big peaks in a row and we were already low on water. As we followed the ridge past Black Crag then to Pillar, Ennerdale was beautifully mapped out below, its blue water and deep green surrounding woods so sharp that they could almost be touched. A perfectly clear sky and blue to blue horizon were the very best the Lake District could offer and barely a soul to be seen. Beyond the rugged summit of Pillar we dropped down to Black Sail Pass, searching the bog in vain for a drop of clear running water.

We marched up Kirk Fell in the increasing morning heat. The descent to Beck Head followed, then we recommenced our search for water. Just then we heard a shout and the sound of mocking voices from below but they were magnanimous and realising our plight John Keighley jogged over with two litres of water. We drained the bottles and thanked them profusely. We then headed up the steep path to Great Gable. The scramble to the high point of the day became easier as the water worked its way into our blood, together with calories scoffed while on the move.

My Route (7-8 hours)

Recently I climbed these Top 500 Summits during our three day Bob Graham Round. We started at the Wasdale Head Inn, crossed the river behind the hotel, walked 200m towards Wast Water, then climbed the steep 2,000ft ascent of Yewbarrow.

The summit of Yewbarrow was reached after an hour. This was followed by a short and steep descent off Stirrup Crag. From here we climbed Red Pike and made a short detour to climb Steeple. After descending to Windy Gap we climbed ENE to the summit of Pillar. A long descent ESE took us to Black Sail Pass, then we turned south climbing a gully on the east side of the main ridge to Kirk Fell.

After Kirk Fell we dropped 600ft to Beck Head then continued steeply to the top of Great Gable. From here it is possible to follow a path back to the Wasdale Head Inn. However, on this occasion we continued over Green Gable, Brandreth and Grey Knotts to Honister Pass.

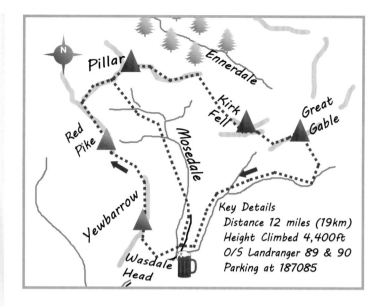

Key Details
Distance 12 miles (19km)
Height Climbed 4,400ft
O/S Landranger 89 & 90
Parking at 187085

Looking down Ennerdale from Great Gable (New Year's Day, 1977).

PLACES TO STAY/DRINK

The Wasdale Head Inn and campsite is close to the start of the walk and is a good place to eat, drink, and stay. However, it is necessary to book early in the summer months. Jo booked it a year in advance for our Bob Graham Round.

SCAFELL PIKE

Esk Hause on the ascent of Scafell Pike, Great Gable behind.

SCAFELL PIKE (3,210ft)

» Scafell Pike is the highest mountain in England and is a superb mountain. It forms part of the 'Three Peaks Challenge': Ben Nevis, Snowdon and Scafell Pike.

» Its near neighbour, Scafell, does not qualify as a Top 500 Summit as the drop between the two mountains is less than 500ft. However, Scafell is a fine mountain in its own right.

» The summit of Scafell Pike can be very crowded on weekends in the summer.

Personal View – Bob Graham Round (Jo)

Numerous walkers were wandering amongst the ill-defined paths over the boulders on the lofty plateau with the summit cairn of Scafell Pike within reach. Neville and I, straining our lungs, marched up the final slope to bag the highest peak in England, with Barry flagging in our wake. We were not alone. The hot dry weather with perfect skies had drawn out the day trippers. Over one hundred people crowded the summit and surrounding boulders. To my surprise, I appeared to be the oldest on the mountain. I recalled my first ascent, aged 12, when I was the youngest. But despite our vintage, we had made good time, seven hours from Dunmail Raise with only Scafell remaining.

The classic route to Scafell is a descent to the col at Mickledore followed by a simple rock climb. Although Neville and Barry had been up before we were not certain of the line. We decided to take the rough route up Lord's Rake and scrambled up the boulder filled switchback past the renowned leaning stone (the National Trust warned in 2001 that this could fall at some time) and on to the top. From there we tackled the steep descent straight down the mountain to Wasdale Head and the end of day one of our three day round.

My Route (5-6 hours)

I have climbed Scafell Pike at least ten times. My usual route is the classic 'Corridor Route' from Seathwaite and I followed this route with a party from work on a recent ascent.

We parked by the roadside at Seathwaite and walked south, arriving at Stockley Bridge after one mile. The path crossed the bridge and turned SW to ascend to Sty Head Tarn at 1,400ft. After passing Sty Head Tarn on the west side we turned left towards Esk Hause. After a short distance the path went right and up the Corridor Route.

We crossed a number of streams on the Corridor Route as it ascended Scafell Pike. We turned left at the col between Lingmell and Scafell Pike and climbed a broad ridge to the summit of Scafell Pike, England's highest mountain.

From the summit we turned NE passing over Broad Crag before descending to Esk Hause. We walked north towards Sprinkling Tarn but, before reaching it, turned down Grains Gill to follow the path back to Stockley Bridge and Seathwaite.

POINTS OF INTEREST

I am told that on a clear day the Mourne Mountains in Northern Ireland can be seen from the summit of Scafell Pike, but I have never seen them!

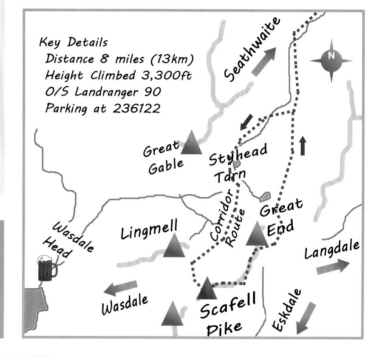

Key Details
Distance 8 miles (13km)
Height Climbed 3,300ft
O/S Landranger 90
Parking at 236122

Seathwaite

Great Gable

Styhead Tarn

Wasdale Head

Lingmell

Corridor Route

Great End

Langdale

Wasdale

Scafell Pike

Eskdale

Summit of Scafell Pike on a busy summer day (2014).

Yewbarrow, Great Gable, Lingmell
and The Screes above Wast Water
(*Heather Thomas-Smith*).

CONISTON OLD MAN

CONISTON OLD MAN (2,635ft)

» Coniston Old Man and its neighbours lie south of the main range of Lake District fells.

» The 'Old Man' is the most southerly Top 500 Summit in the Lake District.

» There is evidence of earlier copper and slate mining on its slopes.

» The summit is the highest point of the compact and isolated group of Coniston fells.

POINTS OF INTEREST

Coniston Old Man is the highest point in the old county of Lancashire. Swirl How had been thought higher but recent listings confirm Coniston Old Man as the higher.

My Route (3-4 hours)

On my first ascent of Coniston Old Man we started from Coniston and followed the footpath NW along the south side of Church Beck. After 1km it turned west to head straight for the summit. The path went west past Crowberry Haws and after 2km reached a mountain tarn, Low Water. From here we ascended steeply SSW to the summit.

We continued north then west to Goat's Hawse, then south past Goat's Water to the bottom of the Old Man's southern slopes. From here we walked east for 3km to return to Coniston village.

Personal View

Coniston Old Man stands south west of the main Lake District fells isolated from the high fells surrounding Scafell Pike. I can only recall climbing Coniston Old Man three times and have never climbed its near neighbour, Swirl How.

My last visit was in 2004 on a sponsored walk with St Basil's which helps young homeless people around Birmingham. These are always popular walks with hundreds of people taking part. They tend to be long, in this case a 28 mile walk from Windermere traversing Coniston Old Man. We made it back to the start as darkness started to fall.

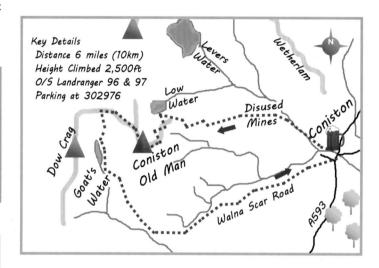

Key Details
Distance 6 miles (10km)
Height Climbed 2,500ft
O/S Landranger 96 & 97
Parking at 302976

Disused copper mine on Coniston Old Man (Heather Thomas-Smith).

29

CHEVIOT

THE CHEVIOT *(2,674ft)*

» Cheviot is in Northumberland, close to the Scottish border.

» These are rolling hills with good views but Cheviot has a flat summit covered with peat.

My Route (3-4 hours)

I drove past Morpeth on the A1 and turned left on to the A697 to Wooler. A few miles south of Wooler I turned left off the A697 past North Middleton, then left up the Hope Valley towards Langleeford. Just before Langleeford there was parking on the left before a small bridge.

I walked up the road for a further 200m and found a path going off right which climbed west up the hillside towards Scald Hill. From Scald Hill a path led SW up the hillside to a paved section over the flat, but potentially boggy summit area, to the trig point (see below). I returned the same way but an alternative would be to return via Hedgehope Hill.

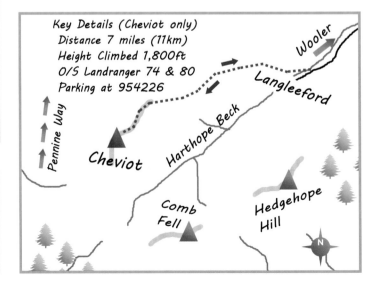

PLACES TO STAY/DRINK

There are interesting places to stay on the Northumberland coast in particular Bamburgh and Newton.

Personal View

Cheviot stands north of Newcastle and close to the Scottish border. It is the highest point for miles around and on a clear day the views are magnificent.

Despite living in Newcastle for the first twenty-five years of my life, I had only climbed Cheviot once. So, on a beautiful August evening in 2013, I drove up the Hope Valley listening to the Ashes Test match on the radio intending to climb this isolated summit again. It was dry underfoot and I made good progress over Scald Hill. Soon I could see for miles towards the coast north and east of Cheviot. The path was paved for the final part of the route so a trek over the infamous peat bogs was avoided. From the summit I ran down and stopped off for a bar snack at Longhorsley.

View east from near the summit of Cheviot.

Key Details (Cheviot only)
Distance 7 miles (11km)
Height Climbed 1,800ft
O/S Landranger 74 & 80
Parking at 954226

Pennine Way

Wooler

Langleeford

Cheviot

Harthope Beck

Comb Fell

Hedgehope Hill

N

PENNINES

CROSS FELL *(2,930ft)*
MICKLE FELL *(2,585ft)*

Jonathan's Routes

CROSS FELL *(4-5 hours)*

I started at Kirkland (ref. 647326, O/S Landranger 91) and followed the path as it bent north then ENE going past High Cap. I reached the Pennine Way 1km north of Cross Fell and it was then easy to go south to the summit.

I continued over Cross Fell going SE for 1km until a path crossed at Tees Head. I followed this SW over Wildboar Scar after which the path turned west. I continued to Wythwaite then walked north back to Kirkland.

MICKLE FELL *(3-4 hours)*

The main difficulty when climbing Mickle Fell is access. Red flags fly when firing is in progress. The signs at the start advise all walkers to contact the range officer at Warcop Training Area, Warcop, Appleby, CA16 6PA to obtain permission to walk to the summit.

My brother and I have climbed the mountain on separate occasions. We both started at the county border on the B6276 between Brough and Middleton-in-Teesdale (ref. 831199, O/S Landranger 91) and walked NNW for over 5km to the summit ridge. On both our visits, visibility was poor and there was little definition until the final summit slopes. There was no obvious path and a compass was an essential requirement.

On the way up Mickle Fell.

Personal View (Jonathan)

Cross Fell and Mickle Fell lie in the Pennines not far from where I live. Cross Fell is on the Pennine Way and makes an enjoyable walk from Kirkland.

Mickle Fell is the most miserable spot in England where you will either drown in peat hags or be shot by the Army! Whilst Mickle Fell could not claim to be one of the best mountains in Britain there is some great countryside nearby including two spectacular waterfalls, Cautley Spout between Kirkby Stephen and Sedbergh and High Force near Middleton-in-Teesdale.

I started my ascent of Mickle Fell from the B6276 at the County Border. Signs warned me not to touch the mountain when red flags were flying. I headed up beside a fence and into the cloud. The compass was essential and the underfoot terrain was terrible; a never ending morass of deep ravines, peat hags and mud. Eventually a ridge of sorts was reached with a cairn which I assumed was the summit. I had seen pictures of the summit and in good weather it looks a pleasant spot but today it was grim. If I had lost my compass I think I would still be there.

Glyders from Llyn Bochlwyd.

WALES

There are 21 Top 500 Summits in Wales including Snowdon, the highest mountain in the British Isles outside Scotland. They are divided into 12 walks as follows:

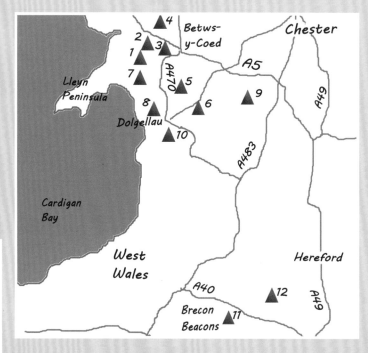

WALKS 1 TO 12

	Walk	Feet	Pg.
1	Snowdon	3,560	36
	Y Lliwedd	2,946	
2	Glyder Fawr	3,279	38
	Y Garn	3,107	
	Elidir Fawr	3,029	
	Tryfan	3,002	
3	Moel Siabod	2,861	40
4	Carnedd Llewelyn	3,490	42
	Pen Llithrig y Wrach	2,622	
5	Arenig Fawr	2,801	43
6	Aran Fawddwy	2,970	44
	Glasgwm	2,557	
7	Moel Hebog	2,566	45
	Moelwyn Mawr	2,527	
8	Y Llethr	2,480	46
9	Cadair Berwyn	2,723	47
10	Cadair Idris	2,929	48
11	Pen y Fan	2,906	50
	Fan Brycheiniog	2,630	
	Waun Rydd	2,523	
12	Waun Fach	2,660	52

For many people living in the south of England and the Midlands the Welsh mountains are nearer than any other mountain area. Weekends and even day trips can be made to them. The nearest mountain to my home in Loughborough in the Top 500 list is Cadair Berwyn which is reached in style driving west along the A470.

The greatest of the Welsh mountains are in Snowdonia. Mighty Tryfan rises steeply out of the moorland as sharply as anything in the rest of Britain and Ireland. Snowdon can be climbed by one of the classic Welsh walks, the 'Snowdon Horseshoe'. This includes Crib Goch, possibly the toughest ridge walk outside of Scotland. For the most energetic, an attempt at the classic Welsh 3,000 foot summits walk is a must and this can be completed in a hard day.

Down in the south of Wales lie four Top 500 Summits of which the best known is Pen y Fan. A good path leads to the summit and hundreds of people can be seen climbing Pen y Fan on most weekends. Also in the south lie the Black Mountains. Do not be put off by the name, these are rolling mountains, beautiful on a sunny day.

Crib Goch from the Miners Track.

SNOWDON HORSESHOE

Snowdon across Llyn Llydaw.

SNOWDON *(3,560ft)*
Y LLIWEDD *(2,946ft)*

» **Snowdon is the highest mountain in the British Isles outside Scotland.**

» **Snowdon is probably the busiest mountain in the British Isles.**

» **A funicular railway runs all the way to the summit. At the summit there is a cafe which was rebuilt ten years ago.**

» **The 'Snowdon Horseshoe' is one of the great mountain walks in the British Isles.**

Personal View

Snowdon is the highest peak in Wales and has everything that a British mountain could have; a railway climbing spectacularly to its summit, a cafe at the summit open in summer, a magnificent ridge over Crib Goch and of course most beloved of all by walkers, a high start point at Pen-y-Pass! As it is also accessible from a number of large cities it is not surprising that it is such a popular mountain and probably the most visited summit in the British Isles.

My first ascent of Snowdon was with a group from university in May 1976. We crossed Crib Goch in thick cloud and, as this was my first visit to Snowdonia, I had no idea how severe the ridge was. From there we continued over Snowdon and Y Lliwedd to complete the 'Snowdon Horseshoe', the sun coming out on our descent.

Later I traversed Crib Goch with my son, James, and only then did I appreciate the severity and spectacular nature of the ridge as we struggled along it on a summer evening. For those with a good head for heights the Snowdon Horseshoe is one of the best one day circuits in Britain. In winter it is a serious undertaking only for experienced climbers.

My Route (6-8 hours)

In this section I have described the route traversing Crib Goch. However, less experienced climbers should follow the Pyg track or the Miners' track all the way to the summit of Snowdon.

In 1976 we parked at Pen-y-Pass and followed the Pyg track in a westerly direction heading for Crib Goch. At Bwlch y Moch the path forked. We went right, up steep rocky slopes, to reach the main ridge of Crib Goch. It was not possible to keep to the crest all the way so we stayed on the southern side of the ridge.

After bypassing the pinnacles at the end of the ridge

we arrived at a col. From here the going was easier, the path carried on along the ridge to Garnedd Ugain, bypassing a rock wall on the south side. From this summit we descended a short distance. After joining the railway line we ascended south to the summit of Snowdon.

We descended SW from the summit cafe on the Rhyd Ddu

path and after a short distance picked up the Watkin path which went left towards Y Lliwedd. There followed a steep and loose descent to the col. We climbed SE to Y Lliwedd going over its twin top before descending NE to a col at 2,300ft. Finally we turned off the ridge at a cairn and descended NNE to the Miners' track and back to Pen-y-Pass.

POINTS OF INTEREST

The Snowdon Mountain Railway was built in 1896 and runs nearly five miles from Llanberis to the summit station.

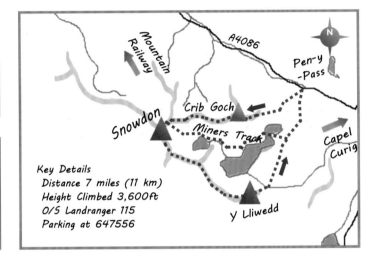

Key Details
Distance 7 miles (11 km)
Height Climbed 3,600ft
O/S Landranger 115
Parking at 647556

Summit of Y Lliwedd from the east.

PLACES TO STAY/DRINK

Snowdon is the only mountain in the British Isles with a cafe at the summit. There is also a tea room/snack bar at Pen-y-Pass. There is plenty of accommodation at Llanberis and a youth hostel at Pen-y-Pass. There are parking charges at Pen-y-Pass.

TRYFAN AND GLYDERS

'Castle of the Winds', Glyders *(Kyle Pattinson)*.

GLYDER FAWR *(3,279ft)*
Y GARN *(3,107ft)*
ELIDIR FAWR *(3,029ft)*
TRYFAN *(3,002ft)*

» These four 3,000 foot mountains form an impressive ridge and would make a superb one day walk from Ogwen Cottage.

» Known as the 'Glyders' this is the central section of the Welsh 3,000ft peaks walk.

» Tryfan is an impressive peak requiring some scrambling to reach the summit.

Personal View (Ella)

I remember our day on the Glyderau vividly. We started with the hikers route up Tryfan to reach its Adam and Eve monoliths. These are twin rock pillars which you would think nothing of jumping from one to the other were they on a flat piece of ground. However, they are not on a flat piece of ground but instead positioned on the edge of a mountain making them extremely exposed. Jumping from one to the other is not for the fainthearted, Barry says he would never attempt it, but we made it safely - though not without butterflies -not least from climbing onto the top of one of the pillars.

After the excitement on Tryfan we ascended via Bristly Ridge to the Glyder Fach plateau and its crazy cantilever stone and the 'Castle of the Winds' pinnacle formation. A stop for the obligatory 'surfing pose' photos on top of the slab of cantilevered rock followed. It was a glorious sunny day with grand views to Snowdon in the south and the Carnedds to the north. We tramped happily along the ridge westwards to tick off Glyder Fawr, Y Garn and Elidir Fawr before descending back to the road. At Betws-y-coed the campsite suddenly filled up with bikers and the sky with rain. The next day we beat a hasty retreat as we couldn't see the hills. The curtains of precipitation were very firmly drawn.

On our next visit to North Wales we climbed Tryfan again. This time via a scrambling route and as part of a weekend warm up and briefing for a trip to Nepal. It was telling that our guides did not allow us on 'their watch' to make the step between Adam and Eve! Another scramble up Bristly ridge and we were declared fit and able to go and attempt some trekking peaks in the Himalayas.

My Routes

TRYFAN AND GLYDER FAWR
(5-6 hours)

All my routes up the Glyders have started at the car park at Ogwen. For Tryfan and Glyder Fawr we walked 1km east along the A5 to a parking area. From there we climbed east under Milestone Buttress to a ladder stile in the wall. Beyond the wall a path ascended steeply SSW to the north ridge of Tryfan. We kept left to avoid the direct route which appeared to be a more difficult scramble.

From the summit we descended SSW down the south ridge to Bwlch Tryfan which links Tryfan and the Glyders. Ahead was the Bristly Ridge. We entered a gully and the route up was well marked. From the top it was a simple walk to Glyder Fach. Now heading WSW we continued past the 'Castle of the Winds' to Glyder Fawr, the highest of the Glyders.

Y GARN AND ELIDIR FAWR
(5-6 hours)

I climbed Y Garn and Elidir Fawr together, and started by following the path which goes west from Ogwen Cottage up Y Garn. Beyond Y Garn the ridge goes north with Elidir Fawr ahead on the left. I continued along the ridge over Foel-goch and down to Bwlch y Brecan. A path then skirted Mynydd Perfedd and headed west to Elidir Fawr. The return route descended ESE from Foel -goch to Cwm Cywion and then to Ogwen.

The map shows the route over all four Top 500 Summits, estimated time (7-9 hours).

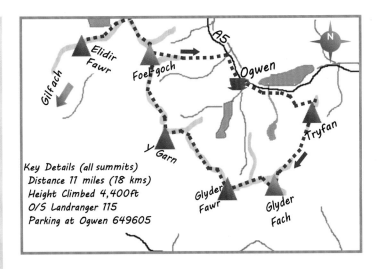

Key Details (all summits)
Distance 11 miles (18 kms)
Height Climbed 4,400ft
O/S Landranger 115
Parking at Ogwen 649605

PLACES TO STAY/DRINK

There is a cafe and a Youth Hostel at Ogwen. Capel Curig and Betws-y-coed, a few miles down the A5, have a number of hotels, pubs and restaurants.

Tryfan showing the north ridge.

POINTS OF INTEREST

The summit of Tryfan is famous for the twin monoliths of Adam and Eve, a pair of rocks some three metres high and just over a metre apart.

MOEL SIABOD

Looking down the east ridge of Moel Siabod (2014).

MOEL SIABOD (2,861ft)

» Moel Siabod is a fine and popular peak just to the east of the main Snowdonia 3,000ft mountains.

» It is close to the A5 near Capel Curig and has good views, nearly all the Welsh 3,000ft mountains can be seen without moving your head.

» Moel Siabod gives a good half day circuit achieved by going through the old quarries and up the east ridge. The descent then takes you down the north ridge.

Personal View

Moel Siabod is south of the A5 near Capel Curig and is easily missed on the drive from Betws-y-Coed, perhaps to Pen-y-Pass to climb Snowdon or to Ogwen to climb Tryfan and the Glyders. However, its ascent gives an excellent half day circuit.

My first visit to Moel Siabod was on a wet Sunday in 2004. I saw very few walkers and assumed that Moel Siabod had been passed over by most people heading for the nearby Welsh 3,000 footers including Snowdon and Tryfan. However, this theory was proved wrong when I decided to climb the mountain again one Sunday ten years later. I counted at least fifty people walking up Moel Siabod and enjoying the spring sunshine. Clearly this is a popular half day walk and Moel Siabod is one of the best Welsh mountains.

My ascent route passed some old slate quarry workings and a quarry pool on its way to the fine east ridge of Moel Siabod. There is some scrambling on this ridge. The ridge deposits you directly at the summit cairn with its great views of the Welsh 3,000ft mountains.

MOEL SIABOD continued

My Route (3-4 hours)

I turned right out of the car park and crossed the river at Pont Cyfyng. I continued past a footpath, going right just after the bridge, and took the second right over a cattle grid to pick up a sign to Moel Siabod.

The narrow road turned into a path and passed two cottages. The path now headed directly towards Moel Siabod entering open land at a gate and stile. Just before the next gate the path split.

The most direct route to Moel Siabod is to the right and continues SW up the NE ridge to the summit. However, to create a circular walk I followed the path to the left past a quarry and eventually past Llyn y Foel. From here I turned west up the east ridge (Daear Ddu ridge) to the summit. I returned by the NE ridge.

Key Details

» Distance 5.5 miles (9km)
» Height climbed 2,500ft
» O/S Landranger 115 Snowdon
» Parking at Bryn Glo car park, 737570.

POINTS OF INTEREST

The start point for Moel Siabod is Capel Curig, supposedly the wettest place in Britain. Capel Curig was named after Saint Julitta's church founded by St Curig.

PLACES TO STAY/DRINK

There are pubs and cafes near the start at Capel Curig. Betws-y-Coed nearby has a selection of hotels, guest houses and restaurants.

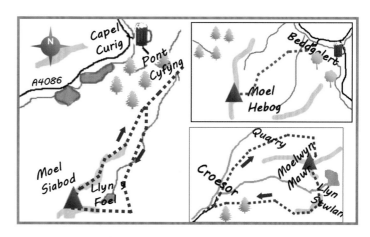

Canoeists under the bridge at the start of the walk at Capel Curig.

CARNEDDS

CARNEDD LLEWELYN
(3,490ft)
PEN LLITHRIG Y WRACH
(2,622ft)

» The Carnedds create a high plateau south of Conwy and the coast of North Wales.

» Carnedd Llewelyn is the second highest summit in Wales.

» Good mountain walking with great views.

My Routes

CARNEDD LLEWELYN
(5-6 hours)
I climbed Carnedd Llewelyn and Pen Llithrig y Wrach separately, although they could be combined, as shown on the map. For Carnedd Llewelyn I parked at Ogwen Cottage and followed the steep path which climbs to the summit of Pen yr Ole Wen. From that summit the Carnedds can be completed by a relatively easy walk. I continued in a NE direction over Carnedd Dafydd to Carnedd Llewelyn returning the same way.

PEN LLITHRIG Y WRACH
(2-3 hours)
To climb Pen Llithrig I parked the car just off the A5 4km NW of Capel Curig. From here I climbed NE, gradually at first but steeper near the summit.

POINTS OF INTEREST

The two highest mountains in Carneddau are Carnedd Llewelyn and Carnedd Dafydd named after the 13th century Prince of Wales, Llywelyn and his grandson Dafydd. Dafydd was executed by King Edward in 1283 ending independence for Wales.

The Carnedds seen from Bangor.

Personal View

Carnedd Llewelyn and Carnedd Dafydd are the most northerly and the least fashionable of the Welsh 3,000 footers. There is a steep climb from Ogwen Cottage to the ridge but then the walking becomes much easier. Pen Llithrig y Wrach is an outlier but can be added to Carnedd Llewellyn to create a circular walk although it would help to have transport at both ends.

When climbing Carnedd Dafydd and Carnedd Llewelyn I started from Ogwen Cottage and climbed the steep ascent to Pen yr Ole Wen. Once on the summit of Pen yr Ole Wen the hard climbing is over. On a sunny day it is an enjoyable walk over these hills perhaps finishing in Conwy if transport can be arranged.

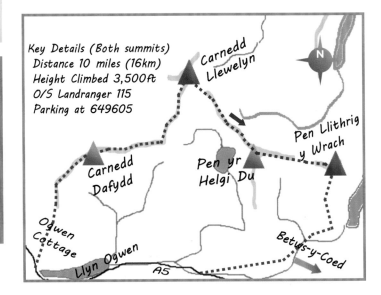

Key Details (Both summits)
Distance 10 miles (16km)
Height Climbed 3,500ft
O/S Landranger 115
Parking at 649605

Carnedd Llewelyn

Pen Llithrig y Wrach

Carnedd Dafydd

Pen yr Helgi Du

Ogwen Cottage

Llyn Ogwen

A5

Betws-y-Coed

ARENIG FAWR

ARENIG FAWR (2,801ft)

» Arenig Fawr stands in remote country west of Bala.

» Its near neighbour Moel Llyfnant (2,464ft) is thirteen feet short of Top 500 status.

Arenig Fawr from Moel Llyfnant.

My Route (3-4 hours)

I drove up the A4212 from Bala and turned left down a minor road after passing Llyn Celyn. After parking I walked east down the road for 1.5km, then abandoned the road and headed south down a grassy track. This turned SSE to reach the east side of Llyn Arenig Fawr. I walked along the east side of the lake to a small building near the dam outflow, turned right and followed the path up a ridge.

I continued past Y Castell to the NE ridge of Arenig Fawr. Finally I followed a line of fence posts which ran SW to the summit. I descended north to return to the car.

Personal View

I climbed Arenig Fawr on a wet day in 2004 returning to Bala for a well earned drink. Later on a beautiful December day I climbed Moel Llyfnant to take some pictures of Arenig Fawr (see above) and in case Moel Llyfnant (2,464ft) is ever promoted to the Top 500 list. Currently it is number 505 on the list of summits.

Key Details

» **Distance 6 miles (10km)**

» Height climbed 1,700ft

» O/S Landranger 124 and 125

» Parking at 832392.

PLACES TO STAY/DRINK

There are plenty of hotels, pubs, cafes and restaurants in Bala which is ten miles from the start.

POINTS OF INTEREST

A memorial on the summit of Arenig Fawr commemorates eight American airmen who died when their Flying Fortress bomber crashed on the hill on 4 August 1943.

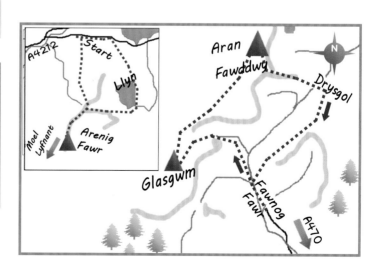

ARAN SUMMITS

ARAN FAWDDWY (2,970ft)
GLASGWM (2,557ft)

» The Arans form a high and interesting ridge between Bala and Dolgellau.

» There is good ridge walking between Aran Fawddwy to Aran Benllyn.

» The best approaches appear to be from the north or the south rather than from the west.

My Route (5-6 hours, including Aran Fawddwy)

I turned right off the A470 at Dinas Mawddwy. The route up Glasgwm started just past Fawnog Fawr. I parked in a field and followed the lane north. The path went NW across the hillside then WNW to the col between Glasgwm and Aran Fawddwy. From here I climbed Glasgwm.

Aran Fawddwy can be added by returning to the col, then heading NE along a line of fence posts for 3km to the summit. It would be possible to return by the same route, but an alternative descent would be to descend south to Drws Bach then east to Drysgol. From here it should be straightforward to descend SW to the start.

For reference, see the Arenig Fawr map on page 43.

Key Details (both summits)

» Distance 10 miles (16km)
» Height climbed 3,300ft
» O/S Landranger 124 and 125
» Parking at 853189.

POINTS OF INTEREST

Aran Fawddwy (2,970ft) is the highest sub 3,000 foot summit or 'Corbett' in the British Isles outside Scotland.

Personal View

On my first visit to the Arans I climbed Aran Fawddwy from the west side starting from the Bala to Dolgellau road. This was a poor route, there were no paths and I was chased over a fence by a large flock of aggressive sheep, all very embarrassing. My advice is to avoid this route.

A few years later I climbed Glasgwm from the south driving to Welshpool then along the A458 and A470 to Dinas Mawddwy. It would be possible to add Aran Fawddwy to this walk and I have suggested this under 'my route'.

Aran Fawddwy in February from the slopes of Foel Hafod-fynydd.

SOUTH OF SNOWDON

MOEL HEBOG *(2,566ft)*
MOELWYN MAWR *(2,527ft)*

» Both mountains can be climbed in the same day or as two half day climbs.

My Routes

MOEL HEBOG (2-3 hours)

From the road junction at the centre of Beddgelert, I drove 500m up the A4085 and turned left across a bridge over the Colwyn. I parked at the end of the tarmac road and walked a further 400m, over a small gauge railway and through some trees. Just after a barn at 581479 I turned right through a gate. After a short distance there was a left fork up the hillside and a good path led all the way to the summit.

MOELWYN MAWR (2-3 hours)

I parked at the car park at Croesor, then followed the track to the cafe. I turned left up the lane and on reaching the farm turned right to a stile. The route continued to another stile, then followed a grassy path up the hillside to Rhosydd quarry ruins. I followed the path to the summit of Moelwyn Mawr and continued to Moelwyn Bach.

For reference, see the Moel Siabod maps on page 41.

Key Details

» Total distance for both summits 10 miles (16km)
» Height climbed 4,800ft
» O/S Landranger 115 and 124
» Parking at 583481, Moel Hebog, and 631447, Moelwyn Mawr.

Looking down to Beddgelert from Moel Hebog.

Personal View

Both these mountains are enjoyable hills to climb with good sea views. Moel Hebog, in particular, is an underrated mountain. Even on a sunny August Bank Holiday I saw only two people climbing it, despite large crowds in Beddgelert nearby and queues reported on Snowdon.

Croesor, the start point for Moelwyn Mawr, is a beautiful spot and it is well worth adding Cnicht, 'the Matterhorn of North Wales', to create a circular walk when climbing Moelwyn Mawr.

POINTS OF INTEREST

Blaenau Ffestiniog, a possible start point for Moelwyn Mawr, is known as 'the town that roofed the world' and there are trips down its slate mines.

Moelwyn Mawr from Cnicht.

45

RHINOGS

Y LLETHR *(2,480ft)*

» Y Llethr is the highest point on the Rhinogs, a long ridge running north to south near the Irish Sea coast in West Wales.

» The heathery and rocky slopes of Rhinog Fawr and Rhinog Fach give this ridge great character.

In the heart of the Rhinogs (2012).

My Route (4-5 hours)

We parked at Graigddu-isaf, a couple of miles off the A470 between Dolgellau and Ffestiniog. From Graigddu-isaf we followed a good path south and then SW, through the forest to the top of the pass between Rhinog Fawr and Rhinog Fach.

A few hundred metres past the top of the pass we turned left along a path which led to Llyn Hywel. We kept to the west side of the loch, then ascended steep slopes to the SE ridge of Y Llethr. This ridge is easily followed to the summit. After descending to the col between Y Llethr and Rhinog Fach (this descent required care) we climbed Rhinog Fach.

From the summit a path led east to below the east side of the ridge. From there the path descended north before bending west to reach the top of the pass and our ascent route.

PLACES TO STAY/DRINK

Dolgellau, 10 miles from the start, has hotels, pubs, cafes and guest houses.

POINTS OF INTEREST

The Rhinogs range are protected as a Special Area of Conservation and National Nature Reserve and walkers are discouraged from leaving the paths.

Personal View

The Rhinogs are a superb ridge of mountains running north to south in west Wales north of Dolgellau. On one of my many revisions to the list I noted that Y Llethr should be added so I had an excuse to visit these mountains. Jo joined me for an ascent of Y Llethr and Rhinog Fach in December 2012. The mist hung about on the summits but it was a good day for walking.

Although we found the summit of Y Llethr disappointing the rest of the walk was superb and particularly the traverse over Rhinog Fach. We tried to prove that there was sufficient drop for Rhinog Fach to be a Marilyn but unfortunately it fell two metres short of the 150 metres drop required.

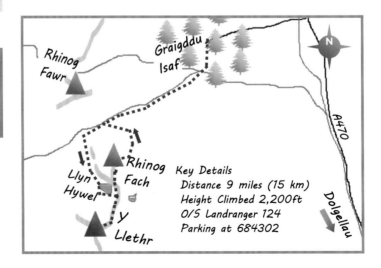

Key Details
Distance 9 miles (15 km)
Height Climbed 2,200ft
O/S Landranger 124
Parking at 684302

CADAIR BERWYN

CADAIR BERWYN *(2,723ft)*

» Cadair Berwyn is the highest point in the Berwyn mountains.

» Pistyll Rhaeadr is the highest waterfall in Wales.

My Route (2-3 hours)

From the entrance to the car park at Tan-y-Pistyll (charge) a path climbed through the trees heading for the top of the Pistyll Rhaeadr Falls. We followed the path onto open hillside. As it started to head down to the top of the falls, we took a grassy path up the wide ridge which led to Moel Sych.

From Moel Sych we walked NE for 1km along a wide ridge, to pass over the actual summit and reach the trig point for Cadair Berwyn.

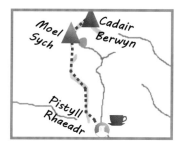

Key Details

» Distance 5.5 miles (9km)
» Height climbed 1,800ft.
» O/S Landranger 125 Bala
» Parking at 076294.

POINTS OF INTEREST

In 1987 Bernard Wright from Cheshire noted the trig point for Cadair Berwyn (827m) was not the true summit. This is 200m south at a height of 830m.

Personal View

Cadair Berwyn is best climbed from Tan-y-Pistyll to the south of the mountain. The drive to Tan-y-Pistyll along the single track road passes through spectacular alpine scenery. After coffee and cake at the beautiful tea room we walked to the top of the waterfall. It was a warm sunny day with many families above the waterfall swimming or risking a look over the edge. We had an enjoyable walk up the mountain but it was an anticlimax after the beauty of Tan-y-Pistyll.

PLACES TO STAY/DRINK

There is a tea room and guest house at Tan-y-Pistyll as well as camping, caravanning and a holiday cottage.

Pistyll Rhaeadr waterfall from the tea room at Tan-y-pistyll (2013).

CADAIR IDRIS

The summit of Cadair Idris on a beautiful January day, the Arans in the background (2013).

CADAIR IDRIS *(2,929ft)*

» Cadair Idris, also known as Pen y Gadair, is one of the most popular mountains in Wales.

» The route described starts at Minffordd and gives a classic circular walk around Cwm Cau. There is a National Trust tea shop at the finish but this was closed in January when I climbed the mountain.

» Cadair Idris is a superb mountain with rugged beauty and great views.

PLACES TO STAY/DRINK

The Cadair tea room is found near the start of the walk (may be closed in winter). There is also a hotel in Minffordd and a good selection of pubs, restaurants and accommodation in Dolgellau.

Personal View (Jonathan)

Many people will remember where they were when Charles and Diana were married, in my case I was climbing Cadair Idris. I was seventeen years old and the wedding seemed unimportant but our leader, an English teacher, thought differently. At 11.20 a.m. he stopped our party of twenty-five in order to have a ten minute silence while the wedding ceremony took place. This bizarre scene is etched in my memory but I guess most of us were happy to have a rest.

It was of course 1981 and we were on a school camp at Dolgellau. Sean was there and many years later we visited the Alps together although our attempt on Mont Blanc failed in atrocious weather. However, on that day we baked in the sunshine on Cadair Idris. Having headed up from Minffordd we continued north from the summit to complete a through route. On the descent we ran down to Llyn y Gadair for a swim.

Today I recollect Cadair Idris as a fantastic mountain, aesthetically pleasing and with that sense of isolation that make the best mainland mountains stand out. Examples of this include An Teallach, Ladhar Bheinn and Blencathra. Hopefully I will find an excuse to return to Cadair soon.

CADAIR IDRIS continued

My Route (4-5 hours)

I started at the National Trust car park near the junction between the A487 and the B4405 at Minffordd. I followed the signs to Cadair Idris and soon arrived at the Visitors Centre and Tearoom. After passing the front of the tea-room the path climbed steeply uphill through woodland (an 8,000 year old Oak Wood) to a gate. I continued along the path and near a stream I took the left hand fork to Cwm Cau.

The path entered Cwm Cau. 1km after the fork but before reaching Llyn Cau I turned left up the hillside towards the ridge on the left hand skyline. On reaching the ridge I followed it WSW then NW to go over Craig Cau (a Hewitt). From Craig Cau the path descended 250ft before climbing 600ft to the summit of Cadair Idris.

I walked ENE for 1.5km to Mynydd Moel then descended SSE turning south. Finally I followed a fence to a stile at 732125. From here a path returned to the start.

POINTS OF INTEREST

Legend has it that the mountain's name refers to a giant called Idris and he was so big that Cwm Cau was his chair.

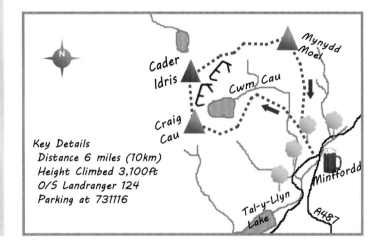

Key Details
Distance 6 miles (10km)
Height Climbed 3,100ft
O/S Landranger 124
Parking at 731116

A small footbridge near the end of the circuit of Cwm Cau.

BRECON BEACONS

Pen Y Fan from Fan Fawr on a busy day in February.

PEN Y FAN *(2,906ft)*
FAN BRYCHEINIOG *(2,630ft)*
WAUN RYDD *(2,523ft)*

» These are grassy hills in South Wales lying between Brecon and Merthyr Tydfil.

» Pen y Fan and its neighbours Corn Du and Cribyn are popular hills which are particularly busy on summer weekends.

» Waun Rydd and Fan Brycheiniog are much quieter hills although Fan Brycheiniog is grandly situated above Lynn y Fan Fawr.

Personal View

Pen y Fan is the best known mountain in South Wales and there always seem to be large numbers of people climbing it from the car park just off the A470. I understand that over 500,000 people climb it each year which puts strain on the car parking and paths. Waun Rydd and Fan Brycheiniog are less well known.

Waun Rydd could be combined with Pen y Fan as a good ridge walk but it would be advisable to have a car at both ends. Fan Brycheiniog is best climbed separately from a small deserted car park on the minor road from Trecastle to Glyntawe. There is a sharp contrast between this car park and the constant activity at the car park signifying the start of Pen y Fan.

I climbed each mountain separately including two ascents of Pen y Fan. On all four ascents the weather was poor with cloud on the summits. Despite this Pen y Fan was always crowded but I did not see anyone else on Waun Rydd or Fan Brycheiniog. It took a fifth visit to take some pictures and visit Blaenavon, a magnificent World Heritage site on the east side of the Brecon Beacons.

BRECON BEACONS continued

My Routes

PEN Y FAN (2-3 hours)
I started from the car park off the A470 just south of the Storey Arms (ref. 989199, O/S Landranger 160). An obvious path headed NE up the hillside to a small col just south of Corn Du. I went over Corn Du then turned ENE and ascended Pen y Fan.

WAUN RYDD (3-4 hours)
I drove to Llanfrynach (ref. 075257, O/S Landranger 160) then walked up to Tregaer. At Tregaer I turned left onto the hillside. A path went SSW for nearly 5km to reach the summit.

FAN BRYCHEINIOG (3-4 hours)
The route started from the car park (ref. 856223, O/S Landranger 160) on the minor road from Trecastle to Glyntawe. I walked WSW to the south end of the lake, Llyn y Fan Fawr. From the lake a track led up to Bwlch Giedd turning NNW to the summit trig point and shelter.

PLACES TO STAY/DRINK

There are a number of places to stay including Brecon and Merthyr Tydfil. My preference would be to combine the Brecons and the Black Mountains and stay at Crickhowell, a beautiful village near Abergavenny.

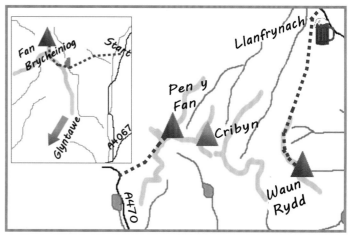

Big Pit at Blaenavon in the Brecon Beacons national park.

POINTS OF INTEREST
Blaenavon is a World Heritage Site standing high in the Brecon Beacons. It contains a number of interesting sites including Big Pit which employed 1,300 workers in its heyday.

BLACK MOUNTAINS

WAUN FACH *(2,660ft)*

» Waun Fach lies near the centre of a plateau of rolling hills north west of Abergavenny, the Black Mountains.

» The Black Mountains are less popular than their near neighbours, the Brecon Beacons.

Trusha on the way up Waun Fach in the Black Mountains.

Jonathan's Route (2-3 hours)

I parked just off the A479 at Cwmfforest and followed a path east through trees. The path ascended the broad shoulder of Pen Trumau to a col at 2,000ft, between Pen Trumau and Mynydd Llysiau. I climbed north over Pen Trumau, a minor top, and continued as the path turned east to Waun Fach and its strange summit area. The top appears to be marked by an area of brown peat and a large stone shaped like a massive mushroom.

I returned by the same route. This could be varied by heading NW from Waun Fach along the broad ridge for 2km, then west down Y Grib to the start.

PLACES TO STAY/DRINK

There is a pub near the start of the walk. However, Crickhowell is a lovely place to visit and has a good selection of hotels and cafes.

Personal View (Jonathan)

A high start from near the riding centre at Cwmfforest had meant pleasant and easy walking to the peat hag which posed as the summit of Waun Fach. I suspected that the walk from the south along the long, wide ridges of the Black Mountains would give a good day. This was the route Barry had come on his 28 mile 'Red Dragon' walk, although I assumed he had lost his way to end up walking that many miles on a straightforward hill like Waun Fach!

I had a busy day ahead so this was not the day to explore the long grassy ridges of these mountains. Instead I headed down to Cardiff for a football match and then to Devon for a Halloween party, a fine day in many ways.

POINTS OF INTEREST

There are a number of historical sights in the area including:

» The Skirrid Mountain Inn, a few miles north of Abergavenny, dates back to 1100 AD and is thought to be the oldest pub in Wales.

» The remains of Castell Dinas, a castle built on the site of an Iron Age hillfort near to the start of the walk.

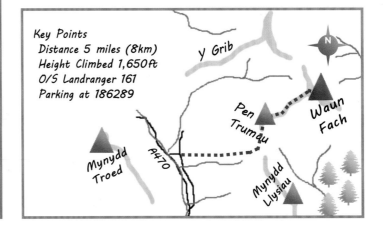

Key Points
Distance 5 miles (8km)
Height Climbed 1,650ft
O/S Landranger 161
Parking at 186289

Y Grib

Pen Trumau

Waun Fach

Mynydd Troed

A470

Mynydd Llysiau

N

Doolough between the Sheeffry Hills and Mweelrea.

IRELAND

There are 29 Top 500 Summits in Ireland, 27 in Southern Ireland and 2 in Northern Ireland. They are divided into 16 walks:

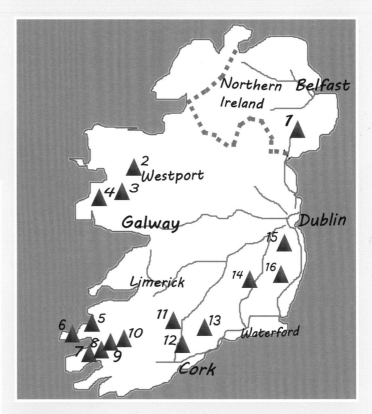

WALKS 1 TO 16

	Walk	Feet	Pg.
1	Slieve Donard	2,796	56
	Slieve Commedagh	2,516	
2	Nephin	2,646	58
	Croagh Patrick	2,507	
3	Barrclashcame	2,533	59
4	Mweelrea	2,671	60
	Ben Lugmore	2,634	
5	Baurtregaum	2,792	62
	Beenoskee	2,710	
6	Brandon Mountain	3,127	64
	Brandon Peak	2,756	
7	Stumpa Duloigh	2,572	66
	Mullaghanattin	2,539	
	Coomacarrea	2,533	
8	Carrauntoohil	3,414	68
	Cnoc na Peiste	3,240	
9	Purple Mountain	2,739	70
10	Mangerton Mountain	2,766	71
11	Galtymore	3,018	72
	Greenane	2,631	
	Temple Hill	2,575	
12	Knockmealdown	2,605	74
13	Fauscoum	2,597	75
	Knockanaffrin	2,477	
14	Mount Leinster	2,610	76
15	Mullaghcleevaun	2,788	77
	Tonelagee	2,680	
	Kippure	2,484	
16	Lugnaquilla	3,039	78

I visited Ireland a number of times when climbing the 29 Top 500 Summits located there, and enjoyed every trip. My favourite area is the south west including the Ring of Kerry and the Dingle Peninsula. 11 out of the 29 Top 500 Summits lie in this area including the highest peak, Carrauntoohil, and the most westerly summit in the British Isles, the Brandon Mountain. These are great mountains with superb views. Near Killarney lies Mangerton Mountain and Purple Mountain. On the Dingle Peninsula approaching Brandon Mountain lie Bautregaum and Beenoskee, lower profile mountains in fabulous situations.

Away from the south west there are many great mountain areas in Ireland. The Mourne Mountains in Northern Ireland lie in a spectacular location above Newcastle, County Down. I recall visiting Slieve Donard, the highest peak in Northern Ireland on a beautiful summer day, and there was a buzz of excitement as people reached the summit. From Cork it is an easy drive to Galtymore and the varied terrain of Fauscoum and Knockmealdown. Finally in Galway the great Mweelrea stands above the cliffs facing west, a summit that should not be missed.

Brandon Mountain from
Brandon Peak.

MOURNE MOUNTAINS

Descending from Slieve Donard next to the Mourne Wall (2013).

SLIEVE DONARD *(2,796ft)*
SLIEVE COMMEDAGH
(2,516ft)

» Slieve Donard is the highest mountain in Northern Ireland.

» The Mourne mountains contain the only two Top 500 Summits in Northern Ireland.

» The route up Slieve Donard from Newcastle, County Down is popular as befits Northern Ireland's highest summit.

» The Mourne Wall was built between 1910 and 1922 and is kept in excellent condition.

Personal View

The Mourne Mountains lie one hour's drive from Belfast next to Newcastle, County Down. Like many other places in Ireland the Mourne Mountains give great walking. Slieve Donard, the highest mountain in Northern Ireland, is deservedly popular and the summit is a superb spot overlooking the sea.

My first attempt to climb Slieve Donard was in late March 2013 in the unseasonably cold weather that occurred that spring. It was a windy day of heavy snow showers and at times clearer periods. The route up to the saddle was treacherous with ice beneath the snow. I reached the saddle but without crampons and in blizzard conditions I gave up after taking a picture of the six foot high Mourne Wall just appearing above the snow.

I returned to the Mourne Mountains in early June and enjoyed the walk immensely. I climbed Slieve Donard first and although it was a weekday there were about fifty people on the summit from a number of different countries. I continued to Slieve Commedagh, a peaceful summit with nobody to be seen. I returned to Newcastle and walked along the seafront, stopping for lunch in a cafe.

My Route (3-5 hours)

I started at the car park at Donard Park (no charge). This lies at the south end of the main street through Newcastle, County Down. From there I walked SW and followed the Glen River through the woodland (crossing to the left then back to the right of the river). After a few hundred metres the trees on my left disappeared and soon I was on open hillside.

The path continued to the saddle between Slieve Donard and Slieve Commedagh. I turned left to follow the Mourne Wall to the summit of Slieve Donard. I returned to the saddle and climbed Slieve Commedagh. Slieve Donard was a short and sharp 850ft climb from the saddle, and Slieve Commedagh was a more gentle climb of 550ft.

I found the summit of Slieve Commedagh 100m north of the Mourne Wall. After continuing along the north ridge for 1km, I descended east to where the main path from Donard Park came out of the woods.

POINTS OF INTEREST

On the Sunday after the May Bank Holiday over 2,000 people used to complete the Mourne Wall walk. However, this was stopped in 1984 because of fears about damage to the environment.

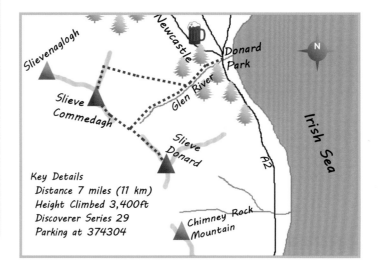

Key Details
Distance 7 miles (11 km)
Height Climbed 3,400ft
Discoverer Series 29
Parking at 374304

The Mourne Wall in late March 2013, the snow has reached the top of the six foot high wall.

AROUND WESTPORT

NEPHIN *(2,646ft)*
CROAGH PATRICK *(2,507ft)*

» Croagh Patrick is a prominent summit near Westport. A broad stoney path known as the Pilgrim's route leads to the summit chapel.

» Nephin is an isolated summit between Westport and Sligo.

Personal View

I love to return to Westport, a peaceful Irish town with the sea surrounding it. It is dominated by Croagh Patrick which soars above the town. Known as The Reek to the locals Croagh Patrick is also referred to as the Pilgrims' Mountain. The July Pilgrimage has been taking place for over 1,000 years. Donald and I climbed Croagh Patrick using the Pilgrims' route one evening while on a golf holiday in 2008. Fortunately the weather was good as we climbed higher in evening sunlight. The chapel at the summit was closed but we had great views out to sea. After staying for twenty minutes we returned to Westport for dinner.

Seven years later I returned to Westport and after a glorious day on Mweelrea, Nephin became my last Top 500 Summit in Ireland. Nephin is unique amongst the higher mountains of the British Isles for its pure isolation. It rises steeply up from the valley floor on all sides. There are no subsidiary peaks or ways to start a little higher, 2,400ft of climbing is needed from any direction. From the south it looked like Blencathra but the broad summit ridge is shorter than Blencathra. No doubt there are magnificent views on a clear day.

Ascending Croagh Patrick (2008).

My Routes

CROAGH PATRICK *(3-4 hours)*

We started at a large car park on the south side of the R335 at Murrisk. From here a broad path led all the way to the summit going south for over a mile then turning west and becoming stoney and steeper as it neared the summit.

» **Distance 5 miles (8km)**

» **Height climbed 2,500ft**

» **Discovery Series 30**

» **Parking at Murrisk (919817).**

NEPHIN *(2-3 hours)*

I drove up the R312 Castlebar to Bangor road turning right a mile after the junction with the R317 to Newport. I stopped at reference 115055 where there was a stone clad cottage with a farm behind. A good track went past the right hand side of the farm and stopped at a barbed wire fence. I climbed the fence and headed steeply up open hillside NNW. After the initial 600ft of climbing the going improved as I ascended a broad ridge to the summit plateau.

» **Distance 4 miles (6km)**

» **Height climbed 2,400ft**

» **Discovery Series 31**

» **Parking at 115055.**

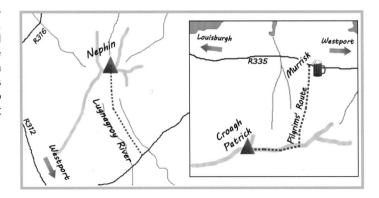

SHEEFFRY HILLS

BARRCLASHCAME *(2,533ft)*

» Barrclashcame is the highest point on the Sheeffry Hills which lie close to Mweelrea in County Mayo.

» These are rolling grassy hills giving excellent ridge walking with good views.

My Route (3-4 hours)

I drove north on the R335 from Leenaun. There is a small parking area next to Doolough, 300m north of the right turn to the Sheeffry Pass. I walked north up the road for 100m until I was clear of the trees then climbed east to reach a broad ridge. This climbed steeply to the summit plateau of Barrclashcame.

From the summit of Barrclashcame I walked east for just over 1km to a large trig point at the centre of the Sheeffry Hills. The trig point marks the summit of an Irish Hewitt called Tievummera. I returned to the car by the same route.

Key Details

» **Distance 5.5 miles (9km)**
» **Height climbed 2,500ft**
» **Discovery Series 37**
» **Parking at 845677.**

Summit of Barrclashcame.

Personal View

The Sheeffry Hills lie just to the east of Mweelrea. They are grassy hills and the long summit ridge is a joy to walk along, the views stretching from Croagh Patrick with its white summit chapel in the north to the Twelve Bens of Connemara in the south.

I parked at a small car park beautifully situated overlooking Doolough and headed straight up the steep hillside to the highest point, Barrclashcame, A narrow grassy ridge went off east and about a mile away stood a large trig point. At the very least I thought I should walk to that. It was Tievummera, an Irish Hewitt. Returning to Barrclashcame I met the first walker I had seen on the mountains for three days. He had arrived from Poland eight years ago intending to stay only six months but clearly enjoyed life in Ireland. I made a quick descent to the car and returned to Leenaun for high tea overlooking the estuary.

MWEELREA HORSESHOE

Mweelrea from the summit of Ben Lugmore (2015).

MWEELREA (2,671ft)
BEN LUGMORE (2,634ft)

» Mweelrea is the highest mountain in Connaught. Its situation, overlooking Killary Harbour, and flanked by east facing cliffs, is magnificent.

» Ben Lugmore has a sharp summit ridge and makes a fitting end to a superb horseshoe.

» The views are superb and ever changing, Mweelrea looks south to the Maum Turks and Bens of Connemara.

Personal View

There are many truly iconic high level walks in Ireland, including the end to end traverse of MacGillycuddy's Reeks, the Brandon Mountain and Peak, Slieve Donard and the Mourne Wall, and this gem. Mweelrea forms a superb horseshoe above the sea with its near neighbours, Ben Bury and Ben Lugmore.

I had never known how to pronounce Mweelrea but always wanted to climb it and was lucky enough to catch a gorgeous October day in 2015 for the circuit. Walking to the slopes of Mweelrea from Delphi Lodge was tedious but thereafter the circuit was a pure delight. Steep slopes overlooking Killary Harbour led me to the surprisingly flat summit of Mweelrea.

I relaxed down easy slopes before ascending Ben Bury, my eyes now drawn to the blue sea and islands to the north, then I turned inland to see the sharp ridge which ran along to the summit of Ben Lugmore. Cliffs plunged down to Doolough on my left and in front of me stood the Sheeffry Hills bringing back memories of those days of endless sunshine in April. Finally I descended to the car at Delphi Lodge to find the coffee shop open and very welcoming. It had been a superb day on one of the greatest mountains in Ireland.

My Route (5-6 hours)

I started at the car park at the Delphi Mountain Resort and walked round the right hand side of the building. A gravel track led into the forest and continued along the south side of the Owennaglogh River. After passing a clearing in the trees I turned left at a junction and followed the track to the south side of the second band of trees. I continued along the south side of the trees until the track petered out.

I walked NW over rough ground, at times boggy, for 1km, then climbed west heading for the col between point 495m and the steep slopes leading up Mweelrea. At the col I followed a path which climbed quickly to the summit ridge. The ridge led north over the summit then descended to the col between Mweelrea and Ben Bury.

Easy slopes now led NE up Ben Bury with fine views north and west. The sun was shining as

I descended a short distance SE then reascended to the sharp ridge of Ben Lugmore. I followed the ridge SE over the summit and continued ENE along the ridge now descending. I descended SSE directly towards the Delphi Mountain Resort and crossed some awkward ground. Finally the Owennaglogh River had to be crossed to reach the gravel track back to the car.

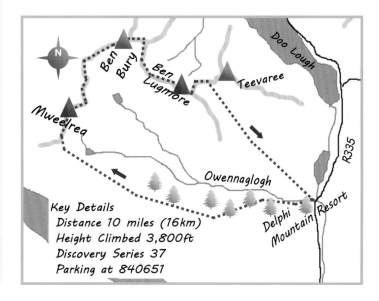

Key Details
Distance 10 miles (16km)
Height Climbed 3,800ft
Discovery Series 37
Parking at 840651

Looking across to the Sheeffry Hills from the slopes of Ben Lugmore (2015).

DINGLE PENINSULA

Beenoskee from Bautregaum (2015).

BAURTREGAUM *(2,792ft)*
BEENOSKEE *(2,710ft)*

» Baurtregaum and Beenoskee are both isolated mountains on the Dingle Peninsula overlooking Tralee Bay to the north and Dingle Bay to the south.

» Baurtregaum and Slieve Donard are the highest mountains in Ireland under 3,000ft, surprisingly there are no 2,800ft or 2,900ft mountains in Ireland.

» Both climbs are half day walks with superb views.

Personal View

My first attempt to find the start point of Beenoskee foundered when I bottomed the car down on a minor 'road' which appeared to lead to Loch Cam. This forced me into a tricky reverse down the narrow stony track. In fact I needed to take the minor road signposted to Glanteenassig Woods and follow the road to a car park at Loch Cam. Thus it was nearly 5 p.m. when I started climbing. The car park was almost full when I arrived with families playing around the side of the small lake. However, it emptied as I climbed higher which seemed strange as it was a glorious evening.

I reached the magnificent summit of Beenoskee overlooking the sea and a small loch, then followed the short ridge to Stradbally, before returning quickly to the car by 7 p.m. However, I had not realised that the gates to the wood closed at 6 p.m. and I was very fortunate to be allowed out.

On the following day, Easter Sunday, beautiful weather greeted me again. I had an early breakfast at the hotel and started walking up Baurtregaum from the parking area in Derrymore at 9 a.m. Soon I found the Dingle Way, then headed up the Derrymore River eventually crossing it to ascend to the summit. I returned quickly as I needed to climb Brandon Peak later.

My Routes

BAURTREGAUM (3-4 hours)

I drove west along the N86 out of Tralee turning left up a minor road, a few hundred metres after crossing the Derrymore River. There was space for cars near a left turn at 742107.

A path went west past a cottage, then turned south up the hillside reaching the Dingle Way after a short distance. I turned left along the Dingle Way to the Derrymore River. A path climbed up the west side of the river. When west of point 723m, I crossed the river and climbed the hillside turning SSE to climb to the summit of Baurtregaum. I returned over point 819m and Scragg but the heathery and awkward ground after Scragg slowed down my descent.

BEENOSKEE (2-3 hours)

Driving from Tralee I took the N86, then turned right along the R560. After 6km there was a sign left to Glanteenassig Woods up a minor road. At the second attempt I followed this and after 5km turned right through a gate. I drove up the road to Loch Cam where there is a good car park.

I walked left out of the car park and followed the boardwalk for 300m. Just after passing some viewing seats I climbed steeply NW up the hillside. On reaching the col between Beenoskee and Stradbally Mountain I followed the edge, climbing Beenoskee first then Stradbally Mountain.

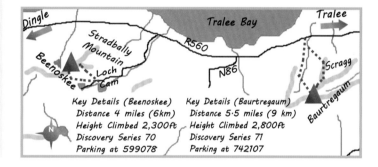

Key Details (Beenoskee)
Distance 4 miles (6km)
Height Climbed 2,300ft
Discovery Series 70
Parking at 599078

Key Details (Baurtregaum)
Distance 5·5 miles (9 km)
Height Climbed 2,800ft
Discovery Series 71
Parking at 742107

Looking to MacGillycuddy's Reeks from Beenoskee (2015).

BRANDON MOUNTAIN

The ridge running between Brandon Mountain and Brandon Peak from the east (2015).

BRANDON MOUNTAIN
(3,127ft)
BRANDON PEAK (2,756ft)

» Brandon Mountain is the most westerly of the Top 500 Summits in Britain and Ireland. It is also the highest mountain in Ireland outside the 'Reeks'.

» Brandon Mountain and Brandon Peak combine to give a great ridge walk.

» The views looking out to the Atlantic and inland along the Dingle Peninsula are magnificent.

Personal View

The walk over the Brandon Mountain and Brandon Peak is a must for hill walkers visiting Ireland. In 1983 Donald and I followed the Saints' Route to the summit of Brandon Mountain. The thick mist and drizzle cleared briefly to give a view of Brandon Peak from near the summit. Although the weather was poor, climbing Brandon Mountain was memorable for both of us and I always wanted to return to experience this magnificent mountain in clear weather.

In April 2015 the weather was superb. I climbed Bautregaum in the morning then drove to the south end of the Brandon ridge. From here a good path led up from a farm to Gearhane, then an impressive ridge took me to Brandon Peak. A runner passed me near the summit of Gearhane otherwise I was undisturbed in this awesome place. From the Brandon Peak I could see along the whole of the Dingle Peninsula to Tralee; further south MacGillycuddy's Reeks could be clearly seen. To the west lay the sea and the Blasket Islands. After that there was just the Atlantic Ocean stretching to America.

My Routes

In 1983 Donald and I climbed Brandon Mountain from the south west parking at grid reference 435095. There is now parking marked on the map. We followed a good path NE to the summit and returned the same way. This route is known as the Saints' Route. We could have added Brandon Peak and this route is shown on the map.

Thirty-two years later I climbed Brandon Peak from the end of a minor road. This ran from Cloghane finishing at a farm at reference 471068. From here a good path led west. After 200m I turned north through a gate to follow an equally good path which led up the hillside to a plateau at 2,000ft. I climbed NE to the summit of Gearhane, then continued NE along a narrow ridge to Brandon Peak.

A classic traverse of Brandon Mountain and Peak starts at Faha which is due east of the summit of Brandon Mountain. The ridge can be followed over Brandon Mountain and Brandon Peak dropping down to the farm. Two cars are needed for this traverse.

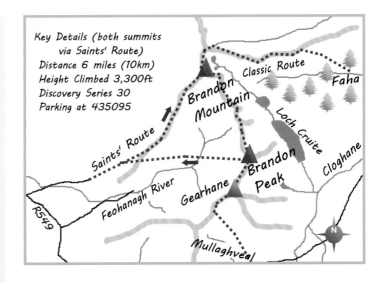

Key Details (both summits via Saints' Route)
Distance 6 miles (10km)
Height Climbed 3,300ft
Discovery Series 30
Parking at 435095

Classic Route
Faha
Brandon Mountain
Loch Cruite
Saints' Route
Cloghane
R549
Feohanagh River
Gearhane
Brandon Peak
Mullaghveal
N

PLACES TO STAY/DRINK

I would choose to stay at Dingle, a lovely small town by the sea, when climbing the Brandon Mountain.

Looking west from Brandon Peak.

POINTS OF INTEREST

Mount Brandon is named after Saint Brendon and is at the end of a christian pilgrimage known as Cosan na Naomh. The traditional pilgrimage from Dingle ended at the summit of Brandon Mountain but the route now finishes at the foot of the mountain.

RING OF KERRY

Looking west to Mullaghanattin from the start point for Stumpa Duloigh, very few cars seem to use this road!

STUMPA DULOIGH *(2,572ft)*
MULLAGHANATTIN *(2,539ft)*
COOMACARREA *(2,533ft)*

» These three individual summits lie in the mountain region south and west of the Reeks.

» All the mountains can be climbed as half day walks. The walks can be extended to give great ridge walking.

» Mullaghanattin is known as the 'Matterhorn of Kerry' because of its triangular form. Its ridge includes Beann which misses out on Top 500 status by a few feet.

Personal View

I climbed these mountains on separate days but they could be completed by determined walkers on the same day. It was very windy on Mullaghanattin and an unpleasant February blizzard hit me on Coomacarrea. I have described my ascents of Mullaghanattin and Stumpa Duloigh below.

MULLAGHANATTIN: It was April but the wind howled across the ridge as we edged our way towards the summit of Mullaghanattin. From time to time we were sheltered in the lee of the ridge and able to appreciate Mullaghanattin as a hidden gem. The final slopes led to a trig point and views all around of the magnificent Ring of Kerry, one of the best mountain regions in the British Isles.

STUMPA DULOIGH: The following February I returned to Ireland stopping at pretty Kenmare for a late lunch. Kenmare is a colourful town and the coffee shop where I had lunch buzzed with life. From there I drove to a point close to Stumpa Duloigh abandoning the car by the side of a minor road. I saw no other cars pass along the road for the full two and a half hours that it took to climb to the summit and back. Stumpa's summit ridge was a great highway sitting below the Reeks with a fence to guide walkers.

My Routes

STUMPA DULOIGH (2-3 hours)

I drove to the top of the pass between Stumpa Duloigh and Knocklomena, finding a parking place just west of the road's high point. I walked back to the top of the pass and climbed just west of north to the low point of the ridge east of Stumpa Duloigh. From there I climbed to the summit ridge and followed the fence posts to the summit.

MULLAGHANATTIN (3-4 hours)

We started at a gate 2km SE of Ballaghbeama Gap and climbed NW over two fences to reach the 462m point above the gap. It is possible to make a direct ascent from the gap but it looked steep with some scrambling so we did not attempt it. We then followed a wide ridge in a westerly direction, passing two small summits at 594m and 693m, before the final climb to the trig point.

COOMACARREA (2-3 hours)

I took a wrong turning out of Killorglin and finished south of Coomacarrea rather than to the north at Coomasaharn lake. I drove up a minor road towards Coomaspeara and stopped near some woods, directly south of the col between Coomacarrea and Meenteog. From here a good track led past a sheep shed and north to a col between Meenteog and Coomacarrea. I turned west into driving wet snow and ascended to the summit by a fence, returning by the same route.

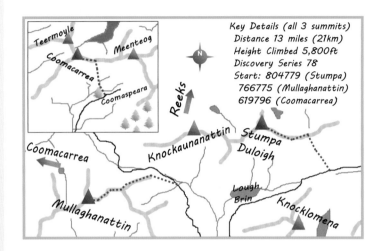

Key Details (all 3 summits)
Distance 13 miles (21km)
Height Climbed 5,800ft
Discovery Series 78
Start: 804779 (Stumpa)
766775 (Mullaghanattin)
619796 (Coomacarrea)

Sheltering from the wind on Mullaghanattin (Ceryse Griffith).

MACGILLYCUDDY'S REEKS

Looking towards Carrauntoohil (on the right) from near the start at Cronin Yard.

CARRAUNTOOHIL (3,414ft)
CNOC NA PEISTE (3,240ft)

» Carrauntoohil, the highest mountain in Ireland, can be climbed on its own from Cronin Yard. This is a popular climb.

» The main ridge of MacGillycuddy's Reeks contains eight tops over 3,000ft.

» The ridge is a classic traverse over the highest mountains in Ireland with constantly varying scenery.

» The ridge walking around the Big Gun is fantastic but this is a difficult and exposed section particularly in mist.

Personal View

It is hard to beat 'The Reeks'. JP had completed a classic clockwise circuit from the Hag's Glen with Ella kicking off with the tricky section around the Big Gun. They reached Cnoc na Peiste in time for a stop for lunch. After this they made good time to Carrauntoohil before tackling the ridge to Beenkeragh and then descending to Hag's Glen, 'Proper hills and great bars in Killarney', he said afterwards.

I had climbed Carrauntoohil on a family holiday at Killarney from Cronin Yard and expected to climb Cnoc na Peiste in the same way. However, Jo and I both wanted to traverse the full ridge of the Reeks and we were joined by John Delamere and Graham Mead.

We started with a fast ascent of Caher then made our way over the various summits slowing down to traverse the narrow ridges of the Big Gun. We were surprised by the sharpness of the ridges during this stage of the walk but they could be traversed with care. By this time John's ankle was giving him problems and he found even more trouble by trying to take a shortcut down a wooded cliff near the end. Eventually, we found him and were back for dinner after a great day.

My Route (9-12 hours)

The taxi dropped us off at the west end of the Reeks (ref 771871) where a path climbed up the hillside. We followed the path ESE then south to cross a river, and continued south onto the ridge which led up Caher.

From Caher we walked east then NE as the ridge dropped 300ft, then climbed 450ft to the summit of Carrauntoohil. From the summit we descended 1000ft SSE to the col at the top of the Devil's Ladder, the 'tourist route up Carrauntoohil'.

We were now on the easterly section of the Reeks walking east to pass over Cnoc na Toinne, Cnoc an Chuillin and Maolan Bui. Soon we turned NE to Cnoc na Peiste, the second Top 500 Summit on the Reeks. After Cnoc na Peiste there was some exposed ridge walking and scrambling as we climbed over the Big Gun. This required care but the weather was good so it did not present many problems.

From Cruach Mhor we descended ENE to Cnoc an Bhraca, then walked north for two miles to a track which led down to the road.

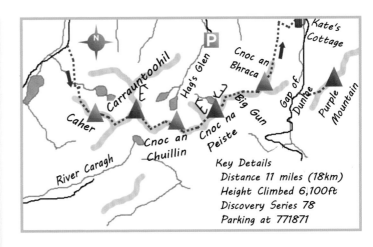

Key Details
Distance 11 miles (18km)
Height Climbed 6,100ft
Discovery Series 78
Parking at 771871

Ridge walking near the Big Gun (2009).

PLACES TO EAT/DRINK

The traverse of MacGillycuddy's Reeks west to east finishes near Kate Kearney's cottage, a pub/restaurant. Apparently Kate was a well known beauty in Ireland around 1845 distilling Kate Kearney's mountain dew.

PURPLE MOUNTAIN

PURPLE MOUNTAIN (2,739ft)

» Purple Mountain is separated from MacGillycuddy's Reeks by the spectacular Gap of Dunloe.

» It could be added to a walk over the Reeks but this would be a very long day.

My Route (2-3 hours)

I drove past Kate Kearney's Cottage continuing to the highest point on the road through the Gap of Dunloe. It is advisable, if driving up in summer, to set off early in the morning or in the evening as the crowds make this a difficult drive at peak times. At the highest point on the road there were places to park. A path climbed west up the Reeks and another one went east up Purple Mountain.

I followed the Purple Mountain path which passed Glas Lough, then climbed to the wide SW ridge of Purple Mountain. I passed over a small bump then walked ENE to the summit. It would be possible to continue over Tomies Mountain to Kate Kearney's Cottage but I returned the same way to retrieve the car.

For reference, see the MacGillycuddy's Reeks map on page 69.

Key Details

» Distance 4 miles (6km)
» Height climbed 2,000ft
» Discovery Series 78
» Parking at 872835.

Sheep block the way on my ascent of Purple Mountain (2014).

Personal View

It was early on a sunny August morning. The head of the Gap of Dunloe dividing the Reeks from Purple Mountain looked spectacular in the bright sunshine. Most of the visitors to Killarney were still having breakfast so the drive to the head of the Gap was quiet. From there I followed a path past an enclosed lochan, Glas Lough, to the summit of Purple Mountain.

I stopped to take some photos on the way down but was still back at 10 a.m., time for a leisurely coffee at the cafe opposite Kate Kearney's Cottage. The crowds were now out with walkers, cyclists and horse-drawn traps all making their way up the Gap of Dunloe and who could blame them, for in good weather this is a truly beautiful place.

POINTS OF INTEREST

The Gap of Dunloe is 11km (7 miles) long and passes five lakes. Between the 1st and 2nd lake, Coosaun Lough and Black Lake is an old arch bridge called the 'Wishing Bridge' so named as it is said that wishes made there come true.

MANGERTON MOUNTAIN

MANGERTON MOUNTAIN
(2,766ft)

» Mangerton Mountain is close to Killarney and is a half day walk.

» This is an interesting mountain with good paths and views over Killarney and its lakes.

My Route (3-4 hours)

We started near the Tooreen-cormick Battle Field Site where it was easy to park. A good path ran south rising gradually and heading directly towards Mangerton Mountain. The path turned SW after 2km to avoid going over point 762m.

The path rose more steeply to reach the Devil's Punch Bowl at 2,200ft. We followed the path as it climbed south round the edge of the Bowl. When it became clear we were not going to find the trig point without heading away from the edge, we went 200m south finding it easily. We descended north to complete a circuit of the Devil's Punch Bowl before returning to the car.

POINTS OF INTEREST

There are a number of interesting places to visit near Mangerton Mountain including Muckross House, Muckross Friary and Torc Waterfall.

Looking down at the Devil's punchbowl *(Cornell Griffith)*.

Personal View

Trusha, Ceryse and Cornell joined me for a long weekend in Ireland in April 2014. We took an early flight to Cork and were able to start climbing Mangerton Mountain after lunch. Mangerton Mountain is the most easterly of the summits around Killarney and the Ring of Kerry, an area sometimes compared to the English Lake District. We turned off the main road near Muckross and followed minor roads to the start point near Tooreencormick Battle Field Site.

The sun shone as we walked along a good path, through gorse, crossing streams and gradually rising to the Devil's Punch Bowl. A stiff wind greeted us as we walked along the edge of the cliffs guarding the Devil's Punch Bowl. We tramped south through boggy ground to reach the trig point which would be challenging to locate in mist. As we walked down, the lakes of Killarney glistened in the late afternoon sunshine.

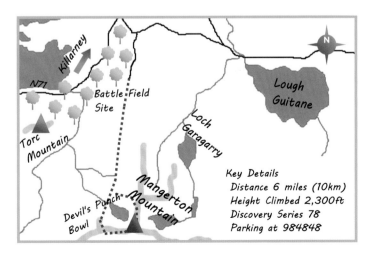

Key Details
Distance 6 miles (10km)
Height Climbed 2,300ft
Discovery Series 78
Parking at 984848

GALTEE MOUNTAINS

Galtymore and Galtybeg from O'Loughnan's Castle (2014).

GALTYMORE *(3,018ft)*
GREENANE *(2,631ft)*
TEMPLE HILL *(2,575ft)*

» The Galtee mountains form a long ridge running east to west thirty miles NE of Cork.

» There are three Top 500 Summits on the ridge. Galtymore is the highest but Greenane and Temple Hill also qualify as the drops between them and Galtymore are over 500ft.

» Greenane and Temple Hill are at opposite ends of the ridge so transport at both ends is necessary to complete all three summits in one walk.

Personal View

The Galtee mountains lie just north of the motorway from Dublin to Cork and are only one hour's drive from Cork. They are topped by Galtymore, one of Ireland's three 3,000ft summits which lie outside MacGillycuddy's Reeks. Probably the best way to enjoy these mountains is to start at the west end by climbing Temple Hill and finish near Cahir on the east side. However, I had climbed Temple Hill four months earlier so only needed to add Galtymore and Greenane on this visit.

I started by flying into Cork airport. Cork is one of my favourite airports, small, efficient and friendly. Twenty minutes after stepping out of the plane I was driving towards the Galtee mountains in a hire car. Unsure of exactly where to start, I followed signposts off the R639 to Galtymore. These led to a car park directly south of the summit. From here a path, at times invisible, went north and led to the main ridge from where it was a short climb to the summit.

It was the end of February and the snow level was just over 2,000ft. The hail showers briefly cleared as I passed Galtymore summit then climbed Galtybeg, a good peak with a narrow ridge. Finally it was a long trudge to Greenane via O' Loughnan Castle and I nearly drowned having fallen waist deep into a peat bog on the way back.

My Routes

GALTYMORE AND GREENANE (5-6 hours)

I turned off the R639 directly south of Galtymore and followed signs to Galtymore. These led to a car park (2 euro charge in 2014) and a hut serving tea and snacks. From here a track led north onto open hillside. I climbed north and followed a broad ridge which joined the main Galtymore ridge just east of its summit.

I walked over Galtymore and Galtybeg, then descended to 2,100ft before climbing O'Loughnan's Castle. From here I walked east for 1.5km in worsening weather to the summit of Greenane. I returned over O'Loughnan's Castle to the col, contoured round Galtybeg, then descended south to pick up a track which led back to the start.

TEMPLE HILL (2-3 hours)

I had climbed Temple Hill the previous year from the nearest point on the road which was NW of the summit.

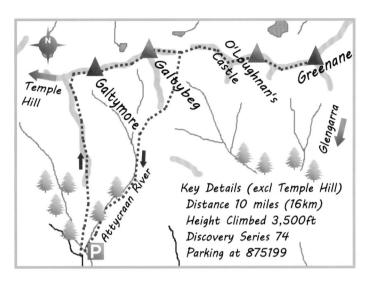

Key Details (excl Temple Hill)
Distance 10 miles (16km)
Height Climbed 3,500ft
Discovery Series 74
Parking at 875199

Cross at the summit of Galtymore (2014).

PLACES TO STAY/DRINK

Tea and snacks were sold from a hut next to the car park at the start. The nearest towns are Cahir and Mitchelstown. Not much further away is Clonmel which has a good choice of hotels and restaurants.

POINTS OF INTEREST

Cahir Castle, south east of Galtymore is one of the largest castles in Ireland. It was built in 1142 by Conor O'Brien, Prince of Thomond.

KNOCKMEALDOWN

KNOCKMEALDOWN *(2,605ft)*

» The Knockmealdown mountains lie NE of Cork and south of Galtymore.

» Knockmealdown is a short climb from the top of the pass known as the Vee Gap.

Nearing the summit of Knockmealdown after starting at Vee Gap.

My Route (2-3 hours)

I started at the car park at Vee Gap on the R668 south of Clogheen. From the car park I crossed the road and followed a substantial path heading steeply up the hillside in an easterly direction. The path climbed 1,000ft in less than 1km to the summit of Sugar-loaf Hill.

From the summit of Sugarloaf Hill I followed another substantial path which descended SSE to a col. The path then led SE up gradual slopes to the top of Knockmealdown. There was a false top with a small cairn a few hundred metres before the main summit.

Personal View

The Knockmealdown mountains form a fine east to west ridge south of the Galtee mountains with the sight of Sugarloaf Hill from the north being one of its most impressive features. On the day of my first visit in 2013 the cloud level remained at 1,500ft all day and rain swept in from the south west.

This was disappointing as these are fine mountains, particularly Sugarloaf Hill which was a direct ascent from the Vee Gap. After climbing Sugarloaf Hill I followed a wide path south east to Knockmealdown, eventually finding a trig point that left me in no doubt that I was at the summit. I returned quickly to the car putting the heater on full blast to dry out as I drove to Fauscoum.

Eighteen months later I returned to the Knockmealdown mountains to see what I had missed in 2013. The Vee Gap was crowded with cars and walkers, but the summits were peaceful with extensive views round southern Ireland.

Key Details

» Distance 5 miles (8km)
» Height climbed 1,800ft
» Discovery Series 74
» Parking at 030100.

POINTS OF INTEREST

These mountains are an important breeding ground for two rare species, the Red Grouse and the Hen Harrier.

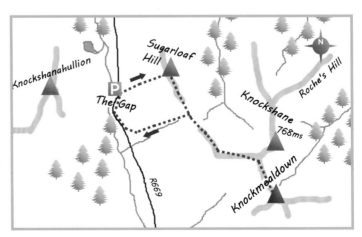

COMERAGH MOUNTAINS

FAUSCOUM *(2,597ft)*
KNOCKANAFFRIN *(2,477ft)*

» The Comeragh mountains lie approximately fifty miles north east of Cork.

» Knockanaffrin is the lowest Top 500 Summit at 2,477ft.

My Routes

KNOCKANAFFRIN (2-3 HOURS)

I started at a car park 3km east of Hanora's cottage and followed the path NE up the hillside for a short distance to a gate. I did not go through the gate (which leads to The Gap) but climbed NE for 2km to the Knockanaffrin ridge at 2,050ft. I followed the ridge NNW to the summit, then returned along the ridge and descended SE to The Gap. If just climbing Knockanaffrin it would be straightforward to return to the start from here.

From The Gap I went too far east instead of climbing directly to the north summit of Fauscoum. By climbing to the north top of Fauscoum and then continuing across the peat hags to the main summit, both these mountains could be completed easily in a day.

FAUSCOUM (2-3 hours)

I returned the next day parking directly south of Fauscoum near the river Mahon. From here it was a short climb (2.5km) directly north to the summit cairn of Fauscoum. Unfortunately the mist was low so I had no views.

PLACES TO STAY/DRINK

I stayed at Hanora's Cottage which lies just west of the Comeragh mountains.
This guest house was very welcoming with a superb breakfast.

Personal View

The Comeragh mountains lie south of the Galtee mountains. From what I could see (the mist level was 1,500ft throughout my visit) they appear to be beautiful and interesting mountains. However, the area surrounding the highest point, the summit of Fauscoum at 2,597ft, is a large area of flat peat hags, similar to the summit of Cheviot or Kinder Scout.

I blame a number of factors for my failure to climb Fauscoum at the first attempt; no visibility, lack of a proper map, a misleading 'scenic' route on the internet, lack of daylight etc. However, none of this could excuse the fact that at 4.30 p.m. on an October Sunday I was scrambling up near vertical grass hillside below the north summit of Fauscoum. Thereafter my attempt to find Fauscoum from the north, in thick mist across flat bogland, was doomed. I returned the next day to climb it from the south.

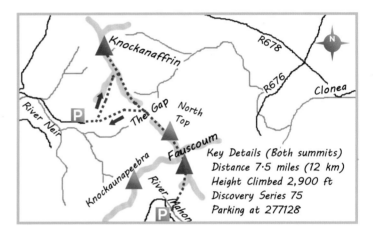

Key Details (Both summits)
Distance 7.5 miles (12 km)
Height Climbed 2,900 ft
Discovery Series 75
Parking at 277128

A brief clearing in the clouds on the Comeragh mountains.

MOUNT LEINSTER

MOUNT LEINSTER *(2,610ft)*

» Mount Leinster is situated south of the Wicklow mountains.

» There is a road all the way to the summit but a locked gate prevents cars continuing past the car park at Nine Stones.

My Route (1-2 hours)

I stayed the night at Kilkenny driving to Borris early in the morning to pick up signs to the Mount Leinster Heritage road. The Nine Stones car park was at the highest point of the road. I found a narrow road with two locked gates preventing access for cars. It went SSE from the car park and led all the way to the summit. Just before reaching the compound I turned right and walked 50 metres south to the trig point.

Key Details

» Distance 3 miles (5km)
» Height climbed 1,200ft
» Discovery Ireland 68
» Parking at 816546.

Personal View

It is harder to drive to Mount Leinster than to climb it. Mount Leinster is an isolated mountain south of the Wicklow mountains with one near neighbour, Blackstairs Mountain, another solitary mountain just to its south. It is a long drive to these mountains from Dublin, the nearest airport and ferry terminal depending on how Ireland is reached. In addition I found it a challenge to find the Nine Stones car park which lies at the highest point of the Mount Leinster Heritage road.

There is however, a certain romance and adventure when visiting the more remote parts of Ireland. I don't suppose I will stay in Kilkenny again, a true Irish town (come to think of it this could be said about any town in Ireland!) or visit the remote villages which surround this strange and brooding mountain.

After an interesting journey to the Nine Stones car park it was a straightforward walk up the road to the summit. The main problem was that the single track road had become icy particularly near the summit and I kept having to leave the road to stay upright. I reached the summit in ghostly conditions. In the snow and mist the telecommunications mast looked like a scene from the James Bond film *Goldeneye*.

Nine Stones car park, a road to the right of the trees leads to the summit (2014).

POINTS OF INTEREST

The cairn at the top is supposedly the burial chamber of the king of Leinster killed in 693 AD.

WICKLOW MOUNTAINS

MULLAGHCLEEVAUN
(2,788ft)
TONELAGEE *(2,680ft)*
KIPPURE *(2,484ft)*

» These three mountains lie in the Wicklow mountains south of Dublin.

My Routes

MULLAGHCLEEVAUN (3-4 hours)

I started from the military road which runs from Laragh to the Sally Gap. My start point was below Carrigshouk just south of a forest. Starting at 1,300ft I climbed NW to the east top of Mullaghcleevaun then WNW to the summit.

Key Details

» Distance 5.5 miles (9km)
» Height climbed 1,600ft
» Discovery Ireland 56
» Parking at 101051.

TONELAGEE (1-2 hours)

On both my visits I have started from the Wicklow Gap which has a height of nearly 1,500ft. Therefore this is one of the easiest of the Top 500 Summits. From the Wicklow Gap I followed a path, boggy at first, which goes NNE to the summit.

Key Details

» Distance 2 miles (3km)
» Height climbed 1,200ft
» Discovery Series 56
» Parking at 076002.

KIPPURE (1-2 hours from R115)

I drove to the crossroads at the Sally Gap and continued 4km north on the R115 towards Dublin. I turned left and drove 3km up a minor road to the summit. However, it is no longer possible to drive up the minor road to the summit so this final section would have to be walked or cycled.

Summer in the Wicklow mountains, Mullaghcleevaun from Tonelagee (2015).

Personal View

The Wicklow mountains lie south of Dublin. They are rolling hills, very different in character from the mountains in the west of Ireland but with similarities to the Brecon Beacons and Black Mountains in South Wales.

My last visit was in August 2015. I needed some pictures of the mountains and fortunately the weather was kind. The Wicklow mountains are a great region to explore. We visited Enniskerry, a beautiful village in the north east corner of the region, and the Powerscourt Waterfall. The following day we climbed my favourite summit in the Wicklow mountains, Tonelagee, then visited the amazing Glendalough region. We drove back to Dublin through the mountains and past Sally's Gap in evening sunshine.

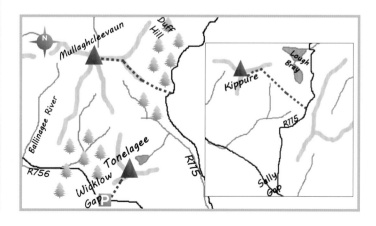

LUGNAQUILLA

LUGNAQUILLA (3,039ft)

» Lugnaquilla is the highest mountain in the Wicklow mountains south of Dublin.

» It is one of only five 3,000ft mountains in Ireland with a 500 foot drop on all sides.

» The ascent from the west is straightforward.

My Route (3-4 hours)

I drove to the start from Dublin following the N51 south then turning off to Donard, 25 miles south of Dublin. I followed the road SE to the start in Glen Imaal. I parked just over 5km west of the summit.

The route followed a track ESE over Camara Hill and continued east to the summit of the mountain. It was an easy climb in the clear conditions and I was regularly overtaken by fell runners. However, the route finding could be challenging in mist and a compass would be needed.

POINTS OF INTEREST

Views on a clear day can extend across the Irish sea to Snowdonia and west to the Reeks. There are steep glacial corries on both sides of the mountain known as the 'North Prison' and the 'South Prison'.

PLACES TO STAY/DRINK

As it was a Sunday and there was nothing open in Donard, I stopped in a pub near Blessington for lunch and a drink.

View of Lugnaquillia from Tonelagee.

Personal View (JP)

Lugnaquilla is the highest mountain in the Wicklow mountains. It lies 30 miles south of Dublin but it can be seen from the higher points further north as clearly the biggest mountain in the range. We took a flight from Stansted to Dublin, picked up the hire car, drove along the coast to Laragh, then a grassy, easy tramp and we were on the summit by midday. Now that is the way to kick off a weekend!

Lugnaquilla is not enthralling as hill walks go, open and squelchy, but very satisfying nonetheless. It is best kept for decent weather. We were back down in time for lunch and a wander around Glendalough. Good spot this, interesting ruins and monkish history, well hidden amongst the hills. We stayed locally in a welcoming bed and breakfast then headed off for a day ticking Dublin's must dos including the Brewery and the Craic tour. Memories are fragmented but good.

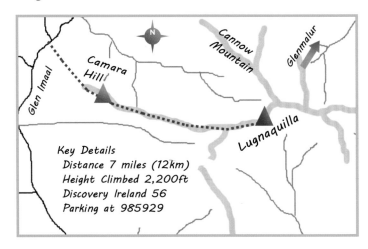

Key Details
Distance 7 miles (12km)
Height Climbed 2,200ft
Discovery Ireland 56
Parking at 985929

Ben Oss and Ben Dubhchraig from
Ben Lui *(Heather Thomas-Smith)*.

SCOTLAND: SOUTH SCOTLAND

South Scotland covers the Southern Uplands and the South Highlands as far as Glen Lochay. There are 64 Top 500 Summits divided into 20 walks:

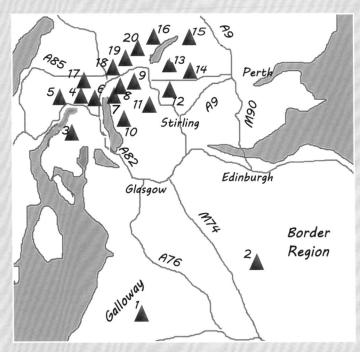

WALKS 1 TO 11

	Walk	Feet	Pg.
1	The Merrick	2,766	82
	Corserine	2,669	
	Cairnsmore of Carsphairn	2,614	
	Shalloch on Minnoch	2,543	
2	Broad Law	2,756	84
	White Coomb	2,694	
	Hart Fell	2,651	
3	Ben Donich	2,778	86
	The Brack	2,582	
	Beinn Bheula	2,556	
	Cnoc Coinnich	2,497	
4	Beinn Ime	3,318	88
	Beinn Narnain	3,038	
	The Cobbler	2,899	
	Beinn Luibhean	2,815	
5	Beinn Bhuidhe	3,111	90
	Beinn an Lochain	2,956	
	Stob Coire Creagach	2,680	
6	Ben Vorlich	3,093	91
	Ben Vane	3,004	
7	Cruach Ardrain	3,432	92
	An Caisteal	3,264	
	Beinn Chabhair	3,061	
	Meall an Fhudair	2,508	
8	Ben More	3,852	94
	Stob Binnein	3,821	
9	Meall an t-Seallaidh	2,794	95
	Creag Mac Ranaich	2,654	
	Stob a' Choin	2,850	
	Beinn Stacath	2,531	
10	Ben Lomond	3,194	96
	Beinn a' Choin	2,525	
11	Ben Ledi	2,883	97
	Benvane	2,694	

South Scotland covers the area from the Scottish borders to Glen Lyon, in particular the mountainous regions of the Southern Uplands and the South Highlands. There are 7 Top 500 Summits in the Southern Uplands and 57 Top 500 Summits in the South Highlands.

SOUTHERN UPLANDS

The Southern Uplands struggle to reach 2,500ft but, on a number of occasions, the summits rise above that level with the highest summit being the Merrick in south west Scotland with a height of 2,766ft. A mere 10ft lower is Broad Law which is a few miles south of Edinburgh. All 7 summits are Corbetts.

SOUTH HIGHLANDS

In the South Highlands there are 57 Top 500 Summits including 28 Munros, 27 Corbetts and 2 Grahams. The highest mountain is Ben Lawers at 3,984ft followed by Ben More at 3,852ft. Other well known summits include 'The Cobbler' with its unique appearance and scramble to the summit and Ben Lomond, a popular mountain close to Glasgow.

WALKS 12 TO 20

	Walk	Feet	Pg.
12	Ben Vorlich	3,231	98
	Stuc a' Chroin	3,199	
	Beinn Each	2,667	
	Meall na Fearna	2,654	
13	Creagan na Beinne	2,913	99
	Creag Uchdag	2,883	
	Shee of Ardtalnaig	2,490	
14	Ben Chonzie	3,054	100
	Auchnafree Hill	2,589	
15	Meall Tairneachan	2,582	101
	Farragon Hill	2,569	
16	Ben Lawers	3,984	102
	Meall Garbh	3,668	
	Meall Corranaich	3,507	
	Meall Greigh	3,284	
	Meall nam Maigheach	2,558	
17	Ben Lui	3,708	104
	Ben Oss	3,376	
	Beinn Dubhchraig	3,209	
	Beinn Chuirn	2,887	
18	Ben Challum	3,363	106
	Meall Glas	3,145	
	Sgiath Chuil	3,021	
	Beinn nan Imirean	2,785	
19	Beinn Heasgarnich	3,536	107
	Creag Mhor	3,435	
	Meall nan Subh	2,645	
20	Meall nan Tarmachan	3,425	108
	Meall Ghaordaidh	3,410	
	Beinn nan Oighreag	2,982	

Ben Lomond from Tarbet.

GALLOWAY HILLS

The Merrick from Forest Road.

THE MERRICK *(2,766ft)*
CORSERINE *(2,669ft)*
**CAIRNSMORE OF
CARSPHAIRN** *(2,614ft)*
SHALLOCH ON MINNOCH
(2,543ft)

» Four Corbetts south of Glasgow
in the Galloway Hills.

» The Merrick is the highest
mountain in the Southern
Uplands. The route from
Shalloch on Minnoch goes
over a demoted Corbett, now
a Marilyn, Kirriereoch Hill
(2,579ft).

» Corserine and Cairnsmore of
Carsphairn are two Corbetts
climbed separately near
Carsphairn.

Personal View

It was late September 2006 when I drove up to the Bell Memorial car park from the Lake District arriving after lunch and rather later than I intended. Shalloch on Minnoch was a straightforward ascent but the traverse to the Merrick over Kirriereoch Hill took a long time. From the Merrick I made a direct descent to the single track forest road, a mistake, it would be better to go back over Kirriereoch Hill. Anyway the descent off the Merrick was slow and it was nearly dark when I reached the deserted single track forest road. Setting off on the four mile trudge back to the start in the dark was unnerving, so I was delighted to see a car which took pity on me and gave me a lift back to my car.

The weather was stormy with flooding forecast as I drove towards Corserine three months later. As the roads started to flood it looked as though I may not reach the mountain. However, the rain eased and it was possible to climb the mountain in strong winds which turned gale force near the trig point. The way down was difficult and I lost any sense of direction in the high wind. I had to wade streams which had turned into torrents to get back to the start. Cairnsmore of Carsphairn had been an easier climb on a cold March day two years earlier.

My Routes

THE MERRICK (7-8 hours)

The route I chose went over both the Merrick and Shalloch on Minnoch. I drove past Glentrool village and along the forestry road for eight miles to the Bell Memorial car park. From the car park I walked a short distance north then turned right up a forest track to Shalloch on Minnoch farm. I followed the south bank of the Shalloch burn NE then east up the broad west ridge of Shalloch on Minnoch. The summit was 300m SE of the trig point.

I left the summit in a SE direction to go over Tarfessock then SSE to Kirriereoch Hill. Finally, a 500ft descent and reascent led to the Merrick. I should have returned over Kirriereoch Hill, rather than head directly to the road from the summit.

CORSERINE (4-5 hours)

I left the A713 at Polharrow Bridge and drove along the single track road to Forest Lodge car park. From the car park I walked west along the road keeping south of the Polharrow Burn. After taking the right fork past Loch Harrow I continued to grid reference 525875. A path led west across a gully and through a fire break. The route continued west to the summit after reaching open hillside.

Key Details

» **Distance 7 miles (12km)**
» **Height climbed 2,300ft**
» **O/S Landranger 77**
» **Parking at 532863.**

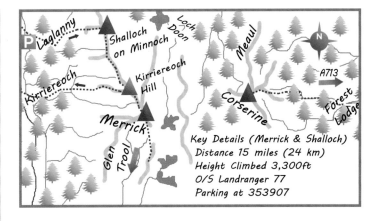

Key Details (Merrick & Shalloch)
Distance 15 miles (24 km)
Height Climbed 3,300ft
O/S Landranger 77
Parking at 353907

CAIRNSMORE OF CARSPHAIRN (3-4 hours)

I started from the A713 just to the north of Carsphairn at Green Well of Scotland (walkers are discouraged from mid April to mid May due to lambing). I walked NE along a track past Willienna and Dunool. After continuing past the end of the track, I crossed a burn and followed a wall NE to the summit.

Key Details

» **Distance 6 miles (10km)**
» **Height climbed 2,000ft**
» **O/S Landranger 77**
» **Parking at 558944.**

Ascending the Merrick.

MOFFAT HILLS

The Grey Mare's Tail on the way up White Coomb (2014).

BROAD LAW *(2,756ft)*
WHITE COOMB *(2,694ft)*
HART FELL *(2,651ft)*

» Three Corbetts in the Southern Uplands east of the A74 and one hours drive south of Edinburgh.

» The mountains are usually climbed individually although Hart Fell and White Coomb could be linked by a high level walk.

» All three summits could be climbed in one day.

Personal View (Stuart)

I was enjoying a quick power kip on the way to the Ryder Cup at Gleneagles when I was awoken to ask if I minded a quick diversion for a gentle walk near Moffatt. No problem, I replied, as a walk would loosen my travel tightened legs. We passed through Moffatt, a pleasant town and the last outpost of Tory rule in Scotland and parked at a National Trust car park underneath the Grey Mare's Tail Waterfall. As my host packed water, chocolate and donned a woolly hat it dawned on me that this may be different from a dawn stroll with my Labrador dogs.

The walk started pleasantly, we acknowledged fellow walkers and followed a well constructed path. Sadly I was then told to leave the path and cross the fast flowing Tail Burn to avoid a long detour. A slip led to a paddle in icy water up to my knees. Now wet, I had to scramble up peat and heather following the course of a wall to a broad summit. John took it upon himself to power ahead as though it was some sort of race.

At last we reached the summit and I surveyed the splendour of the vista with views of the adjoining ridges and over to Loch Skeen. Maybe this was one of Barry's better calls! Refreshed from the basic provisions, water and chocolate, we started our descent which was easier, particularly as I spent most of the time sliding down on my backside. One Corbett down, 220 to go.

MOFFAT HILLS continued

My Routes

BROAD LAW (2-3 hours)
I drove up the A701 to Tweedsmuir, from where a minor road goes past Talla Reservoir to the Megget Stone at 1,300ft. From there I followed a fence leading north over Fans Law and Cairn Law to the trig point.

WHITE COOMB (2-3 hours)
We parked at the National Trust car park on the A708 under the Grey Mare's Tail (£2 charge in 2014). A path ascended the steep NE side of the waterfall. When the path levelled off we crossed the burn and went west beside a wall to Upper Tarnberry. After a short descent, we ascended to White Coomb.

HART FELL (3-4 hours)
I drove up the A708 from Moffat and parked just over the bridge from Capplegill. I walked NNW up the east side of the Blackhope burn and climbed NW. Steeper slopes led to the summit. On the return I walked south over the hills past Swatte Fell.

Key Details
» Total distance for all three ascents 13.5 miles (22km)
» Height climbed 5,500ft
» O/S Landranger 72, 78 and 79
» Parking at 151203 (Broad Law), 185145 (White Coomb) and 147098 (Hart Fell).

PLACES TO STAY/DRINK
Moffat is a good base for climbing these hills and has hotels, guest houses, restaurants and cafes.

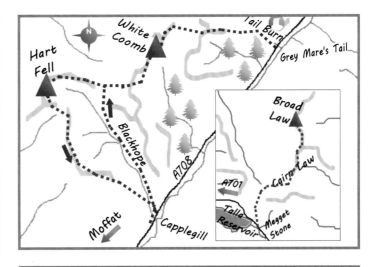

POINTS OF INTEREST
The Grey Mare's Tail is the UK's fifth highest waterfall and lies at the start of the walk up White Coomb. In *Marmion*, Walter Scott describes the scene 'Where deep deep down, and far within, toils with the rocks the roaring linn; Then issuing forth one foamy wave, and wheeling round the giant's grave, white as the snowy charger's tail, drives down the pass of Moffatdale.'

Stuart and John at the summit of White Coomb (2014).

REST AND BE THANKFUL

The Brack from across Loch Long.

BEN DONICH *(2,778ft)*
THE BRACK *(2,582ft)*
BEINN BHEULA *(2,556ft)*
CNOC COINNICH *(2,497ft)*

» Three Corbetts and a high
Graham close to Glasgow.
They would normally be divided
into three half day walks.

» Beinn Bheula is the most
southerly Corbett and Top
500 Summit in the Scottish
Highlands.

» The start point for Ben Donich
and The Brack is the top of the
'Rest and be Thankful' pass
built in 1753.

Personal View

These four Top 500 Summits lie south of the 'Rest and Be Thankful'
pass and close to the shores of Loch Goil and Loch Long. I climbed
them in three half day walks.

I enjoyed my walk over Ben Donich and traverse to The Brack but
the descent from The Brack was tortuous. Recklessly I decided to
descend through the dense forest on the lower northern slopes
of The Brack and got stuck in thick woods. After much effort and
some expletives I forced a way through the woods to the forest
track. In retrospect this was probably a fair punishment for sloppy
route finding.

I ascended Beinn Bheula and Cnoc Coinnich in 2008 and 2011
respectively. In June 2008 I drove up from the Lake District climbing
Beinn Bheula and later Stob Coire Creagach, a second Corbett. It
was misty and humid climbing Beinn Bheula and I struggled with the
route finding on the lower slopes.

The centre of the village at Lochgoilhead was a good start point for
Cnoc Coinnich and a rare opportunity to start from the sea. There
was a school party apparently learning to canoe on Loch Goil. At the
summit there was a superb cairn overlooking a cliff face.

My Routes

BEN DONICH AND THE BRACK (5-6 hours)

From the 'Rest and Be Thankful' Pass I walked south for a few hundred metres down the Lochgoilhead road to a sign saying 'Hill access to Ben Donich'. From this point there was a path with white marker posts which led south all the way to the summit. There was some indistinct sections of the path and a tricky area with a downwards scramble to negotiate.

From the summit of Ben Donich I descended east to the 1,250ft col between Ben Donich and the Brack, the Bealach Dubh-lic. From the Bealach I climbed SE to the summit of the Brack.

Key Details

» Distance 7.5 miles (12km)

» Height climbed 3,300ft

» O/S Landranger 56

» Parking at 230074.

BEINN BHEULA (3-4 hours)

I turned off the main road at Lettermay and drove a short distance south to park at the edge of the forest, ref 188999. I walked west up the forest track for 1km, then went right for 200m to the Lettermay Burn. A narrow path led along the south bank of the Burn for 1km to open hillside. I climbed SW up the shoulder of Beinn Bheula to reach the north ridge a few hundred metres north of the summit.

Key Details

» Distance 6 miles (10km)

» Height climbed 2,500ft

» O/S Landranger 56

» Parking at 188999.

CNOC COINNICH (3-4 hours)

I parked opposite the Post Office in Lochgoilhead. The route went to the right of the public toilet block, up a small lane and over a stile. I crossed a forest track and went through a gate. A path went NE then east up the hillside with the forest on the left. When the path descended and crossed a bridge I took the right fork marked Coilessan. Soon the path climbed up a firebreak to a stile before reaching open hillside. I walked east to the pass between the Brack and Cnoc Coinnich, then SE up a broad ridge to the summit cairn.

Key Details

» Total distance 5.5 miles (9km)

» Height climbed 2,500ft

» O/S Landranger 56

» Parking at 200013.

Ben Donich from Loch Restil.

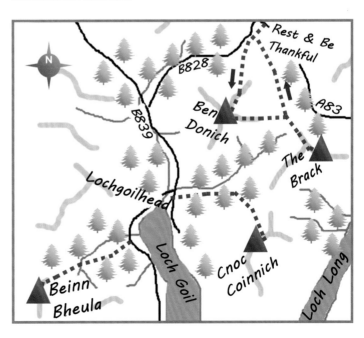

ARROCHAR ALPS

Beinn Narnain and the Cobbler *(Heather Thomas-Smith)*.

BEINN IME *(3,318ft)*
BEINN NARNAIN *(3,038ft)*
THE COBBLER *(2,899ft)*
BEINN LUIBHEAN *(2,815ft)*

» This is a compact circuit of two Munros and two Corbetts near Arrochar that can be completed in one day.

» The summit of The Cobbler is reached by scrambling through a hole in the rock followed by a short traverse along a ledge.

» The Cobbler with its three rocky summits is one of the best known of the Scottish mountains, and is featured in Alastair Borthwick's book about Scottish climbing in the 1930s, *Always a Little Further.*

Personal View (Alistair)

The walk shown by the map below is a superb walk over two Munros and two Corbetts. The Cobbler is the stand out mountain with its three summits, the North Peak, the Centre Peak (which is the highest point and thus the Corbett) and the South Peak. I had climbed the North Peak of The Cobbler and Beinn Narnain with Barry in 1982 so today I only needed to climb Beinn Ime, the second Munro in the group.

I drove up the road towards the summit of Rest and be Thankful thirty-two years after my last visit, but now with only twenty-one Munros to go! I stopped in the small parking area where the stream running down from the Bealach a' Mhaim goes under the A83. However, my positive state of mind was spoilt by a poor start. I bottomed the car on a large protruding rock in the parking area. It was difficult to get it off, chassis damage or so I thought.

There was a good path on the NW side of the stream but I did not see it and trudged up the boggy east side. To be frank, a tedious climb to the col between Narnain, The Cobbler and Ime. Then, perhaps the widest path I had seen for some years led to Ime's summit where there was a stone structure equivalent to a 'viewing platform'. Great views, at least when I was there, but it was a relief to get back to my car and find that it was still driving normally.

ARROCHAR ALPS continued

My Routes (6-7 hours for all four summits, see map)

It took me two attempts to complete these mountains as I only climbed the North Peak of The Cobbler and missed Beinn Luibhean on my first visit in 1982. On both occasions I started from the car park on the A83 at a bridge directly west of The Cobbler. The map shows the route to complete all four summits in the same day, a fine round which should be completed even by those focussing on Munros.

On my first visit Alistair and I followed a path by the side of the stream up to 1,400ft. We climbed steeply SE up the hillside to the col between the North Peak and the summit of The Cobbler. We ascended the North Peak (we did not know in those days that the Centre Peak was the summit) then descended north to Bealach a' Mhaim. From the Bealach we climbed 900ft ESE to the summit of Beinn Narnain returning to the same Bealach.

Alistair needed to go back thereby leaving Beinn Ime for thirty-two years. I ascended NNW up long grassy slopes, covered in snow for the last 600ft, to the summit of Beinn Ime. Beinn Luibhean could have been added but I wasn't climbing Corbetts back in 1982.

My second trip was in 2004 on a beautiful day in August. I climbed to the summit of The Cobbler then climbed Beinn Luibhean.

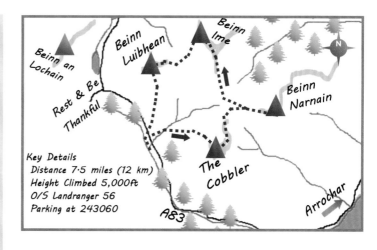

Key Details
Distance 7.5 miles (12 km)
Height Climbed 5,000ft
O/S Landranger 56
Parking at 243060

POINTS OF INTEREST

The centre peak of The Cobbler requires some tricky scrambling and a good head for heights to reach the summit. Technically this is probably the second hardest Top 500 Summit to reach after the Inaccessible Pinnacle.

Strange summit of The Cobbler (2004).

NEAR LOCH FYNE

BEINN BHUIDHE *(3,111ft)*
BEINN AN LOCHAIN *(2,956ft)*
STOB COIRE CREAGACH
(2,680ft)

» One Munro and two Corbetts near Loch Fyne.

My Routes

BEINN BHUIDHE *(6-8 hours)*
We parked in the car park just off the minor horseshoe road which leaves the A83, and walked along the road on the east side of the River Fyne. After 3km the road crossed the river and we continued up the glen to Inverchorachan. Just beyond Inverchorachan, we climbed up the south side of a stream until it emerged from a wooded gully. We crossed the stream and climbed WNW. A path led up steep ground to the ridge between Beinn Bhuidhe and its NE summit. We followed the ridge to the summit.

BEINN AN LOCHAIN *(2-3 hours)*
I climbed Beinn an Lochain directly from the top of Rest and Be Thankful. The route led quickly to the south top and then it was a short walk to the summit.

STOB COIRE CREAGACH *(2-3 hours)*
I parked just off the A83 west of the bridge over Kinglas Water. The route went north through a plantation, crossed a stile then climbed up a grassy gully. Finally I went NW up the hillside to the summit avoiding a few small crags.

Key Details

» **Distance 13 miles (Bhuidhe) and 6 miles (Lochain and Creagach)**

» **Height climbed 3,100ft (Bhuidhe) and 4,300ft (Lochain and Creagach)**

» **O/S Landranger 56**

» **Parking at 193127 (Bhuidhe), 230074 (Lochain) and 234096 (Creagach).**

Colin on the way up Beinn Bhuidhe in 1995, his hat may still be on the mountain!

Personal View

Colin and I left Sedgefield to climb Beinn Bhuidhe at 7 a.m. early in April 1995. We stopped briefly for breakfast and arrived at the end of the private road up Glen Fyne at 11.45 a.m. Unfortunately the private road was closed to cars so we set off walking. It was nearly five miles to the foot of the mountain then, as we climbed higher, we started tiring in what was becoming a very strong wind. On reaching the summit ridge the wind hit us in gale force gusts. The ground steepened and I kicked steps up a snow slope. We moved quickly but the wind hit us again and Colin's hat disappeared never to be seen again. Finally the summit appeared so we turned and fled running back along the private road.

I was gasping for breath as I climbed the steep east facing slopes of Beinn An Lochain having already climbed The Cobbler and Beinn Luibhean on a beautiful summer day in 2004. Once on the summit ridge I enjoyed walking over the summit and then down the North East ridge. Four years later I climbed Stob Coire Creagach on a pleasant late afternoon from Glen Kinglas.

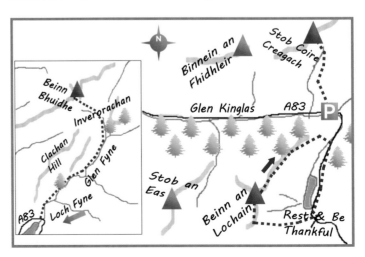

LOCH SLOY

BEN VORLICH *(3,093ft)*
BEN VANE *(3,004ft)*

» Ben Vorlich and Ben Vane are two Munros in the north part of the Arrochar Alps.

» They are situated either side of Loch Sloy and can be climbed as two half day walks or in one day.

My Routes

BEN VORLICH (4-5 hours)

Donald and I climbed Ben Vorlich in 1985. We started from Ardvorlich because this appeared to be the closest point to the summit. We followed a direct line to the summit with cloud cover from 1,000ft. It would be better to start from Inveruglas, walk or cycle to the head of Loch Sloy and climb Ben Vorlich from there.

BEN VANE (3-4 hours)

There is parking 500m north of Inveruglas Bridge. After walking back towards the bridge I followed the Hydro-Electric Board's private road towards Loch Sloy. After 2km I turned left and crossed Inveruglas Water. I walked for 500m then ascended to the summit of Ben Vane by its ESE ridge.

Both mountains could be climbed in one day as shown on the map.

PLACES TO STAY/DRINK

There is a cafe and small visitors centre at the car park at Inveruglas. In addition there are guest houses and hotels along the shores of Loch Lomond.

Personal View (JP)

September, a clear and crisp day with not a cloud in the sky. I left the car at Loch Sloy power station and marched off alone up the glen's access track, trying to ignore the pylons that blotted the landscape. I kept my eyes fixed on the mountain dominating the view ahead. Ben Vane is not the biggest but is a proper treat, a steep and rocky little gem. Leaving the Land Rover track you wind up its east ridge dodging between rock outcrops on a thin path, easy going the whole way, with views opening behind and to the north and south.

Topping out at 3,004ft I was surprised by the extent of the view. The landscape is sharp up and down so you have a real sense of height as you watch people looking very small in the world below. I had a longer day in mind than just Ben Vane and headed west to the head of Glen Uaine. Beinn Ime and Narnain were my targets, Ben Vorlich would be left for another day.

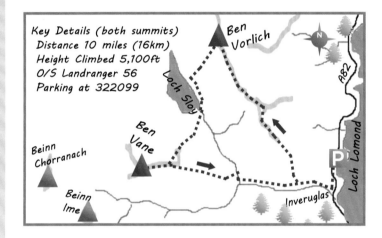

Key Details (both summits)
Distance 10 miles (16km)
Height Climbed 5,100ft
O/S Landranger 56
Parking at 322099

Ben Vane from near Inveruglas *(Heather Thomas-Smith).*

POINTS OF INTEREST

Rob Roy's Cave lies just to the north of Inveruglas. Legend has it that Rob Roy used the cave as a hide-out during his cattle rustling years.

CRIANLARICH HILLS

Alistair, Jonathan and I about to set off with JP (taking picture) up Cruach Ardrain (1986).

CRUACH ARDRAIN *(3,432ft)*
AN CAISTEAL *(3,264ft)*
BEINN CHABHAIR *(3,061ft)*
MEALL AN FHUDAIR
(2,508ft)

» There are five Munros south of Crianlarich and on the other side of the A82 lies a Corbett, Meall an Fhudair. Four of these mountains are Top 500 Summits (see above).

» The mountains lie next to Ben More and Stob Binnein and could be combined with them.

» The route from Inverlochlarig to Cruach Ardrain allows the second Munro, Beinn Tulaichean (3,104ft) to be added.

» Beinn a' Chroin (3,085ft), a third Munro, can be added to An Caisteal and Beinn Chabhair.

Personal View

Cruach Ardrain and its near neighbour, Beinn Tulaichean, lie west of Ben More and Stob Binnein and gave a good walk from Inverlochlarig in August 1986. These Munros were the first of many Munros the four of us climbed together. JP and Jonathan climbed in trainers without a compass and learnt that this was not a good idea.

It was raining as we sat having breakfast at the Little Chef near Cumbernauld and it continued raining all day. We started from Inverlochlarig Farm and climbed into cloud at 1,500ft traversing Beinn Tulaichean and carrying on to Cruach Ardrain. We had difficulty finding the cairn at the top of Beinn Tulaichean in the cold east wind and heavy showers 'merging' but still reached the summit in under two hours. From there the compass was employed full time as we continued to Cruach Ardrain, at times a path appeared which helped to guide us. A large cairn looked like the summit but the SMC Guide suggested that we should carry on. Fortunately we continued, descending fifty feet then climbing to the true summit. The walk, including the descent, took 4 hours 15 mins.

The three Glen Falloch Munros lie near Glasgow so on a free Sunday in April 1993 Jonathan and I decided to drive up there. We parked in a layby at Derrydaroch climbing An Caisteal first followed by Beinn a' Chroin and finally Beinn Chabhair. The cloud lifted when we arrived at Beinn Chabhair to give a limited view.

CRIANLARICH HILLS continued

My Routes

CRUACH ARDRAIN (4-5 hours)

We parked 750m east of Inverlochlarig and walked west past the farm. After passing the farm we climbed NW up grassy slopes, continuing between crags and boulders higher up to Beinn Tulaichean. From the summit of Beinn Tulaichean we walked NNW along a path which drops to the col before Cruach Ardrain. We continued up a grassy ridge to a small cairn, then turned east passing more cairns before the summit. We returned over Beinn Tulaichean, an additional climb of 400ft.

Key Details

» Distance 7 miles (11km)
» Height climbed 3,800ft
» O/S Landranger 51 and 56
» Parking at 441183.

AN CAISTEAL AND BEINN CHABHAIR (6-7 hours)

We parked just off the A82 near Derrydaroch and crossed the bridge over the River Falloch. After climbing SSE to Stob Glas we followed the ridge SE, turning east at 2,600ft to the summit of An Caisteal. After descending the SSE ridge, we climbed to the rocky west end of the summit ridge of Beinn a' Chroin. The summit was 1km to the east. After returning to the col between Beinn a' Chroin and An Caisteal we headed west to a lower col at 2,000ft. From there we climbed WSW to the summit of Beinn Chabhair.

Key Details

» Distance 9.5 miles (15km)
» Height climbed 4,250ft
» O/S Landranger 56
» Parking at 352220.

MEALL AN FHUDAIR (3-4 HOURS)

There was limited parking by the side of the A82 near Glenfalloch Farm (ref. 319196, O/S Landranger 56). I walked up the private hydro track and turned right on joining a higher road. I walked along this for a short distance before climbing NW steeply to the east ridge of Troisgeach. From Troisgeach I continued WNW for nearly 1km towards Meall nan Caora, then SW to a wide plateau and finally west to the summit of Meall an Fhudair.

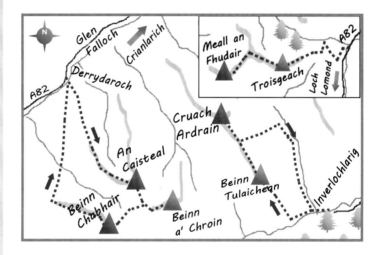

Beinn a' Chroin from An Caisteal *(Heather Thomas-Smith)*.

BEN MORE

BEN MORE *(3,852ft)*
STOB BINNEIN *(3,821ft)*

» Ben More is the highest mountain in the British Isles south of Ben Lawers.

» Ben More and Stob Binnein are prominent peaks which can be seen from all directions in the Southern Highlands.

» Both mountains are close to the road so the distances are not long.

POINTS OF INTEREST

There have been two air crashes on Ben More, in 1973 a British European Airways test flight crashed near the summit and in 2012 a microlight aircraft crashed into the mountain.

My Route (5-6 hours)

We left the A85 at a stile 150m east of Benmore Farm and climbed SE for over 3,000ft up steep grassy slopes to the NW shoulder of the mountain. We continued SE to the summit of Ben More.

From the summit we descended to the Bealach-eadar-dha-Beinn. We climbed just east of south up the north ridge of Stob Binnein. The cairn was at the south end of the summit plateau. After returning to the Bealach we descended NW to the Benmore Burn. The Burn could be followed back to the start.

PLACES TO STAY/DRINK

There are bars and accommodation at Crianlarich nearby. Alternatively Killin is an attractive place to stay.

Ben More and Stob Binnein from the north.

Personal View (Alistair)

Ben More and Stob Binnein are high and prominent summits near Crianlarich requiring 3,300ft of continuous climbing direct from the A85 road. In 1982 I had booked a cottage at Portnellan next to the A85 and it turned out to be directly below Ben More.

There was no talk of Munros in those distant days but Ben More was the highest point in the area and had to be climbed. So one morning the five of us who were staying at the cottage set out, crossed the road, and just went straight up, and up, and up until the top was finally reached and we lay on the ground and groaned and felt relieved it was over. Barry and I continued to Stob Binnein. The 1,000 foot drop and rise seemed nothing after what we had done already, and soon we were back for a hot bath and later the pub in nearby Crianlarich.

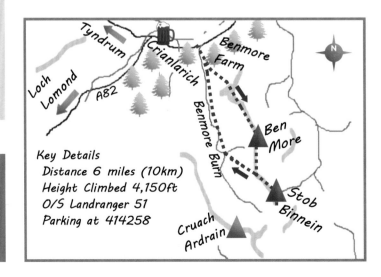

Key Details
Distance 6 miles (10km)
Height Climbed 4,150ft
O/S Landranger 51
Parking at 414258

BALQUHIDDER

MEALL AN T-SEALLAIDH
(2,794ft)
CREAG MAC RANAICH
(2,654ft)
STOB A' CHOIN (2,850ft)
BEINN STACATH (2,531ft)

» Four Corbetts near Balquhidder.

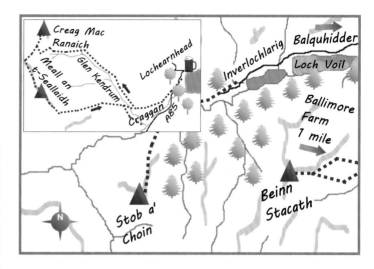

My Routes

MEALL AN T-SEALLAIDH AND CREAG MAC RANAICH (5-6 hours)

After parking at Lochearnhead I walked up a minor road 400m past a church to a bridge. I went under the bridge and followed a track to the disused railway line. This was followed SW for 1km, then I crossed a bridge to Glen Kendrum. From there a track led up Glen Kendrum to the bealach between the two Corbetts. It was a steep climb NNE to Creag Mac Ranaich whose summit lay 300m to the north. I returned to the bealach and climbed SW over rough ground to the col west of Cam Chreag. It was an easy walk south for 1km to Meall an t-Seallaidh.

Key Details

» Distance 12 miles (19km)
» Height climbed 3,200ft
» O/S Landranger 51
» Parking at 589233.

STOB A' CHOIN (3-4 hours)

I parked 750m east of Inverlochlarig farm and headed west along a good path on the north side of the River Larig. 1km past the farm I crossed a footbridge over the river, and made a rising traverse SW (hard work) to a platform on the north ridge at 630m. Finally I climbed the north ridge to the summit.

Key Details

» Distance 5.5 miles (9km)
» Height climbed 2,500ft
» O/S Landranger 56 and 57
» Parking at 441183.

Personal View

There are four Corbetts around Balquhidder which divide into three walks, the best of which is the round of Meall an t-Seallaidh and Creag Mac Ranaich from Lochearnhead. On Creag Mac Ranaich, I was surprised to be stopped by a man driving a small red motorised vehicle concerned that I had disturbed the deer. It hadn't occurred to me that stalking continued into February.

The following January I climbed Beinn Stacath in the worst weather I have encountered in fifty years of walking in the mountains. The heavy rain, hail and wind meant I kept being blown many yards sideways when only halfway up the mountain and I only just made it to the summit.

BEINN STACATH (4-5 hours)

This hill is not named on maps but is shown as a 771m trig point. I started from Ballimore farm (ref 529176, O/S Landranger 57) and followed a good track west to a footbridge across the Allt Fathan Glinne. I continued west to the east ridge of Beinn Stacath, then followed the ridge WSW to point 684m and finally to the trig point. The return journey was seven miles with 2,100ft of climbing.

Beinn Stacath seen from near the top of The Stob, a high Graham.

BEN LOMOND

BEN LOMOND *(3,194ft)*
BEINN A' CHOIN *(2,525ft)*

» After Ben Nevis, Ben Lomond is probably the most popular mountain in Scotland. It is also the most southerly Munro.

» Beinn a' Choin is a Corbett lying just north of Ben Lomond. Both mountains lie on the east shore of Loch Lomond.

My Routes

BEN LOMOND *(4-5 hours)*
I parked at the public car park just north of the Rowardennan Hotel. A good path went NE from the hotel to the south ridge and I walked north along this. The path took me all the way to the summit with zigzags up the steeper slopes. I varied the route back by continuing NW then SSE to go back over the Ptarmigan.

BEINN A' CHOIN *(3-4 hours)*
I followed a minor road along the north side of Loch Arklet, parking by the roadside about 100m east of the Dam at the west end of the loch. I climbed to the summit of Stob an Fhainne and continued north along a broad ridge to the Bealach a' Mheim. The route climbed NW between rock out-crops to arrive at a fence which I followed north. As the fence missed the summit on the east side, I left it at a tiny lochan and walked NW for less than 100m to the summit.

Key Details

» Distance 7 miles (11km (Ben Lomond) and 4.5 miles (7km) (Beinn a' Choin)

» Height climbed 3,100ft (Ben Lomond) and 2,300ft (Beinn a' Choin)

» O/S Landranger 56 Loch Lomond

» Parking at 360985 (Ben Lomond) and 357096 (Beinn a' Choin).

Looking down on Loch Lomond *(Chris Wood)*.

Personal View

Ben Lomond is one of the most popular Munros with thousands of people climbing it each year. It is conveniently situated just north of Glasgow with excellent views along Loch Lomond. On a clear day it is visible from places as far apart as Glasgow to the south and Ben Nevis to the north. One Sunday in 1983 I drove from Newcastle to Rowardennan and followed the excellent 'tourist path' all the way to the summit. A number of people were climbing the mountain but unfortunately there was no view above 2,500ft. I varied the route by going down over the Ptarmigan although this route tends to become muddy and is rocky in places.

Twenty-four years later in February 2007 I again travelled up to Scotland on a Sunday from Newcastle to climb Beinn a' Choin. Mist and deep snow drifts made the traverse along the ridge and the final ascent to the summit challenging. It was difficult to keep to the route and tiring to hack through the snow drifts. After a quick descent I was glad to get back to the car and warm up.

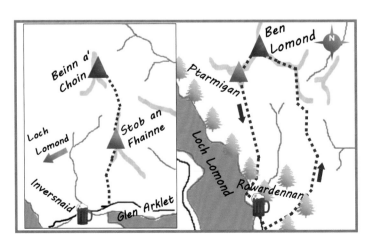

CALLANDER CORBETTS

BEN LEDI *(2,883ft)*
BENVANE *(2,694ft)*

» Ben Ledi, near Callander, is
a prominent and well known
mountain.

Personal View (Trusha)

It had seemed a good idea at
the time, a pleasant walk in winter sunshine on a Scottish hill.
It is not too long and there is
a good path, Barry had assured
me. As we stepped out of Edinburgh Airport we were greeted
by a biting cold wind and rain.

I began to regret my decision to
join this day out from work. Not
much chance of the boys agree-
ing to an alternative day shop-
ping in Edinburgh: Peter Dobson
liked to compete in Ironman tri-
athlons, Chris Franks was virtually a professional mountaineer
and climbed seemingly all over
the world and Barry had climbed
more Scottish mountains than
most people had had hot din-
ners. Not so sure this was a
good group to hang out with!

We drove north to Callander,
the car splashing through the
wet roads, and stopped for coffee and cake before going on
to the car park near Ben Ledi.
Actually the initial climb to the
ridge was not too bad, I think we
must have been sheltered from
the strong west wind. Then we
hit the south ridge of Ledi. The
wind howled across ferociously
and I was being blown ten feet
at a time.

The boys took charge and made
sure I was 'helped' up the mountain. Eventually the cairn and trig
point appeared. To my surprise
someone else was there and we
exchanged brief words. I learnt
that he had last climbed Ledi
thirty years ago. We sheltered
for a couple of minutes before
an equally windswept and wet
descent.

My Routes

I would recommend traversing these two mountains, as shown by
the map, but I climbed them separately.

BEN LEDI (3-4 hours)

To climb Ben Ledi we drove three miles north from Callander turning
left to cross the river at the Coireachrombie bridge, where there is a
car park. A good path west up the hillside reaching the SE ridge
of Ben Ledi at 1,800ft. We climbed NW up the ridge to the summit,
1,000ft higher.

BENVANE (3-4 hours)

To climb Benvane I started at Ballimore and climbed south up easy
slopes continuing up the long north ridge of Benvane to the summit.

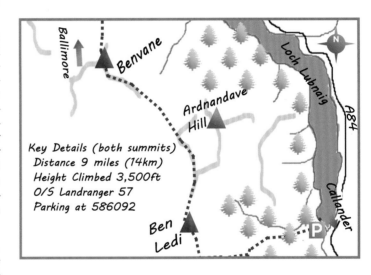

Key Details (both summits)
Distance 9 miles (14km)
Height Climbed 3,500ft
O/S Landranger 57
Parking at 586092

Ben Ledi from Callander.

BEN VORLICH GROUP

BEN VORLICH *(3,231ft)*
STUC A' CHROIN *(3,199ft)*
BEINN EACH *(2,667ft)*
MEALL NA FEARNA *(2,654ft)*

» Two Munros and two Corbetts between Loch Earn and Loch Lubnaig.

» All the summits can be climbed as one walk if transport can be arranged at Loch Lubnaig and Loch Earn.

Nearing the summit of Ben Vorlich *(Chris Wood).*

My Routes

It took me three walks to climb these four summits. In 1971 we were driven to the head of Glen Artney and camped between Stuc a' Chroin and Ben Vorlich. The following morning we climbed Ben Vorlich and were transported across Loch Earn to Lochearnhead.

On my second visit to these mountains I started from a layby on the A84 near Ard-chullarie More. A right of way climbed steeply through the trees and joined a forest track north to Glen Ample. 500m past the trees I turned east and followed the north side of the burn steeply up the hillside. Then I went NNE for 300m to join a line of fence posts which led to the summit of Beinn Each. I followed a knobbly ridge 2.5km north then NE to Stuc a' Chroin before returning.

Finally on a beautiful summer day I climbed Meall na Fearna from Ardvorlich. The route was straightforward. I walked south down Glen Vorlich, climbed east to the wide ridge between Beinn Domhnuill and Meall na Fearna, then SE to the summit.

The map shows a potentially fine traverse from Loch Lubnaig to Loch Earn over all four summits. I estimate that this route would take 7-8 hours.

Personal View

These summits lie between Loch Lubnaig and Loch Earn and can be reached easily from Stirling. Ben Vorlich and Stuc a' Chroin were my first Munros back in 1971 although I am not sure that we climbed Stuc a' Chroin.

In 1971 we were on a school trip staying at Cultybraggan, an old World War POW camp near Comrie. The accommodation was basic (the image of margarine blocks swimming in cold water for breakfast has stayed with me all my life!) so the two day trip over Stuc a' Chroin and Ben Vorlich, including an overnight camp, was an attractive prospect. We walked up Gleann an Dubh Choirein then climbed Stuc a' Chroin (probably) before pitching the tents below Ben Vorlich. The following morning we climbed Ben Vorlich and then descended to Loch Earn, taking an army landing craft from there back to Lochearnhead.

It was over thirty years before I returned to the area climbing Beinn Each in February 2005 and Meall na Fearna in July 2007. I added Stuc a' Chroin after climbing Beinn Each in case I had not climbed it in 1971.

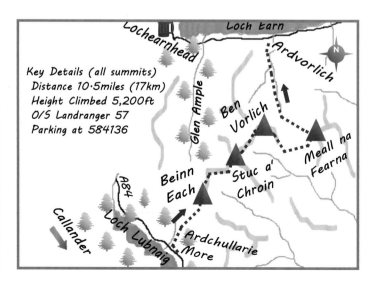

Key Details (all summits)
Distance 10·5miles (17km)
Height Climbed 5,200ft
O/S Landranger 57
Parking at 584136

SOUTH LOCH TAY

CREAGAN NA BEINNE
(2,913ft)
CREAG UCHDAG *(2,883ft)*
SHEE OF ARDTALNAIG
(2,490ft)

» Two Corbetts and one Graham
lying south of Loch Tay.

» Creag Uchdag can be climbed
separately although it would be
possible to combine all three
mountains in one walk.

My Routes

*CREAGAN NA BEINNE AND
SHEE OF ARDTALNAIG
(5-6 hours)*
From Ardtalnaig I drove a few
hundred metres up the road
towards Claggan and parked.
I climbed SE up the hillside
from just past Claggan to the
summit ridge of The Shee.
The summit was at the south
end of the wide ridge. After
descending SE to just north of
Dunan I returned over Creagan
na Beinne on a good path.

CREAG UCHDAG (3-4 hours)
There was parking at the dam
at the south end of Loch Lednock. I walked along the north
shore to a circular stone enclo-
sure and then made a rising
traverse north to the summit.

PLACES TO STAY/DRINK

Comrie and Crieff are well
placed for climbing Creag
Uchdag. Killin or Aberfeldy
would be good places to
stay if climbing The Shee of
Ardtalnaig and Creagan na
Beinne. There is also a hotel
in Ardeonaig and a guest
house in Ardtalnaig.

Personal View

These three mountains lie between Comrie and Loch Tay. I climbed
them all in poor weather and found The Shee of Ardtalnaig (The
Shee) the most interesting of the three summits. I started at Ardtalnaig to climb The Shee and Creagan na Beinne. It was straightforward to reach the summit ridge of The Shee which was covered
in peat hags. Since the ridge was grassy with peat hags it was a
surprise when, out of the mist, a remarkable cleft in the cliffs on
the east side of the mountain appeared. I descended to Dunan then
climbed Creagan na Beinne.

In February 2008 an early start from Loughborough enabled me to
reach Glen Lednock in time to climb Creag Uchdag. It was a cold
day and there were white hares on the mountain. I recall enjoying
coffee in Comrie afterwards.

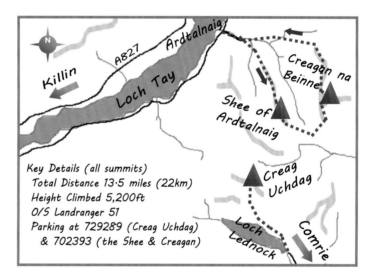

Key Details (all summits)
Total Distance 13·5 miles (22km)
Height Climbed 5,200ft
O/S Landranger 51
Parking at 729289 (Creag Uchdag)
& 702393 (the Shee & Creagan)

Looking across Loch Tay to Ardtalnaig and Creagan na Beinne.

BEN CHONZIE

BEN CHONZIE *(3,054ft)*
AUCHNAFREE HILL *(2,589ft)*

» Auchnafree Hill can be climbed on the way to or from Ben Chonzie.

» Crieff is a good base for these hills.

POINTS OF INTEREST

In February 1746 the Jacobite Army was quartered around Crieff with 'Bonnie Prince Charlie' holding his final war council before Culloden in the Old Drummond Arms.

My Routes

Ben Chonzie and Auchnafree Hill are best climbed together from Glen Turret. This route is shown on the map. I climbed them separately parking at Loch Turret dam, then taking the track along the east side of the loch on both occasions.

BEN CHONZIE *(4-5 hours)*

To climb Ben Chonzie we continued up the Turret Burn after passing Loch Turret. 500m before reaching Lochan Uaine we climbed west up the hillside. After 1km we turned NW to the large summit cairn.

AUCHNAFREE HILL *(3-4 hours)*

To climb Auchnafree Hill I walked 2km beside Loch Turret, then turned right up the hillside to Ton Eich. From Ton Eich I followed a track for a few hundred metres then went NNW to the summit.

PLACES TO STAY/DRINK

Crieff is only a few miles away and a good place to stay. Crieff Hydro has an excellent range of activities and caters well for children.

Ben Chonzie from Loch Turret.

Personal View (Colin)

Ben Chonzie is one of the more accessible summits in Scotland, standing just north of Crieff. We were staying at Crieff Hydro as was Barry, a friend and squash opponent. We had just finished playing squash when Barry, who was a seasoned climber, asked me whether I wanted to join him for a walk up Ben Chonzie the following afternoon.

As a total novice, and with no equipment, I arrived ready for the climb as agreed at 3.30 p.m. with my squash trainers. I was determined to hold a good account of myself and, as Barry pushed on hard up the mountain, I managed to keep up. It was a summer's day and the views were outstanding.

We finished off with a run back to the car then a short drive back to Crieff for a well-earned dinner. I have climbed many more Munros with Barry but Ben Chonzie remains my favourite mountain.

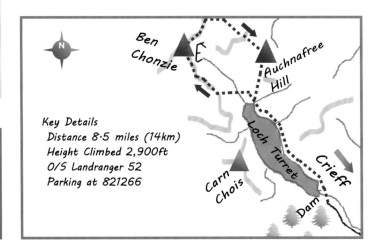

Key Details
Distance 8·5 miles (14km)
Height Climbed 2,900ft
O/S Landranger 52
Parking at 821266

ABERFELDY CORBETTS

MEALL TAIRNEACHAN
(2,582ft)
FARRAGON HILL *(2,569ft)*

» These Corbetts lie on a long ridge which fills the high ground between Aberfeldy and Loch Tummel.

» Meall Tairneachan and the Farragon Hill are usually climbed separately.

My Routes

MEALL TAIRNEACHAN
(2-3 hours)
There was parking near the junction between the B846 and the road leading to Schiehallion. We ascended along the edge of the forest to a small top. We traversed north of Meall Odhar Mor and the path led to a horseshoe shaped ridge and the trig point.

FARRAGON HILL *(4-5 hours)*
On a quiet day in February I parked near a point marked Lurgan on the map. It would be advisable to check with the Estate before doing this. I went NW along a good track which led past the west side of Loch Derculich. From the highest point of the track I climbed WSW up craggy slopes to the summit.

POINTS OF INTEREST
There is much to see around Aberfeldy. The town is known for 'Wade's Bridge' built in 1733 but also includes a memorial to the 'Black Watch' and a distillery.

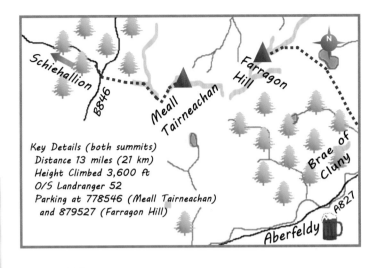

Key Details (both summits)
Distance 13 miles (21 km)
Height Climbed 3,600 ft
O/S Landranger 52
Parking at 778546 (Meall Tairneachan)
and 879527 (Farragon Hill)

Personal View

Both these Corbetts lie north of Aberfeldy and are glimpsed from the A9 when driving towards Pitlochry from the south. Meall Tairneachan is a short climb from the road but the Farragon Hill is a much longer walk.

Keith, a friend of mine since schooldays, and I decided to climb Meall Tairneachan in a break before supper when on a holiday at Kenmore in April 1989. By running the flat and downhill sections we managed to get back in time for supper but probably did not do justice to this hill. Sixteen years later in February 2005 I climbed the Farragon Hill on a cold but dry February day. There was thick snow above 2,000ft which made the last few hundred feet from the top of the track hard work.

Keith running up Meall Tairneachan, Schiehallion in the background (1989).

BEN LAWERS GROUP

On the Ben Lawers group.

BEN LAWERS *(3,984ft)*
MEALL GARBH *(3,668ft)*
MEALL CORRANAICH
(3,507ft)
MEALL GREIGH *(3,284ft)*
MEALL NAM MAIGHEACH
(2,558ft)

» These are rounded grassy hills to the north of Loch Tay which give excellent walking.

» There are three additional Munros in the group, An Stuc (3,668ft), Beinn Ghlas (3,619ft) and Meall a' Choire Leith (3,038ft).

» Ben Lawers is the highest mountain in Britain south of Ben Nevis.

» With a car at both ends seven Munros and one Corbett can be completed in one day.

Personal View

The Ben Lawers Group fills the high ground north of Loch Tay. The mountains are easy to reach from the road and Ben Lawers itself is the highest mountain in the Southern Highlands. This is an excellent Munro bagging area with seven Munros and one Corbett, all of which could be completed in one day.

Without the benefit of two cars or indeed a full day to devote to the task, I climbed the Ben Lawers Munros in two walks. In September 1988 I climbed Ben Lawers, Meall Garbh, An Stuc and Meall Greigh when on a family holiday at Kenmore. It was a wet day with low cloud. I could hear claps of thunder as I approached An Stuc and was starting to become scared but suddenly the mist cleared and I saw Ben Lawers ahead, a great relief after two hours in mist. It began to rain heavily but I was encouraged by the break in the clouds and walked quickly up the final 1,000ft to the summit of Ben Lawers.

I completed the Munros in the Ben Lawers Group the following year in far better weather finishing on Beinn Ghlas, a popular hill due to the high start and proximity to the Visitor Centre. My diary records that these were relatively easy Munros to 'tick off'. Eighteen years later I climbed Meall nam Maigheach, the only Corbett in the Group. It was a short climb from the road with only 900ft of ascent.

BEN LAWERS GROUP continued

My Routes

JP and Jonathan completed all these mountains in one day using transport at both ends. Their route is shown on the map. However, it took me three days. On two of those days I started at the bend on the minor road just north of the Lochan na Lairige. This gave a high start.

BEN LAWERS, MEALL GARBH, MEALL GREIGH (6-7 hours)

On my first visit to Ben Lawers I started from Lawers and ascended north, initially along the Lawers burn, to Meall Greigh. From this summit I descended west and climbed west then SW to Meall Garbh. A short up and down took me to An Stuc with thunder and lightning close by. Finally I descended SSW off An Stuc and climbed south to Ben Lawers. I descended straight back to Lawers.

MEALL CORRANAICH (4-5 hours)

I started from the north end of Lochan na Lairige and walked NE to Allt Gleann da Eig. The route continued in the same direction to the summit of Meall a' Choire Leith. From this summit I followed the ridge SSE then south for 3km to Meall Corranaich. I then descended SE to a bealach at 2,500ft and back up to Beinn Ghlas.

MEALL NAM MAIGHEACH (1-2 hours)

The ascent of Meall nam Maigheach was an easy climb NNW from just north of Lochan na Lairige.

POINTS OF INTEREST

The Ben Lawers Visitor Centre was demolished in 2012 and replaced by a series of information boards.

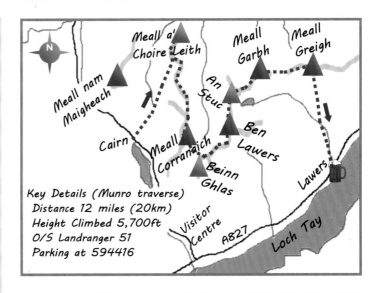

Key Details (Munro traverse)
Distance 12 miles (20km)
Height Climbed 5,700ft
O/S Landranger 51
Parking at 594416

PLACES TO STAY/DRINK

Killin is a good place for exploring these mountains and has hotels, guest houses, restaurants and cafes. The Ben Lawers Hotel situated by Loch Tay is a good place to start or finish the walk.

Ben Lawers from Kenmore.

BEN LUI GROUP

Ben Oss, Ben Lui (in cloud), and Beinn Chuirn from Beinn Odhar.

BEN LUI *(3,708ft)*
BEN OSS *(3,376ft)*
BEN DUBHCHRAIG *(3,209ft)*
BEINN CHUIRN *(2,887ft)*

» Ben Lui is one of the most spectacular Scottish mountains and is popular with walkers.

» An additional Munro can be climbed, Beinn a' Chleibh (3,005ft), which lies just to the west of Ben Lui.

» There are a variety of options for climbing all four Munros in one day.

» Beinn Chuirn is usually climbed separately but could be added to the four Munros by energetic walkers.

Personal View

Ben Lui stands tall and impressive on the left hand side of the A85 on the drive north from Crianlarich to Tyndrum. Munroists can claim four Munros in a day when climbing Ben Lui by adding Ben Oss, Ben Dubhchraig and Beinn a' Chleibh. It would also be possible to climb all four Munros plus Beinn Chuirn in a classic horseshoe from Dalrigh. This would be a tough but satisfying day requiring over 7,000ft of climbing.

It took me three ascents to complete the four Munros and one Corbett that form the Ben Lui Group. On the first two ascents I was joined by Colin on half day trips when we were staying at Crieff. On both trips we had to run part of the way in order to be back in time for dinner.

When we climbed Ben Lui we came across two lads from Cumbria. They had driven up from Cumbria that morning, biked it to Cononish and were climbing the four Ben Lui Munros. When we asked whether they were climbing all the Munros they said 'possibly, in thirty-five years or so'. Such is the nature of Munro climbing in the early years, no real plan is possible because there seem to be so many mountains to climb. Many years later in 2011 I 'ticked off' the Corbett, Beinn Chuirn, which was a short but steep climb from Glen Lochy.

BEN LUI GROUP continued

My Routes

BEN OSS AND BEN DUBHCHRAIG (5-7 hours)

We parked at Dalrigh to climb Ben Oss and Ben Dubhchraig and walked south. We crossed the bridge over the River Fillan, then followed a rough road west to a bridge over the railway. We left the road and headed west crossing the Allt Coire Dubhchraig at a footbridge. After following the NW side of the burn through trees we arrived at open hillside, then climbed to the shoulder of Beinn Dubhchraig. The ridge led SW to the summit. We descended NW along the ridge to a col before climbing to the summit of Ben Oss.

Key Details

- » Distance 11 miles (18km)
- » Height climbed 3,500ft
- » O/S Landranger 50
- » Parking at 343291.

BEN LUI AND BEINN A' CHLEIBH (4-5 hours)

The following year we climbed Ben Lui and Beinn a' Chleibh from Glen Lochy parking near the A85. We followed a path SE through the woods to the open hillside of Ben Lui. After reaching the summit we descended SW to climb Beinn a' Chleibh.

Key Details

- » Distance 6 miles (10km)
- » Height climbed 3,700ft
- » O/S Landranger 50
- » Parking at 239279.

BEINN CHUIRN (2-3 hours)

There was parking off the A85 (ref. 263305, O/S Landranger 50). After following a path beside the Allt Garbh Choirean I climbed steeply east to the summit. The return journey was 2.5 miles (4km) with 2,200ft of climbing.

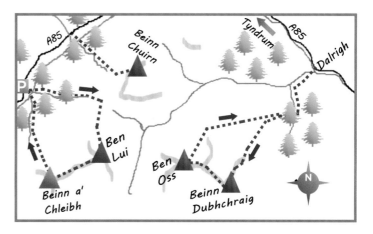

POINTS OF INTEREST

In 1306 Robert the Bruce, King Robert the First of Scotland, lost a battle at Dalrigh with the Clan MacDougall of Argyll, who were at that time allies of the English. This followed an earlier defeat for Robert at the Battle of Methven near Perth. Robert the Bruce recovered from these setbacks to defeat the English at the Battle of Bannockburn (1314).

Beinn Dubhchraig from Ben Oss *(Heather Thomas-Smith)*.

GLEN LOCHAY SOUTH

BEN CHALLUM *(3,363ft)*
MEALL GLAS *(3,145ft)*
SGIATH CHUIL *(3,021ft)*
BEINN NAN IMIREAN
(2,785ft)

» Three Munros and one Corbett
lying between Glen Dochart
and Glen Lochay.

» It is a long walk to complete all
four summits in one day.

Ben Challum from Meall Glas *(Chris Wood)*.

My Routes

BEN CHALLUM, MEALL GLAS, SGIATH CHUIL *(8-10 hours)*

I parked just before the gates
(now locked) at the end of the
road up Glen Lochay. The track
led 2km SW down the glen to
cross the River Lochay at a
footbridge near Lubchurran. I
climbed SE up grassy slopes
to the north ridge of Sgiath
Chuil and followed this ridge
south over Meall a' Churain to
the summit.

After returning north for a few
hundred metres I dropped
down steep slopes to the
bealach between Meall a'
Churain and Beinn Cheathaich. I headed just north of
Beinn Cheathaich to avoid a
steep and rocky section near
its summit, then went SE and
east to Meall Glas.

I returned to the col just east
of Meall Glas and descended
SW to the col below Beinn
nan Imirean (the summit was
only 600ft above). A descent
west took me to the low pass
(1,300ft) east of Ben Challum. Finally I climbed NW to
the summit returning to the
pass and a long walk back to
the start.

BEINN NAN IMIREAN
(3-4 hours)

Many years later I climbed
Beinn nan Imirean in thick
snow from Auchessan in Glen
Dochart.

Personal View

In April 1990 I stayed in Killin for the night before attempting the
three Munros lying south of Glen Lochay. This was to be one of my
hardest days on the Munros. There was snow above 2,000ft which
sapped any energy I had and by the time I started ascending Meall
Glas (the second Munro) I needed regular stops for water. Even the
final climb of 250ft up Meall Glas seemed tough.

I missed out Beinn nan Imirean (climbed seventeen years later) and
descended to just over 1,000ft before climbing Challum. Leaving
the rucksack by a wall and a group of bare trees so I could find it I
edged up the hillside. I climbed one hundred feet at a time, picking
out a rock and then collapsing for a rest. At times I felt sick. My diary
records 'The last 300ft were the hardest, scrambling and kicking
steps up a steep snow slope, what a relief to reach the summit!' I
descended a snow slope between the main summit and the south
summit as it seemed an easier route down. Soon I started to feel
better picking up the rucksack two and a half hours after leaving it.
It was a long walk down Glen Lochay to complete an eight hour day.

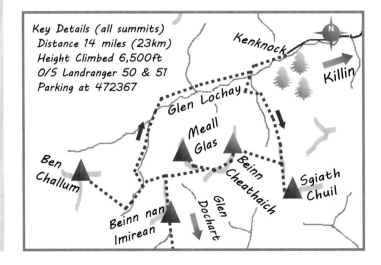

Key Details (all summits)
Distance 14 miles (23km)
Height Climbed 6,500ft
O/S Landranger 50 & 51
Parking at 472367

GLEN LOCHAY NORTH

BEINN HEASGARNICH (3,536ft)
CREAG MHOR (3,435ft)
MEALL NAN SUBH (2,645ft)

» Beinn Heasgarnich and Creag Mhor lie at the head of Glen Lochay.

» It is a tough walk over Beinn Heasgarnich and Creag Mhor.

» Meall nan Subh, a Corbett, can be added after Beinn Heasgarnich or climbed separately.

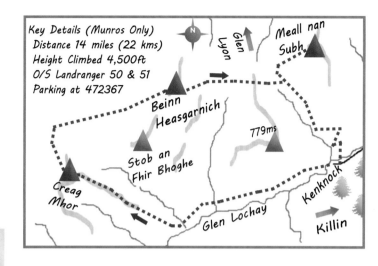

Key Details (Munros Only)
Distance 14 miles (22 kms)
Height Climbed 4,500ft
O/S Landranger 50 & 51
Parking at 472367

My Routes

CREAG MHOR AND BEINN HEASGARNICH (6-7 hours)
We parked just before the locked gates at the end of the road up Glen Lochay and walked 5km up the glen to Bat-avaime.

From Batavaime we climbed steeply NW up grassy hillside to Sron nan Eun, continuing WNW up the ridge to Creag Mhor. From Creag Mhor we headed NW then north for 500m along a broad ridge, then descended east to a low col (2,200ft). From here we climbed east and finally NNE to the summit of Beinn Heasgar-nich. We descended east then SE to reach Kenknock.

MEALL NAN SUBH (from top of Hydro-Electric road 1-2 hours)
When climbing Meall nan Subh I was able to drive to the cairn at the top of the Hydro-Elec-tric Board road (447392). The gate is now locked so it is necessary to walk up the road from Kenknock. From the top of the Hydro-Electric Board road it was a straightforward climb of 900ft to the summit of Meall Nan Subh.

Personal View

It was a sunny morning in August 1987 when Alistair met me at Lochearnhead. We were both unfit and I had developed a headache after the long drive from Newcastle so it seemed a long walk up Glen Lochay. As we ascended Creag Mhor only Alistair's dog, Kizzy, appeared likely to complete the walk! However, the walking became easier when we reached the top of Sron nan Eun and soon we were on the summit of Creag Mhor. It started to cloud over as we ascended Heasgarnich and the descent was frustrating, peaty and riddled with streams. It was a good day though topped off with sau-sage and chips washed down with a couple of beers at Callander.

Twenty years later I climbed Meall Nan Subh. The ascent was nota-ble because I had forgotten my compass. In the mist I had to use the strong west wind as a guide to direction on the upper slopes (not recommended).

Nearing the summit of Creag Mhor on a fine day in August 1987.

LOCHAY TO LYON

MEALL NAN TARMACHAN
(3,425ft)
MEALL GHAORDAIDH
(3,410ft)
BEINN NAN OIGHREAG
(2,982ft)

» Two Munros and a Corbett between Glen Lochay and Glen Lyon.

My Routes

MEALL NAN TARMACHAN
(3-4 hours)

Colin and I drove to the Ben Lawers Visitors' Centre. 500m past it we parked next to a locked gate on a rough road branching off SW. We walked along the road for a few hundred metres, then climbed west up grassy slopes to the broad SSE ridge of Meall nan Tarmachan. We climbed this ridge going over a small knoll at 3,000ft, then descending to the col below the SE face. We climbed this by turning right up a grassy rake, past the upper rocks, to the summit. We carried on to Meall Garbh before returning.

Key Details

» Distance 4.5 miles (7km)
» Height climbed 2,000ft
» O/S Landranger 51
» Parking at 604383.

MEALL GHAORDAIDH AND BEINN NAN OIGHREAG

Colin and I parked near Duncroisk and walked up the west side of the Allt Dhuin Croisg for 1.5km to a fence. From here we climbed directly NW to the summit of Meall Ghaordaidh. The trig point stood within a circular cairn. I returned to Duncroisk to climb Beinn nan Oighreag fourteen years later.

Key Details (combining both mountains in one walk, 5-6 hours).

» Distance 9.5 miles (15km)
» Height climbed 4,100ft
» O/S Landranger 51
» Parking at 527362.

Meall nan Tarmachan from the Falls of Dochart.

Personal View (JP)

Meall Ghaordaidh is a great grassy lump that can easily be climbed in a morning. A track near Duncroisk kicked me off then I picked my way up easy slopes that asked no questions. It was a good viewpoint but I had to hurry as I had a wedding to get to in the Kingdom of Fife. However, I remember Ghaordaidh for another reason, I woke next morning to find Princess Diana had died.

Barry climbed Beinn nan Oighreag on Christmas Day breaking through cold and dense fog into sunshine at 2,800ft, no reindeer on the summit though. He claims there was nowhere to eat afterwards and was grateful to find an Indian restaurant open in Pitlochry. However, a word of warning for Christmas Day hikers, this Indian restaurant has now closed.

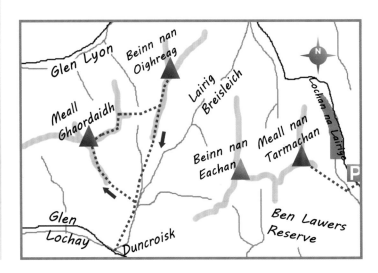

Buachaille Etive Mor across
Rannoch Moor.

SCOTLAND: RANNOCH TO GLENCOE

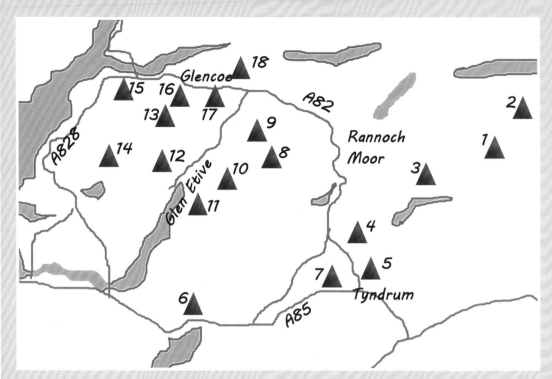

There are 54 Top 500 Summits in the area surrounding Rannoch Moor. They stretch from Glen Lyon in the south east to Glencoe in the north west. They are divided into 18 walks.

Rannoch Moor lies at the centre of this area which includes the mountains around Glencoe, Glen Etive and to the north of Glen Lyon. To the south lie the Orchy Munros and the Orchy Corbetts, two long days which give 10 summits, 5 Munros and 5 Corbetts. To the west lie Glencoe and Glen Etive, 26 summits squeezed into a relatively small area with a large number of sea level starts. 18 further summits make up the total including the mountains north of Loch Awe and Glen Lyon.

There are many great peaks in this area including:

» Bidean nam Bian in Glencoe, the highest summit in this section at 3,773ft;

» Ben Cruachan, sometimes known as 'The Hollow Mountain' because it houses Cruachan Power Station;

» Buachaille Etive Mor, perhaps the most photographed mountain in Scotland; and

» The Aonach Eagach ridge, probably the hardest ridge in mainland Scotland.

The West Highland Way, which runs from Fort William to Loch Lomond, cuts through the centre of the area so many of the hotels become crowded in the summer.

WALKS 1 TO 3

	Walk	Feet	Pg.
1	Carn Mairg	3,419	112
	Carn Gorm	3,377	
	Cam Chreag	2,828	
	Beinn Dearg	2,723	
2	Schiehallion	3,554	114
	Beinn a' Chuallaich	2,926	
3	Stuchd an Lochain	3,150	115
	Meall Buidhe	3,057	
	Meall Buidhe	2,985	
	Sron a' Choire Chnapanich	2,746	

WALKS 4 TO 18

	Walk	Feet	Pg.
4	Beinn a' Chreachain	3,547	116
	Beinn Dorain	3,530	
	Beinn Achaladair	3,404	
	Beinn an Dothaidh	3,294	
	Beinn Mhanach	3,125	
5	Beinn Odhar	2,955	117
	Beinn a' Chaisteil	2,907	
	Cam Chreag	2,900	
	Beinn Chaorach	2,685	
	Beinn nam Fuaran	2,645	
6	Ben Cruachan	3,695	118
	Beinn Eunaich	3,245	
	Beinn a' Chochuill	3,215	
	Beinn a' Bhuiridh	2,942	
7	Beinn Udlaidh	2,755	120
	Beinn Bhreac-Liath	2,633	
	Beinn Mhic-Mhonaidh	2,610	
8	Stob Ghabhar	3,575	121
	Stob a' Choire Odhair	3,100	
9	Meall a' Bhuiridh	3,636	122
	Creise	3,609	
	Beinn Mhic Chasgaig	2,835	
10	Stob Coir' an Albannaich	3,425	123
	Meall nan Eun	3,045	
	Stob Dubh	2,897	
11	Ben Starav	3,538	124
	Glas Bheinn Mhor	3,271	
	Beinn nan Aighenan	3,150	
12	Beinn Fhionnlaidh	3,145	125
	Beinn Trilleachan	2,755	
13	Sgor na h-Ulaidh	3,260	126
	Meall Lighiche	2,533	
	Beinn Maol Chaluim	2,975	
14	Beinn Sgulaird	3,074	128
	Creach Bheinn	2,656	
	Fraochaidh	2,883	
15	Sgorr Dhearg	3,361	130
	Sgorr Dhonuill	3,284	
16	Bidean nam Bian	3,773	131
17	Stob Dearg	3,353	132
	Stob Dubh	3,143	
	Stob Coire Raineach	3,035	
18	Sgorr nam Fiannaidh	3,173	134
	Beinn a' Chrulaiste	2,811	

On the West Highland Way between Tyndrum and Bridge of Orchy.

GLEN LYON

Summit of Meall Garbh, Schiehallion behind *(Heather Thomas-Smith).*

CARN MAIRG *(3,419ft)*
CARN GORM *(3,377ft)*
CAM CHREAG *(2,828ft)*
BEINN DEARG *(2,723ft)*

» There are four Munros and two Corbetts lying to the north of Glen Lyon and these can be completed in two walks.

» The Munro round includes four summits, the other two Munros are Creag Mhor (3,220ft) and Meall Garbh (3,176ft).

» The Corbetts are both in easy reach from the road up Glen Lyon and can be completed on the same day.

Personal View

In May 2001 'Foot and Mouth' had hit Britain. We had to wait to have the car wheels hosed down before driving up Glen Lyon to climb its four Munros. The farmer had been told to allow walkers on the mountains but he did not appear happy about it. Dogs were not allowed so Bracken and Corrie went off with Alistair to climb Schiehallion leaving Jonathan, JP, Ella and I to complete the 'Glen Lyon four'.

The weather started fine as we climbed Carn Gorm but closed in after Meall Garbh, thick mist and heavy rain. Ella suggested stopping for lunch, but in the cold and wet weather we had no enthusiasm for a stop of any description, so we ate the sandwiches while walking. As we climbed Creag Mhor the sun came out giving good views at last. We headed down in improving weather and drove back to Aberfeldy for dinner.

I have good memories of climbing the two Corbetts, Cam Chreag and Beinn Dearg, on a fine August afternoon in 2007. I climbed Cam Chreag first then had afternoon tea at Bridge of Balgie before an early evening ascent of Beinn Dearg. Beinn Dearg was a steeper climb than Cam Chreag and the views to the Ben Alder range to the north and the Ben Lawers range to the south were magnificent.

GLEN LYON continued

My Routes

GLEN LYON MUNROS
(6-8 hours)

We started at the small car park in Invervar. A good track led up the east side of the Invervar Burn. There was a footbridge across the burn at the top of the forest, then we climbed west to the summit of Carn Gorm.

We descended to the col at 2,700ft, bypassed An Sgorr, then climbed NE up Meall Garbh. We followed fence posts east over Meall a' Bharr (1,004m) before the climb to the summit of Carn Mairg.

We descended east then SSE to a col at 2,750ft. A final ascent led to the fourth and last Munro, Creag Mhor. From there we descended to Invervar.

CAM CHREAG (2-3 hours)

I parked by the roadside just north of Gallin and followed the west side of a stream up the hillside. As the hillside became less steep, I headed towards a small top 500m west of the summit. It was a short walk from there to the summit of Cam Chreag.

BEINN DEARG (2-3 hours)

I started a few hundred metres west of Camusvrachan where a forest track ascended through the woods. After coming out of the woods a steep climb led to the SE shoulder of Beinn Dearg. On reaching the summit plateau I continued north to the top which was on the fence line. I returned by the same route but it would be possible to return via Creag Ard.

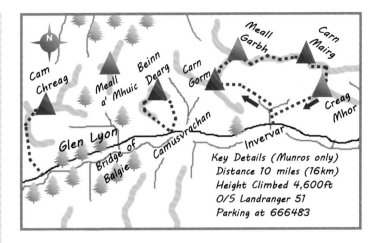

Key Details (Munros only)
Distance 10 miles (16km)
Height Climbed 4,600ft
O/S Landranger 51
Parking at 666483

Finally out of the mist descending Meall Garbh (2001).

KINLOCH RANNOCH

SCHIEHALLION *(3,554ft)*
BEINN A'
CHUALLAICH *(2,926ft)*

» One Munro and one Corbett lying south and north of Kinloch Rannoch.

My Routes

SCHIEHALLION *(3-4 hours)*

In 1978 we started at the car park just east of the Braes of Foss (1,000ft above sea level). There are now signs for the path to Schiehallion. We walked SW across grassy moorland and met a track up from the Braes of Foss. We crossed the track and kept heading in a SW direction up the mountain. As the slope steepened the route went up peaty ground. We turned west when we reached stony ground higher up. The final mile along the ridge was marked by cairns.

Key Details

» Distance 5.5 miles (9km)
» Height climbed 2,500ft
» O/S Landranger 42 and 51
» Parking at 753558.

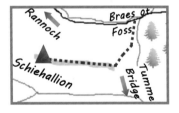

BEINN A' CHUALLAICH
(2-3 hours)

The shortest ascent starts near a sharp bend on the B847 (ref 707616, O/S Landranger 42) where a track leads to a gate in the forestry fence. From there I climbed WNW up the hillside to reach the col between Beinn a' Chuallaich and Meall nan Eun. From the col it was a short climb up the NW ridge to the trig point. The return journey was four miles with 2,000ft of climbing.

View of Schiehallion from near Kinloch Rannoch.

Personal View (Ella)

I love the mountains and so did my new boyfriend (JP), after all we had met in a ski resort. So what could go wrong when he suggested climbing a few hills in Scotland. He mentioned Munro bashing and being 'quite focussed' as the tally to go dwindled. It seemed that climbing a Scottish hill in each other's company might be a (critical) test of suitability! And so it was that I found myself at the bottom of Schiehallion (the Fairy Hill of the Caledonians) feeling positive. I had climbed my first Munro at the age of nine (Ben Alligin in Torridon) even if there had since been a significant gap. In fact Catbells in the Lake District as a student, was the only summit in the meantime.

It seems I passed the test by the skin of my teeth. The ascent was simple, weather cool and cloudy, but great views from the top. It was coming down that I didn't enjoy, inadequate footwear and a lack of experience meant that the descent took twice as long as the ascent over the stony boulder field that covers the upper part. The boyfriend hid his frustration at my slowness at the time but now we are married we each walk at our own pace and rarely see each other! The following day we went up Ben Lomond and my initiation was complete.

Of course later expeditions included some long days in the mountains and I learned to ask (casually), 'How long do you expect it to take?' in order to prepare myself and ensure I had a big enough picnic.

LOCH AN DAIMH

STUCHD AN LOCHAIN (3,150ft)
MEALL BUIDHE (3,057ft)
MEALL BUIDHE (2,985ft)
SRON A' CHOIRE CHNAPANICH (2,746ft)

» Two Munros and two Corbetts which surround Loch an Daimh.

My Routes

EASTERN MUNROS (5-7 hours)
Colin and I parked at the Loch an Daimh dam (height of 1,500ft). Stuchd an Lochain was to be my 200th Munro. We walked past the south end of the dam for 150m then climbed south. A ridge appeared and a line of fence posts. We followed these west over Creag an Fheadain, SSW to Sron Chona Choirein, and finally west and NW to Stuchd an Lochain.

After returning to the dam we climbed north to Meall a' Phuill (2,900ft). From there it was an easy walk west and then NNW to the top of Meall Buidhe.

WESTERN CORBETTS (5-6 hours)
I parked at Pubil and headed along a track on the north side of Loch Lyon for 2km. The route climbed north beside one of the burns and traversed west to the 2,300ft col below Meall Buidhe. A fence led north up the shoulder to the summit plateau. I walked west for 1km to the summit. I returned to the col then walked NE down the Feith Thalain for 1km. A traverse east led to a wide col 1km SW of Sron a' Choire Chnapanich. Finally, I climbed the mossy slopes to the summit.

Personal View (Alistair)

The easiest way to climb the two Munros known to us all as 'The Dam' would have been to climb one, go back to the start, then climb the other. However, we decided on a more aesthetic approach going round the head of Loch an Daimh and taking in the Corbett, Sron a' Choire Cnapanich. JP brought his wife Ella along for this walk. Having a woman along always adds a touch of class to an expedition. For example sandwiches at lunchtime, people looking less scruffy and not being left behind if they weren't keeping up.

We started at Loch an Daimh dam and drifted easily up the Stuchd first. It wasn't wet and we were not rushing. Then it got better, we stopped for lunch, almost unheard of normally, but this was a proper lunch. Ella had brought bread, ham, tomatoes, and a knife to cut the tomatoes, fantastic! Lunch over, we continued on the circuit. Over the Corbett (Sron a' Choire Chnapanich) then down to the head of the loch which had a remote feel, I doubt many visit this spot. After this a sharp ascent took us to the northern ridge above Loch an Daimh and the summit of Meall Buidhe with the weather now wet, very wet in fact.

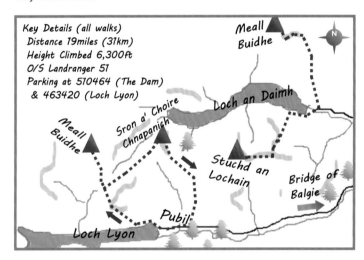

Key Details (all walks)
Distance 19miles (31km)
Height Climbed 6,300ft
O/S Landranger 51
Parking at 510464 (The Dam) & 463420 (Loch Lyon)

Nearing the summit of Meall Buidhe *(Chris Wood)*.

ORCHY MUNROS

BEINN A' CHREACHAIN
(3,547ft)
BEINN DORAIN *(3,530ft)*
BEINN ACHALADAIR
(3,404ft)
BEINN AN DOTHAIDH
(3,294ft)
BEINN MHANACH (3,125ft)

» Five Munros overlooking the Bridge of Orchy that can be completed in one long day or split into two easier days.

Beinn Achaladair (left) and Beinn an Dothaidh from the north.

My Routes

BEINN DORAIN AND BEINN AN DOTHAIDH (5-6 hours)

In 1998 Colin and I started from the station car park at Bridge of Orchy. A path led to the col between Beinn Dorain and Beinn an Dothaidh. We climbed Beinn Dorain first then returned to the col to climb Beinn an Dothaidh.

BEINN MHANACH, BEINN ACHALADAIR, BEINN A' CHREACHAIN (8-9 hours)

A few years later I climbed Beinn Mhanach, Beinn Achaladair and Beinn a' Chreachain from Achallader. I started by climbing to the col east of Beinn an Dothaidh. From there I descended east before climbing over Beinn a' Chuirn to Beinn Mhanach.

I returned west to the watershed and climbed west to point 1002m on Beinn Achaladair. The ridge continued north then NE going over Beinn Achaladair and onto Beinn a' Chreachain. I returned west for 1km then descended to the valley.

Key Details

» Distance 13 miles (21km)
» Height climbed 6,400ft
» O/S Landranger 50
» Parking at 322443.

Personal View (JP)

It was May Bank Holiday as I set off from Orchy and up the easy path to the col. I had loaded the pack having decided to have a night out on the hills but it was a poor forecast and I saw nothing on Dorain and Dothaidh apart from a few snow flurries. It improved on Achaladair and the cloud lifted. I had only been going three hours so was ahead of schedule. A steeper descent east led to easy grassy walking finishing on Chreachain's dome.

I horseshoed Gleann Cailliene to reach lumpy Beinn Mhanach. I had seen no-one all day but sometimes that is the way I like it. South now to the head of Loch Lyon. Eyeing grey clouds to the west I realised that I was in for a wet night. The expected bothy turned out to be a farm but I was ok in the lee of a boulder with my orange sack. The wind and rain hit and grew stronger in the night. I was not looking forward to Creag Mhor and Ben Challum in the morning.

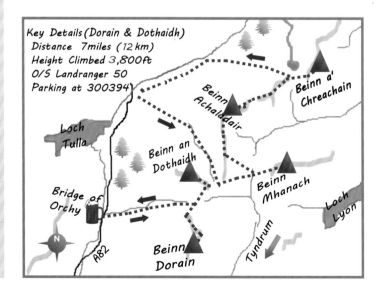

Key Details (Dorain & Dothaidh)
Distance 7 miles (12 km)
Height Climbed 3,800ft
O/S Landranger 50
Parking at 300394

Loch Tulla

Beinn Achaladair

Beinn a' Chreachain

Beinn an Dothaidh

Beinn Mhanach

Loch Lyon

Bridge of Orchy

Beinn Dorain

Tyndrum

A82

N

ORCHY CORBETTS

BEINN ODHAR *(2,955ft)*
BEINN A' CHAISTEIL
(2,907ft)
CAM CHREAG *(2,900ft)*
BEINN CHAORACH *(2,685ft)*
BEINN NAM FUARAN
(2,645ft)

» This is a compact circuit of five Corbetts that can be completed in a day. This is a good place to 'bag' five Corbetts in one walk.

» These are big grassy hills which give a great but strenuous walk.

My Route (8-10 hours)

I parked just off the A82 near its summit north of Tyndrum and walked north for a short distance and under the railway. It was a steep climb SE to the south ridge of Beinn Odhar which I followed north to the summit. From the summit I descended SE for 1,000ft to a lochan, then walked ESE to the col between Beinn Odhar and Beinn Chaorach. From the col I climbed steeply for 1,000ft to the ridge of Chaorach. The fence turned north for 200m to the summit.

The crossing to the next Corbett was the least strenuous of the round. I walked NNE to the col, then NE and east to the summit of Cam Chreag. A pleasant descent down the long NNW ridge of Cam Chreag followed. I crossed the Abhainn Ghlas and climbed north up steeper slopes for 1,300ft to Beinn nam Fuaran. This was a magnificent summit overlooking Loch Lyon.

I followed a fence steeply down SW then continued in the same direction up 1,000ft to the final Corbett, Beinn a' Chaisteil. The return went SE down the ridge for 1.5km, before descending to the glen and the long hike back to the start.

Personal View

I enjoyed my circuit of this fine round of five Corbetts starting from the West Highland Way between Tyndrum and Bridge of Orchy. The Corbetts are close together and near the A82 with Beinn Odhar being a direct ascent from the road. During my round in September 2007, I had resigned myself to not seeing anyone (not unusual on the Corbetts) so I was surprised to see a woman appear out of the mist as I reached the summit cairn on Cam Chreag.

It was Yvonne Holland, a keen climber both abroad and in the UK. As well as completing the Munros she had climbed Mount McKinley (Denali) in Alaska and many other overseas peaks including some in the Himalayas. She stopped for lunch at the stream after Cam Chreag but caught me up again on the summit of the final Corbett in the round, Beinn a' Chaisteil. We completed the walk together as the weather improved and the cloud finally lifted.

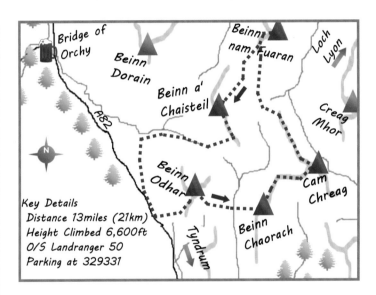

Key Details
Distance 13miles (21km)
Height Climbed 6,600ft
O/S Landranger 50
Parking at 329331

Looking down to Tyndrum from near the summit of Beinn Odhar.

BEN CRUACHAN

Ben Cruachan range from the east *(Heather Thomas-Smith)*.

BEN CRUACHAN *(3,695ft)*
BEINN EUNAICH *(3,245ft)*
BEINN A' CHOCHUILL
(3,215ft)
BEINN A' BHUIRIDH *(2,942ft)*

» Stob Diamh (3,274ft) is the fourth Munro in this group.

» There are two possible routes, the first ('my route') ascends the four Munros and needs transport at both ends.

» The second route and the more natural circuit traverses Ben Cruachan, Stob Diamh and Beinn a' Bhuiridh. Beinn Eunaich and Beinn a' Chochuill are climbed separately.

Personal View (Jonathan)

The classic Ben Cruachan circuit traverses two Munros and one Corbett. It starts and finishes at the Visitor Centre for 'The Hollow Mountain' next to Loch Awe and is a great round that should not be missed. In 1987 JP and I were badly equipped for an Easter climbing trip to Scotland. Cruachan was only my sixth Munro and I did not appreciate the difference between the Lakes and Scotland.

Cruachan is a huge mountain and I felt it as we toiled up beyond the dam deciding to take in the Top, Meall Cuanail, before the final pull to the main summit of Ben Cruachan. Snow was on the ground, the cloud swept in and unusually JP was left behind. I sat down and a passing walker stopped to reprimand me about how irresponsible I and 'that idiot below' was. It was difficult not to agree with him.

We carried on and conquered the horseshoe (excluding Beinn a' Bhuiridh) and I regard this as one of the finest walks in Scotland with the crossing between the two Munros particularly impressive. We returned over twenty years later, better equipped this time to tick off a variety of Munro Tops and of course the lone Corbett, Beinn a' Bhuiridh.

BEN CRUACHAN continued

My Routes

THE FOUR MUNROS
(8-10 hours)

I started from the Cruachan Power Station, parking by the roadside rather than at the Visitor Centre. After going through the left hand arch of the railway bridge, I followed a path up the west side of the burn. At the reservoir I climbed WNW to the south ridge of Meall Cuanail. This was followed to the top of Meall Cuanail. From there I descended 200ft, then continued north up the ridge to the summit of Ben Cruachan.

From Ben Cruachan I followed the ridge in an easterly direction over Drochaid Ghlas to Stob Diamh. The traverse is not difficult but required careful route finding in mist and took longer than expected.

I descended from Stob Diamh to the pass at Lairig Noe. From there it was a hard climb north for 1,500ft to the ridge just east of Beinn a' Chochuill. From Chochuill I descended the gentle east ridge to the bealach between Beinn a' Chochuill and Beinn Eunaich. From there the ascent to the summit of Beinn Eunaich was straightforward. Finally I went south down a broad grassy ridge to the road where transport was waiting.

BEINN A' BHUIRIDH (3-4 hours)

I climbed Beinn a' Bhuiridh separately from the A85 starting at the east end of Loch Awe (Ref 132284, O/S Landranger 50).

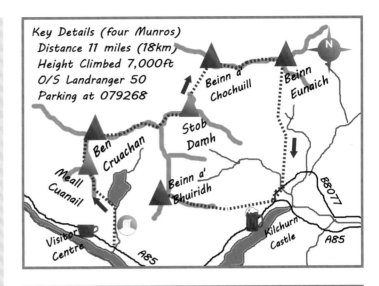

Key Details (four Munros)
Distance 11 miles (18km)
Height Climbed 7,000ft
O/S Landranger 50
Parking at 079268

POINTS OF INTEREST

Ben Cruachan is known as the Hollow Mountain. The world's first high head reversible pumped storage hydro scheme is housed in a gigantic man-made cavern underneath it. There is a Visitor Centre at the power station and guided tours.

Ben Cruachan and the Taynuilt Peak *(Heather Thomas-Smith)*.

TYNDRUM CORBETTS

BEINN UDLAIDH *(2,755ft)*
BEINN BHREAC-LIATH
(2,633ft)
BEINN MHIC-MHONAIDH
(2,610ft)

» These three Corbetts lie close to Tyndrum. They split into two walks.

» Beinn Udlaidh and Beinn Bhreac-Liath are a short climb from Arinabea in Glen Lochy.

» Beinn Mhic-Mhonaidh is climbed separately from the Falls of Orchy.

My Routes

BEINN UDLAIDH AND BEINN BHREAC-LIATH *(4-5 hours)*

I started at Arinabea 3km west of Tyndrum on the A85. There was a gap in the trees so I climbed through the gap, just west of north, to reach the col between the two peaks. Both Corbetts should be climbed from the col although I made a route finding error (see personal view).

BEINN MHIC-MHONAIDH *(4-5 hours)*

There is parking off the B8074 near the Falls of Orchy. I walked over the bridge and down the forestry track for 2km to the Allt Broighleachan. I took the cycle trail over a stream then turned left onto a trail. This led west coming out of the forest at some ruined shielings. I climbed NW to the summit ridge and then NE to the summit.

PLACES TO STAY/DRINK

Tyndrum has accommodation, food and drink. Alternatively I enjoy staying at the Bridge of Orchy Hotel or its bunkhouse. However, this should be booked as it is popular being on the West Highland Way.

Beinn Bhreac-Liath and Beinn Udlaidh from Beinn Odhar.

Personal View

Beinn Udlaidh and Beinn Bhreac-Liath are a natural twosome but it took me two attempts to climb them. In March 2007 on a cold and wet day I veered too far east and thought Beinn Bhreac Liath was the summit of Beinn Udlaidh. This meant that my second summit was Beinn Bheag (just over 2,000ft), a thoroughly incompetent performance! The weather was no better when I returned in June 2008 but this time I found the summit of Udlaidh and the debris of the mast which lies near its summit.

Surprisingly, after two shocking days on Udlaidh and Bhreac-Liath, it was a beautiful day in November 2011 when I climbed Beinn Mhic-Mhonaidh. I shared the summit ridge with some deer in the winter sunshine.

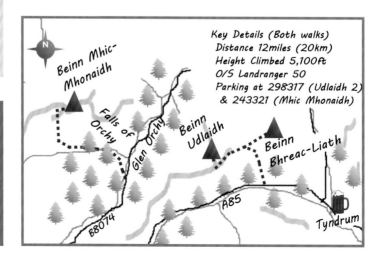

Key Details (Both walks)
Distance 12 miles (20km)
Height Climbed 5,100ft
O/S Landranger 50
Parking at 298317 (Udlaidh 2)
& 243321 (Mhic Mhonaidh)

BLACKMOUNT SOUTH

STOB GHABHAR *(3,575ft)*
STOB A' CHOIRE ODHAIR
(3,100ft)

» Two Munros with good paths
climbed from Forest Lodge
near Bridge of Orchy.

» Both Munros can be seen
when looking south crossing
Rannoch Moor on the A82.

My Route (6-7 hours)

We started at Victoria Bridge
and followed the track west,
along the north side of the
Linn nam Beathach, for 1.5km
to a corrugated hut. We then
followed the path north along
the Allt Toaig for 2km. After
crossing a burn the path led
NNE up the heathery ridge
of Stob a' Choire Odhair. The
heathery ridge turned stony as
we climbed NNE to the summit. We descended west to
the bealach between Stob a'
Choire Odhair and Stob Ghabhar.

After continuing west for 500m
we turned SW to climb more
steeply to Aonach Eagach.
From here a path ran west
along the left side of the ridge.
Finally it climbed NW up the SE
ridge to the summit.

POINTS OF INTEREST

Stob Ghabhar can be climbed
as part of a traverse of the
Black Mount range. This is
a 25 mile walk from the
Inveroran Hotel to the Kings
House Hotel never dropping
below 2,400ft, except at the
start and finish.

Personal View

These two Munros lie a few miles north east of Bridge of Orchy
in an area known as the Blackmount. Stob Ghabhar is the higher
mountain and is a well known and popular Munro.

One Sunday in late October 1997 Alistair and I made an early start
from Callander to climb both Munros from Forest Lodge. We were
surprised to find at least thirty cars parked at Forest Lodge and
assumed most of their occupants were climbing Stob Ghabhar.
The paths were excellent and Alistair was moving quickly despite a
knee operation earlier in the year and six pints the night before. We
left the crowds and climbed deserted Stob a' Choire Odhair first.
We then headed up Stob Ghabhar and found the summit crowded
despite being covered in cloud. Overall this was an enjoyable round
from Victoria Bridge.

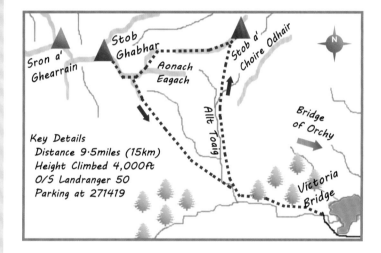

Key Details
Distance 9.5miles (15km)
Height Climbed 4,000ft
O/S Landranger 50
Parking at 271419

The Blackmount from the east.

BLACKMOUNT NORTH

MEALL A' BHUIRIDH
(3,636ft)
CREISE *(3,609ft)*
BEINN MHIC CHASGAIG
(2,835ft)

» This is an enjoyable round with a high start from Rannoch Moor. The route goes up the Meall a' Bhuiridh ski slopes.

» There are good views of Glencoe and north to Ben Nevis as well as the Blackmount.

My Routes

MEALL A' BHUIRIDH AND CREISE *(5-6 hours)*
Colin and I left the A82 and drove up to the ski centre where there was parking and a cafe. If possible leave a car or a bike in Glen Etive to avoid the tedious walk back at the end. We climbed SSW under the ski lifts to Coire Pollach and continued to the summit of Mcall a' Bhuiridh. We descended WSW to a col then climbed west to a ridge. This ran north and after 600m reached the top of Creise.

From Creise it looked possible to add Beinn Mhic Chasgaig by returning 600m south, then descending west to a col at 2,200ft. The Corbett can be climbed from there. However, I left this for another day.

BEINN MHIC CHASGAIG
(2-3 hours)
I climbed Beinn Mhic Chasgaig separately from Glen Etive and started by crossing the river at reference 220520 (O/S Landranger 41).

POINTS OF INTEREST
The Glencoe ski centre is Scotland's oldest ski resort. The main ski area on the high northern slopes of Meall a' Bhuiridh is known as Happy Valley and is ideal for people learning to ski.

Meall a' Bhuiridh and Creise from the north.

Personal View (Jonathan)

JP and I tackled Creise and its neighbour Meall a' Bhuiridh after a heavy night in the Kings House. We still had a large choice of Munros so in the tent decided on 'nearest available'. It had been fun skiing on the slopes of Meall a' Bhuiridh but climbing the slopes under the chairlift was tedious. It was a warm, muggy day but we had the views of Rannoch Moor and the spectacular divide of Glencoe to sustain us. However, we had no water to relieve my increasing dehydration and pounding headache.

Heading west over Creise the ridge came to an abrupt end and a steep and rocky descent took us down to the River Etive. This was the moment I had been looking forward all day, a drink and a dip in the river. I have always drunk from mountain streams and never had any problems. The River Etive proved to be the exception, probably the combination of it being too low and the recent dry spell was fatal. Twenty-four hours later we both suffered serious stomach and vomiting problems, unfortunately I was on a London Tube train!

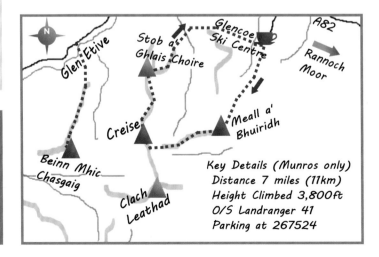

Key Details (Munros only)
Distance 7 miles (11km)
Height Climbed 3,800ft
O/S Landranger 41
Parking at 267524

GLEN ETIVE EAST

STOB COIR' AN ALBANNAICH (3,425ft)
MEALL NAN EUN (3,045ft)
STOB DUBH (2,897ft)

» The Munros are climbed from Glen Etive. They could be added to the Starav or Ghabhar walks but this gives a long day.

» Stob Dubh is a high Corbett climbed separately.

My Routes

Both climbs started two miles from the end of the road down Glen Etive.

STOB COIR' AN ALBANNAICH AND MEALL NAN EUN (6-7 HOURS)

After leaving the car Alistair and I crossed the bridge over the River Etive and turned SW. Before reaching Coileitir Cottage we climbed SE up the hillside on the right hand side of a straight deep gully. At 2,800ft we passed Beinn Chaorach. The route gradually turned ESE to the summit of Stob Coir' an Albannaich. Continuing to Meall nan Eun required careful compass work. We descended east for 500m then north to a bealach at 2,500ft. Finally we climbed ENE over Meall Tarsuinn to Meall nan Eun.

STOB DUBH (3-4 hours)

After crossing the bridge over the River Etive I turned left along a track. This went NE and after 1km led to a bridge over the Allt Ceitlein. I crossed the bridge and turned left towards a house, Glenceitlein. A steep ascent ENE led to the summit.

Key Details

» Distance 10 miles (16km) (Munros) 6 miles (10km) (Stob Dubh)

» Height climbed 4,300ft (Munros) and 2,900ft (Stob Dubh)

» O/S Landranger 50

» Parking at 138469 (both routes).

Personal View (JP)

I included Stob Coir' an Albannaich and Meall nan Eun in a great round from Victoria Bridge on a cool and sunny May day. The Stalkers' track allowed easy going up Stob Odhar but halfway up I was overtaken by a fell runner who said he was doing my round of four Munros plus the Starav three. Wow! I descended west off Odhar into a grand corrie and skirted the impressive rim to Ghabhar.

I set off along the lonely and spectacular four kilometre west ridge, steep grass down to the bealach then easy up flat topped Eun. Continued west over a minor bump then found a gully up the steep north face of Albannaich. It was a good viewing top so I had a Mars bar. Descending to Loch Dochard took me through all sorts of wild terrain, rock outcrops then boggy moor. At the bottom I was still a long way from home and on the forest track I was overtaken again by the fell runner. He was puffing but I was on the verge of collapse; ten hours for the round.

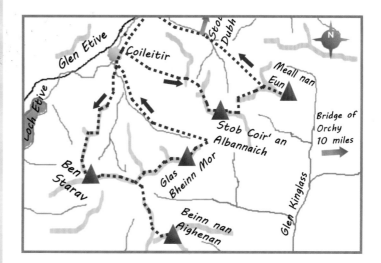

Meall nan Eun from Stob Dubh.

BEN STARAV

BEN STARAV *(3,538ft)*
GLAS BHEINN MHOR
(3,271ft)
BEINN NAN AIGHENAN
(3,150ft)

» This is a hard day on the Munros, Ben Starav is a straight climb of 3500ft from sea level.

» It is worth adding Beinn nan Aighenan to avoid having to return later.

My Route (8-9 hours)

Jonathan and I started from the Glen Etive road two miles from its southern end. It was possible to park by the roadside. We walked east along a good path to cross the River Etive by a bridge. After the bridge the path turned SW. At the Allt Mheuran we climbed SE and after 200m crossed a bridge to the west bank. We walked along the west bank for 500m, then climbed the relentless north ridge of Starav to the summit.

After following the ridge over the top of Stob Coire Dheirg we descended to the col at 2,500ft. A further descent of 500ft SE led to a bealach at 2,000ft, then we climbed the north ridge of Beinn nan Aighenan. After returning to the 2,500ft col on the Starav ridge we climbed east over a minor top to Glas Bheinn Mhor. We continued east for another 500m, then descended north to the Allt Mheuran and followed it back to the start.

For reference, see the Glen Etive east map on page 123.

Key Details

» Distance 11 miles (18km)
» Height climbed 6,100ft
» O/S Landranger 50
» Parking at 138469.

Glas Bheinn Mhor from Glen Etive.

Personal View (Jonathan)

Amongst our group of walkers Starav is my mountain, I have climbed it three times by its north ridge, 3,500ft of ascent, and I doubt that this will ever be beaten by anyone I know! Probably the relentless northern ascent is only matched by ascending Ben More from near Crianlarich. My first ascent was on a cold Easter day in 1987, it was my eighth Munro and the only thing that I am sure about was that JP and I failed to visit Beinn nan Aighenan, the southern outlier.

It wasn't long before I was back to mighty Starav, this time continuing on to Beinn Aighenan which is my favourite Munro of the three. I had then started climbing Munro Tops and in this case they proved to be a navigational challenge. The South Top was the toughest to reach and by the time I returned I had run out of time so I missed Glas Bheinn Mhor on the way back. My final ascent of Starav was in 2002 when I joined Barry for a round of all three Munros described in 'My Route' opposite.

PLACES TO STAY/DRINK

We returned to the Kings House for a drink after climbing these three Munros. An alternative place to drink would be the Clachaig Inn.

GLEN ETIVE WEST

BEINN FHIONNLAIDH
(3,145ft)
BEINN TRILLEACHAN
(2,755ft)

» Beinn Fhionnlaidh is an isolated and hidden Munro which can be climbed from Glen Etive or Glen Creran.

» Beinn Trilleachan is a distinctive and isolated Corbett overlooking Loch Etive.

My Routes

BEINN FHIONNLAIDH
(5-6 hours)
I started at Invercharnan, a drive of ten miles south down Glen Etive from the A82. There is parking just north of the bridge over the Allt Charnan. After passing a house I followed the Forestry Commission road for 3km to a sharp right turn. I followed a path which passed through a firebreak and after 200m reached a stile and open hillside. I climbed west up grassy hillside to a col south of point 841m. From here I climbed north then NW to the summit ridge of Beinn Fhionnlaidh. I followed the ridge west then WSW to the summit.

BEINN TRILLEACHAN
(4-5 hours)
I started at the edge of the forest 300m before the end of the single track road which leads down Glen Etive (ref 111454). It was possible to park by the side of the road. A path climbed 1km NW along the side of the forest. At a height of 600ft I turned SW and started climbing the hillside aiming directly for the summit. At 2,000ft the ridge became rocky and at 2,516ft I reached a cairn at the top of the spectacular Etive slabs. There was a short descent of 250ft, then easy slopes led to the summit of Beinn Trilleachan.

Personal View (Alistair)

Beinn Fhionnlaidh is a forgotten Munro hidden behind Bidean nam Bian and standing a long way back from Glen Etive and Glen Creran. It stands alone and although it has never excited me it needed to be climbed. I approached from Invercharnan, the usual route. I went through Glen Etive Forest on a good track and found it fast going. Then I was in open countryside taking a sharp left across a conflux of streams; wet feet now.

It was a sharp pull to the summit ridge, then the cloud lifted and I was able to appreciate what a great viewpoint this was, west to the sea, north to Glencoe, and south to Etive and beyond. It was lucky that the clouds lifted, but maybe lonely Fhionnlaidh deserves better than to be considered just a tick.

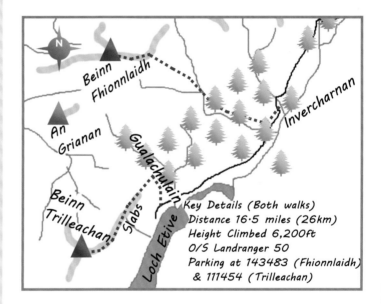

Key Details (Both walks)
Distance 16·5 miles (26km)
Height Climbed 6,200ft
O/S Landranger 50
Parking at 143483 (Fhionnlaidh) & 111454 (Trilleachan)

Summit ridge of Beinn Trilleachan with its slabs (2009).

'HOOLEY' TO ETIVE

JP and Jonathan complete the Munros on Sgor na h-Ulaidh in 2003, Mike Pyman (JP's father) hands out the champagne.

SGOR NA H-ULAIDH *(3,260ft)*
MEALL LIGHICHE *(2,533ft)*
BEINN MAOL CHALUIM
(2,975ft)

» One Munro and two Corbetts lying just to the south of Glencoe.

» Sgor na h-Ulaidh was the final Munro for Jonathan and JP in 2003. It is a 'hidden' Munro in Glencoe less well known than Bidean nam Bian. Meall Lighiche lies just to the north of Sgor na h-Ulaidh.

» Beinn Maol Chaluim is a high Corbett between Glencoe and Glen Etive.

Personal View (Jonathan)

Sgor na h-Ulaidh is an isolated Munro near Glencoe. In 2003 it was the final Munro for JP and I so we were joined by JP's parents, and my father met us on the way down. I am not sure why I left 'Hooley' to be my final Munro, possibly because it was close to the Clachaig Inn and accessible for those who wished to join us on the day. I was delighted that JP's father made it to the summit aged 75 as he had been a major influence on my early life and had himself been walking and skiing the Glencoe hills for nearly sixty years. Another twenty-five years walking sounds good to me!

We started with the neighbouring Munro Top of Stob an Fhuarain and the climb seemed endless, typical of many Scottish mountains I have climbed over the years. I am sure everyone has their own distractions to help them climb slopes like these but mine involved reciting the words of a song from The Jam 'Private Hell'. From the top it was an easy crossing to the Munro and that was that, Munros done! After climbing 'Hooley' Barry hauled me up the nearby Corbett before a few celebratory pints in the Clachaig and the Kings House.

My Routes

SGOR NA H-ULAIDH AND MEALL LIGHICHE (6-7 hours)
We started from the A82 road 3km SE of Glencoe village. A track ran along the west bank of the Allt na Muidhe crossing to the east bank after 1km. We continued SW for 1km, then turned south down the glen for a further 1.5km. We climbed left up the hillside reaching the ridge just north of Stob an Fhuarain. We went over this summit and SW to a bealach at 860m before ascending to Sgor na h-Ulaidh.

We continued west for 500m to Corr na Beinne, then descended steeply north (not an easy descent) to a col. Jonathan and I ascended 800ft NW to the summit of Meall Lighiche. We returned over Creag Bhan, then descended north to reach the outward route.

Key Details
» Distance 8.5 miles (14km)
» Height climbed 4,300ft
» O/S Landranger 41
» Parking at 118565.

BEINN MAOL CHALUIM (3-4 hours)
I started from the road which runs down Glen Etive at grid reference 149496. At this point there was a gap in the forest on the west side. I climbed steeply from the north end of the gap following a faint path which ran up near the trees. From the top of the forest I climbed NW to the broad south ridge of Beinn Maol Chaluim. I continued north across a slight dip to the SE top at 2,780ft, then followed an easy ridge to the summit.

Key Details
» Distance 5 miles (8km)
» Height climbed 2,700ft
» O/S Landranger 41 and 50
» Parking at 149496.

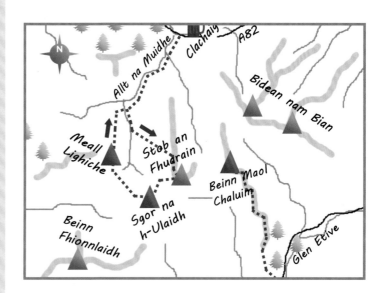

Summit ridge of Maol Chaluim (2009).

PLACES TO STAY/DRINK
We returned to the Clachaig Inn after climbing Sgor na h-Ulaidh. Later we drove to the Kings House, where we were staying, so that the drivers could have a few drinks.

APPIN

Final summit ridge of Fraochaidh (2014).

BEINN SGULAIRD *(3,074ft)*
CREACH BHEINN *(2,656ft)*
FRAOCHAIDH *(2,883ft)*

» One Munro and two Corbetts in Appin with good views over Loch Linnhe and out to sea on a clear day.

» These tend to be lonely summits lying to the south of the more fashionable Glencoe peaks.

» Fraochaidh is a substantial Corbett with dips on the ascent giving 4,000ft of climbing and making it one of the tougher Corbetts to reach in this area.

Personal View

Beinn Sgulaird and Creach Bheinn would be best climbed together giving a good ridge walk between the two mountains with fine views over Loch Linnhe and out to sea. However, I ascended them separately, both from sea level. I climbed Beinn Sgulaird when on a family holiday and found it hard work in misty and humid conditions. As usual I had not left enough time and tried to take a shortcut on the way down. Predictably this backfired and despite jogging some of the extra distance I was late back. Fourteen years later I climbed Creach Bheinn from Druimavuic House. The summit ridge on a clear evening late in March was beautiful with good views out to sea.

Fraochaidh is a mighty Corbett with three tops to traverse, all just over 2,000ft, when ascending the mountain from Ballachulish. It is one of the tougher Corbetts south of the Great Glen but on a fine day well worth the walk. Rusty fence posts can be followed from the first top. I reached the summit of Fraochaidh in hazy sunshine on a late March day. Unfortunately the day was marred by falling on wet and slippery ground on the way down and cracking a couple of ribs. Two strong coffees and some cake at Glencoe was needed to relieve the pain!

My Routes

BEINN SGULAIRD (4-5 hours)

I climbed Beinn Sgulaird in 2001 starting at the Invercreran Hotel. From the hotel I took a direct route to the ridge just south of the summit.

CREACH BHEINN (4-5 hours)

To climb Creach Bheinn I started from the A828 just north of Druimavuic House. A gate leads to a track (almost a road) through the trees. 300m past the upper end of the forest I crossed to the south side of the stream and climbed steeply south to the ridge near Meall Garbh (734m). From there it was an easy walk to the summit.

The map shows the route combining Beinn Sgulaird and Creach Bheinn.

FRAOCHAIDH (6-7 hours)

I left the A82 at Ballachulish and drove south on a minor road along the west side of the River Laroch, parking at the end of the road. I followed a track for 3.5km, then descended to the River Laroch and crossed it. There was a cairn which signified where to leave the track which was easy to miss.

I climbed SSW on a path until just before a stile into the forest. From here I ascended SW to the first top at 626m. Rusty fence posts now guided the way SSW over a top at 718m, then SW to a top at 671m. Finally I climbed steeply WNW beside an old fence to the summit of Fraochaidh. It was a long return journey to Ballachulish.

Key Details (Fraochaidh)

» Distance 11 miles (18km)
» Height climbed 3,400ft
» O/S Landranger 41
» Parking at 080576.

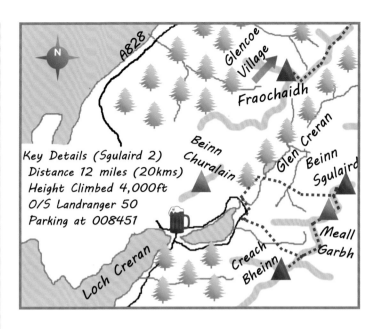

Key Details (Sgulaird 2)
Distance 12 miles (20kms)
Height Climbed 4,000ft
O/S Landranger 50
Parking at 008451

Start point for Sgulaird and Creach Bheinn, Druimavuic House across Loch Creran.

BEINN A' BHEITHIR

SGORR DHEARG *(3,361ft)*
SGORR DHONUILL *(3,284ft)*

» This is an enjoyable circuit over two Munros with superb views.

» Beinn a' Bheithir dominates the view south from Onich on the north side of Loch Leven.

» The mountains are close to Ballachulish so there is no need to drive far to the pub or accommodation.

Beinn a' Bheithir from Onich across Loch Leven.

My Route (6-7 hours)

We used two cars for this climb leaving one at South Ballachulish (reference 047590) then driving to Ballachulish village (reference 076583). However, two cars are not necessary as both Munros can be climbed from South Ballachulish.

From Ballachulish village we climbed SW to the south ridge of Sgorr Bhan. Just over 3,000ft of climbing took us to the summit of Sgorr Bhan, then we followed a good ridge to the summit of Sgorr Dhearg.

We descended to the col at 2,500ft between the two Munros, then climbed to Sgorr Dhonuill, the second Munro. After returning to the col it was possible to descend directly to South Ballachulish.

Personal View

Sgorr Dhearg and Sgorr Dhonuill are prominent Munros that are seen clearly from Ballachulish Bridge when crossing it on the drive south from Fort William. As we struggled to remember or even pronounce the names of the Munros they were always known as 'the sea'.

It was during the summer of 1997 that Alistair, Jonathan, JP and I climbed the Munros of Beinn a' Bheithir. We started with a coffee at the Ballachulish Hotel before setting off up Sgorr Dhearg. Soon we were sweating in the muggy air on a path up the south ridge of Sgorr Bhan. We climbed over Sgorr Bhan, a Munro Top, then a final 400ft of climbing took us to Sgorr Dhearg. A descent of 800ft and reascent led to Sgorr Dhonuill, the ridge steep and at times exposed. The mist and sunshine fought for supremacy as we ate our Mars bars on the summit. We returned to the col and jogged down in time to see the Lions lose to South Africa.

POINTS OF INTEREST

Ballachulish Bridge was opened in 1975 and this meant the end of the ferry which had run across Loch Leven from Ballachulish since 1733.

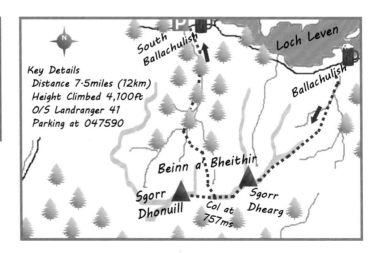

Key Details
Distance 7·5miles (12km)
Height Climbed 4,100ft
O/S Landranger 41
Parking at 047590

BIDEAN NAM BIAN

BIDEAN NAM BIAN *(3,773ft)*

» Stob Coire Sgreamhach (3,517ft) is also a Munro having been promoted in 1997. It is advisable to include this summit when climbing Bidean.

» Bidean nam Bian is one of the best known and popular mountains in Scotland.

My Route (for both Munros, 4-5 hours)

Douglas, my uncle, seemed unconcerned by the appalling weather as he set a fast pace up Bidean nam Bian in 1981. Julian and I trudged on behind in the rain and thick mist. We had started from the car park just west of Allt-na-reigh on the A82 road. A path went over the bridge and into the valley between Beinn Fhada and Gearr Aonach. We continued past a flat area known as the Lost Valley used by the Macdonalds to hide stolen cattle.

We reached the bealach between Stob Coire Sgreamhach and Bidean nam Bian, and turned right to ascend Bidean nam Bian. However, Stob Coire Sgreamhach could easily have been added from the bealach. We descended over Stob Coire nam Beith and down to Achnambeithach near the Clachaig Inn. This is a good route if you have transport at the Clachaig.

I returned many years later to climb Stob Coire Sgreamhach.

PLACES TO STAY/DRINK

It is best to stay in Glencoe after a walk over Bidean. The Clachaig Inn is conveniently placed and popular with walkers and climbers.

Personal View (JP)

Bidean, or the Auld Biddy as I like to call it, is perhaps my favourite mountain. Covered with steeps, a multiplicity of ridges and the boulder strewn hidden valley, it is the view that captures the heart. You could be on Dorsal Arete in deep snow, glissading down Beinn Fhada, taking Gearr Aonach's 'wiggly way' but always you have Glen Coe, Glen Etive and a vast array of mountains beneath you.

I approached Sgreamhach on a winter's day via Fhada's ridge, the powder snow was deep and unbroken, light clouds playing in the sunshine and the Glen's piper playing below, wonderful stuff. Coire nan Lochan offers loads of playgrounds in winter and summer but take care in nam Beith, that's avalanche country. Whichever way you go Bidean has plenty of highways but probably you will come from the north where most of the real interest lies, and of course the Clachaig Inn which will give a fitting end to the day.

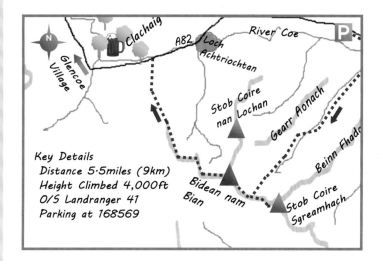

Key Details
Distance 5·5miles (9km)
Height Climbed 4,000ft
O/S Landranger 41
Parking at 168569

Bidean nam Bian from the north.

BUACHAILLE RIDGES

Buachaille Etive Mor from the Kings House.

STOB DEARG *(3,353ft)*
STOB DUBH *(3,143ft)*
STOB COIRE RAINEACH
(3,035ft)

» The Buachaille Etive Mor ridge
includes two Munros following
the addition of Stob na Broige
(3,136ft) in 1997.

» The east face of the Buachaille
Etive Mor is one of Scotland's
most photographed scenes.

» The Buachaille Etive Beag ridge
also includes two Munros, Stob
Dubh and Stob Coire Raineach.

» From the ridge of Buachaille
Etive Mor it is possible to
cross to Buachaille Etive Beag
to complete four Munros in
the day.

Personal View (JP)

I like Rannoch Moor, a rough watery landscape sheltered by high
peaks offering brilliant isolation from our urban world. Going north
there is always the anticipation of Glencoe and the sentinel is the
Buachaille. This is a hill that cries out to be climbed. The standard
route is up Coire na Tulaich (Barry's route). This is a rocky and
enclosed pull in summer and a place to be careful in deep snow,
but it leads easily and quickly to the summit.

It was March and the weather had been clear for a few days so
Curved Ridge beckoned. It was clear of snow and dry, an absolute
joy to scramble up. We were roped up, our guide making sure Sean
and I didn't fall off. The views back over Rannoch were great, and
the rock scenery superb. We hit snow for the last switch back pitch
to the top, then descended around the corrie rim.

On a previous summer jaunt I had traversed the whole ridge and
descended steeply into Lairig Gartain, whipping up Stob Dubh on
Buachaille Etive Beag from there. Gird your loins if you go that way,
it is a fair pull. I missed Stob Dubh's close neighbour Raineach
that time, so went back for another winter ascent. This time we
climbed good easy angled snow all the way from the A82, maybe
skis next time.

BUACHAILLE RIDGES continued

My Routes

BUACHAILLE ETIVE MOR
(3-4 hours for Stob Dearg only)

Alistair and I climbed Stob Dearg in beautiful snow conditions in November 1979. We started at Altnafeadh on the A82 road and followed the track across the bridge over the River Coupall. After a few hundred metres we took the right fork to the Coire na Tulaich. We continued past a few rock outcrops to a snow covered scree slope at 2,300ft, then kicked steps up the snow slope and arrived at the bealach on the main ridge. The summit was a short distance east then north east.

If climbing Stob na Broige the main ridge can be followed SW over three tops to its summit. When I climbed Stob na Broige I climbed to the ridge before Stob Coire Altruim and continued to the summit of Stob na Broige.

BUACHAILLE ETIVE BEAG
(4-5 hours for both Munros)

My cousin Julian and I started from the A82 road where there is now a sign 'Lairig Eilde to Glen Etive'. After following this path for 500m we turned uphill, traversing slightly east of south, to ascend to the col between the two Munros. We climbed SW up to a small top at 920m and walked along a ridge for 1km to Stob Dubh, then returned to the car.

I did not climb Stob Coire Raineach until 1997, but It is a short climb of 600ft from the 2,500ft col to add this second Munro.

Key Details (both Munros)

» **Distance 5.5 miles (9km)**
» **Height climbed 3,100ft**
» **O/S Landranger 41**
» **Parking at 188562.**

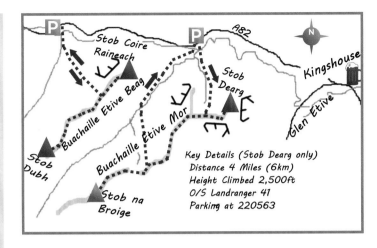

Key Details (Stob Dearg only)
Distance 4 Miles (6km)
Height Climbed 2,500ft
O/S Landranger 41
Parking at 220563

POINTS OF INTEREST

The craggy north east face of Stob Dearg, or the Buachaille as it is known, has been popular with climbers for the last hundred years. Iconic climbs include Curved Ridge and Crowberry Ridge, a severe rock climb.

Buachaille Etive Beag ridge, looking south to Stob Dubh (*Chris Wood*).

AONACH EAGACH

**SGORR NAM FIANNAIDH
(3,173ft)
BEINN A' CHRULAISTE
(2,811ft)**

» There is a second Munro on the Aonach Eagach ridge Meall Dearg (3,128ft).

» Beinn a' Chrulaiste is a short half day expedition from the Kings House.

My Routes

SGORR NAM FIANNAIDH
(6-7 hours)

In 2004 I started from a car park on the A82 road a few hundred metres west of Allt-na-reigh. A signposted path climbed steeply NE up the hillside. The path reached the SE ridge of Am Bodach and started to become rocky. The descent WNW from Am Bodach involved some scrambling. The difficulties continued all the way over Meall Dearg to the col before Stob Coire Leith.

From the col I ascended Stob Coire Leith and continued along the ridge to Sgorr nam Fiannaidh (the Top 500 Summit). I descended south to Loch Achtriochtan and walked back along the A82 to the start.

BEINN A' CHRULAISTE
(2-3 hours)

A group of us from work climbed Beinn a' Chrulaiste. We started from the car park at the Kings House. A path went north up the west side of the Allt a' Bhalaich for 1.5km, then we climbed WNW up the broad ridge. This was more rugged than we expected but the summit soon appeared. We returned by the same route as the rain started.

Key Details

» Distance 4 miles (6km)
» Height climbed 2,000ft
» O/S Landranger 41
» Parking at 259547.

The Aonach Eagach ridge in winter from Glencoe.

Personal View (Alistair)

For experienced climbers, the Aonach Eagach ridge is a classic traverse in winter. However, we were five inexperienced students from the Newcastle University Exploration Society when we traversed this ridge on a cold January weekend nearly forty years ago. We travelled overnight to Glencoe in a very old Landrover with no heating and a top speed of 40 mph. Periodically the two in the back rotated with the two in the front to avoid shivering and frostbite.

On arrival we traversed the Aonach Eagach east to west with ice axes and crampons. Starting with Am Bodach and finishing with Sgorr nam Fiannaidh was slow but dramatic on a clear winter day with snow covering the ridge. We were young and relatively fearless but the dangers were clear and I was pleased to reach the Clachaig Inn in one piece for a pint. We then set off for Ben Nevis spending a very cold night by the large Lochan halfway up the Ben, before climbing one of the north east facing gullies to reach the summit. A weekend I have not forgotten but will never repeat!

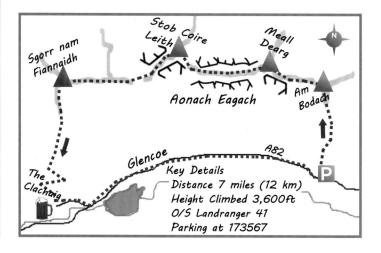

Key Details
Distance 7 miles (12 km)
Height Climbed 3,600ft
O/S Landranger 41
Parking at 173567

Climbing Ben Nevis.

SCOTLAND: CENTRAL HIGHLANDS

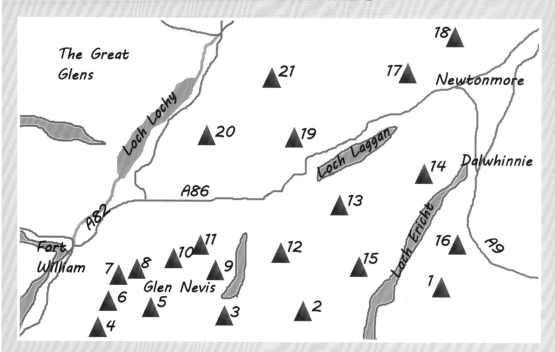

In the Central Highlands there are 52 Top 500 Summits divided into 21 walks. They include Ben Nevis, the highest mountain in Britain and Ireland at 4,411ft.

The Central Highlands cover a large area from Rannoch Moor in the south to Inverness in the north and from Ben Nevis in the west to the A9 in the east. There are 52 Top 500 Summits in this area including the highest mountain in the British Isles, Ben Nevis at 4,411ft. This is the only area outside the Cairngorms where there are any mountains over 4,000ft.

Apart from Ben Nevis there are a number of other Munro giants in the area including Ben Alder, Creag Meagaidh and Carn Mor Dearg. There are also challenging ridge walks over multiple Munros on the Grey Corries and Mamore ridges.

The majority of the mountains in the Central Highlands are over 3,000ft but there are 22 Corbetts. Many of these lie in the north of the area around the Monadhliath, Glen Roy and the Corrieyairack Pass.

The main towns in the area are Fort William and Newton-more and many of the mountains are close to one of these places. The A86 road splits this area into two mountain regions and makes driving from Fort William to Newtown-more straightforward.

WALKS 1 TO 5

	Walk	Feet	Pg.
1	Stob an Aonaich Mhoir	2,805	138
	Beinn Mholach	2,759	
	Meall na Leitreach	2,544	
2	Stob Gaibhre	3,133	139
	Carn Dearg	3,087	
	Meall na Meoig	2,848	
3	Leum Uilleim	2,972	140
	Glas Bheinn	2,597	
4	Garbh Bheinn	2,844	141
	Mam na Gualainn	2,611	
5	Binnein Mor	3,706	142
	Sgurr Eilde Mor	3,313	
	Binnein Beag	3,093	

WALKS 6 TO 21

	Walk	Feet	Pg.
6	Sgurr a' Mhaim	3,606	143
	Stob Ban	3,278	
7	Ben Nevis	4,411	144
8	Aonach Beag	4,049	146
	Carn Mor Dearg	4,002	
9	Stob Coire Easain	3,660	147
10	Stob Choire Claurigh	3,862	148
	Sgurr Choinnich Mor	3,592	
	Stob Ban	3,205	
11	Cruach Innse	2,812	150
	Sgurr Innse	2,654	
12	Chno Dearg	3,435	151
	Beinn na Lap	3,074	
13	Beinn a' Chlachair	3,566	152
	Geal Charn	3,443	
14	The Fara	2,989	153
	Creag Dhubh	2,479	
15	Ben Alder	3,765	154
	Geal Charn	3,714	
	Carn Dearg	3,391	
	Beinn Bheoil	3,343	
16	Beinn Udlamain	3,314	156
	Sgairneach Mhor	3,251	
	Geal Charn	3,008	
	Sow of Atholl	2,634	
17	Carn Dearg	3,100	157
18	Carn an Fhreiceadain	2,879	158
	Geal-charn Mor	2,703	
	Carn a' Chuilinn	2,677	
	Carn na Saobhaidhe	2,660	
19	Creag Meagaidh	3,707	160
	Beinn a' Chaorainn	3,445	
	Beinn Teallach	3,002	
20	Carn Dearg	2,736	162
	Beinn Iaruinn	2,625	
	Carn Dearg	2,680	
	Carn Dearg	2,520	
21	Gairbeinn	2,940	164
	Meall na h-Airse	2,828	

Looking west down Loch Laggan in the centre of the region from Creag Ruadh, a Graham.

LOCH GARRY TO ERICHT

STOB AN AONAICH MHOIR
(2,805ft)
BEINN MHOLACH *(2,759ft)*
MEALL NA LEITREACH
(2,544ft)

» Three Corbetts between Loch
Garry and Loch Ericht.

My Routes

STOB AN AONAICH MHOIR
(with bike 4-5 hours)

There is parking at the Bridge
of Ericht near a locked gate
and sign 'Talladh-a-Bheithe
Estate'. I cycled seven miles
north along a private road to
the high point on the road,
just over 1km from the summit. I climbed 700ft WNW to
the summit before making the
long but much easier return
journey.

Key Details

» Distance 16 miles (26km)

» Height climbed 2,100ft

» O/S Landranger 42

» Parking at 521583.

BEINN MHOLACH
(with bike 4-5 hours)

There is parking at Dalnaspidal. I cycled south down the
west side of Loch Garry. At the
south end of the loch I left the
bike and carried on by foot. I
crossed the Allt Shallainn and
climbed SW up the mountain
to its massive cairn. There was
a path but it kept disappearing. After reaching the summit
I had to take careful compass
bearings for the descent as
the terrain was confusing.

MEALL NA LEITREACH
(2-3 hours)

I parked at Dalnaspidal and
followed the track towards
Loch Garry. I turned left before
the loch to cross a bridge
to reach the hillside. It was
a short climb south to the
summit plateau. The cairn
was a further 1km in a SSW
direction.

View over Loch Ericht from Stob an Aonaich Mhoir (2014).

Personal View

On a beautiful day of unbroken sunshine in April 2014 I cycled up
the Hydro road to Stob an Aonaich Mhoir from Bridge of Ericht. I
can't remember a better day in Scotland, people were sitting outside cafes and the views were fantastic. However, the cycling soon
became hard work. There was 1,400ft of climbing to reach the high
point on the road. I was soon breathless and wondering how 'Tour
de France' riders cope with the Alps and the Pyrenees. Eventually I
reached the top of the Hydro road and saw an array of bikes; clearly
I was not alone on the mountain. From the top of the Hydro road it
was a short 700ft ascent to the summit. As I reached the summit on
this perfect April day a magnificent view unfolded over Loch Ericht.

The previous year I had cycled along Loch Garry before climbing
Beinn Mholach in horrendous weather. There was no mistaking the
summit of Beinn Mholach with its massive cairn. I was able to enjoy
five minutes of comfort sheltered beside it before a very unpleasant
walk down into the teeth of the wind and rain.

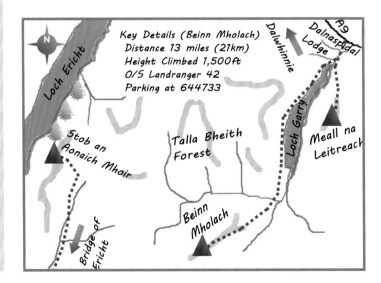

Key Details (Beinn Mholach)
Distance 13 miles (21km)
Height Climbed 1,500ft
O/S Landranger 42
Parking at 644733

RANNOCH FOREST

SGOR GAIBHRE *(3,133ft)*
CARN DEARG *(3,087ft)*
MEALL NA MEOIG *(2,848ft)*

» Two Munros, Stob Gaibhre and Carn Dearg and one Corbett, Meall na Meoig.

» They can be climbed together from just east of Rannoch Station.

My Routes

SGOR GAIBHRE AND CARN DEARG *(6-7 hours)*

We climbed these two Munros from Corrour Station walking to the east end of Loch Ossian. We continued east for a short distance on a stalkers' path until we were clear of the trees. From there we climbed ESE to the summit of Sgor Choinnich (a Munro Top) then south to Sgor Gaibhre. After descending WSW to a col at Mam Ban we climbed Carn Dearg. A direct route west took us back to Corrour station.

MEALL NA MEOIG *(4-5 hours)*

To climb Meall na Meoig I started 2km east of Rannoch Station and cycled along a private track NW then north. After 3km I reached a bridge over the Allt Eigheach and left the bike. From there I climbed up Beinn Pharlagain and on compass bearings went east and then north to Meall na Meoig.

The map opposite shows the continuation from Meall na Meoig over Sgor Gaibhre and Carn Dearg, probably the best route over these three summits.

PLACES TO STAY/DRINK

Rannoch and Corrour Station both have tea rooms. There is also accommodation but this would need to be booked.

Personal View (JP)

It was the second morning of my four day crossing from Dalwhinnie to Fort William. Two Munros were on my route, Stob Gaibhre and Carn Dearg, so an easier day beckoned. It was a sunny day with a howling southerly. The Munro Top, Sgor Choinnich, was a test with the pack. I had to crawl in places. It was calmer by the time I hit peaty Mam Ban and just easy pathless walking was left as I went over Carn Dearg to the hostel at Corrour.

Continue walking or take a train, I could do with a pint or three at Spean Bridge? Too far though, I must be going mad even to think of it. Of course I had overcooked myself and spent a sick night in the upstairs room of the tiny bothy.

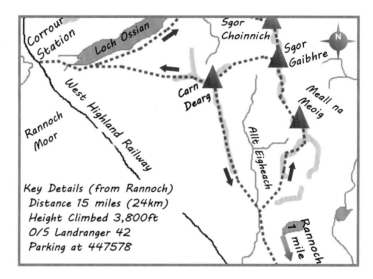

Key Details (from Rannoch)
Distance 15 miles (24km)
Height Climbed 3,800ft
O/S Landranger 42
Parking at 447578

My brothers and their dogs at Corrour Station after our ascent of the Rannoch Forest Munros (2001).

RANNOCH CORBETTS

LEUM UILLEIM *(2,972ft)*
GLAS BHEINN *(2,597ft)*

» Two Corbetts just north of Rannoch Moor between Corrour Station and Kinlochleven.

My Routes

LEUM UILLEIM *(2-3 hours)*

From Corrour Station Leum Uilleim was a straightforward climb. I walked SW for 2km to the wide rocky NE ridge of Leum Uilleim which led to the summit.

Key Details

» Distance 5 miles (8km)
» Height climbed 1,700ft
» O/S Landranger 41
» Start at Corrour, 356664.

GLAS BHEINN *(5-6 hours)*

I parked on the north side of Kinlochleven and followed signs to Loch Eilde Mor. I kept left after passing a chair, then climbed ENE to the main track to Loch Eilde Mor. Before the loch a path went right which led to the Loch Eilde Mor dam. I walked over this and continued 3km east along a stalkers' path, leaving it just before Meall na Cruaidhe to ascend NE to the summit.

Key Details

» Distance 11 miles (18km)
» Height climbed 2,500ft
» O/S Landranger 41
» Parking at 188623.

Leum Uilleim and Corrour Station (2014).

Personal View

I stepped out of the wind and rain at Rannoch Station and into the warmth of the train which would take me to Corrour Station. It was another world, people eating snacks, taking pictures or just glad to be inside as the rain swept over Rannoch Moor. Twelve minutes later I was at Corrour, the train back was in three hours, enough time to climb Leum Uilleim. In the event Leum Uilleim turned out to be an easy climb from Corrour despite a day of high winds and heavy showers.

Earlier in the year I had followed good paths from Kinlochleven nearly all the way to Glas Bheinn. Without the paths this would have been a tough Corbett. The route crossed the Loch Eilde Mor Dam built in 1916. Eventually I reached the summit slopes and was greeted by a herd of deer crossing close by.

Loch Eilde Mor Dam built in 1916.

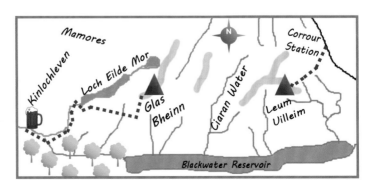

LOCH LEVEN CORBETTS

GARBH BHEINN *(2,844ft)*
MAM NA GUALAINN *(2,611ft)*

» Garbh Bheinn has unexpected character and a fine west ridge leading to the summit.

» Mam na Gualainn is an enjoyable half day walk.

» There are good views from both Corbetts over Loch Leven, the Aonach Eagach and the Mamores.

My Routes

GARBH BHEINN *(3-4 hours)*

I started from the B863 at a road bridge 200m west of the caravan site at Caolasnacon. From the east side of the bridge I followed a path beside the Allt Gleann a' Chaolais for 1km, then climbed north to the first col on the ridge. From here a path led up the ridge to the summit. If transport can be arranged the NE ridge could be followed to Kinlochleven.

Key Details

» Distance 4 miles (6km)
» Height climbed 2,800ft
» O/S Landranger 41
» Parking at 143608.

MAM NA GUALAINN
(3-4 hours)

The climb started near Callert, three miles down the B863 from North Ballachulish. There was parking near some trees, 300m past Callert House. I followed the path, which commenced from the west end of the trees, and climbed north towards the col. Before reaching the col I turned right up the hillside to a ridge which led to the trig point at the summit.

Key Details

» Distance 5 miles (8km)
» Height climbed 2,600ft
» O/S Landranger 41
» Parking at 096603.

Personal View

Garbh Bheinn is an underrated Corbett just north of the Aonach Eagach ridge. It is climbed from the road to Kinlochleven and has a fine and interesting west ridge. The summit overlooks Rannoch Moor and the Aonach Eagach ridge. I drove up from Loughborough and set out at 5 p.m. in threatening weather which improved as I climbed higher. On the way down the weather stayed cloudy but clear and I made it back to the hotel in time for dinner.

I climbed Mam na Gualainn on a cloudy morning in May 2012, the cloud eventually lifting to nearly 2,500ft. There was a good path to the col between Mam Na Gualainn and Tom Meadhoin. From there I climbed through patchy snow (it had snowed the previous night) to the west ridge of Mam Na Gualainn and a great tramp through wet snow to the summit.

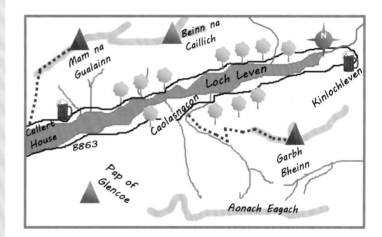

Looking down to Loch Leven from Garbh Bheinn (2011).

MAMORES EAST

BINNEIN MOR *(3,706ft)*
SGURR EILDE MOR *(3,313ft)*
BINNEIN BEAG *(3,093ft)*

» A fine walk over three classic Munros, Binnein Mor, Sgurr Eilde Mor and Binnein Beag.

» A further four Munros can be added to make this a long day. The additional Munros are Na Gruagaichean (3,465ft), An Gearanach (3,222ft), Am Bodach (3,386ft) and Stob Coire a' Chairn (3,219ft).

My Route (9-10 hours)

We parked at Kinlochleven and walked ENE along a track which joined a Landrover track 1km west of Loch Eilde Mor. From there a stalkers' track climbed NE to Coire an Lochain. From the north end of the loch we climbed 900ft up steep and bouldery quartzite to the summit of Sgurr Eilde Mor.

We returned to the north side of the loch and climbed north across the slopes of Binnein Mor to the col between Binnein Mor and Binnein Beag. A 600ft climb NE up scree and boulders took us to the summit of Binnein Beag. We returned to the col and climbed to the bottom of the ridge bounding the small NE corrie of Binnein Mor. We ascended the ridge and continued to the other four Munros descending to Kinlochleven from Am Bodach.

Personal View

This is a great traverse over at least three Munros and potentially seven Munros which can be completed in one day. I completed the walk with Alistair in 2003 when we were staying in Kinlochleven. An Gearanach is one of only five Munros that I have climbed three times.

An Gearanach and the Steall waterfall from Ben Nevis.

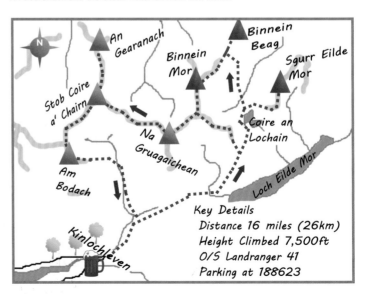

Key Details
Distance 16 miles (26km)
Height Climbed 7,500ft
O/S Landranger 41
Parking at 188623

MAMORES WEST

SGURR A' MHAIM *(3,606ft)*
STOB BAN *(3,278ft)*

» Mullach nan Coirean (3,080ft) can be added so that three Munros are completed.

» The walk up Sgurr a' Mhaim over the Devil's Ridge is a superb walk but there are some exposed sections.

My Routes

STOB BAN *(4-5 hours)*
We started 300m east of Achriabhach in Glen Nevis. A path followed the east bank of the Allt Coire a' Mhusgain to the col between Stob Ban and Sgurr an Iubhair. From there it was a 600ft climb west to the summit of Stob Ban.

SGURR A' MHAIM *(4-5 hours)*
On my ascent of Sgurr a' Mhaim I followed the same route to the col between Stob Ban and Sgurr an Iubhair. This time I turned east to climb Sgurr an Iubhair. From there I traversed the Devil's Ridge to Sgurr a' Mhaim descending NW back to Achriabhach.

I climbed Stob Ban and Sgurr a' Mhaim in 1976 when I had little knowledge of the Munros and plenty of time. In reality it would be best to combine these summits in one walk as shown on the map.

Key Details (both summits)

» Distance 7.5 miles (12km)
» Height climbed 4,400ft
» O/S Landranger 41
» Parking at 146684.

Personal View

Sgurr a' Mhaim and Stob Ban lie at the south end of Glen Nevis. They were two of my earliest Munros climbed in 1976 and Stob Ban was Alistair's first Munro. From the youth hostel we walked up Glen Nevis and met Dave Dalton, a friend who agreed to join us on Stob Ban. Dave had climbed Stob Ban many times in the previous couple of months whilst doing a geological survey of the area so route finding was not a problem! The summer of 1976 was hot and sunny in England but not in Scotland and Dave used to cycle to the pub in Fort William for some respite from the midges and rain.

I climbed Sgurr a' Mhaim a few days later traversing the Devil's Ridge before descending directly into Glen Nevis. In the afternoon Dave and I rock climbed on the Polldubh cliffs on the opposite side of Glen Nevis.

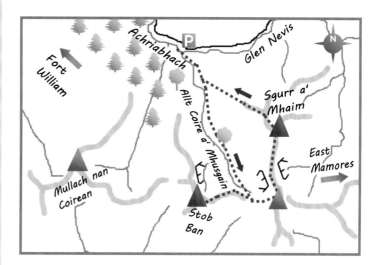

Dave's campsite in Glen Nevis (1976).

BEN NEVIS

Kiran and friend near the top of Ben Nevis, looking towards Fort William and beyond.

BEN NEVIS (4,411ft)

» Ben Nevis is the highest summit in Britain and Ireland and has magnificent cliffs and ridges.

» Rock climbers can appreciate the full splendour of Ben Nevis by climbing Tower Ridge.

» Summer weekends can see over 1,000 people climbing Ben Nevis, many on the National Three Peaks Challenge.

Personal View

Ben Nevis looks impressive and has fantastic ridges and climbing on its north and east side. It also has fine views as illustrated in the photo provided by Kiran Sondhi although 'she had lost the will to live' when this picture was taken.

My first ascent was in 1973 when on a holiday camp. A party of thirty of us were taken up via a scrambling route on the North Face. Three of the party descended but the rest of us made it to the summit up an 'unknown route'. My next two ascents (2001 and 2007) were by the Tourist Route. In 2001 we went up late in the evening as the first leg of our Three Peaks trip (Ben Nevis, Scafell Pike and Snowdon) and in 2007 I took a party from work up Ben Nevis.

Finally in 2014 we climbed Tower Ridge on a beautiful day in late May, assisted by guides as this is a serious climb requiring ropes. Then we traversed the Carn Mor Dearg Arete to the summit of Carn Mor Dearg before descending to the valley.

BEN NEVIS continued

My Routes
(Tourist Route 6-8 hours)

On my first ascent back in 1973 we followed the path next to the Allt a' Mhuilinn before finding our way up the North Face to the summit. We returned by the Tourist Route to Fort William. I am not sure of the route taken but do not recommend venturing on to the North Face without a professional guide.

On my next two ascents we started at Glen Nevis Youth Hostel and followed the Tourist Route to the summit and back. This route follows an excellent path which climbs the flanks of Meall an t-Suidhe to the broad bealach containing Lochan Meall an t-Suidhe. From there a series of zigzags ascend broadly ESE. We followed the path across a deep gully, then the path continued to zigzag up bouldery ground to the summit plateau.

On my fourth ascent we climbed Ben Nevis from the CIC Hut via Tower Ridge. This is a spectacular route but exposed with rock climbing. The climbing included a very awkward step over Tower Gap near the summit. I was glad to be with a guide and roped up. We crossed to Carn Mor Dearg via the Carn Mor Dearg Arete and descended from there.

PLACES TO STAY/DRINK

There are plenty of hotels and guest houses in Fort William. There is also a youth hostel and campsite in Glen Nevis at the start of the Tourist Route up Ben Nevis.

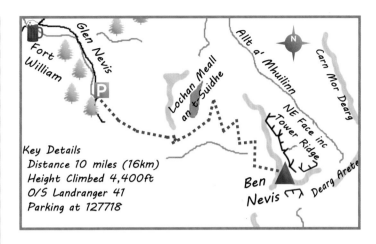

Key Details
Distance 10 miles (16km)
Height Climbed 4,400ft
O/S Landranger 41
Parking at 127718

POINTS OF INTEREST

At the summit there is the remains of an Observatory which was staffed continually between 1883 and 1904. The average temperatures during that period were just below freezing and average annual rainfall was 171 inches.

JP climbing Tower Ridge above Tower Gap (2014).

CARN MOR DEARG

AONACH BEAG *(4,049ft)*
CARN MOR DEARG *(4,002ft)*

» Aonach Mor (4,006ft) is also a Munro and should be added as part of the route.

» The northern slopes of Aonach Mor are now a ski area.

» Carn Mor Dearg is the near neighbour of Ben Nevis. These three Munros can be climbed as one walk with Ben Nevis.

View of Fort William and Loch Linnhe from the Snow Goose Restaurant on Aonach Mor.

My Route (7-8 hours)

We left the A82 between Fort William and Spean Bridge and drove to the ski centre car park. A walk south through the trees took us to the bottom of the long north ridge of Carn Mor Dearg.

We climbed south up the ridge traversing Carn Beag Dearg and Carn Dearg Meadhonach to Carn Mor Dearg. From the summit we descended east down a steep ridge for 500ft, then a further descent took us to the bealach at 2,800ft.

We climbed steeply ESE to the col between the Aonachs. A walk north took us to Aonach Mor, then we walked south over Aonach Beag. Finally we descended to Steall via Stob Coire Bhealaich and Sgurr a' Bhuic.

POINTS OF INTEREST

Carn Mor Dearg can be linked to Ben Nevis. The best route is to climb Carn Mor Dearg then cross to Ben Nevis via the Carn Mor Dearg Arete; an excellent ridge walk.

Personal View (Alistair)

These three 4,000ft Munros make a fine walk from the Nevis car park so I headed off early on a quiet September morning, the forecast promising and my feet dry. I followed mountain bike tracks half the way to the Snow Goose restaurant then saw a sign for walkers directly under the Gondola pylons. It was not an inspiring path, in fact it kept giving up the ghost so I went back to the yellow cycle route. Above the restaurant the mountain was in cloud but a snow fence guided me to the summit plateau of Aonach Mor.

A good path took me on to Aonach Beag; no view just occasional glimpses of snow on the east facing gullies. From the col between Mor and Beag I descended down and back up to Carn Mor Dearg, a mighty mountain but still no view. Then I reversed the route to return over Aonach Mor, why, because I thought returning on the ski lift seemed attractive but then my brothers would never have let me get away with it! As it happened the mist cleared and I plodded down with great views and not a soul in sight.

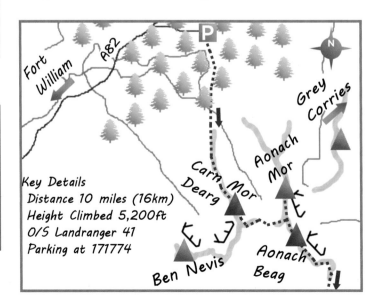

Key Details
Distance 10 miles (16km)
Height Climbed 5,200ft
O/S Landranger 41
Parking at 171774

THE EASAINS

STOB COIRE EASAIN
(3,660ft)

» The second Munro, Stob Coire a' Mheadhoin (3,626ft) will be added to the walk but the drop is less than 500ft so it does not qualify as a Top 500 Summit.

» The Easains can be climbed using the West Highland line starting at Corrour Halt and finishing at Tulloch.

My Route (5-6 hours)

I left the A86 five miles east of Roy Bridge and drove almost to Fersit near Loch Treig. I walked south along the west bank of the River Treig to the north end of Loch Treig. A climb west avoiding the crags took me to the NNE ridge of Mheadhoin which I followed to the summit.

From Mheadhoin I descended SW to the col at 3,150ft and then climbed a rocky ridge to the summit of Stob Coire Easain. There seemed little alternative but to return by the same route.

Key Details

» **Distance 9 miles (14km)**
» **Height climbed 3,800ft**
» **O/S Landranger 41**
» **Parking at 349782.**

POINTS OF INTEREST

The Easians stand over Loch Treig which means Loch of Death. Loch Treig was dammed in 1929, submerging two communities at its southern end.

Personal View (Jonathan)

These two graceful peaks stand isolated between the Grey Corries massif and the deep valley holding Loch Treig. Generally they give a straightforward walk with the satisfaction of two Munros ticked. I climbed them with Alistair and our two dogs, Bracken and Corrie.

It was Easter Sunday with substantial snow on the mountains and we came across an unusual problem. Both dogs started to 'ball up' with snow and became increasingly immobile. The snow stuck to the longer hair on their legs and stomach and literally stopped their forward movement. We ended up knocking great chunks of snow off them and carrying them for part of the way. Thus we had a challenging day and took longer than the suggested route time.

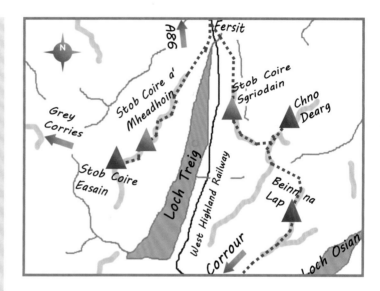

Stob Coire a' Mheadhoin *(Heather Thomas-Smith)*.

GREY CORRIES

The Grey Corries from the Commando Memorial near Spean Bridge.

STOB CHOIRE CLAURIGH
(3,862ft)
SGURR CHOINNICH MOR
(3,592ft)
STOB BAN *(3,205ft)*

» The Grey Corries are very distinctive mountains east of Ben Nevis and Aonach Beag and Mor.

» They could be combined with those mountains in a fine but long one day crossing from Fort William to the east end of the Grey Corries.

» Our walk took in a fourth Munro, Stob Coire an Laoigh (3,662ft) and was a long day.

Personal View (JP)

The Grey Corries lie to the east of Ben Nevis and present an awkward challenge as they are set well back from the road. In addition they run parallel to the road and offer no easy circuit meaning that there is a long walk back to the car. However, I was avoiding all these problems by crossing Scotland from Dalwhinnie to Fort William over the mountains.

After my dodgy night at the hostel at Corrour (see Rannoch Forest) I traversed the Easains. Then I reversed onto Stob Ban and was crouched between two rocks when an eagle flew by, no more than twenty yards away, fantastic. A steep descent to the col from Stob Ban followed then up to Claurigh. There were old snows along the stony and aptly named Grey Corries, a great high level route. Tiring now I camped on Aonach Beag's eastern shoulder overlooking the Mamores. The following day I took in the Aonachs and headed over to the Ben, it had been a grand crossing.

I was to climb Stob Ban and the Grey Corries again, with the three brothers in 1999, but it was a long way from the road. Much better to climb these mountains when crossing Scotland, maybe on a Scottish coast to coast walk.

My Route (8-10 hours)

There was parking 2km south of Corriechoille Farm at a junction of the private roads. We walked SE along the track down the Lairig Leacach for nearly 8km to a bothy, passing Cruach Innse on the left and the Grey Corries on the right.

Soon after passing the bothy the track forked. We took the right fork, walked 100m, then climbed SW up the hillside. At 2,000ft the hillside turned into a ridge. We continued up the ridge to the summit of Stob Ban. From Stob Ban we descended north to a bealach at 2,600ft, then climbed north up a steep ridge to Stob Choire Claurigh, our second Munro of the day.

We were now on the main ridge of the Grey Corries and walked WSW over three tops to our third Munro, Stob Coire an Laoigh. From here the ridge went WNW over Stob Coire Easain, a Munro Top, before dropping SSW to a col. An ascent SW led to our fourth and final Munro, Sgurr Choinnich Mor. We returned over Stob Coire Easain and down its north ridge to the car.

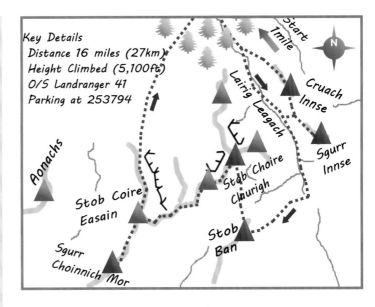

Key Details
Distance 16 miles (27km)
Height Climbed (5,100ft)
O/S Landranger 41
Parking at 253794

Traversing the Grey Corries (*Heather Thomas-Smith*).

POINTS OF INTEREST

The Grey Corries derive their name from the pale grey quartzite screes on their higher slopes. They can be combined with Ben Nevis, Carn Dearg and the Aonachs in a long day walk.

INNSE CORBETTS

CRUACH INNSE *(2,812ft)*
SGURR INNSE *(2,654ft)*

» Cruach Innse and Sgurr Innse are situated east of the Grey Corries and Ben Nevis.

» They are straightforward Corbetts close together.

» These Corbetts are surrounded by Munros.

My Route (4-5 hours)

From Spean Bridge I drove along the road on the south side of the River Spean to Corriechoille. 3km down a private track there was parking near a dismantled tramway. I continued on foot through the forest crossing the Allt Leachdach at a bridge. Then I climbed up the hillside to the NW ridge of Cruach Innse, and followed the ridge to the summit.

I descended SE then south through rocky terrain to the broad col at 1,900ft. After crossing the col I climbed SE to the steep upper rocks of Sgurr Innse. A narrow path traversed left across scree and boulders and then to the summit. It was a straightforward return to the 1,900ft col and then west to the Lairig Leacach.

For reference, see the Grey Corries map on page 149.

Key Details

» Distance 7.5 miles (12km)
» Height climbed 3,000ft
» O/S Landranger 41
» Parking at 256788.

Cruach Innse from near the bridge over the Allt Leachach.

Personal View (Jonathan)

I volunteered for a walk over the Innses recently as Barry had no pictures of them. It was an enjoyable day with some great views over the Easains and a closeup of the eastern flank of the Grey Corries. This reminded me of my tricky descent from the Grey Corries a few years ago in the snow after climbing an outlying Munro Top. Back to the present as I aimed for the col between the two Corbetts and tackled lower Sgurr Innse first. Then I headed south towards Cruach Innse and messed around taking some photographs.

Unfortunately the light was flat so it was difficult to capture the quiet beauty of these Corbetts. My efforts to photograph some lovely pink heather were rejected by the Editor. Still I passed the Wee Minister twice (see below). This is supposed to bring good fortune to all those who pass.

CORROUR TO TULLOCH

CHNO DEARG *(3,435ft)*
BEINN NA LAP *(3,074ft)*

» This walk takes in three Munros between Corrour and Tulloch railway stations.

» Stob Coire Sgriodain (3,213ft) is the third Munro.

My Route (6-8 hours)

From Corrour Station we followed the track east towards Loch Ossian, then took a left fork to the north side of the loch. We climbed north to 2,300ft, then ENE up a broad ridge to the summit. We continued NNE for 1.5km, then descended NW to the Allt Feith Thuill. From here an ascent north took us to Meall Garbh (a Munro Top). After descending 300ft we climbed NE to Chno Dearg.

To climb Stob Coire Sgriodain we went back to the col between Chno Dearg and Meall Garbh, then headed west followed by WNW along a broad ridge to point 956m. We continued NW then finally ascended north to the summit of Stob Coire Sgriodain. Careful route finding was required in the mist. From the summit we descended north to Fersit.

For reference, see the Easians map on page 147.

Key Details

» Distance 12 miles (20km)
» Height climbed 4,300ft
» O/S Landranger 41
» Start at Corrour 356664.

Personal View

At just before 1 p.m. Jonathan and I got off the British Rail 'Sprinter' at Corrour. It was damp and overcast with the cloud just below 3,000ft. With the benefit of the high start we were soon on the summit plateau of Beinn na Lap. There followed a tough crossing to Chno Dearg as we had to descend to the Glen at 1,650ft. From the top of Chno Dearg careful route finding was required in the mist to find the final Munro, Stob Coire Sgriodain. At last the mist cleared and we were able to jog parts of the way down to Fersit.

> ### POINTS OF INTEREST
> Corrour Station was opened in 1894 when guests of the Corrour Sporting Estate were taken from the Station to Loch Ossian by horse-drawn carriage and steamer. Corrour is the highest Station in Britain at 1,339ft.

Looking down Loch Treig from Stob Coire Sgriodain *(Heather Thomas-Smith)*.

LOCH LAGGAN MUNROS

BEINN A' CHLACHAIR
(3,566ft)
GEAL CHARN *(3,443ft)*

» A long walk over three Munros
south of Loch Laggan.

» Creag Pitridh (3,032ft) is the
third Munro.

My Route (7-8 hours)

There is parking 1km SW of
Moy Lodge just past the end
of Loch Laggan. We walked
up the rough road on the east
side of the Abhainn Ghuilbinn
for 1km. We turned left and
walked east for 500m, then
turned right along a track which
led to the SW end of Lochan na
h-Earba. After leaving the track
we followed a stalkers' path
SE for 1.5km, then climbed
south to the NE ridge of Beinn
a' Chlachair. We followed the
wide ridge to the summit.

The descent went NE down the
ridge continuing until the ridge
reached a large crag. Here we
turned north and descended
to the stalkers' path. A right
fork led to the col between
Geal Charn and Creag Pitridh.
We climbed Geal Charn first
then returned to the col for the
short climb up Creag Pitridh.

POINTS OF INTEREST
Loch Laggan is featured as
the centrepiece for *Monarch
of the Glen* and more
recently in *Harry Potter*.

PLACES TO STAY/DRINK
We stayed at a hotel near
Laggan renamed the
'Monarch Hotel and Church
Ruin'. There are other hotels
and guest houses around
Laggan.

Loch Laggan Munros from the west, far left is Binnein Shuas, a high Graham.

Personal View (Alistair)

These three Munros lie south of Loch Laggan next to *Monarch of
the Glen* country. They tend to be unfashionable and left to 'Munro
Baggers' but they make a good day walk from near Moy Lodge. We
had climbed the 'Meggy' three the previous day, now it was the turn
of these three.

It was a crisp October morning with frost still on the ground as we
set off along the rough road from the A86, the going was quick and
the views ahead reminded me of the Monadh Liath. It was a long
trek to Chlachair, the first of the trio, with the views to the south and
the Ben Alder six disappearing as we climbed to the misty summit.
From there we bashed on to Geal Charn and then to Pitridh, one
of the easiest Munros I have climbed. It was dark by the time we
reached the cars and midnight before I reached the lights of North
Yorkshire.

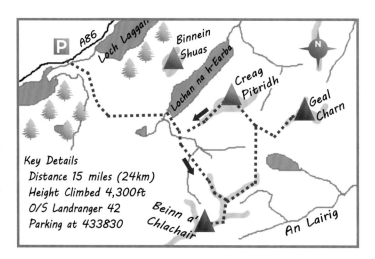

Key Details
Distance 15 miles (24km)
Height Climbed 4,300ft
O/S Landranger 42
Parking at 433830

AROUND DALWHINNIE

THE FARA *(2,989ft)*
CREAG DHUBH *(2,479ft)*

» The Fara is a high Corbett overlooking Dalwhinnie.

» Creag Dhubh is a high Graham near Newtonmore.

My Routes

THE FARA *(3-4 hours)*

From the level crossing near Dalwhinnie Railway Station I followed the private track along the west side of Loch Ericht for 2km. Soon after passing An Tochailt Lodge there was a gap in the trees on the right. I climbed through the gap NW up the hillside. At the top of the forest I continued NW following a broken fence to the summit.

CREAG DHUBH *(2-3 hours)*

I started from a small car park just off the A86 at the north end of Lochan Uvie. I made a rising traverse NE below the cliffs to a plantation and climbed steeply up the side of this. At the top I went left to reach the SW ridge of Creag Dhubh. A path climbed up the ridge to the summit.

For reference, see the Monadh Liath map on page 157.

Key Details

» Distance 5.5 miles (9km) (Fara) and 3 miles (5km) (Creag Dhubh)

» Height climbed 1,800ft (Fara) and 1,600ft (Creag Dhubh)

» O/S Landranger 42 and 35

» Parking at 634850 (Fara) and 673958 (Creag Dhubh).

Personal View

The Fara is an impressive summit visible from the A9 between Dalwhinnie and Newtonmore. It is easily reached from Dalwhinnie from where there is a high start at around 1,200ft. I was staying in Newtonmore when I climbed The Fara in November 2004. It was one of those rare days when it was possible to climb through the clouds and see the summits above a sea of white cloud. My notes record a good day for seeing wildlife including deer, hares, ptarmigan and grouse.

Creag Dhubh is one of the highest Grahams and lies near Newtonmore. It makes an excellent half day walk and it was good timing to climb it on a rare day of sunshine in late October 2012. It was an enjoyable walk after a steep ascent from the road. This had me gasping for breath before I was even a third of the way up. The higher parts of the mountain gave a good ridge walk with views over the Monadh Liath and the Cairngorms.

POINTS OF INTEREST

Cluny's Cave, one of Bonnie Prince Charlie's hideouts after Culloden, is located on the crags of Creag Dhubh, but is very difficult to find. Cluny MacPherson lived in the cave for nine years after Culloden.

The summit of Creag Dhubh (2012).

BEN ALDER

Ben Alder and Beinn Bheoil from across Loch Ericht.

BEN ALDER *(3,765ft)*
GEAL CHARN *(3,714ft)*
CARN DEARG *(3,391ft)*
BEINN BHEOIL *(3,343ft)*

» Normally this is a two day walk over six Munros in the Ben Alder Forest, the other two Munros are Aonach Beag (3,662ft) and Beinn Eibhinn (3,616ft). A bike is useful to avoid a long walk in and out.

» Ben Alder is one of the great remote mountains of Scotland with a vast high plateau.

Personal View (JP)

This was the first day of my four day walk from Dalwhinnie to Fort William. The second day is described under Rannoch Forest and the third and fourth days are covered under the Grey Corries. Starting at Dalwhinnie I set off in the gloaming along Loch Ericht to the Culra Bothy, (memo to self: take a bike next time). From Culra Bothy I left the pack and shot off directly up Carn Dearg. Picked up the pack and crossed the moors to Beinn Bheoil. Ben Alder looked great, huge areas of snow gleaming in the sunshine.

Over Sron, down to the bealach and stomped up the broad ridge of Ben Alder. Hares and ptarmigan abounded as I headed over the plateau. A few standing glissades later I was at the Bealach Dubh about to attack Geal Charn. Eerie, lonely spot, it felt like a lot of history has passed through there.

Zipping up the grassy slopes I finally crested some old snow mounds and topped out. High cloud had arrived but still great wild views on all sides, super stuff. By the time I came off Eibhinn via grassy Craoibhe it was a little dreich so I camped by Uisge Labhair. A wet night passed happily in the peapod.

My Route (2 days)

Alistair and I started from the railway station at Dalwhinnie (I had taken the train from Doncaster). We cycled down Loch Ericht, turning west at Ben Alder Lodge, and left the bikes at a shed 500m before reaching Loch Pattack.

After 3.5km the path crossed the river at a bridge and continued SW past Culra Lodge. Finally we left the path to climb the 'Lancet Edge' to Sgor Iutharn. We then walked west contouring just to the south of Geal Charn to the col between Geal Charn and Aonach Beag. After climbing Aonach Beag we went out and back to Beinn Eibhinn.

A long walk took us back over Geal Charn. We descended ENE on a compass bearing off Geal Charn, continued to Carn Dearg, then descended to Culra Bothy.

The following day we crossed the river and followed a path SW then south to a stream. We crossed it and climbed the ridge to the Ben Alder plateau. After visiting the trig point we continued round the rim for 1.5km and descended to the Bealach Breabag. We climbed NE to a top, Sron Coire na h-Iolaire, then continued NNE over Beinn Bheoil. From there it was a long walk back to the bikes at Loch Pattack and a rapid cycle to Dalwhinnie to catch the train home.

PLACES TO STAY/DRINK

There are two bothies near Ben Alder, Culra Bothy to the north and Ben Alder Cottage to the south. This is a remote area with no roads and the nearest place for food and drink is Dalwhinnie.

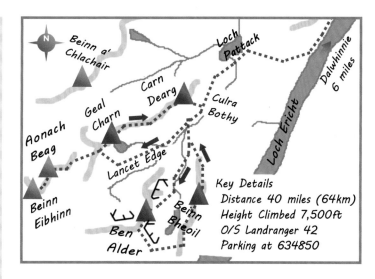

Key Details
Distance 40 miles (64km)
Height Climbed 7,500ft
O/S Landranger 42
Parking at 634850

Aonach Beag and Ben Alder ranges from Loch Ossian *(Heather Thomas-Smith)*.

WEST DRUMOCHTER

BEINN UDLAMAIN *(3,314ft)*
SGAIRNEACH MHOR
(3,251ft)
GEAL CHARN *(3,008ft)*
SOW OF ATHOLL *(2,634ft)*

» The route traverses a fourth Munro, A' Mharconaich (3,200ft).

» This walk gives a rich haul of summits west of Drumochter Pass, four Munros and one Corbett.

Drumochter Pass at just over 1,500ft in winter.

My Routes

MUNROS EXCLUDING SOW OF ATHOLL (6-7 hours)

I left the A9 near the Coire Dhomhain and crossed the railway line to join the track on the north side of the Allt Coire Dhomhain. After 1km I crossed the stream and climbed to the col between the Sow of Atholl and pt 758m.

Omitting the Sow of Atholl I climbed WSW up Sgairneach Mhor. From the summit I walked SW for 500m before going due west to the col at the top of Coire Dhomhain. I continued west to the south ridge of Udlamain and then north to its summit up a broken line of fence posts. From the summit I followed the fence NE along a good path which took me to A' Mharconaich.

From A' Mharconaich I retraced my steps for 500m, then descended NW to a col at 2,400ft. I climbed north for 1.5km to the summit of Geal Charn. A broad ridge descended NE. I turned ESE near the foot of the ridge to return to the road.

SOW OF ATHOLL (2-2.5 hours)

This was a straightforward climb from Dalnaspidal in 2005. I walked SW down the path towards Loch Garry for nearly 1km, then climbed the SE ridge of the Sow of Atholl.

Personal View

This is a straightforward round over four Munros starting from near the summit of Drumochter Pass. It is worth adding the Sow of Atholl as the first summit before the four Munros although I missed it out and had to return later. I climbed the four Munros in late October 1994 leaving Sedgefield early at 4.45 a.m. and arriving at Drumochter Pass soon after 9 a.m.

There was a light dusting of snow and the ptarmigan were already in winter plumage. I found that the path from Udlamain to A' Mharconaich was 'motorway class' with even a fence for guidance. The final Munro, Geal Charn, took longer than expected as the rain drove in from the west over Ben Alder but I was down in time for afternoon tea at the Atholl Arms.

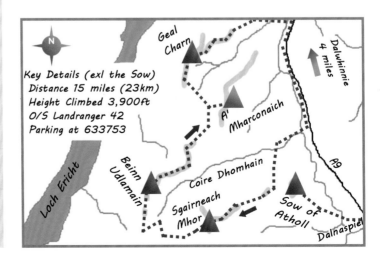

Key Details (exl the Sow)
Distance 15 miles (23km)
Height Climbed 3,900ft
O/S Landranger 42
Parking at 633753

MONADHLIATH MUNROS

CARN DEARG (3,100ft)

» There are three other Munros in the Monadhliath, A' Chailleach (3,051ft), Carn Sgulain (3,018ft) and Geal Charn (3,038ft).

» This is a high moorland plateau with Carn Dearg appearing to be the best summit.

My Route (6-8 hours)

It was only a short drive from Newtonmore up Glen Banchor. I parked where the public road ends at the Allt a' Chaorainn. From here I walked north on a track on the east side of the Allt a' Chaorainn. After 2km I climbed NW up the hillside turning north to the summit of A' Chailleach. I descended north, now walking through deep snow, to the Allt Cuil na Caillich then climbed Carn Sgulain.

I followed fence posts west then SW over Meall a' Bhothain, Carn Ballach and Carn Ban, then finally went SSE to Carn Dearg.

I returned north from Carn Dearg for 500m, then descended NE to the top of Gleann Ballach avoiding the cliffs. From there I descended SE crossing to the Allt Fionndrigh so that I could follow a good track back to the car.

POINTS OF INTEREST

Munro's original tables listed six Munros in the Monadh Liath and five on the walk described. Carn Ban and Carn Ballach were relegated to Tops when the 1980 tables were produced.

Personal View

It was a beautiful March morning in 1988 when I set off to climb the three Munros which comprise the high plateau of the Monadh Liath. Three skiers were brewing up in the tiny stalkers' bothy on A' Chailleach and they soon caught me on the snow covered tops as conditions were perfect for cross country skiing above 2,000ft. Soon after the bothy I was sinking into snow up to my knees and it was a battle to reach the summit of A' Chailleach, white ptarmigan laughing at me on the final summit slopes.

The battle with the deep snow continued up Carn Sgulain, less than 500ft of ascent but it seemed to take an eternity. However, just as I was about to give up and return to the car, the snow became more compact and started holding my weight so I made fast progress across the plateau to Carn Dearg. I took care to avoid the massive cornices on Carn Dearg's east facing corrie, then headed down sinking into waist deep snow before reaching the grassy lower slopes.

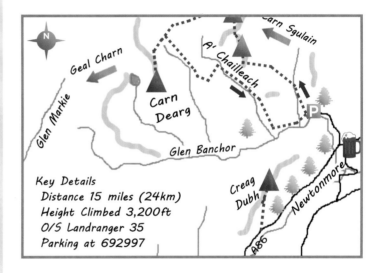

Key Details
Distance 15 miles (24km)
Height Climbed 3,200ft
O/S Landranger 35
Parking at 692997

Alistair's dog Bronte looking windswept at the top of Carn Dearg.

157

NORTH MONADHLIATH

Highland Main Line and A9 crossing the River Findhorn east of Tomatin (2014).

CARN AN FHREICEADAIN
(2,879ft)
GEAL-CHARN MOR *(2,703ft)*
CARN A' CHUILINN *(2,677ft)*
CARN NA SAOBHAIDHE
(2,660ft)

» Four Corbetts lying in a vast expanse of high moorland towards the north of the Monadh Liath.

» The four Corbetts are too far apart to allow them to be combined easily.

» Carn na Saobhaidhe is the toughest of the four Corbetts to reach and a bike is useful.

» The route up Carn an Fhreiceadain passes Kingussie Golf Course. On a sunny day this is one of the most attractive short golf courses in the world.

Personal View

These four Corbetts lie west of the A9 between Newtonmore and Inverness. Carn an Fhreiceadain and Geal-charn Mor are not far from the A9 and can be combined as two half day walks. There are good tracks and a short drive between them. I climbed them on dull days with the cloud at 2,500ft so neither walk was particularly memorable.

Carn na Saobhaidhe is a strange Corbett which took me down Strathdearn, a valley I had never previously visited. The river Findhorn flows down the valley which is at a constant height of 1,300ft, one of the highest in Britain. It is a good place to see Golden Eagles and other birds. I cycled down the valley passing well maintained estate buildings. After abandoning the bike near a locked bothy it was still a long walk to the summit. There was a feeling of remoteness and desolation as I neared the summit broken only by a few deer; then I saw a wind farm lying a few miles to the north!

Carn a' Chuilinn is an isolated summit near Fort Augustus. On a quiet May evening I found that an estate track followed by a stalkers' path gave a straightforward ascent to an attractive summit. I climbed the mountain from the north side and found the sheep and the birds aggressive, perhaps because it was the lambing and nesting season.

My Routes

CARN AN FHREICEADAIN
(4-5 hours)

There is parking near the Kingussie Golf Club. I walked past the clubhouse and crossed the stream to the road on the east side. At Pitmain Lodge I took the track to the right. I climbed north then NW to Beinn Bhreac, then west to the summit of Carn an Fhreiceadain. I walked SW from the summit past a large cairn. A track followed the Allt Mor back to Pitmain Lodge.

GEAL-CHARN MOR (3-4 hours)

I started from Lynwilg just off the A9 and followed the track up the north side of the Allt na Criche. When the track reached the bealach between Geal-charn Mor and Geal-charn Beag there was a memorial. From there I climbed SW for 1km to the summit.

CARN A' CHUILINN (4-5 hours)

I parked near a cattle grid (ref 408087, O/S Landranger 34) where there is a small gate on the SE side of the road. An ascent south through a grassy field led to the main track as it came out of a wood. I followed the track for 3km. Just before it crossed a bridge I took a stalkers' path which continued south beside a stream, eventually climbing to the summit.

CARN NA SAOBHAIDHE
(with bike 5-6 hours)

From Coignafearn Old Lodge where there is parking (ref 710179, O/S Landranger 35) I cycled 8km to Dalbeg where I left the bike. From Dalbeg I walked west up a track that followed the Allt Creagach. After 2km I took a left fork over a bridge on a good path that petered out after 1.5km. Finally I climbed NW to the summit.

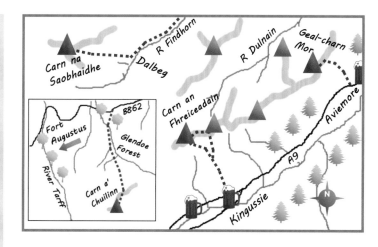

Early evening in May near the summit of Carn a' Chuilinn (2014).

'MEGGY'

Coire Ardair, Creag Meagaidh *(Chris Wood)*.

CREAG MEAGAIDH *(3,707ft)*
BEINN A' CHAORAINN
(3,445ft)
BEINN TEALLACH *(3,002ft)*

» Two additional Munros can be added, Carn Liath (3,301ft) and Stob Poite Coire Ardair (3,458ft).

» If climbing all five Munros in one walk two cars would be useful as the walk runs parallel to the A86 between Newtonmore and Spean Bridge.

» Coire Ardair beneath Creag Meagaidh has spectacular cliffs which provide many good winter climbing routes.

Personal View (Alistair)

Creag Meagaidh is the king of the mountains between the A86 and Inverness and it is possible to climb all five of the Munros in the group in one day. The route starts at Aberarder and finishes at Roughburn so it is best to have transport at both the start and the finish. However, Barry and I were completing the five Munros in two walks.

It was October, a dusting of snow covered the high tops and the nights were starting to draw in. From the Creag Meagaidh Trust car park we slogged up Carn Liath and were glad of the relatively high start. There followed a long walk, not unlike the crossing of the Monadhliath nearby, to Stob Poite Coire Ardair. The views around the Lochan at the head of historic Coire Ardair were dramatic as snow speckled the cliffs making the area look cold and forbidding.

We descended to The Window and up to the plateau crossing to 'Meggy's' cairn which was on the west side. From the summit the ridge ran south of east leading back to the car park after a long day. A long evening in the hotel followed with a musician playing Scottish songs well into the night. Three Munros completed today and three more south of Loch Laggan beckoning tomorrow.

'MEGGY' continued

My Routes

CREAG MEAGAIDH (6-7 hours)

Alistair and I parked at Aberarder and walked up the private road past the farm. We climbed north towards Na Cnapanan and continued to Carn Liath. We walked west and WSW for nearly three miles along a broad ridge to Stob Poite Coire Ardair. After continuing for 500m we descended south to The Window. Finally we climbed steeply south to the top of the plateau and walked SW and west to the summit of Creag Meagaidh.

Key Details

» **Distance 15 miles (24km)**

» **Height climbed 4,400ft**

» **O/S Landranger 34**

» **Parking at 483874.**

BEINN A' CHAORAINN (5-6 hours)

In 1986 Donald and I started from Roughburn and climbed Beinn a' Chaorainn first. We followed the forestry road for 750m, then climbed north passing Meall Clachaig, turning NE to reach the south summit. From there it was an easy walk to the Munro summit. We continued to the north top and descended NNW for 1km, then west down to the col at 2,000ft. We climbed directly west to the NE ridge of Beinn Teallach, then followed the ridge SW to the summit.

Key Details

» **Distance 11 miles (18km)**

» **Height climbed 3,800ft**

» **O/S Landranger 34**

» **Start at 377813.**

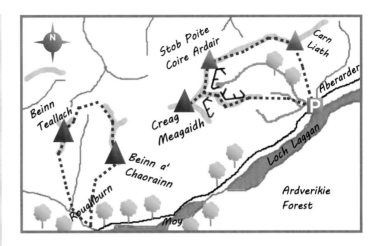

POINTS OF INTEREST

Creag Meagaidh is designated as both a Special Protection Area and a National Nature Reserve. There is native woodland of birch, alder, willow, rowan and oak and the area is an important breeding ground for many birds, in particular the dotterel.

Donald studies the map on the summit of Beinn a' Chaorainn (1986).

GLEN ROY

Looking north to the head of Glen Roy (2012).

CARN DEARG *(2,736ft)*
BEINN IARUINN *(2,625ft)*
CARN DEARG *(2,680ft)*
CARN DEARG *(2,520ft)*

» Four Corbetts, three with the same name, on either side and at the head of Glen Roy.

» All four Corbetts could be climbed in one long day or split into two or three easy days.

» The tracks and ruined buildings which are seen on the two northern Corbetts give a sense of history.

Personal View

There are no Munros up Glen Roy so it tends to be ignored by walkers until they start climbing Corbetts. There are four Corbetts (three called Carn Dearg) that are climbed from the Glen, and energetic walkers could complete all four in one day. The two more southerly Corbetts could be viewed as a ticking exercise but they are both interesting in their own way. The route up Beinn Iaruinn followed the steep ridge to the left of Coire nan Eun but took me to the summit quickly. In contrast on a lovely May evening I took more time to climb the highest Carn Dearg of the three in this Glen and enjoyed the views over the 'Meggy' group.

The two northern Corbetts at the head of Glen Roy are steeped in history and made for a good walk on a November day with snow above 2,000ft. There were large numbers of deer above me as I climbed the more northern Carn Dearg (2,675ft) and the views north were restricted by cloud. After crossing to the second and lower Carn Dearg I was able to run down to Turret Bridge. It was a straightforward circuit which I completed in half a day, but it took a long time to drive up and down the glen from Roy Bridge.

GLEN ROY continued

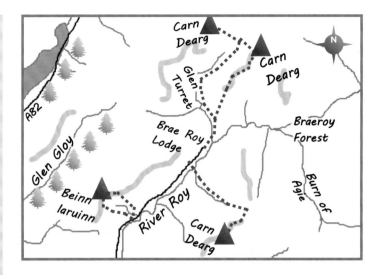

My Routes

BEINN IARUINN (2-3 hours)

The route up Beinn Iaruinn started seven miles up Glen Roy at a road bridge under Coire nan Eun. I followed the steep ridge up the left side of the Coire to the summit plateau. From there I walked north over the summit and continued for a few hundred metres before descending to the road.

CARN DEARG (3-4 hours)

Nine miles up Glen Roy a footbridge crosses the River Roy. I crossed the bridge and followed the path up the left side of the burn in Coire nan Reinich. From the burn I climbed SE to the col north of Carn Dearg then walked SW to the summit.

NORTHERN CARN DEARGS (4-5 hours)

I parked 300m before Brae Roy Lodge and walked up the private road past the lodge. I continued over Turret Bridge and took a left fork up Glen Turret. A track led up the Glen crossing the Allt Eachach at a small bridge. I traversed the slopes NE above the stream to reach a col at 1,800ft.

From the col I ascended the northern Carn Dearg first climbing NNW from the col. The cairn was set back 150m from the top of the hillside. After returning to the col I ascended the southern Carn Dearg. From the summit it was an easy descent SW down the broad ridge.

POINTS OF INTEREST

The area at the head of Glen Roy is steeped in history. First, Brae Roy Lodge, a 19th century shooting lodge, is passed. Turret Bridge is then crossed, an 18th century hump backed bridge used as part of a military highway from Dalwhinnie. Finally there are remains of stone houses on the way up to the Corbetts.

Summit of the most northerly Carn Dearg above Glen Roy looking south east (2012).

Key Details (all summits)

» Total distance 16 miles (26km)

» Height climbed 6,800ft

» O/S Landranger 41 and 34

» Parking at 309891 (Iaruinn), 330909 (Carn Dearg) and 334912 (Northern Deargs).

CORRIEYAIRACK HILLS

GAIRBEINN *(2,940ft)*
MEALL NA H-AISRE *(2,828ft)*

» Two Corbetts climbed separately. They lie north of the route to the Corrieyairack pass.

» Gairbeinn is the more interesting of the two mountains.

» It may be best to climb them on the same day to avoid having to drive the single track road from Laggan twice.

My Routes

GAIRBEINN (2-3 hours)
I parked at Melgarve where the tarmac road ends. For 1km I continued up the track then left it at the Allt a' Mhill Ghairbh. I climbed north then NE up steep slopes to reach the summit.

MEALL NA H-AISRE (3-4 hours)
The route up Meall na h-Aisre started at Garva Bridge. I walked north on a track which began at the west side of the bridge and crossed to the east side of the river after 1km at a footbridge. From here I climbed north to the SE ridge and followed this NW over a top at 844m to the summit.

PLACES TO STAY/DRINK

The nearest hotel is at Laggan but it would also be convenient to stay at Newtonmore or Kingussie.

POINTS OF INTEREST

This area has considerable history. General Wade was responsible for the building of the Corrieyairack Pass and Garva Bridge in the eighteenth Century.

Meall na h-Aisre from near Garva Bridge (2009).

Personal View

These were both Sunday morning Corbetts climbed before leaving Scotland to return to Loughborough. Meall na h-Aisre was an uneventful climb from Garva Bridge in poor weather. The rain eased on the descent and I was able to take the picture above when nearing the end of the walk.

The weather was better on Gairbeinn and the mountain was teeming with deer. It was a short climb with a pleasant summit ridge. It might have been possible to take some decent pictures but unfortunately I destroyed my camera by leaving it in the rucksack with an open bottle of water. The camera never recovered!

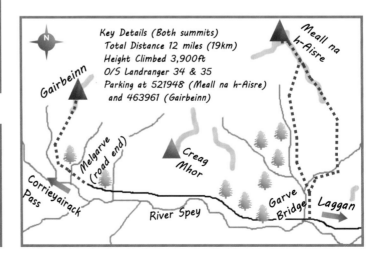

Key Details (Both summits)
Total Distance 12 miles (19km)
Height Climbed 3,900ft
O/S Landranger 34 & 35
Parking at 521948 (Meall na h-Aisre) and 463961 (Gairbeinn)

Summit of Cairngorm.

SCOTLAND: EAST HIGHLANDS

East of the A9 there are 59 Top 500 Summits divided into 22 walks. The area includes the Cairngorms. This mountain range contains three out of the four highest mountains in Britain and Ireland.

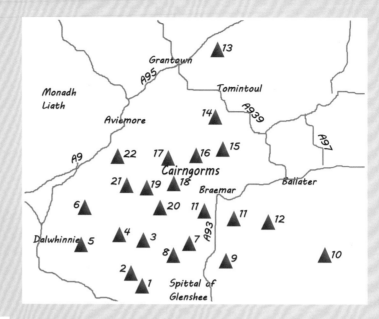

WALKS 1 TO 10

	Walk	Feet	Pg.
1	Ben Vuirich	2,962	168
	Ben Vrackie	2,759	
2	Carn nan Gabhar	3,704	169
	Braigh Coire Chruinn-bhalgain	3,510	
	Carn Liath	3,200	
3	Beinn Dearg	3,307	170
	An Sgarsoch	3,300	
	Carn an Fhidhleir	3,261	
	Carn a' Chlamain	3,159	
	Beinn Mheadhonach	2,956	
4	Beinn Bhreac	2,992	171
5	Leathad an Taobhain	2,991	172
	Carn Dearg Mor	2,813	
	Creag an Loch	2,874	
	An Dun	2,713	
6	Meall Chuaich	3,120	173
	Carn na Caim	3,087	
7	Beinn Iutharn Mhor	3,427	174
	Carn Bhac	3,104	
	An Socach	3,097	
8	Glas Tulaichean	3,449	175
	Carn an Righ	3,377	
9	Glas Maol	3,504	176
	Carn a' Gheoidh	3,198	
	Monamenach	2,648	
	Ben Gulabin	2,645	
10	Mount Keen	3,080	178
	Ben Tirran	2,941	
	Mount Battock	2,554	

The East Highlands cover the area from the A9 to the east coast of Scotland. The best known range of mountains in this area is the Cairngorms. Ben Macdui, Braeriach and Cairn Toul, the second, third and fourth highest mountains in Britain and Ireland, lie in the Cairngorms. On the high Cairngorm plateau the weather can change rapidly. Great care is needed if walking in winter on these mountains. In some of the north-facing Corries, the snow often remains all year round.

To the south of the Cairngorms lie the Grampians, a remote area with few roads. The Ring of Tarf is renowned for containing some of the most remote mountains in Britain including Carn an Fhidhleir and Beinn Bhreac. Further east lies the Balmoral Estate and Lochnagar. Finally, in the far north east, Corbetts are found amongst grassy fields and Whisky distilleries.

Braemar is situated in the centre of the region and gives good access to a number of the mountains. However, many of the summits in this section are a long way from the nearest road. They are best tackled by camping out on the mountains or staying in one of the bothies. This is illustrated by some of the personal views.

WALKS 11 TO 22

	Walk	Feet	Pg.
11	Morven	2,861	179
	Morrone	2,819	
	Creag nan Gabhar	2,736	
12	Lochnagar	3,790	180
	Conachcraig	2,838	
13	Ben Rinnes	2,756	182
	Corryhabbie Hill	2,561	
	Cook's Cairn	2,479	
14	Brown Cow Hill	2,721	183
	Carn Mor	2,639	
	Carn Ealasaid	2,600	
15	Culardoch	2,953	184
	Carn Liath	2,829	
16	Beinn a' Bhuird	3,927	185
	Ben Avon	3,843	
	Carn na Drochaide	2,685	
17	Beinn Mheadhoin	3,878	186
	Bynack More	3,575	
	Beinn a' Chaorainn	3,550	
	Creag Mhor	2,936	
18	Ben Macdui	4,296	188
	Carn a' Mhaim	3,402	
19	Braeriach	4,252	190
	Cairn Toul	4,236	
20	Beinn Bhrotain	3,795	192
	Sgor Mor	2,667	
21	Sgor Gaoith	3,668	193
22	Geal Charn	2,692	194
	Meall a' Bhuachaille	2,657	
	Meallach Mhor	2,522	

Looking up Glen Isla from Monemenach.

PITLOCHRY TO ATHOLL

BEN VUIRICH *(2,962ft)*
BEN VRACKIE *(2,759ft)*

» Ben Vuirich is a high and isolated Corbett south of Beinn a' Ghlo.

» Ben Vrackie is the first mountain seen from the A9 driving north from Perth. It is Pitlochry's local hill with a good path to the summit.

My Routes

BEN VRACKIE (3-4 hours)

Driving east out of Pitlochry we turned left straight after the Moulin hotel then first right to a car park. There was a good path leading north through mixed woodland to a gate onto the hillside. We carried on NNE passing between Meall na h-Aodainn Moire and Creag Bhreac. The route led us to steep slopes just east of the SW face of Ben Vrackie. The path negotiated these slopes to reach the summit plateau and a short walk to the top.

Key Details

» Distance 5 miles (8km)
» Height climbed 2,100ft
» O/S Landranger 43
» Parking at 946599.

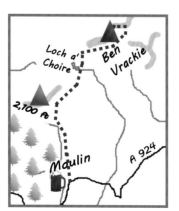

Ben Vrackie from Pitlochry.

Personal View

Ben Vrackie stands to the east of Pitlochry. It signifies the start of a succession of Munros and Corbetts that can be picked out by regular Scottish walkers either side of the A9 all the way to Aviemore. Trusha and I flew to Edinburgh to climb Ben Vrackie but it was a dreadful day, the rain coming across in sheets on a strong west wind and the cloud level at 1,000ft. We opted to delay any walking and tour Blair Castle followed by a long stop in the coffee shop.

In the end we could delay no longer. Fortunately there was a good path from near Moulin up Ben Vrackie. This continued all the way to the summit thereby making the walk bearable. The wind and rain continued until we arrived at the summit then suddenly, with exquisite timing, the clouds ripped apart to reveal a great view to the south.

It was a cold and damp November day in 2006 when I set off from Loch Moraig to climb Ben Vuirich, not the best day for appreciating any mountain. Both the snow level and the mist were just under 2,500ft making the summit climb, which should have been the highlight of the walk, rather tedious. I returned to the warmth of the Atholl Arms for afternoon tea.

BEN VUIRICH (5-6 hours)

From Blair Atholl I drove to the north end of Loch Moraig and parked at reference 907672 (O/S Landranger 43). A good track led ENE for 3km, then the track descended SE to a bridge across the Allt Coire Lagain. I turned left soon after crossing the bridge and followed an estate track across the south slopes of Meall Breac. After passing Meall Breac the track stopped. I continued east to the south ridge of Beinn Vuirich which gave an easy ascent to the summit.

For reference, see map with Beinn a' Ghlo, return trip 13 miles, 2,400ft of ascent.

BEINN A' GHLO

CARN NAN GABHAR *(3,704ft)*
BRAIGH COIRE CHRUINN-BHALGAIN *(3,510ft)*
CARN LIATH *(3,200ft)*

» A good circuit over three Munros east of Blair Atholl but a long way back from Carn nan Gabhar.

My Route (6-8 hours)

In 1985 I climbed these three mountains on a day trip from Sedgefield. The route started 3km NE of Blair Atholl at the north end of Loch Moraig. I walked 2km ENE along the track to a bothy, then climbed NE up steepening slopes to the summit of Carn Liath.

The twisting ridge descended north to a col at 2,400ft, then climbed NE and north to Braigh Coire Chruinn-bhalgain. I continued east and NE along the ridge for 1km, then descended east to a col at 2,750ft. I climbed ESE to the dip between Carn nan Gabhar (Beinn a' Ghlo summit) and Airgiod Bheinn. A walk NE took me to Carn nan Gabhar, the summit marked by a cairn 200m NE of the trig point. I descended south from Carn nan Gabhar to avoid returning over the Munros.

Key Details

» Distance 13 miles (21km)
» Height climbed 4,100ft
» O/S Landranger 43
» Parking at 907672.

POINTS OF INTEREST

In 1844 Queen Victoria said, 'We came upon a lovely view, Beinn a' Ghlo straight before us, and under these high hills the River Tilt gushing and winding over stones and slates...'

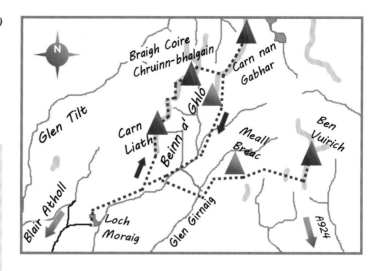

Personal View (JP)

The Linn of Dee is an unusual start point when climbing Beinn a' Ghlo but I was taking a three day tour of the Grampians. Day one was spent on the Ring of Tarf (see page 170). Near Geldie Lodge I crossed the river in a snow shower. Slipped and fell in – never bounced so high! Cursing, I set off up Sgarsoch's northern slopes to the flat stony summit. Over Fhidhleir under blue skies and onto remote Beinn Bhreac then heathery mixed stony ground to Beinn Dearg's sandstone boulders. East over another good Corbett, Mheadhonach, and finally Chlamain. I took the south ridge down to the relatively manicured Glen Tilt and camped.

After an early crossing of the Tilt at Marble Lodge I struggled up easy grass to big old Beinn a' Ghlo but once on its ridges it showed its mettle as a fine range of tops. Now I headed north to aptly named Glen Loch, switch backing over splodgy lands to Carn an Righ. Mars bar and cairn building over, the wind was biting so down to camp in Gleann Mor. The final day took me back to Inverey over Tulaichean, Iutharn and Carn Bhac. A dip in the Dee was tempting after a mighty good walk.

Carn Liath from near the start of the walk *(Chris Wood).*

RING OF TARF

BEINN DEARG *(3,307ft)*
AN SGARSOCH *(3,300ft)*
CARN AN FHIDHLEIR
(3,261ft)
CARN A' CHLAMAIN
(3,159ft)
BEINN MHEADHONACH
(2,956ft)

» A two day walk over remote
mountains between Blair Atholl
and Braemar.

» The walk misses Beinn Bhreac
but this could be added after
Beinn Dearg.

The col between An Sgarsoch and Carn an Fhidhleir in 1995, a remote place.

My Route (2 days)

In 1995 our two day route
started at Old Blair. Thanks to
Reg we had transport arranged
at the finish at the Linn of Dee.
If it is not possible to arrange
transport these mountains are
probably best divided into two
walks. Both would be long days
and a bike would be useful.

From Old Blair we walked up
Glen Banvie, crossed the Banvie burn and followed the track
above Allt an t-Seapail to the
bothy. The path continued NE
to the shoulder of Carn Dearg,
then north to the summit. From
the summit of Beinn Dearg
we walked east, then I made
a detour south to climb Beinn
Mheadhonach. We continued
to Carn a' Chlamain and finally
descended north to the Tarf
Bothy.

After a night in the Tarf Bothy
we set off early the following
morning. We walked beside
the Allt a' Chaorainn to the
col between Carn an Fhidhleir
('the Fiddler') and An Sgarsoch. After climbing 'the Fiddler', nearly missing the summit in the mist, we returned to
the col between 'the Fiddler'
and An Sgarsoch. An Sgarsoch was climbed easily but
the walk out to the Linn of Dee
exceptionally long.

Personal View

In his book, *A Mountain Walk*, Hamish Brown describes the Ring of
Tarf as 'Wild mist moor, unlived-in, lonely as a sad heart, the silence
more crashing than any sound could be'. It is a memorable description of these remote mountains, their summits generally visited only
by those climbing Munros and Corbetts.

We walked over five of the six summits in 1995. Starting from Old
Blair we climbed Beinn Dearg, Beinn Mheadhonach and then Carn a'
Chlamain. From Chlamain (Queen Victoria's first Munro) we headed
north to the Tarf Bothy, the heather and peat bogs making for slow
progress. We arrived at 6.30 p.m. and sat outside reading the Bothy
book: is the white room haunted? It certainly felt haunted when I got
up and went outside for a natural break in the middle of the night. I
was terrified and glad to return to the warm sleeping bag.

The following morning we were away by 7 a.m., a long walk over featureless ground to 'the Fiddler', one of the remotest Munros. Then it
was down to the col and up An Sgarsoch. It took us five hours from
there to the Linn of Dee but it would be much quicker with a bike.

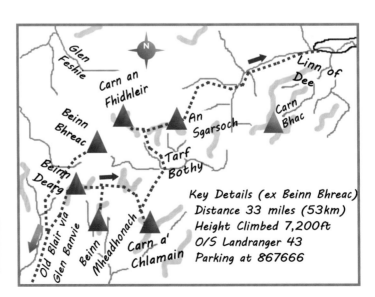

Key Details (ex Beinn Bhreac)
Distance 33 miles (53km)
Height Climbed 7,200ft
O/S Landranger 43
Parking at 867666

BEINN BHREAC

BEINN BHREAC *(2,992ft)*

» Beinn Bhreac is a high and inaccessible Corbett lying north of Beinn Dearg.

My Route (with bike 7-9 hours)

I was joined for this climb by Nick Hopkin. This was his first remote Scottish mountain and he gives his account opposite. We drove up the A9 turning off the main road at Bruar and parked at Calvine, just off a minor road. This led directly to the track which we needed to follow to Bruar Lodge.

We got the bikes out and immediately cycled across the busy A9. This was followed by 2km of uphill cycling and walking, then we free wheeled down the track to Glen Bruar and were able to make good speed along the bulldozed track to Bruar Lodge. 1km past Bruar Lodge we dumped the bikes. A good path climbed NE up the hillside on the north side of the Allt Beinn Losgarnaich.

After 2km the path petered out and we continued through peaty and rough ground for a few hundred metres. Eventually we found better ground and a path, indistinct in places, which ran north on the east side of the stream. This also petered out so we made our way NE across rough ground for 1km to the headwaters of the Tarf.

From here it was a straightforward ascent NE to the remote summit of Beinn Bhreac with its lonely cairn. We returned the same way, four hours for the outward journey and three hours twenty minutes back.

For reference, see Ring of Tarf map opposite.

Personal View (Nick)

Barry invited me on his trip to Beinn Bhreac, the one summit he had not climbed in the remote mountain area sometimes known as the Ring of Tarf. The Corbett is definitely one for triathletes, a good blend of cycling and walking with the chance of a swim at any time! The challenge began with some pleasant cycling along a track for around seventy-five minutes with good views over a modest hydro electric scheme. The cycle ended up just beyond an impressive shooting lodge in the shadow of some imposing black and brown mountains.

Beinn Bhreac itself may be a few feet short of Munro status but this Corbett once conquered gives you a splendid sense of isolation. Getting there was by no means straightforward as once up the initial hill after leaving the bikes there was little in the way of a path. Indeed the terrain is challenging, very boggy and designed to test those muscles which have previously remained dormant. Once beyond Beinn Dearg you know that you are one of only a handful of people to reach Beinn Bhreac that year. Views from the top are daunting, including the Cairngorms to the north. It is easy to imagine you are on a different planet.

The more adventurous may be tempted to bag Beinn Dearg on the way back but there are no easy routes to follow. Descending by the path close to the bikes was tricky due to loose rocks and even the return leg of biking seemed harder than the outbound route. This walk is not to be underestimated but connoisseurs will relish this challenging Corbett.

Key Details

» **Distance 25 miles (40km)**
» **Height climbed 3,000ft**
» **O/S Landranger 43**
» **Parking at Calvine, 804659.**

PLACES OF INTEREST

Glen Bruar Lodge, which is passed on the route, was built in 1789 as a sporting lodge. Now it accommodates up to eighteen people and is available for let.

Nick on the remote summit of Beinn Bhreac (2015).

FESHIE TO GAICK

LEATHAD AN TAOBHAIN
(2,991ft)
CARN DEARG MOR *(2,813ft)*
CREAG AN LOCH *(2,874ft)*
AN DUN *(2,713ft)*

» Four Corbetts lying between Blair Atholl and Kincraig.

Carn Dearg Mor in the distance from near Leathad an Taobhain (2010).

My Routes

LEATHAD AN TAOBHAIN AND CARN DEARG MHOR
(7-9 hours)

The route started at the car park 1km before Achlean. I walked to Achlean and took a path along the east side of the Feshie, crossing a bridge over it after a further 1km. A road led to Glenfeshie Lodge where it turned into a track. I branched right to go SW beneath the slopes of Carn Dearg Mor. The track turned south and eventually reached Meall an Uillt Chreagaich. Here a footpath branched down to a stream, then up to the summit of Leathad an Taobhain. On the way back I climbed Carn Dearg Mor.

AN DUN AND CREAG AN LOCH
(7-8 hours)

The route started at Dulnacardoch Lodge just off the A9. From here a good track led 9km north to Sronphadruig Lodge (a bike would be useful for this section). I climbed the south ridge of An Dun continuing to the summit. 500m down the north ridge I descended steeply to Loch an Duin. A steep climb east led to the summit plateau of Creag an Loch. On reaching the summit plateau I went east then north to the summit. I returned south along the summit plateau of Creag an Loch, descending SW to Sronphadruig Lodge.

Personal View

On a clear day in July 2010 I climbed Leathad an Taobhain and Carn Dearg Mor starting near Achlean. There is nothing better than walking along the Feshie particularly in evening sunshine. It was a long walk but the paths were good and I was able to make fast time returning for a late tea at the hotel in Kincraig.

Three years earlier I had climbed An Dun and Creag an Loch on a day of sunshine and showers. It was a steep climb up An Dun then I descended to remote Loch an Duin. Another steep climb took me to the summit of Creag an Loch before the long walk back.

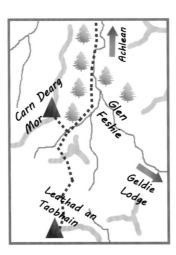

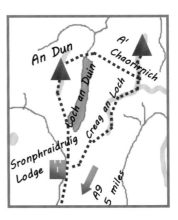

Key Details (Feshie)

» Distance 19 miles (30km)
» Height climbed 3,500ft
» O/S Landranger 35 and 43
» Parking at 851984.

Key Details (Gaick)

» Distance 16 miles (26km)
» Height climbed 3,000ft
» O/S Landranger 42
» Parking at 722703 off the A9.

EAST OF DRUMOCHTER

MEALL CHUAICH (3,120ft)
CARN NA CAIM (3,087ft)

» A'Bhuidheanach Bheag (3,071ft) is an additional Munro which should be added when climbing Carn na Caim.

» The three Munros are on the east side of the Drumochter Pass.

My Routes

MEALL CHUAICH (4-5 hours)
I left the A9 just south of the Chuaich cottages and followed a rough private road from a locked gate. This led to a road which ran just north of east alongside an aqueduct and past a small power station. When nearing the dam at the south end of Loch Chuaich, I turned SE then east to cross the Allt Coire Chuaich. Finally I left the track and climbed heathery slopes to a broad ridge and the summit.

Key Details
» Distance 9 miles (14km)
» Height climbed 2,000ft
» O/S Landranger 42
» Parking at 655868.

CARN NA CAIM (2-3 hours)
I started a few hundred metres south of the turnoff to Dalwhinnie. A good track led east then south and finally SE to a quarry and pt 902m. I went NE over a 914m knoll then slightly downhill and up again to Carn na Caim. After returning to pt 902m A'Bhuidheanach can be added, but this will add around two hours to the time taken.

PLACES TO STAY/DRINK
There is a choice of cafes, bars and hotels at Newtonmore which is a ten minute drive from Drumochter Pass.

Personal View (Jonathan)

I have many happy memories of Dalwhinnie 'the highest village in the highlands' although the pub and even a cafe that used to serve an excellent breakfast have now closed. In 1990 it provided a bed for the night, well actually a bench on the railway station. A late train and lack of planning had meant this was the only option. Sadly I didn't have a sleeping bag, just a rucksack and some water.

This meant that an early start became an attractive option. I crossed the A9 and followed an ugly scarred quarry road to featureless Carn na Caim and A' Bhuidheanach. From there the main challenges were the long crossing between the two Munros and which of the raised lumps of land were the actual summits. I was back at Dalwhinnie by midday. I replicated my steps fifteen years later to climb a Munro Top that I had missed near A' Bhuidheanach.

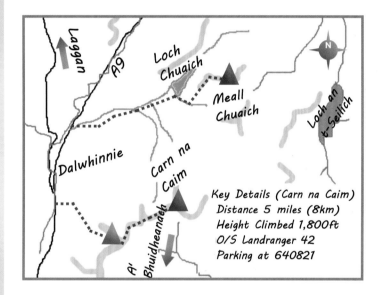

Key Details (Carn na Caim)
Distance 5 miles (8km)
Height Climbed 1,800ft
O/S Landranger 42
Parking at 640821

Near Loch Chuaich with Meall Chuaich behind (*Chris Wood*).

SOUTH OF LINN OF DEE

BEINN IUTHARN MHOR
(3,427ft)
CARN BHAC *(3,104ft)*
AN SOCACH *(3,097ft)*

» This is a long walk over remote country to the west of the Glenshee ski area.

My Route (9-11 hours)

I parked at Inverey and followed the road (turns into a track) up the west side of the Ey burn and Allt Cristie Mor. After nearly 4km I left the track, crossed the Allt Cristie Mor and climbed Carn Damhaireach (2,570ft). A broad ridge led to the SW top of Carn Bhac (3,020ft). A final walk 1km ENE brought me to the Munro summit.

I returned to the SW top then went south over featureless terrain. After 3km I climbed steep scree slopes to reach the summit plateau of Beinn Iutharn Mhor and followed the broad ridge SW to the summit.

I descended SE to reach the Allt Beinn Iutharn and followed this NE below Beinn Iutharn Bheag. When north of Beinn Iutharn Bheag I turned east to cross its lower slopes. Steep slopes then led to the summit plateau of An Socach.

Key Details

» Total distance 21 miles (33km)
» Height climbed 4,100ft
» O/S Landranger 43
» Parking at 086892.

POINTS OF INTEREST

Inverey is split by the Ey burn, the east side (Meikle Inverey) used to be Protestant and the west side (Little Inverey) Catholic.

Summit of An Socach, late afternoon on a beautiful March day in 1989.

Personal View

From the Bridge of Cally Hotel I drove up to Inverey, four miles west of Braemar, on a glorious March morning. I love the country near Braemar, heather, silver birch and clear fast running streams. Ptarmigan and white hare kept me company on the traverse from Carn Bhac to Beinn Iutharn Mhor.

Towards the top of Beinn Iutharn Mhor I kicked steps up a steep snow slope. On An Socach I met two lads from Birmingham who were camped at Loch nan Eun. Finally there was the long walk down Glen Ey to the car with the stream glistening in the evening sunlight. I slumped into the Fife Arms at Braemar and drank two mugs of tea after a memorable day.

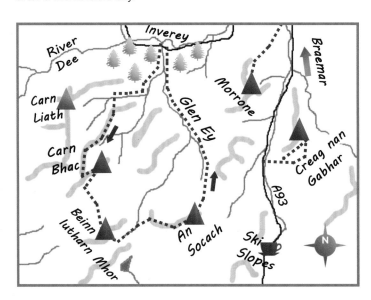

SPITTAL OF GLENSHEE

GLAS TULAICHEAN *(3,449ft)*
CARN AN RIGH *(3,377ft)*

» Two remote Munros between Glenshee and Glen Tilt reached from the Spittal of Glenshee.

My Route (6-7 hours)

In April 1999 Alistair and I parked at Dalmunzie House (a £2 charge applied in 2014). From Dalmunzie we walked up the road past Glenlochsie Farm and along the track of the old railway line to Glenlochsie Lodge.

From here a track went up the hillside to the summit of Glas Tulaichean. We continued along the NNE ridge of Glas Tulaichean then descended NW. A path ran along the south side of Mam nan Carn. We followed this path west to a col just east of Carn an Righ and climbed west to the summit. After descending to Gleann Taitneach we followed a track back to Dalmunzie.

Key Details

» Total distance 13 miles (22km)
» Height climbed 3,400ft
» O/S Landranger 43
» Parking at 091713 (Dalmunzie House).

POINTS OF INTEREST

During the 18th Century it is thought that around 150 people lived near Dalmunzie House. Today there is the estate, a hotel, a cottage and a nine hole golf course.

Personal View (Alistair)

In the halcyon days before the turn of the century I used to find it easy to get company on the Munros. My brothers, Barry and Jonathan, were still climbing them and thus willing to join me! In this case Barry was staying at a cottage in Seahouses so I picked him up for a day on the Munros. This time it was the summits north of the Spittal of Glenshee, Carn an Righ and Glas Tulaichean.

We set off early from the Dalmunzie Hotel at the Spittal of Glenshee. With a starting height of 1,300ft at the Spittal the route to Tulaichean and Righ is not difficult or strenuous although maybe being only 40 years old helped. There was an excellent track to the top of Tulaichean then we made our way to Carn an Righ. I felt a sense of isolation at the summit, as always in this part of the Grampians, but it was a comforting isolation not a threatening one. I returned to the car still feeling reasonably fresh.

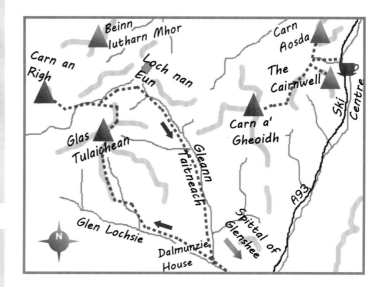

On the way down Gleann Taitneach (1999).

AROUND GLENSHEE

Alex and James at the summit of Monamenach, Creag Leacach and Glas Maol behind (June 2016).

GLAS MAOL *(3,504ft)*
CARN A' GHEOIDH *(3,198ft)*
MONAMENACH *(2,648ft)*
BEN GULABIN *(2,645ft)*

» Two Corbetts and two Munros near Glenshee all with high start points.

» The Munros are climbed from the Glenshee cafe which is at a height of 2,000ft.

» Three further Munros can be added, Creag Leacach (3,240ft), the Cairnwell (3,061ft) and Carn Aosda (3,009ft).

» The Corbetts both lie close to the road and are easy climbs.

Personal View

Around Glenshee there are many Munros and two Corbetts, Monamenach and Ben Gulabin. Monamenach was my final Corbett and Top 500 Summit. My two boys, Alex and James, joined me for the climb. We had a great day, starting by running the Edinburgh Parkrun, a fine run along the shores of the Firth of Forth, with 500 other runners. The sun came out on the drive up Glen Isla. At Auchavan a puncture forced us into a quick tyre change then we made our way to the summit. A bottle of champagne was consumed at a leisurely pace at Monamenach's summit.

Glas Maol and Creag Leacach can be climbed from the high start at the Glenshee ski centre without difficulty. In February 1986 the weather was good for skiing and walking, windless with some sunshine. I walked over Meall Odhar to the summit of Glas Maol. There were two skiers on the summit 'off piste' (the ski tows had not reached Glas Maol back in 1986). I continued to Creag Leacach seeing ptarmigan and white rabbits before dropping down to the road. I slogged back up the road and dived into the Glenshee cafe for a coke and two cups of tea.

Carn a' Gheoidh sits behind the Cairnwell and Carn Aosda and must feel unloved by the thousands of people who ski at Glenshee each year. Snow conditions were fabulous when I climbed Carn a' Gheoidh but the isolation and calmness as I walked clear of the skiers and over Carn nan Sac was incredible.

My Routes

GLAS MAOL (3-4 hours)

I started from the south end of the large car park at Glenshee and ascended ESE over a knoll, into a dip, then climbed Meall Odhar. The route continued SE to Glas Maol. The summit cairn was 500m SE across the stony plateau. A line of fence posts then led SSW along a ridge which narrowed near Creag Leacach. The return distance was six miles with 2,000ft of climbing.

CARN A' GHEOIDH
(2-3 hours)

I climbed Carn a' Gheoidh from the ski centre at Glenshee. From the ski centre I climbed west to reach a ridge which ran SW to Carn nan Sac. A wide ridge continued west to the summit of Carn a' Gheoidh.

Key Details

» Distance 6 miles (10km)

» Height climbed 1,900ft

» O/S Landranger 43

» Parking at 139782.

For reference, see map with Spittal of Glenshee on page 175.

MONAMENACH (1-2 hours)

We started at Auchavan at the end of the public road and followed a track NW to a bealach at just over 600m. From there a good path climbed NW to the summit.

Key Details

» Distance 2.5 miles (4km)

» Height climbed 1,500ft

» O/S Landranger 43

» Parking at 192697.

BEN GULABIN (1-2 hours)

There was parking just off the A93 north of the Spittal of Glenshee at ref 114715. From here a gate gave access to the hillside and a good track led NNW to the col between Ben Gulabin and Creagan Bheithe. From the col we climbed SW on a grassy track turning NW on the summit ridge to Ben Gulabin.

Key Details

» Distance 3 miles (5km)

» Height climbed 1,500ft

» O/S Landranger 43

» Parking at 114715.

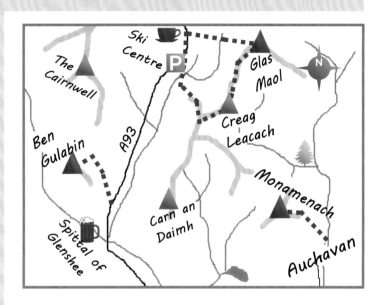

Creag Leacach from the A93.

FURTHEST EAST

MOUNT KEEN *(3,080ft)*
BEN TIRRAN *(2,941ft)*
MOUNT BATTOCK *(2,554ft)*

» Mount Keen is the most easterly Munro and Mount Battock the most easterly Corbett.

My Routes

MOUNT KEEN (5-6 hours)

The route started at the car park in Auchronie. We walked west to the road junction then NW up Glen Mark. After 3.5km we reached 'Queen's Well', a monument to Queen Victoria who drank the waters in 1861. After bearing right past the last house in the Glen we followed the track NNW up the Ladder Burn. We climbed the slopes to emerge onto moorland with Mount Keen ahead to the north. A right fork took us to the summit. The return distance was ten miles with 2,300ft of climbing.

BEN TIRRAN (3-4 hours)

I started from the B955 at Wheen. A track led north up the hillside reaching Loch Wharral in just over 3km. From Loch Wharral I climbed east up the hillside to a cairn which was 500m SW of the summit. A path led NE from the cairn to the summit with its shelter and trig point. The return distance was six miles with 2,200ft of climbing.

MOUNT BATTOCK (4-5 hours)

The route started just past Millden Lodge. Immediately after crossing the bridge I turned right and parked north of the house, Fernybank. I walked along the road forking right past Muir Cottage up the west side of the Burn of Turret. I continued north on a good path to point 717m then east to the summit. The return distance was eight miles with 2,700ft of climbing.

Summit of Ben Tirran, sometimes known as 'The Goat' (2014).

Personal View

These three mountains lie on the east side of Scotland and are climbed from Glen Clova (Ben Tirran) and Glen Esk (Mount Keen and Mount Battock). Good paths, often landrover tracks, lead up the mountains and in winter white hares can be seen in abundance. I have always enjoyed visiting this part of Scotland with its gentle mountains and historical sights, such as Glamis Castle, the childhood home of the Queen Mother.

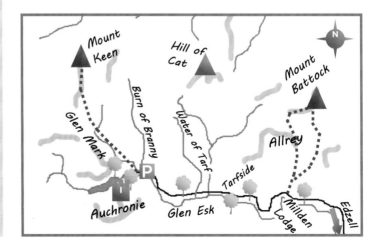

RIVER DEE CORBETTS

MORVEN *(2,861ft)*
MORRONE *(2,819ft)*
CREAG NAN GABHAR
(2,736ft)

» Morven is an isolated hill to the north of Ballater.

» Morrone and Creag nan Gabhar are short walks from near Braemar.

Personal View

Morven is situated just north of Ballater and is a popular local mountain. Although it was late afternoon at the end of February when I climbed it the weather was benign, sunny spells and very little snow. Initially the climb was steep but the walking became easier and the views were superb.

The other two Corbetts are near Braemar and have high starts. On Boxing Day 2006 I had a clear day on Creag nan Gobhar with the weather warm on the summit. Two years later, in February 2009, I climbed Morrone after a long drive to Braemar from Loughborough. Unfortunately there was thick cloud and no views.

My Routes

MORVEN *(2-3 hours)*

I drove to the foot of the mountain from Ballater, turning left off the A97 when 1km south of Logie Coldstone. I parked at Balhennie from where I could see the abandoned farmhouse on the hillside. A path led past the south side of the farmhouse and ascended 1,000ft steeply up heathery slopes. From there I followed an old fence line to the east ridge, then walked west following fence posts to the summit. I returned the same way in fading light.

Key Details

» Distance 5 miles (8km)

» Height climbed 2,100ft

» O/S Landranger 37

» Parking at 410044.

The abandoned farmhouse at the start of the climb up Morven.

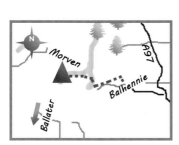

MORRONE *(2-2.5 hours)*

I drove to Braemar and parked next to the Duck Pond at the top of Chapel Brae. A private track went through the Morrone Birkwoods before turning uphill. A good path then led all the way to the summit of Morrone.

CREAG NAN GABHAR *(2-3 hours)*

I parked near the bridge at Reference 140834 and followed the path east up an unnamed glen leading to Glen Callater. The path followed the south side of the stream crossing to the north side after 1.5km. I continued for another 1km, then climbed north up the hillside to a col below the summit. From there I went WNW for a further 1km to the summit. A direct but steep descent WSW led back to the car.

Key Details (both Corbetts)

» Distance 9 miles (14km)

» Height climbed 3,100ft

» O/S Landranger 43

» Parking at 142907 (Morrone) and 140834 (Creag Nan Gabhar).

Morrone and Creag Nan Gabhar are shown on the map for south of Linn of Dee on page 174.

LOCHNAGAR

Lochnagar from the north.

LOCHNAGAR *(3,790ft)*
CONACHCRAIG *(2,838ft)*

» The following Munros can be added in a long day of 30km from Glen Muick, Carn a' Coire Boidheach (3,668ft), Carn an t-Sagairt Mor (3,435ft), Cairn Bannoch (3,320ft) and Broad Cairn (3,274ft).

» Lochnagar is one of the great Scottish mountains with many famous climbing routes. It lies entirely within the Balmoral Estate.

» Conachcraig is a short and easy climb of just over 500ft from the path up Lochnagar.

Personal View

Lochnagar is the highest mountain in Scotland east of the A93 and lies in the Royal Estate of Balmoral. Everything about Lochnagar and Conachcraig is high quality befitting the royal estate of Balmoral. The paths and the signposting seem to make the walking easier than normal.

Lochnagar was my fourth Munro, in the summer of 1975. Over forty years later my recollections of the walk are limited but I recall that the summit was in cloud and was further and harder to reach than I expected.

I returned to Glen Muick in March 2014 to climb Conachcraig. It was a beautiful winter morning with the ice just starting to melt after a very cold night. A herd of deer crossed the path in front of me soon after I left the Glenmuick car park. Thereafter I was constantly disturbed by white hares and grouse. It was a straightforward ascent, a narrow path leaving the Lochnagar 'motorway' track at a col and climbing 500ft to the summit. From the summit I ran down so that I could enjoy lunch in Ballater before an afternoon ascent of the Corbett, Carn Mor, from the Lecht.

The map shows the route over all five Munros in this area and Conachcraig, the Corbett.

My Routes

The route to Conachcraig started at the car park at the Spittal of Glenmuick (2014 charge of £3 per day). I followed the private road SW for 200m past the Visitor Centre, then turned right and crossed the glen to Allt-na-giubhsaich.

There were signs to Lochnagar through the trees. I followed a vehicle track in a westerly direction crossing to the north side of the burn after 1km. On reaching the col I found a cairn. From here a narrow path led NE to the top of Conachcraig.

In 1975 we followed the same route for Lochnagar but missed Conachcraig. We climbed to the col south of Meikle Pap. The path then went left and ascended SSW to the summit ridge of Lochnagar. We continued around the rim of the Corrie and after 1km ascended NW to Cac Carn Mor then the summit, Cac Carn Beag.

Key Details (Conachcraig and Lochnagar only)

» Distance 12 miles (19km)
» Height climbed 3,100ft
» O/S Landranger 44
» Parking at 309851.

POINTS OF INTEREST

Balmoral Estate was purchased by the Royal Family in 1852. It is a working estate including grouse moors, forestry, farmland and managed herds of deer and highland cattle.

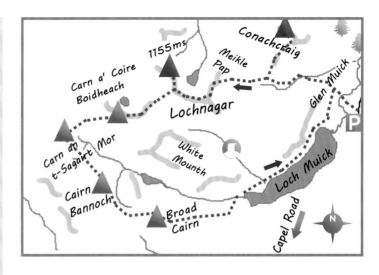

The Lodge soon after leaving the Spittal of Glenmuick (2014).

WEST OF DUFFTOWN

BEN RINNES *(2,756ft)*
CORRYHABBIE HILL *(2,561ft)*
COOK'S CAIRN *(2,479ft)*

» Two Corbetts and one high Graham near Dufftown.

» Cook's Cairn was a Corbett but was demoted to a Graham following a remeasurement.

Donald near the summit of Ben Rinnes (2012).

My Routes

BEN RINNES (2-2.5 hours)
We turned right off the B9009 5km SW of Dufftown and drove 500m up a minor road to a car park. A good path climbed 500ft up Round Hill. We crossed a flat section over Roy's Hill and finally ascended 1,000ft to the summit of Ben Rinnes.

Key Details
» Distance 4 miles (6km)
» Height climbed 1,800ft
» O/S Landranger 28
» Parking at 284360.

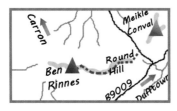

CORRYHABBIE HILL AND COOK'S CAIRN (5-6 hours)
I turned south down a minor road off the B9009 and parked at a T junction. Opposite the farm a track headed SE. I followed this for a few hundred metres until on open hillside, then turned south up the Hill of Achmore. The ridge swung SSE up Muckle Lapprach and finally east to the summit shelter and trip point. I descended SE to the valley at 1,700ft, then climbed Cook's Cairn returning to Corryhabbie Hill the same way.

Personal View

Following a game of golf at Dufftown, Donald and I climbed Ben Rinnes late in the afternoon on a pleasant day in July. When we set off there were a number of families with young children walking down the mountain; the wide path and easy walking makes Ben Rinnes ideal for children. The views to the north over the Moray Firth and to the south over the Cairngorms were fantastic. It took us just over two hours to climb the mountain and return to the car.

Corryhabbie Hill and Cook's Cairn are gentle undulating hills rising from agricultural land and make for an enjoyable walk from Ellivreid. On my visit in 2014 I was surprised to find three parties out for a Sunday walk on Corryhabbie Hill on a windy March day. I climbed Corryhabbie Hill and found there was no easy way of avoiding climbing it again after I had made the journey over to Cook's Cairn. Thus I descended and reascended 850ft twice. Needless to say I found nobody on Cook's Cairn, maybe it attracted more visitors when it was a Corbett.

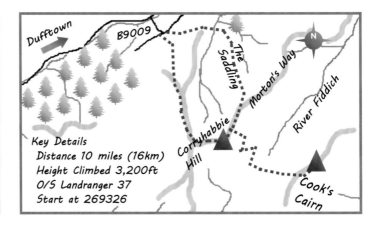

Key Details
Distance 10 miles (16km)
Height Climbed 3,200ft
O/S Landranger 37
Start at 269326

AROUND THE LECHT

BROWN COW HILL *(2,721ft)*
CARN MOR *(2,639ft)*
CARN EALASAID *(2,600ft)*

» Three summits lying near the road from Tomintoul to Braemar.

My Routes

BROWN COW HILL (3-4 hours)

I parked at reference 258087 just south of Cock Bridge and left the A939 by a gateway. A grassy track went SW to the main gravel track leading SSW on the west side of the Cock Burn. After 2km the track veered to the west and started to ascend to the col between Carn Oighreag and Brown Cow Hill at 2,000ft. A line of grouse butts led south over rising moorlands. I went SW to the heathery summit area, the summit was the middle top.

Key Details

» Distance 9 miles (14km)
» Height climbed 1,400ft
» O/S Landranger 36 and 37
» Parking at 258088.

CARN MOR (3-4 hours)

From the car park at the top of the Lecht pass (2,090ft) I climbed NE past Meikle Corr Riabhach. After 1km I reached a long wide ridge which ran NNE for nearly 5km, passing over Carn Liath and another small summit, before arriving at Carn Mor.

CARN EALASAID (2-3 hours)

From the top of the Lecht pass I headed west past the ski slopes and Beinn a' Chruinnigh. The route turned south descending slightly before the final ascent to Carn Ealasaid.

Personal View

The Lecht is probably best known for winter weather reports telling the UK that the A939 is blocked at 'The Lecht'. It is also a small but attractive ski resort. Carn Mor and Carn Ealasaid can be climbed easily from the top of the pass at the Lecht. Carn Mor is a short climb then a long walk at the 2,500ft level. When I visited Carn Mor I found fascinating views over the far north east of Scotland and saw white hares in abundance.

My enthusiasm for Brown Cow Hill was dampened by being bitten by a small dog on the way down. I was nearly back when the dog, one of five dogs out for a walk, raced up to me from 100 yards away and without breaking its stride jumped as high as it could and buried its teeth into my leg, a strange incident! Despite this I enjoyed climbing Brown Cow Hill on a mainly sunny February morning.

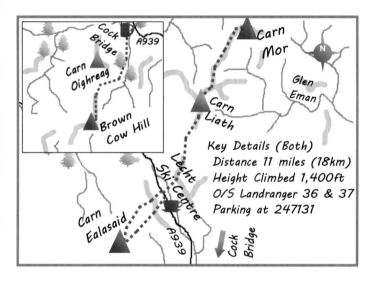

Key Details (Both)
Distance 11 miles (18km)
Height Climbed 1,400ft
O/S Landranger 36 & 37
Parking at 247131

The top of the pass at the Lecht (2014), Carn Mor and Carn Ealasaid can be climbed from here.

183

BRAEMAR CORBETTS

CULARDOCH *(2,953ft)*
CARN LIATH *(2,829ft)*

» Two Corbetts to the east of the main Cairngorm range.

» An estate track running through the middle of them helps access.

My Route (5-6 hours)

I turned off the A93 three miles east of Braemar and left the car just before Keiloch. The estate track led NW then I took the track signposted Loch Builg which went north. I followed this for nearly 4km. The track dipped and crossed a wooden bridge. After a further 500m I climbed NW to the summit of Carn Liath.

I descended ENE to the Bealach Dearg and continued NE along the track for 1km. I made a route finding error here and should have continued until the track made a turn to the left. Eventually I arrived at this point and ascended 550ft east to the summit of Culardoch.

POINTS OF INTEREST

Nearby Crathie Kirk (below) is known as the place of worship for the Royal family when they stay at Balmoral.

Keiloch, the start point for Culardoch and Carn Liath.

Personal View

I was staying at Braemar in February 2008 and got away at first light to climb these two Corbetts. Good progress up Carn Liath was destroyed by missing the turn to Culardoch and wasting 30 minutes down a valley which must be rarely visited. Eventually I found a good track which led to the summit of Culardoch where I was surprised to find some walkers and a friendly border collie. I was back down for a late lunch and the long drive back to Loughborough.

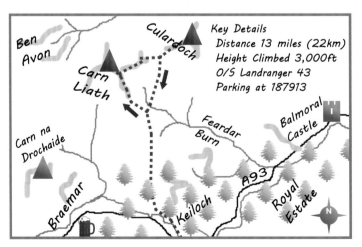

Key Details
Distance 13 miles (22km)
Height Climbed 3,000ft
O/S Landranger 43
Parking at 187913

BEN AVON ROUND

BEINN A' BHUIRD *(3,927ft)*
BEN AVON *(3,843ft)*
CARN NA DROCHAIDE
(2,685ft)

» This is a long, high level walk in the eastern Cairngorms traversing two Munros and a Corbett.

» Ben Avon is the highest point of a vast plateau with granite tors.

» Beinn a' Bhuird is characterised by its east facing cliffs.

My Route (9-11 hours)

We climbed both Munros and Carn na Drochaide in 1997. I set off from Newcastle at 5 a.m. and met Jonathan and JP in the Fife Arms at Braemar for morning tea. JP had just completed a three day tour of the Grampians bringing his Munro total to 200 (see Beinn a' Ghlo).

We started from Linn of Quoich, following the track up the west side of Glen Quoich for 7km before climbing onto An Diollaid. From An Diollaid the track ascended NE up a broad ridge to the north top and highest point of Beinn a' Bhuird. We walked east for a short distance, then descended NE then east again to the Sneck. From the Sneck we climbed east then NE to Ben Avon's plateau and its summit tor.

We returned SSW over high ground then descended south down to the glen. Eventually we reached a ruin under Meall an t-Slugain. Carn na Drochaide was now between us and the Linn of Quoich, so I persuaded Jonathan and JP to climb it. It was a miserable ascent in the rain but the sun came out as we descended to the car.

Personal View (Alistair)

Two walkers, two dogs, two tents but only one bike and it belonged to me! Jonathan is six years younger than me, fitter, and has had no knee operations so the bike was not going to be shared. For me a bike helps to take the grind out of a long walk in and this one was at least seven miles. So my younger brother moaned all the way from Tomintoul to Inchrory where there was a fantastic estate house. Shortly after this I dumped the bike and later we camped on the edge of the River Avon, just before the Bruach top where the path leaves for Beinn a' Bhuird. It was an idyllic and truly remote spot with tumbling water echoing in our ears as we fell asleep.

The next morning we headed off for Bhuird together but Jonathan abandoned me part way to the North Top to head east collecting Munro Tops. I wandered over the north and south tops of Bhuird enjoying the tranquillity then set off to Ben Avon where we met at the summit. It was a lunar and unique landscape. Soon we were heading back and more moaning from Jonathan after I picked up my bike. In the end I cycled ahead and drove back a few miles to pick him up.

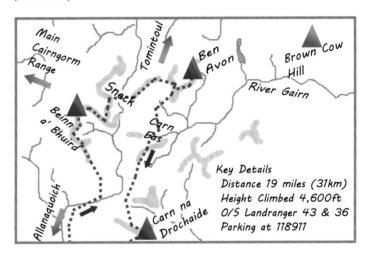

Key Details
Distance 19 miles (31km)
Height Climbed 4,600ft
O/S Landranger 43 & 36
Parking at 118911

Summit tours of Ben Avon *(Heather Thomas-Smith)*.

LOCH AVON SUMMITS

Summit tors of Beinn Mheadhoin in sunshine, April 2003.

BEINN MHEADHOIN *(3,878ft)*
BYNACK MORE *(3,575ft)*
BEINN A' CHAORAINN
(3,550ft)
CREAG MHOR *(2,936ft)*

» Three Munros and one
  Corbett lying just to the east
  of Cairngorm. The fastest route
  back from Beinn Mheadhoin
  is over Cairngorm (4,084ft),
  a fourth Munro.

» Beinn Mheadhoin is the most
  spectacular of these mountains
  with its rock tors and views
  over Loch Avon.

» The four summits can be
  completed in one long day.

Personal View (JP, a Cairngorm crossing)

With the rucksack, bag, tent and a few Mars bars I set off on a two
day walk over the Cairngorms. An undemanding trudge took me up
Cloich-Mhuilinn, Munro's last hill which he did not climb, then on
to Bhrotain with the curlews calling overhead. I had other things
in mind though taking in Monadh Mor before turning north. Soon
I was on the plateau rim. This is big country with big cliffs holding
cornices into June. The plateau itself had snow cover making navigation tricky in intermittent cloud and flat light. The cloud lifted as
I retraced from Braeriach by the dramatic east rim above mighty
Garbh Coire to Angel's Peak and Cairn Toul, dramatic summits.
Finally I glissaded down old snow from Devil's Point and camped
outside Corrour Bothy.

The following morning tired legs were forced up Mhaim and then to
MacDui. I skirted the Coire to Derry Cairngorm then went north to
Loch Etchachan's outflow. So Mheadhoin became my tenth Munro
of this tour. On its western slopes I met reindeer and on the summit
I played on the tors and the tops with the brilliant Loch Avon in the
eyeline. I dropped steeply east to the col of Glen Derry then slogged
up Chaorainn, short turf, easy walking. Three miles of boggy moor
then a tiny rise to Beinn Bhreac. On the way back I swear I saw a
wildcat in the Glen Derry woods.

My Routes

BEINN MHEADHOIN, BYNACK MORE (7-9 hours)

There is a car park at the foot of Coire na Ciste and a path goes NE to the north end of Lochan na Beinne. After crossing between the 737m and 692m spot heights, I descended to Strath Nethy. From here I climbed Bynack Beg and Bynack More.

After Bynack More I walked over A' Choinneach then descended to the north end of Loch Avon. From here I crossed over the river by a bridge and ascended Beinn Mheadhoin. The return to the car was via the north ridge of Cairngorm.

BEINN A' CHAORAINN (7-8 hours)

I climbed Beinn a' Chaorainn from the Linn of Dee. After walking to Derry Lodge I continued north for nearly 3km up Glen Derry. A climb NE led to Beinn Bhreac. From this summit a long traverse north took me to Beinn a' Chaorainn. There was low cloud so route finding was difficult. I was fortunate to run into a couple of guys with GPS who pinpointed my spot on the way up Chaorainn.

CREAG MHOR (6-8 hours)

To climb Creag Mhor I set off from the Cairngorm ski lift car park. I passed the Ptarmigan restaurant before descending to the head of Loch Avon. After walking to the Fords of Avon I climbed NE to reach the summit of Creag Mhor.

POINTS OF INTEREST

Beinn Mheadhoin is noted for its summit tors. The highest point is the top of one of the largest tors and requires an easy scramble to reach it.

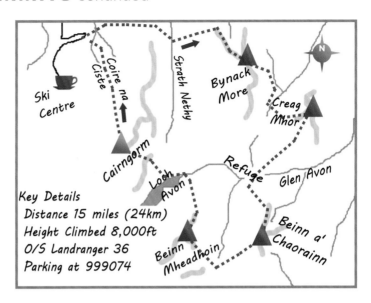

Key Details
Distance 15 miles (24km)
Height Climbed 8,000ft
O/S Landranger 36
Parking at 999074

The map shows a possible one or two day route over the four summits.

The new refuge at the Fords of Avon.

BEN MACDUI

Looking up Loch Avon towards Carn Etchachan and the plateau just below Ben MacDui.

BEN MACDUI *(4,296ft)*
CARN A' MHAIM *(3,402ft)*

» Ben MacDui is the second
highest mountain in Britain and
is also famous for its ghostly
Grey Man.

» Derry Cairngorm (3,790ft),
a third Munro, can be added
to this walk.

» These summits can be
ascended from the Linn of
Dee but if climbing Ben MacDui
on its own, it is easier to start
from the Cairngorm ski car
park on the Aviemore side.

Personal View (Jonathan, an Easter ascent of Ben Macdui)

It was Easter so four of us had driven up from London for a long
weekend skiing in the Cairngorms. I left my mates skiing in order
to climb Ben MacDui and possibly Cairngorm (although this proved
hopelessly optimistic). From the ski car park I headed up the Fiacaill
a' Choire Chais to the 1,141m point and then around the head wall
until a path headed south to MacDui. For three miles I walked on
hard packed snow before eventually reaching the summit. In the
wispy cloud I half expected the Grey Man to appear. In fact I have to
admit I was becoming a little scared, the conditions were spooky, I
was well behind the clock and cold. This is a big place and the hours
just seemed to roll by.

I took a more direct route back and dropped down to Loch Avon
accepting some additional climbing. I sensed that this route may
be easier to navigate and I could not afford to get lost. It proved a
little easier and once I reached Coire Raibert it was 'just' a 1,500
foot climb to the col then down to the car park. Needless to say the
1,500 foot climb seemed endless in the snow but once at the col I
was able to run down to the car park. I was late back and my mates
were of course fed up at the wait for a beer but I was relieved to be
back. Many years later I returned to Ben MacDui in a heatwave, a
complete contrast to my earlier winter ascent.

My Route (8-10 hours)

It was the summer of 1987. We had spent a wet night at the Garbh Coire bothy (it leaked in the middle) following our descent from Cairn Toul in darkness the previous evening (see page 191). From the bothy we walked to the Lairig Ghru and then found a way up steep slopes to the top of Ben Mac-dui. From the summit a path went east then NE until we were above Loch Etchachan. We turned SE, descended 100ft, then ascended Derry Cairngorm.

We continued down the south ridge of Derry Cairngorm for 2.5km, then descended SW to the Luibeg Burn. I left the others and made a slow and tired 1,700ft climb west to the top of Carn a' Mhaim.

A descent SE down a broad ridge took me to Luibeg Bridge and a long walk out to the Linn of Dee via Derry Lodge. We arrived back at Linn of Dee at 4.30 p.m. A bike would have been useful for the section to Derry Lodge.

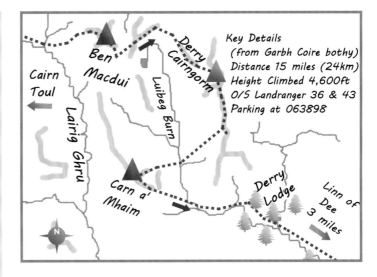

Key Details
(from Garbh Coire bothy)
Distance 15 miles (24km)
Height Climbed 4,600ft
O/S Landranger 36 & 43
Parking at 063898

The map shows my route over Ben Macdui, Derry Cairngorm and Carn a' Mhaim.

Loch Morlich and the Cairngorms.

POINTS OF INTEREST

Up until the 19th century it was thought that Ben MacDui could be higher than Ben Nevis but detailed mapping confirmed Ben Nevis as the higher. Ben MacDui is also well known because of rumours concerning the grey man. Those who have seen 'the big grey man' claim it resembles a broken spectre or a Yeti.

GARBH CHOIRE

Descending from Braeriach.

BRAERIACH (4,252ft)
CAIRN TOUL (4,236ft)

» Two further Munros, Angel's Peak (4,127ft) and The Devil's Point (3,294ft) could be added when climbing Braeriach and Cairn Toul.

» Braeriach and Cairn Toul are the third and fourth highest mountains in Britain.

» This walk goes round the rim of Garbh Choire, the highest plateau in Britain and Ireland.

Personal View

A traverse of the high Cairngorms is one of the best walks in Scotland. Transport needs to be arranged at both ends but the walk can be completed during a long summer day. I completed a Cairngorm crossing in May 2001 turning right after Angel's Peak in order to traverse Beinn Bhrotain and Monadh Mor.

The traverse from Braeriach round Garbh Choire was magnificent, partially in cloud with some of the plateau covered by snow. This is the highest and potentially the most dangerous plateau in Britain. To the south west lies high empty moorland, to the east the cliff faces of Garbh Choire. The snow has only completely melted from Garbh Choire five times in the last 100 years.

I left Jonathan after we passed Carn na Criche, the second highest Munro top at 4,150ft, and soon after that my mobile phone must have dropped out the bottom of my rucksack, maybe it is still there on the high Cairngorm plateau. I passed over Angel's Peak, Monadh Mor and Beinn Bhrotain before the long walk back to the Linn of Dee. I was passed by a young family on bikes after White Bridge before reaching the Linn of Dee ten hours after setting out.

GARBH CHOIRE continued

Cairngorm Crossing Route (10-12 hours)

I had climbed Cairn Toul and Devil's Point from the Linn of Dee as part of a two day expedition in 1987. On that occasion I had set off late with Reg and another friend after driving up to the Linn of Dee from Newcastle. We finished the day by descending from Cairn Toul to the bothy in Garbh Coire at 11 p.m. The weather had deteriorated with heavy rain falling and we were fortunate to find the bothy in gathering darkness.

To climb Braeriach Jonathan and I started at the Cairngorm ski centre car park. From the car park we followed the path towards Coire an t-Sneachda. A path then led west to the Chalamain Gap and through to the Lairig Ghru.

We crossed the Lairig Ghru and followed the path south over Sron na Lairige and round to the summit of Braeriach. We continued round the rim of Garbh Coire to Carn na

Criche, a Munro Top. At this point Jonathan returned and I continued to Angel's Peak.

From Angel's Peak I traversed Monadh Mor, Beinn Bhrotain and Carn Cloich-mhuilinn. Alternatively and maybe easier would be to go over Cairn Toul and The Devil's Point, as shown by the map below. From The Devil's Point it is straightforward to descend to the Corrour Bothy and the long walk out to Linn of Dee.

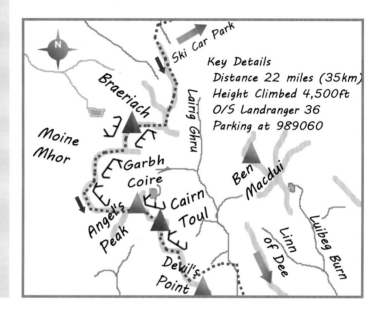

Key Details
Distance 22 miles (35km)
Height Climbed 4,500ft
O/S Landranger 36
Parking at 989060

Chalamain Gap on the way to Braeriach.

PLACES TO STAY/DRINK
The Corrour Bothy lies on the route below the Devil's Point so it could be used for accommodation leaving the walk out to the Linn of Dee for the following day. Braemar is a good base for food and accommodation.

BEINN BHROTAIN

BEINN BHROTAIN *(3,795ft)*
SGOR MHOR *(2,667ft)*

» A second Munro, Monadh Mor (3,652ft), would normally be added to this walk.

» A bike could be used for 7km each way.

» If possible Sgor Mhor should be added to the two Munros to avoid a long trip back later.

My Routes

Monadh Mor and Beinn Bhrotain were climbed on my walk across the Cairngorms in 2001 (see page 191).

I climbed Sgor Mhor from the Linn of Dee a few years later Starting from the car park at Linn of Dee I walked to White Bridge then along the south side of the Dee for another 3km. After crossing the River Dcc it was straightforward to climb 1,000ft directly to the summit of Sgor Mhor.

It would be possible to combine Beinn Bhrotain with Sgor Mhor as shown on the map.

POINTS OF INTEREST

Carn Cloich-mhuilinn was demoted from Munro status in the 1981 tables as the rise from Beinn Bhrotain is only 250ft. Sir Hugh Munro had left this summit for his last Munro but he died in 1919 without climbing it.

The Linn of Dee at the start of the walk.

Personal View (Jonathan)

I climbed Beinn Bhrotain on the second day of my two day tour of the Cairngorm massif from the Linn of Dee in 1999. A hot spell of weather covered the highlands and it was warm enough to spend the night on the col between The Devil's Point and Cairn Toul. At 10 p.m. the views from The Devil's Point were something special. I had a sleeping bag but no tent so tied my dog, Bracken, to the rucksack. It never seemed to get fully dark but I managed a few hours sleep. The following morning, hoping to avoid the heat by climbing high early, I headed over Cairn Toul and Angel's Peak before tackling Beinn Bhrotain.

First though I headed west to the very remote Munro Top of Tom Dubh. Crossing to Monadh Mor from this remote spot I had a strange, surreal feeling of total isolation heightening the senses to a level I had never experienced (although of course it might have been sunstroke!). I crossed Monadh Mor and Beinn Bhrotain then dived into the River Dee fully clothed.

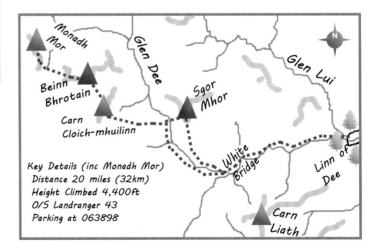

Key Details (inc Monadh Mor)
Distance 20 miles (32km)
Height Climbed 4,400ft
O/S Landranger 43
Parking at 063898

SGOR GAOITH

SGOR GAOITH (3,668ft)

» Sgor Gaoith is one of the two Cairngorm Munros climbed from Glen Feshie, the other is Mullach Clach a' Bhlair (3,345ft).

» The two Munros are a long distance apart although the drop between the two mountains is less than 500ft.

» Sgor Gaoith sits in a magnificent setting above Loch Einich.

My Route (6-8 hours)

The route started at the car park 1km north of Achlean. We walked south to the farm at Achlean and followed the path east up the hillside to the top of Carn Ban Mor, a deleted Munro. We continued NE to the summit of Sgor Gaoith.

As we were adding Mullach Clach a' Bhlair, we headed back over Carn Ban Mor. A track led SW and finally south to Mullach Clach a' Bhlair. The traverse from Carn Ban Mor to Mullach Clach a' Bhlair was 5km but felt considerably further. To return to the car we descended past Meall nan Sleac which was shorter than following the main track back to Glen Feshie.

PLACES TO STAY/DRINK

We stayed at Kincraig which is the nearest place for food and accommodation. However, there is plenty of accommodation along the Spey Valley.

Personal View

We climbed these two Munros on a glorious day in June 1991. The sun reflected off the snow as we ascended to the top of Sgor Gaoith. A long walk south over easy terrain to Mullach Clach a' Bhlair followed, the great bulks of Monadh Mor and Beinn Bhrotain clearly visible to the left tempting me to try to tick them off as well.

The summit of the Mullach was a great viewpoint, to the south lay the 'Ring of Tarf' and remote Carn an Fhidhleir, to the west the window of Creag Meagaidh was prominent. To the north the view was restricted by the high plateau joining Braeriach and Angel's Peak. From the Mullach we descended over Meall nan Sleac to reach Glen Feshie one mile from Achlean. We drove back to Kincraig for tea and scones at the local hotel.

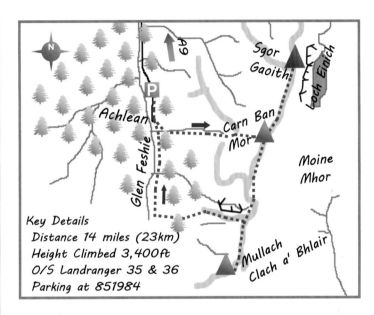

Key Details
Distance 14 miles (23km)
Height Climbed 3,400ft
O/S Landranger 35 & 36
Parking at 851984

Summit of Sgor Gaoith (1991).

CAIRNGORM CORBETTS

GEAL CHARN *(2,692ft)*
MEALL A' BHUACHAILLE
(2,657ft)
MEALLACH MHOR *(2,522ft)*

» These three Corbetts lie to the north and west of the Cairngorm massif and are normally climbed separately.

My Routes

GEAL CHARN *(3-4 hours)*

There was parking at the turning place at the end of the road to Dorback Lodge. I started walking to the abandoned building at Upper Dell. From here a good track ran SSE. I crossed the Allt na h-Eirghe and ascended south up the lower slopes of Geal Charn to a plateau, then turned NE to the summit.

MEALL A' BHUACHAILLE
(2-3 hours)

There was parking just past Glen Mor Lodge. A good path led NE through the forest reaching Ryvoan Bothy after 3km. A path went left at the bothy and ascended 1,500ft west to the summit. From the summit I descended west to a col then turned left down the hill to Glen More.

MEALLACH MHOR
(with bike 4-5 hours)

I parked near Glentromie Lodge (but I should have parked at Tromie Bridge) then cycled 8km down the glen until directly west of Meallach Mhor. I left the bike and climbed up the hillside in an easterly direction. After climbing 1,000ft I reached a broad ridge which led ENE to the summit.

Key Details (Meallach Mhor)

» Distance 15 miles (24km)

» Height climbed 1,700ft

» O/S Landranger 35

» Parking at 790995, Tromie Bridge.

Cycling to Meallach Mhor, the summit in view (2013).

Personal View

JP found a novel route to Meall a' Bhuachaille mountain biking from the Boat of Garten past the Ospreys and Abernethy Forest. From Ryvoan Bothy he climbed the Bhuachaille before returning past Loch Morlich and the Queens Forest. He exited onto the B970 at West Croftmore to return to Boat of Garten. My walks over Meall a' Bhuachaille and Geal Charn were less interesting. However, on Geal Charn I disturbed two deer in undergrowth less than ten yards away which shocked them as much as me.

The following year I left Loughborough at 6.30 a.m. with the bike for the long drive to Kingussie and the start point for Meallach Mhor. There was no sign indicating a private road at Tromie Bridge so I drove up the glen for a couple of miles. I was parking when a man appeared and told me it was still a private road but fortunately he allowed me to park. I cycled to the foot of the mountain and climbed to the summit in high winds. On returning to the car I met a man who had been helping the RSPB and I gave him a lift back to Kingussie.

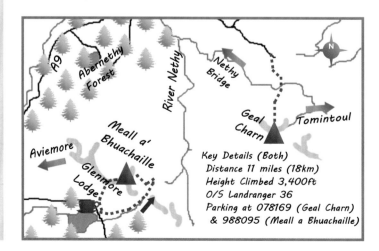

Key Details (Both)
Distance 11 miles (18km)
Height Climbed 3,400ft
O/S Landranger 36
Parking at 078169 (Geal Charn)
& 988095 (Meall a Bhuachaille)

Looking west down Loch Arkaig.

SCOTLAND: FAR WEST HIGHLANDS

The Far West Highlands cover the area between Fort William and the Western Isles. The mountains run from Morven in the south to Arnisdale in the north. There are 57 Top 500 Summits divided into 23 walks:

WALKS 1 TO 11

	Walk	Feet	Pg.
1	Creach Bheinn	2,798	198
	Fuar Bheinn	2,512	
2	Garbh Bheinn	2,903	199
3	Sgurr Dhomhnuill	2,914	200
	Carn na Nathrach	2,579	
4	Beinn Resipol	2,772	201
5	Rois-Bheinn	2,895	202
	Sgurr na Ba Glaise	2,867	
	An Stac	2,671	
6	Beinn Odhar Bheag	2,895	204
	Beinn Mhic Cedidh	2,569	
	Sgurr Ghiubhsachain	2,784	
	Sgorr Craobh a' Chaorainn	2,543	
	Druim Tarsuinn	2,525	
7	Stob Coire a' Chearcaill	2,528	206
	Beinn na h-Uamha	2,500	
	Sgurr a' Chaorainn	2,497	
8	Beinn Bhan	2,612	207
	Meall a' Phubuill	2,540	
9	Gulvain	3,238	208
	Braigh nan Uamhachan	2,510	
10	Sgurr an Utha	2,610	209
11	Sgurr Thuilm	3,160	210
	Sgurr nan Coireachan	3,136	
	Streap	2,982	

The Far West Highlands cover the area west of Fort William including Knoydart and Moidart. The area is split by the A830 as it runs from Fort William to Mallaig.

To the south lies Moidart, Ardgour, Sunart and Morven. There are no Munros here but there are 17 Top 500 Summits, 16 Corbetts and 1 Graham. These are rugged hills and fine Corbetts. The best known mountains are Rois-Bheinn, Beinn Resipol, and Garbh Bheinn.

North of the A830 lies a more varied selection of mountains, more rounded in the east but rocky and remote in the west of the region around Knoydart. Great Munros such as Ladhar Bheinn and Sgurr na Ciche lie in and around Knoydart and there are also some tough Corbetts including Ben Aden and Streap. The area includes the only village in mainland Britain that cannot be reached by road, Inverie, next to the Sound of Sleat.

WALKS 12 TO 23

Walk		Feet	Pg.
12	Sgurr Mhurlagain	2,886	212
	Fraoch Bheinn	2,815	
	Sgurr Cos na Breachd-Laoidh	2,739	
	Bidean a' Chabhair	2,844	
	Carn Mor	2,719	
13	Sgurr na Ciche	3,412	214
	Garbh Chioch Mhor	3,323	
	Sgurr nan Coireachan	3,125	
14	Beinn Bhuidhe	2,805	216
15	Sgurr Coire Choinnichean	2,612	217
	Beinn na Caillich	2,575	
16	Ladhar Bheinn	3,345	218
17	Ben Aden	2,910	220
	Sgurr nan Eugallt	2,946	
18	Meall Buidhe	3,105	222
	Luinne Bheinn	3,082	
	Sgurr a' Choire-bheithe	2,994	
19	Sgurr Mor	3,290	223
	Gairich	3,015	
	Sgurr an Fhuarain	2,956	
20	Meall na h-Eilde	2,749	224
	Geal Charn	2,638	
21	Sron a' Choire Ghairbh	3,074	225
	Meall na Teanga	3,008	
	Ben Tee	2,957	
22	Beinn Sgritheall	3,194	226
	Beinn na h-Eaglaise	2,641	
	Beinn nan Caorach	2,539	
	Beinn a' Chapuill	2,490	
23	Gleouraich	3,394	228
	Sgurr a' Mhaoraich	3,369	
	Spidean Mialach	3,268	

Climbing Beinn Sgritheall *(Chris Wood)*.

GLEN GALMADALE

CREACH BHEINN *(2,798ft)*
FUAR BHEINN *(2,512ft)*

» These Corbetts occupy a superb position in Kingairloch on the east end of the peninsula.

» The round includes two Corbetts, Creach Bheinn and Fuar Bheinn and a Graham, Beinn na Cille (2,138ft).

» This is a classic horseshoe with great sea views.

My Route (6-7 hours)

The route started 15 miles SW of Corran on the B8043. At a bridge over the Galmadale river there was parking. I walked 200m down the road then struck up the hillside beside a plantation. From 200ft above the plantation I climbed NNW to Beinn na Cille, a Graham.

I descended 600ft north then climbed 1,000ft to the summit of Fuar Bheinn. After another descent to the next col at 1,800ft I turned east climbing 1,000ft to Creach Bheinn. The horseshoe was completed by walking south along Meall nan Each until there was an easy descent to the road.

POINTS OF INTEREST

Kingairloch is part of Morven. Morven is an area of approximately 250 square miles and is one of the most remote areas of mainland Britain. The main settlement is Lochaline from where there is a regular ferry to the Isle of Mull.

Looking up Glen Galmadale towards Fuar Bheinn and Creach Bheinn (2009).

Personal View

Kingairloch feels a long way from the beaten track and tends to be rarely visited. My only visit was one Saturday in September 2009 when I drove up from south of Edinburgh. I crossed Loch Linnhe by the Corran Ferry and then drove down the west side of Loch Linnhe to the Galmadale River, the start point for these two lonely Corbetts.

The day started sunny but deteriorated with stormy showers and a strengthening wind as I walked over Meall nan Each after climbing Creach Bheinn. Overall though I found this an interesting and enjoyable circuit yielding two Corbetts and one Graham.

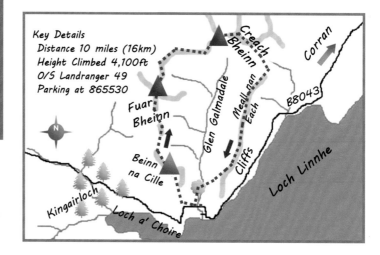

Key Details
Distance 10 miles (16km)
Height Climbed 4,100ft
O/S Landranger 49
Parking at 865530

GARBH BHEINN

GARBH BHEINN (2,903ft)

» Superb peak in Ardgour with glorious views over Glencoe.

» There are a number of different routes to the summit.

My Route (3-4 hours)

On my second attempt to climb Garbh Bheinn I started from the A861 in Glen Tarbert at a small bridge at the edge of the trees (ref 896604). A small path, at times indistinct, led north on the east side of the stream.

I followed this for 1.5km then turned NNE up the hillside. Two streams fell down the hillside at this point and the best route seemed to be up a line of rusty fence posts. These ascended the left side of the second stream.

Continuing in this direction led me to the ridge to the west of Garbh Bheinn. I went over the summit and dropped down to the col before Sron a' Garbh Choire Bhig. From the col I descended through a gully to the route of ascent.

In 1979 our route started at the A861 by the old bridge over the Abhainn Coire an Iubhair. We went up and over Sron a' Garbh Choire Bhig but stopped without attempting the final ascent of Garbh Bheinn.

POINTS OF INTEREST

Many people use the Corran Ferry to reach Garbh Bheinn. This has been running since the 1930s and is now one of the last mainland to mainland ferries in Britain.

Personal View

Garbh Bheinn is a towering Corbett in Ardgour, a short ferry journey from near Fort William. It is well worth the trip over Loch Linnhe to explore this mountain.

Alistair and I were tempted across the Corran Ferry on a cold day of cloud and snow in November 1979 but failed to climb Garbh Bheinn. We reached the final 500 foot climb to the summit but were faced with steep icy rocks in thick mist which we thought wise not to attempt. However, on my second visit thirty-four years later on a beautiful September day that final summit climb did not look daunting. Although the image of having to climb a steep icy cliff face to reach the summit of Garbh Bheinn was destroyed, my memories of a great mountain remain.

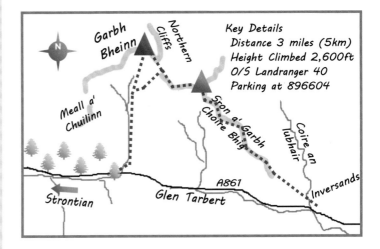

Sunshine and clouds on the summit ridge of Garbh Bheinn (2013).

ARDGOUR

SGURR DHOMHNUILL
(2,914ft)

CARN NA NATHRACH
(2,579ft)

» Sgurr Dhomhnuill is the highest summit in the area south of Glenfinnan.

» It is possible to combine these two Corbetts by starting from the pass north of Strontian.

My Route (6-8 hours)

The route started from the top of the road which goes north out of Strontian to Loch Doilet. I walked ENE over poor terrain, at times small hills and lochans blocking the way. I was unsure whether I was heading in the right direction until, after 3km, Sgurr Dhomhnuill came into view. I went over point 803 metres on Druim Garbh, then descended 300ft SE, before climbing steeply up the last 600ft of Sgurr Dhumhnuill.

I returned to the col, then descended north aiming for the highest point of Gleann na Cloiche Sgoilte. From this bealach it was a steep and pathless 1,300ft ascent to the ridge just west of the summit of Carn na Nathrach. From here it was an easy walk to the summit. I descended to the top of the bealach, then traversed WSW for a mile before climbing back to Druim Garbh.

POINTS OF INTEREST

Strontium (a mineral named after the village) was mined in Strontian in the 18th and 19th century.

On the way to Sgurr Dhomhnuill from the west (2013).

Personal View

These two Corbetts lie at the centre of the area south of Glenfinnan covering Ardgour, Moidart, Morven and Sunart. In total this area contains sixteen Corbetts. Carn na Nathrach can be combined with Sgurr Dhomhnuill but a steep 1,300ft ascent to the summit of Carn na Nathrach is required to achieve this.

I had never been to Strontian until September 2013 and I was impressed both by the place and the mountains. However, the walk over these summits from the pass that bisects Resipol and Dhomhnuill was not straightforward. I found the early terrain around lochans and over small hills very confusing even in good weather and the climb up Carn na Nathrach nearly finished me off! I was pleased to get back to the road and dinner at the Kilcamb Hotel.

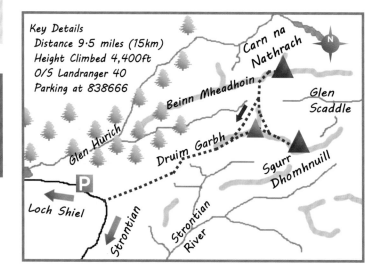

Key Details
Distance 9·5 miles (15km)
Height Climbed 4,400ft
O/S Landranger 40
Parking at 838666

BEINN RESIPOL

BEINN RESIPOL *(2,772ft)*

» Beinn Resipol is a prominent and isolated mountain just north of Loch Sunart.

» The view from the summit includes the Cuillin on the Isle of Skye, Ben More on the Isle of Mull and Ben Nevis.

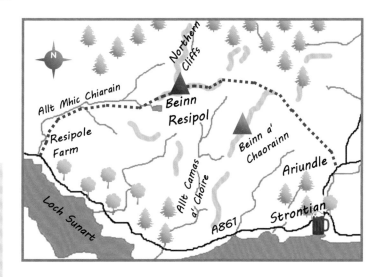

My Route (4-5 hours)

I parked near the gallery at Resipole Farm and crossed the bridge to follow a path on the east side of the Allt Mhic Chiarain. I took a right fork to climb higher up the hillside. A path continued through the woods.

After 2.5km the path reached a second gate and open hillside. I followed the path east along the south side of the Allt Mhic Chiarain. After a further 1.5km I reached the summit slopes of the mountain. At a height of 2,500ft I turned right to climb to the summit, which was at the west end of the ridge. The return was by the same route.

Key Details

» Distance 6 miles (10km)

» Height climbed 2,600ft

» O/S Landranger 40

» Parking at 721642.

Personal View

Beinn Resipol is an isolated Corbett situated in Sunart, which was an area I had never previously visited. It was late October 2013 when I climbed Resipol and judged by the underfoot terrain it had been raining heavily for months. I drove from Strontian to Resipole Farm with an improved forecast of sunshine and showers and parked at the gallery, having obtained permission to park there from its friendly owner.

Apparently there was stalking on the other side of Beinn Resipol that day but I saw only highland cattle as I climbed through the woodland. After reaching open countryside I followed a good path beside a stream to the steep summit slopes of Beinn Resipol. Thirty minutes later I stood on the summit of Resipol in sunshine, a great climb to a beautiful summit.

Beinn Resipol from the east (2013).

POINTS OF INTEREST

Beinn Resipol is a maritime mountain with a Norse name thought to mean 'farmstead'. The mountain is popular with the local residents and holidaymakers. On both sides of the mountain there are pathed walks through the Atlantic Oakwoods.

ROIS-BHEINN

Summit ridge of Rois-Bheinn looking out to sea (2011).

ROIS-BHEINN *(2,895ft)*
SGURR NA BA GLAISE *(2,867ft)*
AN STAC *(2,671ft)*

» Rois-Bheinn is the most westerly Top 500 Summit in mainland Britain and has great views over the Scottish Islands.

» This is one of the few places where three Corbetts can be completed easily in one walk.

» This walk can be combined with Beinn Odhar Bheag and Beinn Mhic Cedidh so five Corbetts can be climbed if transport is available.

Personal View

Rois-Bheinn lies south of the road from Fort William to Mallaig near a small hamlet with a train station, Lochailort. It is one of my favourite mountains in Scotland because of its fine summit and magical location overlooking the sea. The walk is probably best completed on a long summer evening as the sun goes down over the Islands.

I climbed these three Corbetts in the summer of 2011. The ridge walk west from Druim Fiaclach to Sgurr na Ba Glaise was fabulous. The ridge twisted and turned as it headed towards the sea and the Scottish Islands before climbing to the summit of Sgurr na Ba Glaise. After climbing Sgurr na Ba Glaise it was a straightforward descent and reascent to Rois-Bheinn with its reassuring wall running over the summit and out to its western top.

The drop to the col beneath An Stac and climb of 850ft to the summit was the toughest part of the walk but the underfoot terrain was good and soon I was enjoying the descent of An Stac's north ridge with the sea on my left.

ROIS-BHEINN continued

My Route (6-7 hours)

I parked on the narrow road beside the River Ailort. A track went south bearing right to go round the south side of Tom Odhar and into Coire a' Bhuiridh. I continued south up the west side of the Allt a' Bhuiridh for 1km, then climbed the grassy slopes of Beinn Coire nan Gall, aiming for the col between this hill and Druim Fiaclach.

On reaching the col I climbed south to the summit of Druim Fiaclach (2,852ft). It was a 3km ridge walk to the first Corbett, Sgurr na Ba Glaise, only 15ft higher than Druim Fiaclach.

From the summit of Sgurr na Ba Glaise the ridge dropped NW to another bealach at 2,300ft. It then climbed west to Rois-Bheinn. It was worth visiting the west top of Rois-Bheinn for the views west over the Islands.

From Rois-Bheinn I returned to the bealach at 2,300ft and descended NNW a further 500ft to the col underneath An Stac. A steep ridge led to the summit of An Stac. Then I descended north to Seann Chruach before dropping down to the Allt a' Bhuiridh. From there I followed my route of ascent back to the car.

POINTS OF INTEREST

Apparently 2,000 people lived at Lochailort when the railway from Fort William to Mallaig was being built. This is hard to believe now.

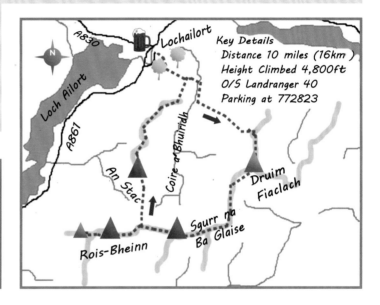

Key Details
Distance 10 miles (16km)
Height Climbed 4,800ft
O/S Landranger 40
Parking at 772823

An Stac and Rois-Bheinn from the north.

LOCH SHIEL

North ridge of Sgurr Ghiubhsachain looking down Loch Shiel (2011).

BEINN ODHAR BHEAG
(2,895ft)
BEINN MHIC CEDIDH
(2,569ft)
SGURR GHIUBHSACHAIN
(2,784ft)
SGORR CRAOBH A'
CHAORAINN *(2,543ft)*
DRUIM TARSUINN *(2,525ft)*

» These five Corbetts lie close to
each other around Loch Shiel.

» Loch Shiel divides the two to
the west, Beinn Odhar Bheag
and Beinn Mhic Cedidh from
the other three.

» Sgurr Ghiubhsachain is seen
in the classic view of the
Glenfinnan Monument
and Loch Shiel.

Personal View

These five Corbetts are spectacularly divided by Loch Shiel and
it took me three walks to complete them. Jonathan had decided
to introduce his new dog Mist to the mountains with the circuit of
Sgurr Ghiubhsachan and Sgorr Craobh a' Chaorainn from close to
the Glenfinnan Monument in 2011. After a pleasant walk along the
lochside it felt a long pull up to Ghiubhsachain perhaps because it
was a sea level start. From the summit it was a very steep descent
to the col then an easy ridge walk to the second peak, Sgurr Craobh
a' Chaorainn.

The following year I climbed the two Corbetts on the west side of
Loch Shiel, Beinn Odhar Bheag and Beinn Mhic Cedidh, on a cloudy
day. The highlight of the walk was the ridge between Beinn Odhar
Bheag and Beinn Odhar Mhor which was airy with spectacular views
over Loch Shiel. The low point was the walk back to the car from
the bottom of Beinn Mhic Cedidh which was slow and awkward.

Finally I climbed Druim Tarsuinn which was a long walk from the
road over an intervening ridge. The final summit ridge reminded me
of Knoydart, it was rocky and had a fence running along it. A false
summit on the way to Druim Tarsuinn was confusing in the mist
but I carried on and found that the actual summit had a cairn on it.

My Routes

BEINN ODHAR BHEAG AND BEINN MHIC CEDIDH (6-7 hours)

The route started three miles west of Glenfinnan village where I found parking at a bend in the road. There was a bridge over the river and railway line. I headed for the NNW ridge on the skyline then followed this up Beinn Odhar Mhor. I descended 350ft on an interesting ridge before climbing to Beinn Odhar Bheag, the first Corbett.

From there I descended 1,200ft to a col then climbed back up to Beinn Mhic Cedidh. I descended by Cedidh's north ridge and crossed the railway line before returning to the car.

Key Details

» **Distance 7.5 miles (12km)**
» **Height climbed 4,400ft**
» **O/S Landranger 40**
» **Parking at 857813.**

SGURR GHIUBHSACHAIN AND SGORR CRAOBH A' CHAORAINN (6-7 hours)

There was parking 2km SE of Glenfinnan near the bridge over the Callop river. We followed the forest track NW to the shore of Loch Shiel then walked over 3km along the side of the loch to Guesa-chan Cottage. From here we climbed the north ridge of Ghi-ubhsachain avoiding the rocky lower part by going round its left hand side.

We descended steeply ESE to the col before Craobh a' Chaorainn and then climbed NE to its summit. A descent NE led to the stalkers' path along the Allt na Cruaiche and back to the start.

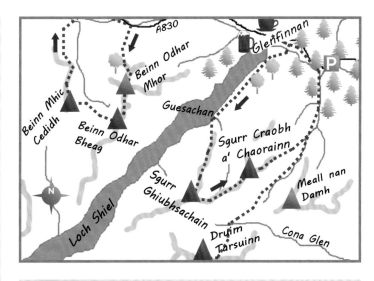

DRUIM TARSUINN (6-7 hours)

I started from the same place as for Sgurr Ghiubhsachain and followed a sign saying Ardgour 18 miles. A good track headed south before being replaced by a stalkers' track when I crossed the Allt Leacaich. I continued over a pass at 1,000ft and descended to cross a river in Cona Glen. After climbing SW to the col between Meall Mor and Druim Tarsuinn, I walked west to the summit.

Key Details (Ghiubhsachain (Walk 2) and Tarsuinn (Walk 3))

» **Distance 10 miles (16km) (Walk 2) and 11 miles (18km) (Walk 3)**
» **Height climbed 3,400ft (Walk 2) and 3,200ft (Walk 3)**
» **O/S Landranger 40**   » **Parking at 925793 (both Walks).**

Looking down to Loch Shiel from Beinn Odhar Bheag (2012).

WEST OF LOCH LINNHE

STOB COIRE A' CHEARCAILL
(2,528ft)
BEINN NA H-UAMHA
(2,500ft)
SGURR A' CHAORAINN
(2,497ft)

» These mountains lie in Ardgour close to Loch Linnhe.

» Beinn na h-Uamha is the lowest Corbett and Sgurr a' Chaorainn is the highest Graham.

My Routes

STOB COIRE A' CHEARCAILL
(3-4 hours)

There was parking next to a cattle grid just over 1km east of Duisky. I walked east for 100m then a gate gave access to the hillside. I went south through open woodland, then headed towards a fence to my right. I followed the fence south to a gate. A ruined fence and intermittent path then led to a wide ridge. This curved SW to the summit.

Key Details

» **Distance 5.5 miles (9km)**
» **Height climbed 2,500ft**
» **O/S Landranger 41**
» **Parking at 022770.**

BEINN NA H-UAMHA AND SGURR A' CHAORAINN
(6-7 hours)

I took the short ferry journey across to Corran and drove to Sallachan where I parked next to the bridge. A good path started at the south side of the bridge and went along Glen Gour past Loch nan Gabhar. I walked along this track for 5km, then crossed over to the north side of the stream and climbed the SE ridge of Beinn na h-Uamha.

From the top of Beinn na h-Uamha I descended 650ft west, then climbed 647ft to the summit of Sgurr a Chaorainn. From here I descended SE to Glen Gour and the long walk back to the car.

Looking down Glen Gour towards Loch Leven and Glencoe (2011).

Personal View

Beinn na h-Uamha and Sgurr a' Chaorainn lie at the head of Glen Gour and give a good round improved by climbing both mountains (which look exactly the same height) rather than the single Corbett. Climbing both mountains would also prevent any regrets in the event of a remeasurement of either or both summits. It is a long walk along Glen Gour on the way to and from the mountains but I enjoyed this circuit on a warm August day in 2011.

In contrast the route up Stob Coire a' Chearcaill from the north was straightforward but the weather was terrible; constant heavy rain and wind which turned into sleet as I neared the top. It was late October and I was surprised to see three people approaching the summit just as I was leaving it.

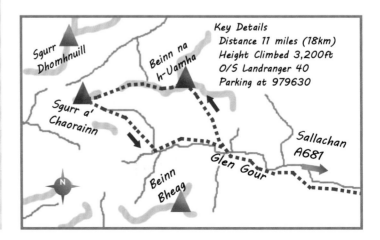

Key Details
Distance 11 miles (18km)
Height Climbed 3,200ft
O/S Landranger 40
Parking at 979630

GLEN LOY

BEINN BHAN *(2,612ft)*
MEALL A' PHUBUILL
(2,540ft)

» Meall a' Phubuill and Beinn
Bhan are two Corbetts that can
be climbed in the same day.

» Meall a' Phubuill is overlooked
by Gulvain and is a much
longer walk than Beinn Bhan.

My Routes

BEINN BHAN (2-3 hours)

I parked at Inverskilavulin. A
path led steeply up the hillside to the right of the burn. It
climbed NE up the corrie then
north on reaching the ridge.
The trig point was on the east
side of the summit plateau. I
returned the same way.

MEALL A' PHUBUILL
(4-5 hours)

I parked at the end of the glen
near Achnanellan. A track
led west past Brian Choille
wood. After passing the wood
I climbed NW up the hillside
to the ridge leading to point
747m. I followed the wall down
to the col and then climbed
Meall a' Phubuill.

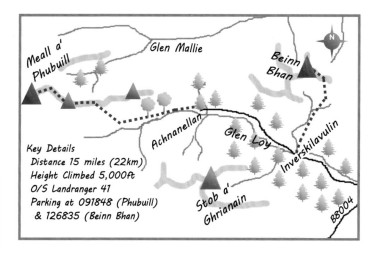

Key Details
Distance 15 miles (22km)
Height Climbed 5,000ft
O/S Landranger 41
Parking at 091848 (Phubuill)
& 126835 (Beinn Bhan)

Personal View

These Corbetts lie up Glen Loy and there is a road as far as
Achnanellan. I climbed both Corbetts on my first and only visit to
Glen Loy. Meall a' Phubuill was further from the end of the road than
I expected and there is a 300ft drop from point 747m making this
east top a 'hump'. On arriving at the summit I was surprised to see
Gulvain close by looking down on Meall a' Phubuill. After returning
to the car I drove to Beinn Bhan which was a straight slog up steep
slopes, hard work as I was tired after climbing Phubuill. There were
good views of Ben Nevis from the summit.

Beinn Bhan from the east.

Point 747m from Meall a' Phubuill
(2011).

GULVAIN

GULVAIN (3,238ft)
BRAIGH NAN UAMHACHAN (2,510ft)

» One Munro and one Corbett lying north of the road from Fort William to Glenfinnan.

» This is an enjoyable circuit and Braigh nan Uamhachan should be included to create a good round and to avoid returning later.

» Gulvain is a shy and retiring Munro not easily seen from the road.

My Route (6-8 hours)

The route started at the main A830 road 1km west of the west end of Loch Eil. We drove along a rough road for 3km although it would be better to walk or cycle this section.

After parking we walked a further 3km up Gleann Fionn Lighe. We climbed NNE up steep grassy slopes to point 855m then continued north to the south top which had a Trig Point. It was a further 1km to the summit.

We descended west and went past Gualann nan Osna before ascending SW to the summit of Braigh nan Uamhachan. We walked south along the ridge going over Sron Liath before descending to the valley.

POINTS OF INTEREST

Old Drove routes run either side of Gulvain and used to connect Loch Eil to Strathan and Achnacarry.

Stopping for a rest on the way up Gulvain in 1999.

Personal View (Alistair)

After climbing Coireachan and Thuilm, we camped at the highest point in Gleann Cuirnean. The following morning Jonathan, JP and his wife Ella deserted me to climb Streap leaving just Corrie, my Beardie dog, and I to make the rough trek to Gulvain, three to four miles on the map, a lot longer on the ground.

Just as we were about to start the steep ascent to the Gulvain ridge, a very large looking fox appeared 50 yards in front of us. I wondered, could it be a lynx? Corrie was nervous, growling and staying close by. The fox (or was it a lynx) disappeared and we continued over Gulvain and the long walk down Gleann Fionn Lighe. It was raining but hopefully my car would be at the end of the Glen. But no sign of the car; Jonathan, my younger brother, had told me to leave it in the wrong place!

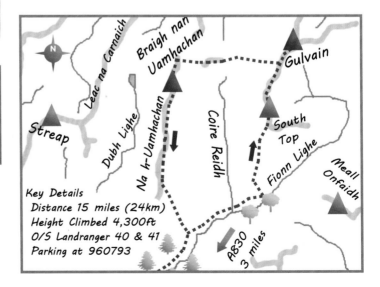

Key Details
Distance 15 miles (24km)
Height Climbed 4,300ft
O/S Landranger 40 & 41
Parking at 960793

SGURR AN UTHA

SGURR AN UTHA *(2,610ft)*

» Sgurr an Utha is a solitary Corbett near Glenfinnan.

» There are great views north and south from Sgurr an Utha in clear weather.

My Route (3-4 hours)

The route started just over one mile west of Glenfinnan village. I left the A830 at the Allt Feith a' Chatha and followed a track up the east side of the stream. After a few hundred metres the path met a good track which I followed north then east up the hillside.

The track stopped abruptly at 1,700ft and I climbed NE up a wide ridge towards Fraoch-bheinn, turning NNW to the col between Fraoch-bheinn and Sgurr An Utha. From the col I went west to the summit. I returned to the col then descended SW near the Allt an Utha to return to the good track and the start.

For reference, see map on Glenfinnan on page 211.

Key Details

» Distance 5.5 miles (9km)
» Height climbed 2,100ft
» O/S Landranger 40
» Parking at 876818.

POINTS OF INTEREST

The area around Fraoch-bheinn is magnetic. Route finding is difficult in the mist so extra care should be taken. Near the summit of Sgurr an Utha the problem disappears.

Personal View (The Compass)

I am eleven years old and have always had the same owner (Barry). He can be grumpy, particularly when I am out of the rucksack and having to show him the way. Frustratingly when the sun shines I am forgotten about, either left in the car or in the back of his rucksack. Generally life is uneventful but I have been in some scrapes. The worst was on a mountain called Sgurr an Utha near Glenfinnan.

It was a terrible November day and I would have preferred to stay in the car but Barry was clearly determined to climb something. After nearly an hour of walking I was removed from the rucksack. It was raining heavily and visibility was down to about ten yards, I knew we should never have left the car. All went well for a while, we followed a bearing of 45 degrees east. I was feeling strong which was just as well as I was being handheld and the rain was turning to snow.

Suddenly I started to feel dizzy, my magnetic head pulled in all directions. Barry was looking at me thinking maybe I was too old for this. I tried to get a grip but it felt hopeless. We wandered about in circles and Barry was becoming very grumpy. I tried to focus telling myself to head 25 degrees west of north then suddenly I started to feel better; what a relief! We marched quickly to the summit of Sgurr an Utha and to this day I don't understand what happened.

The Allt Feith a' Chatha on the ascent of Sgurr an Utha (2012).

GLENFINNAN

Sgurr Thuilm from Carn Mor.

SGURR THUILM *(3,160ft)*
SGURR NAN COIREACHAN
(3,136ft)
STREAP *(2,982ft).*

» Sgurr Thuilm and Sgurr nan
Coireachan give an interesting
round from Glenfinnan with
great views into Knoydart if
the weather is clear.

» Streap is one of the best known
and finest Corbetts in Scotland
often regarded as the steepest
mountain in Britain.

» Bonnie Prince Charlie raised
his standard at Glenfinnan on
19 August 1745 and spent a
night on Sgurr Thuilm after
his defeat at Culloden.

Personal View

Sgurr Thuilm and Sgurr nan Coireachan make a good round from
Glenfinnan which could be speeded up by using a bike up the private
road to the stream running out of Coire Thollaidh. However, on my
round I didn't have a bike or any luck with the weather. Forty days
of dry and sunny weather had just finished as I struggled up Sgurr
Thuilm in heavy rain and a strong SW wind in 1992. At the summit
I drank some water, ate a chocolate bar and turned into the SW
wind. It was shocking, the rain lashed down and I couldn't see anything. Just as I was about to give up a path and line of fence posts
appeared. The rain eased until I was making the final ascent to
Coireachan. After that it was grim going even when I emerged from
the mist at 1,000ft, the streams now raging torrents.

Many years later I returned to climb Streap, a superb Corbett with
steep sides and knife edged ridges. The car park at Glenfinnan was
buzzing when I arrived on Bank Holiday Monday at the end of May.
Unfortunately the midges were joining in so I moved on quickly. I
set off across the bridge and along the private road to Corryhully.
After walking along the tarmac road to Corryhully bothy I was soon
climbing steep grassy slopes to reach the 'ramp' which gave easy
access to Streap's fine summit ridge. The summit was a magnificent
perch before I headed down to rejoin the crowds at Glenfinnan.

My Routes

SGURR THUILM AND SGURR NAN COIREACHAN (6-8 hours)

I started at the Glenfinnan Visitors Centre car park (cost £2 in 2014). The route started with an easy walk up the private road on the west side of the River Finnan past Glenfinnan Lodge. I continued NE at the end of the road and crossed the stream running out of Coire Thollaidh.

From there I climbed the Druim Coire a' Bheithe ridge and headed north to the summit of Sgurr Thuilm. I returned south for a short distance then walked west and NW along the ridge to Sgurr nan Coireachan. Fortunately there was a path and fence posts to guide me.

I descended SE over Sgurr a' Choire Riabhaich keeping to the crest of the ridge. A stalkers' path appeared which took me down to Corryhully Lodge.

STREAP (5-6 hours)

I parked at the Glenfinnan Visitors Centre and followed the private road past Corryhully Bothy. Soon I reached the stalkers' path which led over the pass. After following this for 500m I crossed the stream and climbed steeply east up grassy slopes. After 1,000ft of steep climbing the ramp appeared giving easier climbing to the col between Stob Coire nan Cearc and Streap. A magnificent ridge then led to the summit of Streap.

Key Details

» **Distance 13 miles (21km) (Munros) and 10 miles (16km) (Streap)**
» **Height climbed 4,400ft (Munros) and 2,900ft (Streap)**
» **O/S Landranger 40**
» **Parking at 908807 (both walks).**

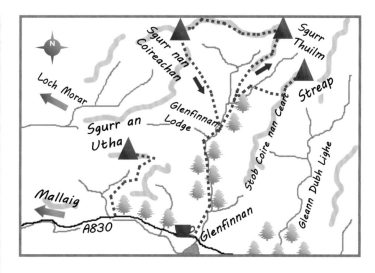

The Glenfinnan Monument at the start point for these summits, Sgurr Ghiubhsachain behind.

GLEN DESSARRY

Looking west from the summit of Bidean a' Chabhair, Loch Nevis on the right (2015).

**SGURR MHURLAGAIN
(2,886ft)
FRAOCH BHEINN (2,815ft)
SGURR COS NA
BREACHD-LAOIDH (2,739ft)
BIDEAN A' CHABHAIR
(2,844ft)
CARN MOR (2,719ft)**

» Five substantial Corbetts at the head of Loch Arkaig, three to the north of Glen Dessarry and two to the south.

» There are low cols between all the Corbetts which means nearly 12,000ft of climbing is needed to complete all five Corbetts.

» Bidean a' Chabhair is the best peak with superb views down Loch Monar and Loch Nevis.

Personal View

The road along the north side of Loch Arkaig to Glen Dessarry is one of the most testing in Scotland, a single track road twisting and turning above the loch side, perfect for the next James Bond car chase! I arrived at the end of the road feeling carsick only to find I had no lunch, just a bottle of water and nearly 6,000ft of climbing ahead. The weather was good though and I enjoyed the challenge of climbing the three Corbetts just to the north of Glen Dessarry in near perfect conditions.

Seven years later I returned along Loch Arkaig to Strathan; once more the weather was perfect. I took the bike out of the car and set off along the forest track meeting some stalkers who were shooting on the hills to the north. I left the bike by a bridge and continued to the eastern foot of Bidean a' Chabhair. The weather was clear and at times sunny, great walking weather. I reached the ridge at 2,000ft and started to approach the summit of Bidean a' Chabhair. This is a magnificent and underrated peak, a sharp summit, a superb long ridge and a glorious setting.

The crossing to Carn Mor was never going to be easy, over 2,000ft of descent down steep slopes then back up again. I had plenty of water, mint cake and an energy drink to keep me going. Finally the summit slopes appeared and there were more great views, this time south over the Glenfinnan Munros.

My Routes

THREE EASTERN CORBETTS
(7-9 hours)

Not far past Strathan a path went off to the right along the east side of the Dearg Allt. After following this for 2.5km to the bealach between Sgurr Mhurlagain and Fraoch Bheinn, I went NE up the hillside for 2km to the summit of Sgurr Mhurlagain. I returned to the bealach then climbed west up steep hillside to the south ridge of Fraoch Bheinn. I followed this to the summit. To descend I went down the south ridge for 1km, then turned west to the foot of the SE ridge of Druim a' Chuirn.

I climbed the SE ridge to Druim a' Chuirn, then the ridge went west to Sgurr Cos na Breachd-Laoidh, the final Corbett. From there I descended to Glen Dessarry and on to Strathan.

TWO WESTERN CORBETTS
(with bike 8-10 hours)

This was a tough walk to complete in one day. I parked at Strathan at the end of Loch Arkaig and cycled through the forest on the south side of the glen to a bridge (930934). I continued on foot coming out of the forest at the east end of Bidean a' Chabhair. From there I climbed west up Meall na Sroine. The undulating ridge of Druim Coire nan Laogh led to the summit of Bidean a' Chabhair.

I retraced my steps down the ridge until I was at a height of 2,000ft. A descent SE down steep grassy slopes led to the stream which divides Carn Mor and Bidean a' Chabhair at 906928. I climbed steeply south to the NE ridge of Carn Mor and followed a line of old fence posts to the summit. From Carn Mor I descended ENE over Meall nan Sparden, continuing NNE to a gap in the forest to collect the bike.

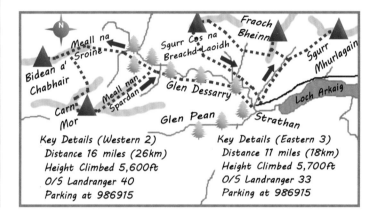

Key Details (Western 2)
Distance 16 miles (26km)
Height Climbed 5,600ft
O/S Landranger 40
Parking at 986915

Key Details (Eastern 3)
Distance 11 miles (18km)
Height Climbed 5,700ft
O/S Landranger 33
Parking at 986915

The Rough Bounds of Knoydart, North Glen Dessarry Corbetts from Bidean a' Chabhair.

SGURR NA CICHE

The Rough Bounds of Knoydart, Sgurr na Ciche from Ben Aden.

SGURR NA CICHE *(3,412ft)*
GARBH CHIOCH MHOR
(3,323ft)
SGURR NAN COIREACHAN
(3,125ft)

» **Three remote Munros in the Rough Bounds of Knoydart.**

» **Sgurr na Ciche is the most spectacular mountain and its pointed summit is prominent from the surrounding hills.**

» **The walk is a long day from Strathan at the head of Loch Arkaig and during the winter months it is hard to complete the walk in daylight.**

» **A prominent wall helps navigation over Garbh Chioch Mhor.**

Personal View

Jonathan, JP and I climbed these Munros on the second day of our two day trip to the Rough Bounds of Knoydart in 1990. At Kinbreack Bothy we had breakfast which comprised biscuits, a bread roll and a cup of tea. We left the bothy at 9 a.m., too late really but the weather had not been inviting. The rain poured down as we waded a river and followed a stalkers' path to the col between Sgurr Beag and An Eag, but it improved briefly as we approached the summit of Sgurr nan Coireachan.

From Sgurr nan Coireachan we descended 700ft then began to climb Garbh Chioch Mhor using the wall as a guide. On and on we walked beside the wall clambering over the rocks in mist. We finally reached the summit over ninety minutes after leaving Sgurr nan Coireachan and more than thirty minutes longer than the time given in the SMC Guide. I guess this section may be easier on a clear day.

We descended from Garbh Chioch Mhor and left the rucksacks at the col before ascending Sgurr na Ciche. The rain became heavier again on Sgurr na Ciche, a magnificent summit. JP wanted to wait for the mist to clear so we could see the views but clearly he had gone mad so we ignored him. We returned to the col in worsening weather, crossed a grassy plateau under Garbh Chioch Mhor, then headed down to Glen Dessarry and a two hour walk back to the car.

My Route (9-10 hours)

We started from Kinbreack Bothy. This is a similar distance as the route from the car park at Strathan and joins the latter route at the summit of Sgurr nan Coireachan. From Kinbreack Bothy we headed west crossing the River Kingie after 1km. We joined the stalkers' path which went west and eventually led to the ridge between Sgurr Beag and An Eag. We followed the ridge to the summit of Sgurr nan Coireachan.

We descended WSW to the Bealach nan Gall and then climbed west up Garbh Chioch Beag and Mhor. The terrain was rocky but a path and a remarkably well built wall guided us. We passed over Garbh Chioch Beag and on to the main Munro summit. We continued beside the wall walking west then NW and dropped to the col below Sgurr na Ciche. A path led up Sgurr na Ciche skirting round towards the west side to avoid the crags.

We returned to the col and descended SW towards Coire na Ciche. At a height of just over 2,000ft we turned SE along a grassy plateau beneath Garbh Chioch Mhor, then descended grassy slopes to Glen Dessary and a long walk back to the car.

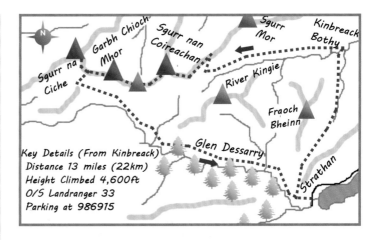

Key Details (From Kinbreack)
Distance 13 miles (22km)
Height Climbed 4,600ft
O/S Landranger 33
Parking at 986915

POINTS OF INTEREST

It is likely that Prince Charles passed close to the site of Kinbreak Bothy during his escape after Culloden in 1746 when he walked over the mountains from Glenfinnan to Loch Quoich.

JP surveys the scene from Kinbreack Bothy before our wet round of these three Munros in 1990.

PLACES TO STAY/DRINK

There is a bothy at Sourlies which would be an alternative starting point for Sgurr na Ciche but it is difficult to reach. There is no accommodation at Strathan so we returned to Spean Bridge.

BEINN BHUIDHE

BEINN BHUIDHE *(2,805ft)*

» Beinn Bhuidhe is a Corbett with a long summit ridge lying south of Inverie.

» The summit ridge has some of the best views in Scotland looking over Loch Ness, the Knoydart Munros and the Isles of Skye and Rum.

Looking west along the summit ridge of Beinn Bhuidhe (2015).

My Route (5-6 hours)

I started from Inverie bunkhouse. This lies 200 metres to the south of where the track heads off from Inverie to Kinloch Hourn via Barrisdale.

Soon after passing the Brocket Memorial, I turned right and followed a path over a bridge and up Gleann Meadail. Just before another bridge back to the north side of the river I left the track and headed SE next to a deer fence.

I crossed the deer fence at a high stile and continued SE crossing the fence again. A steep climb followed beside the west side of a stream. I continued until I reached a triple junction of the stream, then followed the middle stream. This gave a steep ascent to Beinn Bhuidhe's west ridge. The stream to the west is probably easier and I came down this way.

After reaching the ridge I turned east and climbed easy slopes to arrive at the summit trig point.

For reference, see Luinne Bheinn map on page 222.

Personal View

Beinn Bhuidhe is the third Corbett near Inverie lying to the south of the village. It is a bulky Corbett with a long ridge and excellent views over the Isle of Rum. It looked as though there could be a short spell of good weather around Inverie over the May Bank Holiday so I set off north staying at Moffat on Saturday night.

Heavy rain had partially flooded the roads as I drove up from Moffat along the west side of Loch Lomond. Further north the temperature dropped to three degrees as I headed over Rannoch Moor hoping that the weather would improve. After stopping for a coffee at Glencoe I arrived at Mallaig in plenty of time to catch the ferryboat crossing to Inverie.

At last some good news, the boatman said the forecast was for the wind to drop by 6 p.m. and as the cloud had risen to 2,500ft, I thought I should make it to the summit. The boatman also explained that it had been the worst winter for storms in the far west of Scotland that he had known and it had not been possible to cross to Inverie on a number of occasions.

Highland cattle blocked the track to Barrisdale but after that it was an uneventful climb with the weather improving as predicted, giving good views from Beinn Bhuidhe's summit ridge. Surprisingly deer had replaced the cattle on the way back and they appeared very tame, staying within ten yards as I passed by them. I was back at the bunkhouse just after 9 p.m. After a quick shower I made my way to The Old Forge for a couple of drinks and a pizza.

Key Details

» Distance 10 miles (16km)
» Height climbed 3,000ft
» O/S Landranger 33
» Start at Inverie, 776995.

PLACES TO STAY/DRINK

I stayed at the Inverie bunkhouse which was warm, comfortable and friendly and had a pizza at The Old Forge after arriving too late for dinner.

INVERIE CORBETTS

SGURR COIRE CHOINNICHEAN *(2,612ft)*
BEINN NA CAILLICH *(2,575ft)*

» Two Corbetts climbed from Inverie which can be combined.

POINTS OF INTEREST
The Knoydart Foundation purchased the Knoydart Estate in 1997. It is a charity and has an excellent website.

PLACES TO STAY/DRINK
Accommodation at Inverie includes guest houses, a bunkhouse, self catering accommodation and a campsite. There is also a pub, The Old Forge, and a tea shop.

Key Details
» Distance 14 miles (22km)
» Height climbed 5,000ft
» O/S Landranger 33
» Start at Inverie, 776995.

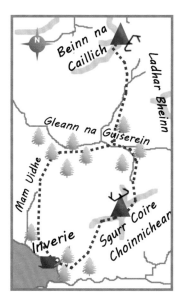

Personal View

It had rained heavily for most of the night but had nearly stopped as I darted over from the bunkhouse to the snack van for a bacon roll. By 8 a.m. I was on my way to Beinn na Caillich. It was a long walk. Just after crossing the bridge near Folach I passed some raging waterfalls. The final climb to Beinn na Caillich was steep but by 11 a.m. I was relieved to be on the summit looking over at Beinn Sgritheall across Loch Hourn.

I returned to Gleann na Guiserein feeling unfit and dreading the ascent of Sgurr Coire Choinnichean. I decided to take a direct route from the bridge near Folach. Initially the ground was soft which was hard to ascend. My water supply ran out when I reached 1,300ft but the streams were full so I splashed water over my face to cool off. I clambered to the summit ridge which was narrow but magnificent, a great place to be in warm afternoon sunshine. I took in the views before the short but steep descent to the coffee shop in Inverie.

View west over Inverie Bay from Sgurr Coire Choinnichean (2015).

My Route (7-8 hours)

From Inverie I followed the Mam Uidhe track for 3km then turned right along another good track down Gleann na Guiserein. After 2.5km I crossed a bridge to follow a path NNE up the glen. I took a left fork towards Mam Li and waded the river. At a height of 1,000ft I turned left to ascend steep stony slopes to the summit ridge of Beinn na Caillich. On reaching the ridge it was a short walk to the summit.

After retracing my steps to the bridge in Gleann na Guiserein, I climbed south following the east side of the Garsley Burn. At 1,500ft the ground became more open and easier to climb. Soon I reached the summit ridge of Sgurr Coire Choinnichean which I followed 1km west to the summit. I descended SW reaching the Barrisdale track a few hundred metres from the bunkhouse.

LADHAR BHEINN

Ascending Ladhar Bheinn in 1992.

LADHAR BHEINN *(3,345ft)*

» Ladhar Bheinn (pronounced Larven) is one of the great Scottish Munros and in my view one of the top five mountains in Britain.

» Ladhar Bheinn is a remote Munro. It is normally climbed from Inverie (a boat trip to get there) or Kinloch Hourn (five mile walk in).

» We combined this walk with Meall Buidhe and Luinne Bheinn and an overnight stop at Barrisdale Bothy.

Personal View (Jonathan)

I hold Ladhar Bheinn in great affection, in my view it is the best mainland mountain in Scotland. We walked in from Inverie to Barrisdale traversing Luinne Bheinn and its mate in the rain but the bothy at Barrisdale was dry and pleasant. The next day dawned bright and sunny and we headed along the shoreline of Loch Hourn before climbing south and then gradually west to reach the fine north east ridge. Here the walk came into its own. I love mountains that drop directly into the sea and Ladhar Bheinn does just that. The best views are from the trig point: The Isles of Skye, Rhum, Eigg and Muck to the west and the mountains of the great glens to the north.

Barry was complaining, five days in the mountains seemed to have taken its toll, so we headed down. The return to Barrisdale was enjoyable with great views along the length of Loch Hourn but there was a sting in the tail. The long five mile walk back to the car at Kinloch Hourn was tortuous with 1,000ft of climbing on the lochside path. Finally we reached the welcome sight of Kinloch Hourn and soon after we sat outside the Cluanie Inn with a pint enjoying the evening sunshine after a special day.

LADHAR BHEINN continued

My Route (return to Barrisdale, 6-7 hours)

From Barrisdale Bothy we took the path to Inverie which crossed a river after 1km. After crossing the river we turned right along a stalkers' path which led to Coire Dhorrcail. The stalkers' path continued for a few hundred metres, then we climbed west to reach the NE ridge of Ladhar Bheinn.

The path made its way up the magnificent NE ridge over Stob a' Choire Odhar and continued to the summit. We walked along the west ridge for 500m to the trig point. Although this is 30ft lower than the summit, the views were fantastic.

We returned by the same route to Barrisdale Bothy and then walked along Loch Hourn to Kinloch Hourn. This was a long way and thus it was six hours between reaching the summit and finishing the walk. Alternatives would be to traverse the west ridge and walk out to Inverie, or arrange a boat from Corran to Barrisdale Bay.

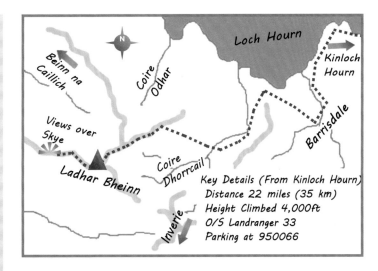

Key Details (From Kinloch Hourn)
Distance 22 miles (35 km)
Height Climbed 4,000ft
O/S Landranger 33
Parking at 950066

Clear waters at Barrisdale Bay *(Heather Thomas-Smith)*.

POINTS OF INTEREST

Ladhar Bheinn is the most westerly Scottish Munro on the mainland. It overlooks Loch Hourn which is often described as the most fjord-like of the sea lochs of north west Scotland.

PLACES TO STAY/DRINK

We stayed in the bothy at Barrisdale which is close to Ladhar Bheinn. The nearest place for food and drink is Inverie where there is a pub and coffee shop or Kinloch Hourn where there is a farm serving tea and snacks.

BEN ADEN

Summit of Ben Aden with Meall Bhuidhe and Luinne Bheinn behind (2016).

BEN ADEN *(2,910ft)*
SGURR NAN EUGALLT *(2,946ft)*

» Ben Aden and Sgurr nan Eugallt are two high Corbetts near the west end of Loch Quoich.

» Ben Aden is one of the great Scottish peaks, a magnificent rocky summit near Sgurr na Ciche and the Rough Bounds of Knoydart.

» Ben Aden is challenging to reach. Using a kayak to the west end of Loch Quoich made the trip more enjoyable.

» Sgurr nan Eugallt is a short ascent from near Kinloch Hourn with a path most of the way to the summit.

Personal View

Ben Aden is one of the great Scottish mountains, a rock peak situated at the remote head of Loch Quoich with great views to its neighbours, including nearby Sgurr na Ciche. It is a challenge to climb Ben Aden, the route along the side of Loch Quoich can be impassable after heavy rain. Alternatively it could be climbed from Barrisdale or Sourlies but neither is easy to reach.

Alistair, however, came up with the answer. Jonathan and I would canoe to the end of Loch Quoich using a Canadian sea kayak. Although Alistair had already canoed to a number of Munros we had not yet used this method of transport. It was superb, we launched the canoe from the roadside and with the loch like a millpond started the five mile trip to the west end of Loch Quoich. Mist, the dog, looked puzzled as she sat in the boat with a life jacket on.

In sunny conditions it took us two hours to reach the magnificent summit of Ben Aden from the west end of Loch Quoich. Sgurr na Ciche towered above to the south and to the west lay Meall Bhuidhe and Luinne Bheinn with the Cuillin ridge behind. A fantastic day completed by staying at Kyleakin on Skye watching the evening sun disappear behind Raasay.

My Routes

BEN ADEN (7-9 hours)

We parked at a car park close to the shore of Loch Quoich and pulled the kayak down to the edge of the lake. We paddled the kayak just over five miles to the west end of Loch Quoich and stepped onto the shore, stiff with the effort.

From the shore we walked nearly 1km along the path towards Lochan nam Breac. From there we climbed up the hillside, arriving at the rocky summit ridge just east of the final 600 foot summit tower. It was possible to avoid all difficulties to reach the cairn at the far west end of the mountain. We returned the same way although with more time we would have traversed the summit ridge over Meall a' Choire Dhuibhe.

SGURR NAN EUGALLT
(3-4 hours)

There was parking west of the ruined cottage of Coireshubh. From the cottage a stalkers' path climbed west then NW and finally SW to the NE ridge at just over 2,000ft. The path reached the ridge at a bealach between Sgurr Dubh and Sgurr nan Eugallt.

After mistakenly climbing most of the way up Sgurr Dubh, I returned to the bealach and climbed SW up Sgurr nan Eugallt arriving directly at the trig point. From here I walked 500m NW on fairly level ground to the summit which is six feet higher than the trig point.

Key Details

» **Distance 5 miles (8km)**

» **Height climbed 2,500ft**

» **O/S Landranger 33**

» **Parking at 959053.**

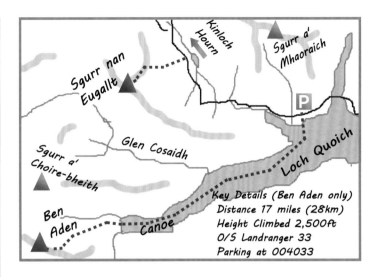

Key Details (Ben Aden only)
Distance 17 miles (28km)
Height Climbed 2,500ft
O/S Landranger 33
Parking at 004033

At the west end of Loch Quoich (2016).

LUINNE BHEINN RIDGE

MEALL BUIDHE *(3,105ft)*
LUINNE BHEINN *(3,082ft)*
SGURR A' CHOIRE-BHEITHE
(2,994ft)

» Three remote and rocky mountains best climbed from Inverie or Barrisdale.

Sgurr a' Choire-bheithe (left) and Luinne Bheinn (right) from Barrisdale Bay (2015).

My Routes

MEALL BUIDHE AND LUINNE BHEINN
(8-10 hours from Inverie)
From Inverie we followed the estate road which ran east up the glen beside the Inverie river. After 3.5km and just past the Brocket Memorial, we took the right hand track, crossed the river and continued to the Mam Meadail at 1,800ft.

We climbed north up steep slopes keeping to the east side to avoid crags and aiming for a col west of Sgurr Sgeithe. From there we climbed the SE ridge to the east top of Meall Buidhe and continued to the summit.

We retraced our steps to the east top, descended the narrow NE ridge to a bealach and climbed 300ft over Druim Leac a' Shith. After descending to Bealach a' Choire Odhair at 2,200ft, we climbed NE to reach the SE top then the summit of Luinne Bheinn. From the summit it was possible to descend directly to Barrisdale.

SGURR A' CHOIRE-BHEITHE
(4-5 hours from Barrisdale)
We arranged a boat from Corran which dropped us off directly below Ladhar Bheinn. This gave an awkward walk along the shoreline to Barrisdale. From here I ascended the long WNW ridge to the summit of Sgurr a' Choire-bheithe in heavy showers. I returned to Barrisdale, met Alistair, and we caught the boat back to Corran.

Personal View

I climbed these three remote mountains in two separate trips using boats to reach the start points at Inverie (Meall Buidhe and Luinne Bheinn) and Barrisdale (Sgurr a' Choire-bheithe). All three mountains are in the heart of Knoydart, remote and beautiful but with a tendency to be very wet, as it was on both my walks.

In 1992, the boat left Mallaig at 10.30 a.m. filled with schoolchildren heading back to Inverie for the holidays. We stepped ashore at Inverie and went straight into the tea room, ordering tea and a fried egg sandwich before a hard day on the hills. After this late breakfast, we climbed Meall Buidhe and Luinne Bheinn finishing at the bothy at Barrisdale. We missed Sgurr a' Choire-bheithe so in 2015 Alistair arranged for a boat to take us over to Barrisdale from Corran. He climbed Ladhar Bheinn and I climbed Sgurr a' Choire-bheithe.

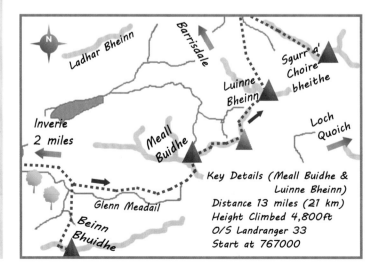

Key Details (Meall Buidhe & Luinne Bheinn)
Distance 13 miles (21 km)
Height Climbed 4,800ft
O/S Landranger 33
Start at 767000

SGURR MOR

SGURR MOR *(3,290ft)*
GAIRICH *(3,015ft)*
SGURR AN FHUARAIN
(2,956ft)

» A long walk over two Munros and a Corbett.

» Gairich could be climbed on its own from Loch Quoich dam.

My Route (10-12 hours for return to Strathan)

We parked at Strathan at the end of Loch Arkaig. Not far past Strathan a path went NE along the Dearg Allt. We followed this and, after 5km, we reached Kinbreack Bothy. The path was indistinct at times over the watershed.

From the bothy we crossed the river and headed west up Glen Kingie for just over 2km, then climbed the hillside to the col between Sgurr Beag and Sgurr Mor. We followed a path over Sgurr Mor and Sgurr an Fhuarain, then descended east off Sgurr an Fhuarain.

We walked north to find another path that led up the west side of Gairich Beag and continued NE to Gairich. After returning to the low col between Gairich and Sgurr An Fhuarain, a stalkers' path led back to Kinbreack Bothy.

Key Details (from Strathan)

» Distance 15 miles (24km)
» Height climbed 7,400ft
» O/S Landranger 33
» Parking at 986915.

POINTS OF INTEREST

Sgurr Mor is one of the most remote Munros in Scotland. Canoeing across Loch Quoich is the shortest route to the mountain.

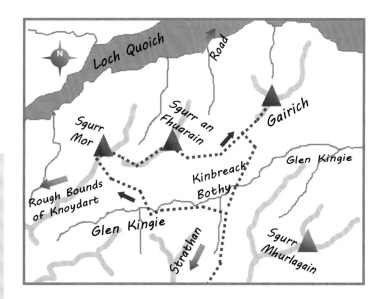

Personal View (Alistair)

I recommend ignoring Barry's route to Sgurr Mor and canoeing across Loch Quoich avoiding over ten miles of wet bog and 1,500ft of climbing. I made the trip in the summer of 2012 finding a track down to the loch from near the start of Sgurr a' Mhaoraich. It was a couple of miles canoeing across the loch to a beach at the start of the Allt a' Choire Bhuidhe. Strangely there was also a hut housing an off road vehicle. Initially I followed a stalkers' track then crossed the stream and followed what must be a relatively untouched route to the ridge.

On the summit plateau I found cycle tracks; that must have been some effort! There were fantastic views from the summit, the mist swirling around showing the Munros to the north and mighty Ben Aden. Then it was down the route of ascent. I was concerned that if my canoe had been tampered with 'I would be up the creek without a paddle' but all was well.

Have we any idea where we are? Jonathan and JP on the way to Gairich in 1990.

THE DARK MILE

MEALL NA H-EILDE *(2,749ft)*
GEAL CHARN *(2,638ft)*

» Two Corbetts climbed from the east end of Loch Arkaig.

» The views to the east are dominated by the Loch Lochy Munros.

» There is a pleasant high level walk between the Corbetts.

My Route (5-6 hours)

The route started from the B8005 just over a mile from Clunes at the Eas Chia-aig waterfalls (see picture). From the car park I followed a path through the forest for 4km to a footbridge at 187928. From here I climbed north to a bealach then NW to the summit of Meall na h-Eilde.

I climbed NW over Meall Coire nan Saobhaidh, then SW to Geal Charn. I descended SE to a track which headed south down the Allt Dubh to the road. It was 2.5km along the road heading east to return to the start.

Key Details

» **Distance 11 miles (17km)**
» **Height climbed 3,400ft**
» **O/S Landranger 34**
» **Parking at 177889.**

Eas Chia-aig Waterfalls near the start of the walk (2009).

Personal View

This circuit takes in two Corbetts on the north side of the road to Loch Arkaig. They are close to the Loch Lochy Munros and very similar in character to those mountains, The area is steeped in history and the Eas Chia-aig waterfalls should be visited.

I completed an enjoyable round of the two Corbetts on a chilly day with occasional snow showers early in May 2009. I had driven up from Belford in Northumberland, a favourite stopover place when I travel to Scotland via the east coast. Although the distance over these Corbetts was long, the walking was easy and I made good time. Traversing the ridge over Meall Coire nan Saobhaidh between the Corbetts was superb.

POINTS OF INTEREST

The waterfalls at the start point denote the west end of 'The Dark Mile', a narrow tree shaded pass through the woods. 'The Dark Mile' was used as the title by D.K. Broster for a novel set in this area after Culloden. There is a cave just off the road where Bonnie Prince Charlie hid in 1746.

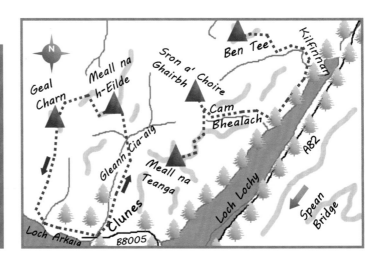

WEST OF LOCH LOCHY

SRON A' CHOIRE GHAIRBH
(3,074ft)
MEALL NA TEANGA *(3,008ft)*
BEN TEE *(2,957ft)*

» The shortest routes to climb all three mountains start from Kilfinnan.

My Routes

SRON A' CHOIRE GHAIRBH AND MEALL NA TEANGA
(5-6 hours)

Kilfinnan lies 4km down a minor road from where the A82 crosses the Loch Laggan swing bridge. From Kilfinnan I walked 3km SW beside Loch Lochy. A path then led up the north side of the Allt Glas Dhoire to a bealach between the two Munros at a height of 2,000ft.

I climbed Meall na Teanga first by ascending south to reach the col between Meall Dubh and Meall na Teanga. Then I climbed SSW to the summit. Returning to the bealach I climbed north up a zigzag path to the summit plateau of Sron a' Choire Ghairbh. I found the summit towards the NW of the plateau.

BEN TEE (3-4 hours) (from Kilfinnan)

I left the road a few hundred metres NE of the Kilfinnan burn and climbed NW on a path up the hillside to a stile over the fence. The route continued WNW over the moorland turning west to reach the east ridge of Ben Tee and the summit.

For reference, see The Dark Mile map opposite.

Key Details

» Distance 11 miles (18km) (Munros) and 5 miles (8km) (Ben Tee)

» Height climbed 3,900ft (Munros) and 2,800ft (Ben Tee)

» O/S Landranger 34

» Parking at 277958 (both walks).

The Loch Lochy Munros seen from the east side of Loch Lochy.

Personal View (Alistair)

In 2001 I set off with my Beardie dog, Corrie, from the car park at the south end of Gleann Cia-aig. I was complacent, two comfortable Munros, good path, no real issues. I climbed Meall Odhar as the cloud came down and the drizzle started. No matter, I continued to the top of Teanga, down to the Bealach and straight up Ghairbh. By now I was looking forward to a pint at the Clachaig Inn. I turned round and headed down the west ridge (or so I thought) intending to join the path of my ascent where it crossed the stream. After thirty minutes I was surprised not to have reached the stream, then some time later I came out of the mist.

I did not immediately recognise where I was so reached for the compass. No compass! I was now very worried, there was no path and no recognisable landmarks, I began to appreciate I had no idea where I was. I checked the map and realised I had come north west off Ghairbh. For some reason I thought the only thing to do was continue. It was dreadful underfoot but eventually I came across a forest and ultimately a forest track which led to a small cluster of houses. From there a very generous guy took pity and drove me back to Glen Garry, thirty miles each way for him, for a mere £20.

Editorial note, Alistair finished thirty miles by road from where he started, surely a record for a six hour climb!

Ben Tee lies just to the north of the two Loch Lochy Munros and can be seen from the road leading west from Invergarry to Kyle of Lochalsh. This Corbett stands out because of its unforgettable name, thought to mean 'Fairy Hill' and conical shape which makes it an excellent viewpoint. I have never climbed Ben Tee and probably never will but Barry climbed it ten years ago. He assures me it is impossible to get lost!

ARNISDALE

Beinn Sgritheall and Beinn na h-Eaglaise from across Loch Hourn *(Heather Thomas-Smith).*

BEINN SGRITHEALL (3,194ft)
BEINN NA H-EAGLAISE
(2,641ft)
BEINN NAN CAORACH
(2,539ft)
BEINN A' CHAPUILL (2,490ft)

» This is the only walk in
the book which contains a
mountain from all three of the
best known lists of Scottish
mountains. The walk includes
one Munro, two Corbetts and
one Graham.

» There are great views over the
Isle of Skye and Knoydart to
the south.

» Arnisdale is a quiet hamlet nine
miles from the nearest shop
in Glenelg.

Personal View (Alistair)

This was a rare occasion when the weather was perfect and what
a great mountain to climb on such an occasion. The views across
Barrisdale Bay to Ladhar Bheinn were stunning. Both my brothers,
JP and the dogs were there. We lounged on the ground below the
Bealach Arnasdail then ambled up to the summit, Barry and Jon-
athan then departing for a Corbett and a Munro Top respectively.

Later we sat in the garden of the Glenelg Inn, the sun setting over
the Isle of Skye, and admired the 'Bonnie Prince Charlie crossing',
a short but interesting crossing as the tidal flow through these
narrows is the second fastest in Scotland.

In July 2014 Barry returned, parking at Balvraid and cycling a further 3.5km down the valley to where he could pick off Beinn a'
Chapuill and Beinn nan Caorach. It was a fine day with only frogs
and deer for company. He started by climbing the ridge to Beinn a'
Chapuill then had some difficulty picking out Beinn nan Caorach
from the jumble of Corbetts and Grahams to the SE. Returning
to 650ft he ascended 2,000ft to reach the summit of Beinn nan
Caorach. Later as the sun came out he drove down to Arnisdale
this time finding a tea hut at Corran.

My Routes

BEINN SGRITHEALL AND BEINN NA H-EAGLAISE (5-6 hours)

In June 2000 we drove to Arnisdale and climbed steeply up to the Bealach Arnasdail on a perfect summer day. From there we climbed Beinn Sgritheall. Jonathan then added a Munro top whilst I decided to climb Beinn na h-Eaglaise. This was a short but steep climb from the Bealach Arnasdail.

Key Details

» Distance 7 miles (12km)
» Height climbed 3,800ft
» O/S Landranger 33
» Parking at 848104.

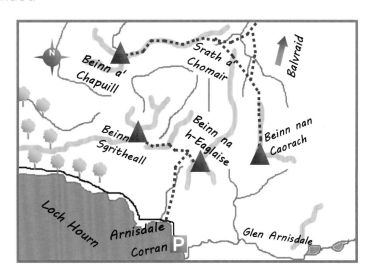

BEINN A' CHAPUILL AND BEINN NAN CAORACH (6-8 hours).

Returning fourteen years later I drove to Balvraid to climb Beinn a' Chapuill and Beinn nan Caorach. As I had the bike with me I cycled along the track towards Kinloch Hourn (reference 874160). However, it would be just as easy to walk this section. From there I followed the track SW for 500m then left the track to cross two streams. On reaching the long east ridge of Beinn a' Chapuill I followed it to the summit.

From there I returned to the bottom of the north ridge of Beinn na h-Eaglaise, then contoured round to the north ridge of Beinn nan Caorach. I followed this ridge to the summit. A line of rusty fence posts appeared near the summit which were a useful guide.

Key Details

» Distance 15 miles (24km)
» Height climbed 4,600ft
» O/S Landranger 33
» Parking at 848166.

POINTS OF INTEREST

Arnisdale is the closest settlement to Camusfearna, the house in which Gavin Maxwell wrote *'Ring of Bright Water'*, the story of his secluded life with his pet otters.

Ascending Beinn Sgritheall *(Chris Wood)*.

NORTH LOCH QUOICH

GLEOURAICH *(3,394ft)*
SGURR A' MHAORAICH
(3,369ft)
SPIDEAN MIALACH *(3,268ft)*

» Three Munros, all Top 500
Summits, north of Loch Quoich
and close to the road.

» The three Munros divide into
two walks but both walks can
be completed in one day.

My Routes

GLEOURAICH AND SPIDEAN MIALACH *(5-6 hours)*

The route started from the
road along the north side of
Loch Quoich just west of the
Allt Coire Peitireach. A good
stalkers' path climbed to
2,800ft on Gleouraich. We
continued up the ridge to a
junction with the north ridge
then climbed SE to the summit
of Gleouraich. We went over
Craig Coire na Fiar Bhealaich, down to Fiar Bhealaich at
2,400ft then climbed SE to
Spidean Mialach.

SGURR A' MHAORAICH *(4-5 hours)*

We parked 1km SW of the
bridge at the north end of Loch
Quoich. A stalkers' path went
north to Sgurr Coire nan-Eiri-
cheallach (891m) and continued to its NW top. We walked
along the ridge in a westerly
direction to Sgurr a' Mhaoraich.

POINTS OF INTEREST

Loch Quoich means 'Loch
of the cup/quaich'. It is now
a reservoir. The dam was
completed in 1962.

Alistair and JP on the summit of Gleouraich (1999).

Personal View (Alistair)

June 1999 and a full turnout for the 'Loch Quoich two or maybe
three'. It was a fine bright day and a great path particularly inspiring
near the summit as it traversed the south-west ridge. Soon we
were on the top of Gleouraich and moving onwards along the ridge
to Mialach. I was enjoying the ridge and the amazing views across
Loch Quoich happy to enjoy the moment.

The others, my brothers and JP, were now keen to climb Mhaoraich,
down to the road and all the way back up. I wasn't, I loitered, sat
down on the path back to the car and fell asleep, happy days! So I
had to return ten years later, now on my own, of course, to Mhaoraich. It was June but still cold, a snow shower passing as I reached
the summit and with worsening weather approaching I hurried down.

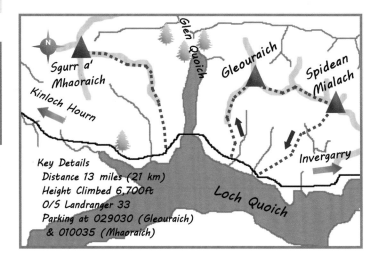

Key Details
Distance 13 miles (21 km)
Height Climbed 6,700ft
O/S Landranger 33
Parking at 029030 (Gleouraich)
& 010035 (Mhaoraich)

Glen Affric in summer.

SCOTLAND: NORTH WEST GLENS

The North West Glens cover the area from Glen Shiel in the south to Glen Carron in the north. There are 53 Top 500 Summits divided into 17 walks:

There are a number of big glens surrounded by mountains lying between the A87 'Road to the Isles' and the A832 and A890 running from Garve to Lochcarron. From south to north the Glens are Glen Shiel, Glen Affric, Glen Cannich, Glen Strathfarrar, Glen Strathconon, and Glen Carron.

In this area there are many challenging walks over multiple Munros including the South Glen Shiel ridge, the Five Sisters, the round of Loch Mullardoch, the Strathfarrar four and trekking to Lurg Mhor, one of the most remote Munros.

The mountains are some of the highest in Britain. They include Carn Eighe, the highest at 3,880ft, Sgurr nan Cea-threamhnan, a complex and remote mountain and Sgurr Fhuaran, the highest of the Five Sisters. It is an area that is dominated by Munros. 31 out of the 53 summits are Munros.

WALKS 1 TO 3

	Walk	Feet	Pg.
1	Druim nan Cnamh	2,592	232
	Meall Dubh	2,585	
2	Aonach air Chrith	3,350	233
	Sgurr an Doire Leathain	3,314	
	Creag nan Damh	3,012	
3	The Saddle	3,314	234
	Sgurr na Sgine	3,104	
	Buidhe Bheinn	2,904	

WALKS 4 TO 17

	Walk	Feet	Pg.
4	Sgurr an Airgid	2,759	236
	Sgurr Mhic Bharraich	2,561	
5	Beinn Fhada	3,385	237
	A' Ghlas-bheinn	3,012	
	Sgurr Gaorsaic	2,752	
6	Sgurr Fhuaran	3,505	238
	Sgurr na Ciste Dubh	3,370	
7	Sgurr a' Bhealaich Dheirg	3,399	239
	Aonach Meadhoin	3,284	
	Ciste Dhubh	3,211	
	Am Bathach	2,618	
8	A' Chralaig	3,673	240
	Sgurr nan Conbhairean	3,639	
	Mullach Fraoch-choire	3,614	
9	Aonach Shasuinn	2,917	241
	Carn a' Choire Ghairbh	2,837	
	Sgurr na Diollaid	2,684	
10	Carn Eighe	3,880	242
	Sgurr nan Ceathreamhnan	3,776	
	Sgurr na Lapaich	3,774	
	An Riabhachan	3,704	
	An Socach	3,508	
	Toll Creagach	3,458	
	Beinn Fhionnlaidh	3,298	
	Carn nan Gobhar	3,255	
11	Aonach Buidhe	2,949	244
	Sguman Coinntich	2,883	
	Faochaig	2,847	
12	Lurg Mhor	3,234	246
	Bidean a' Choire Sheasgaich	3,100	
	Beinn Tharsuinn	2,831	
	Beinn Dronaig	2,615	
13	Fionn Bheinn	3,062	248
	Moruisg	3,045	
	Sgurr nan Ceannaichean	2,995	
14	Sgurr a' Chaorachain	3,455	249
	Maoile Lunndaidh	3,304	
	Sgurr na Feartaig	2,828	
15	Sgurr a' Choire Ghlais	3,554	250
	Sgurr na Ruaidhe	3,258	
	Beinn a' Bha'ach Ard	2,827	
16	Sgurr a' Mhuilinn	2,883	251
	Meallan nan Uan	2,749	
17	Bac an Eich	2,787	252
	An Sidhean	2,671	

Looking north from the South Glen Shiel ridge (*Heather Thomas-Smith*).

CLUANIE CORBETTS

DRUIM NAN CNAMH
(2,592ft)
MEALL DUBH *(2,585ft)*

» Meall Dubh and Druim nan Cnamh are isolated Corbetts between Invergarry and the Cluanie Inn.

» Both are half day expeditions from the A87.

My Routes

DRUIM NAN CNAMH
(with bike 3-4 hours)

I ascended Druim nan Cnamh from the Cluanie Inn. I cycled 6km SE until I was at the highest point of the old road to Loch Loyne and due west of the summit. From there I walked east over peat bogs, heather, grass and rocks. The dry conditions enabled me to make good time to the summit.

MEALL DUBH (2-3 hours)

We climbed Meall Dubh from the A87 parking 2km south of the junction with the A887. There was a gate into the Achlain Beinneun Wood near grid reference 207081. We followed a track for 1km then turned right to emerge from the forest. After 3km of rough going east through heather, we reached the summit.

Key Details (both summits)

» Distance 17 miles (27km)
» Height climbed 3,900ft
» O/S Landranger 33 and 34
» Parking at 076117 (Cluanie Inn) & 207081 (Meall Dubh).

PLACES TO STAY/DRINK

The Cluanie Inn, a well known hotel with a bar, meals and accommodation, lies on the A87 and is well positioned for these Corbetts.

Summit of Druim nan Cnamh looking east (2014).

Personal View

Druim nan Cnamh and Meall Dubh are isolated Corbetts lying between the Cluanie Inn and Invergarry. Druim nan Cnamh can be completed in half a day by cycling 6km up the old road which runs SE from the Cluanie Inn. Meall Dubh is close to the A87 on the route between Invergarry and the Cluanie Inn.

I climbed Meall Dubh on the way back from the Isle of Skye with Jonathan and his dog, Bracken. Meall Dubh was one of Bracken's last mountains. Although she did not climb many Corbetts, she climbed over a hundred Munros and many Munro tops.

A few years later, in 2014, I climbed Druim nan Cnamh on a pleasant summer evening. I started from the Cluanie Inn and found the bike helpful. I was able to cycle most of the way up to the pass and the return journey was brilliant with 6km of descent covered in 15 minutes on the bike.

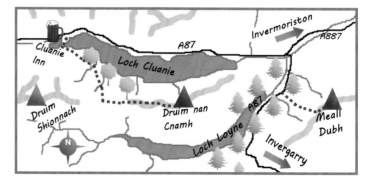

SOUTH GLEN SHIEL RIDGE

AONACH AIR CHRITH
(3,350ft)
**SGURR AN DOIRE
LEATHAIN** *(3,314ft)*
CREAG NAN DAMH *(3,012ft)*

» There are four additional Munros on the South Glen Shiel ridge, Sgurr an Lochain (3,294ft), Druim Shionnach ((3,239ft), Maol Chinn-dearg (3,218ft) and Creag a' Mhaim (3,107ft).

» The traverse of the South Glen Shiel ridge offers a great Munro haul of seven summits which can be completed in one day.

My Route (8-10 hours)

Alistair and I started at the Cluanie Inn. We had left a second car positioned on the A87 at the foot of the final Munro, Creag nan Damh. We walked 3km up the old road. This goes south from just east of the Cluanie Inn and across the bridge over the Allt Giubhais.

After 3km we climbed just west of south to the top of the first Munro, Creag a' Mhaim. From there I followed the ridge all the way to Creag nan Damh at the western end. If there is insufficient time to traverse the ridge it is possible to go down from Maol Chinn-dearg via its NE ridge.

From Creag nan Damh I descended steeply NE to Am Fraoch-choire. At 1,300ft I found a path which led back to the road near the site of the 1719 battle.

POINTS OF INTEREST

The South Glen Shiel ridge used to be regarded as the biggest Munro haul in a single day (for non runners). However the traverse of the Ben Lawers ridge also offers seven Munros following An Stuc's promotion.

Personal View

The A87 or 'The Road to the Isles' as it is sometimes known passes more than twenty Munros on a fifteen mile stretch through Glen Shiel. Seven of these Munros are on the South Glen Shiel ridge and had always appeared to be a good way of increasing my Munro haul. In 2002 I set off with Alistair to complete the ridge.

Starting at the Cluanie Inn we made good progress over the first four Munros then Alistair went down. My progress became slower between Sgurr an Lochain and Creag nan Damh and I was glad we had arranged the cars so there was one waiting for me after the descent.

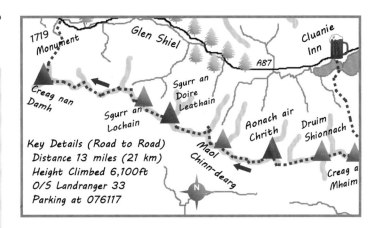

Key Details (Road to Road)
Distance 13 miles (21 km)
Height Climbed 6,100ft
O/S Landranger 33
Parking at 076117

Glen Shiel ridge *(Chris Wood)*.

THE SADDLE

The Forcan ridge on the Saddle, one of the classic Scottish ridges *(Chris Wood)*.

THE SADDLE *(3,314ft)*
SGURR NA SGINE *(3,104ft)*
BUIDHE BHEINN *(2,904ft)*

» The Saddle is a complex mountain with narrow ridges making it one of the best Munros.

» Buidhe Bheinn was listed as the same height as Sgurr a' Bhac Chaolais but a survey in 2012 revealed it as the higher.

» It would be possible to cross from Kinloch Hourn to Glen Shiel over all three summits, the Saddle, Sgurr na Sgine and Buidhe Bheinn. However, this requires transport at both Kinloch Hourn and Glen Shiel.

Personal View

The Saddle was my final Munro in 2004 as it is one of the best Scottish mountains with superb ridges. Unfortunately it rained heavily on our visit and we had no views. Alistair and I climbed Sgurr na Sgine first then, after a slow crossing to The Saddle in atrocious weather, we met Jonathan and JP at the summit for a quick celebration. They had been waiting for us for an hour and were frozen so we headed back down rapidly. Fortunately we had booked dinner at the Glenelg Inn, a lovely spot near the Isle of Skye, so everyone started to feel better when we arrived there and it finally stopped raining.

By 2014 Buidhe Bheinn was winning the height war against Sgurr a' Bhac Chaolais and I drove to Kinloch Hourn to climb it. Kinloch Hourn is 'hard core' with twenty-two miles of deteriorating single track road even to reach it. On arrival I was greeted by walkers' signs to Arnisdale and Inverie. However, these are tough places to reach requiring six hour slogs by walkers who share this remote spot with mountain bikers and canoeists. Buidhe Bheinn is a good mountain with a path most of the way up it but the sea level start meant a tough climb. I was relieved to return to the tea room at the farm, the last refuge in this wild untamed area.

THE SADDLE continued

My Routes

SGURR NA SGINE AND THE SADDLE (6-7 hours)

Alistair and I climbed Sgurr na Sgine and The Saddle from Glen Shiel. As The Saddle was my final Munro it was agreed that Jonathan and JP would meet us at the summit. They were Munro Top bagging. We had an enjoyable climb up Sgurr na Sgine in intermittent sunshine. However, the rain started as we neared the summit and did not let up for the rest of the day.

From the summit of Sgurr na Sgine we headed NW then north along a ridge for 1km. We tried to descend NW to the Bealach Coire Mhalagain but accidentally descended 300ft below it.

After regaining the bealach we climbed NW to the ridge of The Saddle. Jonathan and JP met us at the trig point, although the actual summit may be 100m east of the trig point.

BUIDHE BHEINN (4-5 hours)

Ten years later I climbed Buidhe Bheinn starting at the car park at the end of the road at Kinloch Hourn. I walked back along the road for 500m to cross a bridge then followed the Arnisdale right of way for 1.5km. The second of two stalkers' paths climbed north to 2,200ft. From here I climbed up a gully to the NW ridge and followed the ridge SE over the west top (879m). A rocky ridge led down and back up to the summit.

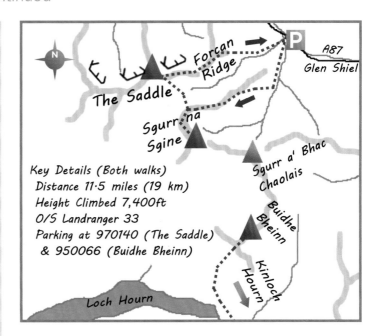

Key Details (Both walks)
Distance 11·5 miles (19 km)
Height Climbed 7,400ft
O/S Landranger 33
Parking at 970140 (The Saddle)
& 950066 (Buidhe Bheinn)

Completion of the Munros on The Saddle on a wet day in 2004.

PLACES TO STAY/DRINK

After climbing The Saddle, we drove to the Glenelg Inn, one of our favourite hotels overlooking the Isle of Skye, for dinner. However, there is accommodation and places to eat much closer, at Shiel Bridge or the Cluanie Inn.

LOCH DUICH CORBETTS

SGURR AN AIRGID *(2,759ft)*
SGURR MHIC BHARRAICH
(2,561ft)

» Two Corbetts near Shiel Bridge.
  Both are half day ascents.

My Routes

SGURR AN AIRGID (3-4 hours)
I parked in Strath Croe and climbed steep slopes finding the stalkers' path at about 1,200ft. After this a path led to the col and on to the summit. I followed the path all the way down to its start which was only 100m along the minor road off the A87.

*SGURR MHIC BHARRAICH
(4-5 hours)*
We started from the campsite at Shiel Bridge, walked south on a good path into a glen and crossed a bridge onto the west side of the stream. After 3km the path turned west and ascended from the glen to Loch Coire nan Crogachan. From there we climbed NW up the slopes to the summit.

Key Details (both summits)

» Total distance 10 miles
  (16km)
» Height climbed 5,200ft
» O/S Landranger 33
» Parking at 945211 (Sgurr
  an Airgid) and 939187
  (Sgurr Mhic Bharraich).

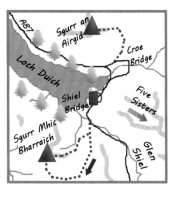

Summit of Sgurr Mhic Bharraich (2009).

POINTS OF INTEREST

There are around 400 breeding pairs of Golden Eagles in Scotland. They are mainly found in the west of Scotland and the Western Isles. There has been a substantial increase in their numbers during my lifetime.

Personal View

These two Corbetts lie to the north and south of Loch Duich near Shiel Bridge. Both are straightforward climbs but the sea level starts mean that completing them in one day is hard work with over 5,000ft of climbing.

Sgurr Mhic Bharraich was the final walk of our Skye trip in June 2009 when we had superb weather every day. It was a Sunday morning climb before returning to the Midlands and we saw two Golden Eagles. Five years later I climbed Sgurr an Airgid and thought it was an underrated mountain with great views. A path runs all the way to the summit from near Shiel Bridge.

PLACES TO STAY/DRINK

The Kintail Lodge Hotel at Shiel Bridge has a bar, food and accommodation including a bunkhouse. There is also a campsite near Shiel Bridge and a youth hostel at Ratagan.

BEINN FHADA

BEINN FHADA *(3,385ft)*
A' GHLAS-BHEINN *(3,012ft)*
SGURR GAORSAIC *(2,752ft)*

» Three Top 500 Summits, two Munros and a Corbett climbed from the head of Loch Duich.

» Sgurr Gaorsaic could be climbed with Ceathreamhnan.

My Routes

BEINN FHADA AND A' GHLAS-BHEINN *(7-8 hours)*

In 1982 Donald and I started at Dorusduain at the end of the public road up Strath Croe. We crossed a bridge and walked 3km up the glen. After turning south, a path climbed the west side of the Allt Coire an Sgairne and onto the ridge south of Meall a' Bhealaich. We climbed SE to the summit of Beinn Fhada.

We descended to Meall a' Bhealaich and then descended to Bealach an Sgairne. From here we climbed NNW up the ridge of A' Ghlas-bheinn past Loch a' Chleirich to the summit.

SGURR GAORSAIC *(5-6 hours)*

Sgurr Gaorsaic could be added after climbing Beinn Fhada by a diversion from the Bealach an Sgairne. However, I started at Dorusduain as for Beinn Fhada and A' Ghlas-bheinn. I walked over the Bealach an Sgairne, before climbing 1,400ft directly to the summit from the south end of Loch a' Bhealaich.

Personal View (Alistair)

In the year 2000 my brothers and JP were ticking off the Skye Munros but these were unsuitable for the dogs, also I did not have the enthusiasm for a long day on the Cuillin ridge. So with two dogs I headed off for mighty Beinn Fhada and its unassuming mate, A' Ghlas-Bheinn. There was an excellent path from the car park at Dorusduain and the day was looking good. A quick ascent and I stood on the summit of Fhada admiring the wilderness to the north and east.

It didn't look far to A' Ghlas-bheinn. Maybe I would be on the top in an hour or so but this proved to be wildly optimistic. Two hours passed as I made an awkward descent to the pass then a tough ascent back up to the summit. Two hours more and I was back at the car with both dogs. In my view I had completed two hard Munros.

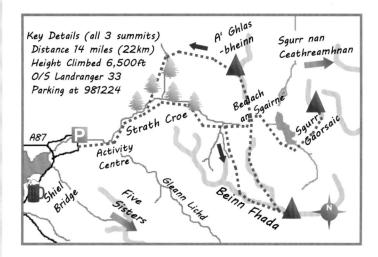

Key Details (all 3 summits)
Distance 14 miles (22km)
Height Climbed 6,500ft
O/S Landranger 33
Parking at 981224

On A' Ghlas-bheinn in 1982, Sgurr nan Ceathreamhnan behind. It was warm enough for a dip.

THE SISTERS OF KINTAIL

SGURR FHUARAN *(3,505ft)*
SGURR NA CISTE DUBH *(3,370ft)*

» The ridge is known as the 'Five Sisters' as there are five peaks, including three Munros which are prominent in the much photographed view across Loch Duich.

» The third Munro is Sgurr na Carnach (3,288ft).

On the Five Sisters ridge *(Chris Wood)*.

My Route (5-6 hours)

In 1976 Alistair and I started at the Suspension bridge on the A87 just east of Loch Duich. We climbed Sgurr nan Saighead, then descended to 2,500ft before making the steep 1,000ft ascent to Sgurr Fhuaran. From here the path dropped 800ft to the col before Sgurr na Carnach.

After some debate (Sgurr na Carnach was not a Munro at the time) we climbed Sgurr na Carnach, then descended to the valley and a long walk back to Shiel Bridge. It would have been better to add Sgurr na Ciste Dubh on this trip. However, I returned twenty-eight years later to climb it together with Saileag directly from the road.

Personal View (Jonathan)

During our traverse of the Five Sisters JP and myself witnessed a remarkable occurrence. The weather was pleasant with cloud lurking around the summits as we tackled the switchback ridge from south to north. Then, in the distance, we heard what sounded like bagpipes. We were in cloud at the time and assumed the sounds were coming from the valley. However, as we hurried along the ridge it was clear that the Piper was on the mountain.

We missed him on the top of Sgurr Fhuaran but caught him on the outlying top of Sgurr nan Saighead. There was a crowd sat around the summit, it was a beautiful evening now and the views to the west added to the surreal atmosphere and a memory I will never forget. I remember little else about the ridge except that there was a succession of steep climbs and descents, particularly around Sgurr Fhuaran, hard work when you are chasing the Piper.

POINTS OF INTEREST

The Battle of Glenshiel was fought in 1719 about a mile east of the foot of Sgurr na Ciste Dubh (the site is marked). The Jacobites, assisted by 300 Spanish troops lost this battle and the uprising came to an end.

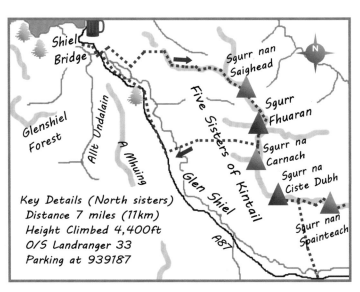

Key Details (North sisters)
Distance 7 miles (11km)
Height Climbed 4,400ft
O/S Landranger 33
Parking at 939187

BROTHERS OF KINTAIL

SGURR A' BHEALAICH DHEIRG (3,399ft)
AONACH MEADHOIN (3,284ft)
CISTE DHUBH (3,211ft)
AM BATHACH (2,618ft)

» Three Munros and a Corbett lying north of the Cluanie Inn. A fourth Munro, Saileag (3,137ft) can be added.

» The ridge is an extension east of the Five Sisters ridge. A traverse of the full ridge is possible in one day and would yield seven Munros.

My Routes

BROTHERS OF KINTAIL (6-7 hours)

Jonathan and I drove 2km west down the A87 from the Cluanie Inn. Just before the forest starts we climbed north up the hillside turning NW after nearly 1km. We followed the Allt Coire Tholl Bhruach, branching right after 1.5km, to go north up the hillside to the col between Sgurr a' Bhealaich Dheirg and Aonach Meadhoin.

We were now on the main ridge and started ticking the Munros by climbing Sgurr a' Bhealaich Dheirg and returning to the col. We continued by climbing Aonach Meadhoin then Sgurr an Fhuarail, a top overlooking the Cluanie Inn. From here we descended NE down a ridge to the Bealach a' Choinich, then climbed north up a narrow ridge to Ciste Dhubh. From this summit it was a long walk back to the Cluanie Inn.

Saileag could be added to this walk.

AM BATHACH (2-3 hours)

I returned in 2007 to climb Am Bathach directly from the Cluanie Inn starting at 6 p.m. It was a wet evening but I was back enjoying dinner at the Cluanie Inn by 8.30 p.m.

Personal View (Alistair)

I cycled down the A87 on a cold but dry November day leaving the bike in the car park below Saileag. There was a good path so I climbed directly for the summit with the snow not too deep. From Saileag the going was hard due to deeper snow and I dropped down south to avoid the worst. Nervously I traversed the final arete to Dheirg (see photo) in thigh deep and virgin snow. The snow continued hindering progress to Meadhoin and Sgurr an Fhuarail (a Munro Top). From Fhuarail it was an easy and fast descent to Cluanie where I had left the car.

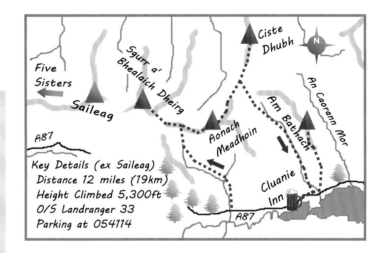

Key Details (ex Saileag)
Distance 12 miles (19km)
Height Climbed 5,300ft
O/S Landranger 33
Parking at 054114

Summit of Sgurr a' Bhealaich Dheirg in winter.

CLUANIE MUNROS

A' CHRALAIG (3,673ft)
SGURR NAN CONBHAIREAN (3,639ft)
MULLACH FRAOCH-CHOIRE (3,614ft)

» Five Munros just north of the Cluanie Inn. The two additional Munros are Carn Ghluasaid (3,140ft) and Sail Chaorainn (3,288ft).

My Route
(road to road 9-10 hours)

We left transport near the Cluanie Inn, as the route started at Lundie five miles east of the Cluanie Inn, and finished one mile east of it. From Lundie we followed the old military road west for 500m, then turned north up a good stalkers' track which led to the summit plateau of Carn Ghluasaid. The cairn was at the north end of the plateau. This was my second ascent of Carn Ghluasaid, my first ascent was seventeen years earlier, in 1981.

We continued west and NW to Sgurr nan Conbhairean, then went north to take in Sail Chaorainn, a Munro. Returning south we bypassed Sgurr Conbhairean by a traverse around its west side. We reached a ridge which led to Bealach Choire a' Chait and then descended to the Bealach.

We were now positioned for the final stretch of the walk over A' Chralaig and Mullach Fraoch-choire. We climbed the ridge to A' Chralaig, then went north to Stob Coire na Chralaig and descended to a col. Finally we climbed north up a narrow ridge with some scrambling to Mullach Fraoch-choire, and then descended to the Cluanie Inn.

PLACES TO STAY/DRINK

The Cluanie Inn is the most convenient place for food and accommodation.

Sgurr nan Conbhairean from Carn Ghluasaid *(Heather Thomas-Smith)*.

Personal View (Alistair)

This turned out to be long day which started with breakfast in the Ben Alder cafe at Dalwhinnie when my beardie dog, on her first trip to the mountains, was accused of eating Barry's watch strap! The lack of sentiment for the young dog was to continue all day and Jonathan's dog kept growling at her if she made any attempt to take the lead on the good path up Carn Ghluasaid.

We went over Conbhairean then Chaorainn in a strong wind, was that it? No, a long drop and a hard pull took us to A' Chlalaig and the Mullach. From the Mullach I would like to have descended to Alltbeithe Hostel in Glen Affric, for me the best youth hostel in Scotland. One evening I was meant to be meeting Jonathan there to climb Ceathreamhnan. He didn't turn up until after 10 p.m. but it wasn't a hardship. Myself and a young Aussie lady sat in the lounge in front of a roaring fire, me demolishing the beer I had brought and she had a dram or two of the whisky. When my brother finally arrived he was none too pleased to find all the alcohol gone!

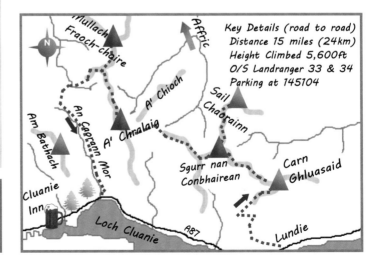

Key Details (road to road)
Distance 15 miles (24km)
Height Climbed 5,600ft
O/S Landranger 33 & 34
Parking at 145104

AFFRIC CORBETTS

AONACH SHASUINN *(2,917ft)*
CARN A' CHOIRE GHAIRBH
(2,837ft)
SGURR NA DIOLLAID
(2,684ft)

» Three Corbetts, two in Glen
Affric and one near Cannich.

My Routes

GLEN AFFRIC CORBETTS
(6-8 hours)

I started at the Forestry Commission car park at the end of the public road, 1.5km east of Affric Lodge. I crossed the bridge and followed the forestry track on the south side of the loch, passing White Cottage and reaching the Allt Garbh after 2km. I followed a poor footpath up the west side of the burn for 1km. The footpath improved as I climbed west up Na Cnapain and SW to Carn Glas Iochdarach. The route continued WSW along a broad ridge before climbing the last 500ft to Carn a' Choire Ghairbh.

I descended south to the col at 2,200ft, then traversed ENE maintaining the same height as the bealach below Aonach Shasuinn. From here it was a steep 800ft climb east to the west summit and a further 750m of flat ground took me to the Corbett.

SGURR NA DIOLLAID
(3-4 hours)

Jonathan and I parked at the bridge in Glen Cannich where the road crosses to the north side of the river at Muchrachd. We climbed slightly east of north to find the best way up the hillside. Towards the summit there was some scrambling as we climbed the final rocky tor at the summit.

Key Details

» **Distance 4 miles (6km)**
» **Height climbed 2,200ft**
» **O/S Landranger 25**
» **Parking at 284336.**

Personal View

Glen Affric is often described as the most beautiful glen in Scotland and is a national nature reserve. Apart from the midges which also seem to love the area, it is a great place to walk. Carn a' Choire Ghairbh and Aonach Shasuinn lie on the south side of the glen and I climbed them on a pleasant summer day.

It was a good circuit with excellent views although the first mile from White Cottage, until I was on the hillside of Carn a' Choire Ghairbh, was awkward and boggy. It was August and there were four stalkers walking up the hill in front of me but they did not seem to object to me being there. Once I reached the summit ridge they disappeared and for the rest of day I was alone. On returning to the car the midges were out in force so I dived into the car and made my way back to Spean Bridge.

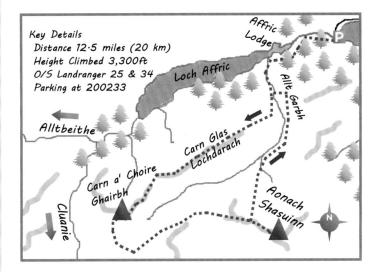

Key Details
Distance 12·5 miles (20 km)
Height Climbed 3,300ft
O/S Landranger 25 & 34
Parking at 200233

Looking east down Glen Affric from Carn Glas Iochdarach (2012).

MULLARDOCH ROUND

Alistair's sea kayak at the west end of Loch Mullardoch. He noted that the high mountains on either side made this a fantastic place to canoe.

CARN EIGHE *(3,880ft)*
SGURR NAN CEATHREAMHNAN *(3,776ft)*
SGURR NA LAPAICH *(3,774ft)*
AN RIABHACHAN *(3,704ft)*
AN SOCACH *(3,508ft)*
TOLL CREAGACH *(3,458ft)*
BEINN FHIONNLAIDH *(3,298ft)*
CARN NAN GOBHAR *(3,255ft)*

» There are four other Munros, Mam Sodhail (3,875ft), Tom a' Choinich (3,649ft), Mullach na Dheiragain (3,224ft), and An Socach (3,022ft).

» The round of Loch Mullardoch covering all the Munros normally takes two or three days in summer.

Personal View (JP)

A late start from the dam at Mullardoch in early November 1989 meant a torchlight ascent northwards to camp on the broad shoulder of Creag Dubh. In the morning whizzed along the ridges north of Mullardoch to An Socach, dense mirk giving way to a beautiful clear day. Down to the atmospheric head of Loch Mullardoch then gird the loins for a grassy slog up the Mullach, the lowering sun giving the Cuillin a crown of gold and red, not a soul to be seen.

Camped on the ridge, the temperatures plunging in the still air. Stags boomed in the Glen and the water bottle froze next to my skin. Pre dawn start for Ceathreamhnan then over the Affric ridges to Carn Eighe. Left the sack on Eighe and took in lonely Fhionnlaidh. Back on Eighe, I was enveloped in damp cloud before charging along the interesting switch back to Tom, which demanded some thinking in the fog. Dark again as I slogged up lumpish Toll Creagach from which I took off north-west down a trackless coire; high heather, boulders and deep mud holes making progress difficult in the dark. Torch batteries fading after a trackless descent, tired and filthy, I stumbled out to the dam but made Cannich in time for a pint... and slept in the car.

My Routes

The round of Loch Mullardoch starts and finishes at the dam at the head of Glen Cannich at the east end of Loch Mullardoch. It is a fine round taking two to three days in summer and is illustrated on the map below. However, I split these mountains into three walks as follows:

NORTH MULLARDOCH MUNROS (11-12 hours from Loch Mullardoch Dam to Killilan)

We climbed the Munros north of Mullardoch from the dam at the east end of Loch Mullardoch walking out to Iron Lodge. This was a long walk, particularly as we also had to walk eight miles from Iron Lodge to Killilan. No cars are allowed past Killilan.

WEST MULLARDOCH (9-10 hours from Loch na Leitreach)

We climbed Sgurr nan Ceathreamhnan and Mullach na Dheiragain from Carnach. On that occasion we took the car down Glen Elchaig but found the gates locked on our return, probably what we deserved! We were saved a problem by a friendly shepherd who had a key to the gates and let us and the car out, much to everyone's relief.

AFFRIC MUNROS (2 days)

We climbed the remaining Munros from Glen Affric. It was too long a walk to complete in a single day so we camped near the summit of An Socach. The following day we climbed An Socach and walked out over the five Munros to the east of An Socach. We finished on Toll Creagach from where we descended to Glen Affric.

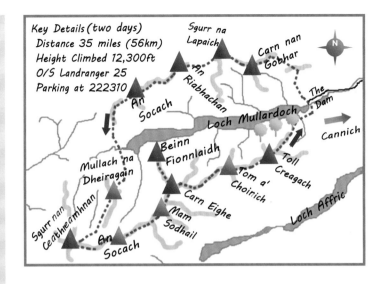

Key Details (two days)
Distance 35 miles (56km)
Height Climbed 12,300ft
O/S Landranger 25
Parking at 222310

Heading towards An Riabhachan from Sgurr na Lapaich *(Heather Thomas-Smith)*.

GLEN ELCHAIG

Summit of Aonach Buidhe, Faochaig in the background (2014).

AONACH BUIDHE *(2,949ft)*
SGUMAN COINNTICH
(2,883ft)
FAOCHAIG *(2,847ft)*

» Three Corbetts lying to the north of Glen Elchaig as it runs from Killilan to Iron Lodge.

» Aonach Buidhe is the most isolated Corbett at the head of Glen Elchaig but can be made easier by cycling to Iron Lodge.

» It is a long walk back from Carnach or Iron Lodge. Cars are not allowed down the valley so there is no hope of a lift!

Personal View

These three Corbetts stand on the north side of the private road from Killilan to Carnach. They are superb mountains but the lack of a tea shop in Killilan to collapse into at the end of the walk is disappointing! I climbed Sguman Coinntich and Faochaig on a beautiful day in early June. The ridge walk from Sguman Coinntich to Faochaig was superb in the sunshine and to my surprise there was a Mountain Marathon taking place. The competitors were returning to their campsite near Carnach as I descended from Faochaig. It was a long walk back to Killilan so I decided that I would cycle up the glen when I climbed Aonach Buidhe.

Aonach Buidhe lies at the east end of Glen Elchaig, close to the Munros north of Loch Mullardoch. As I did not need an early start, I stopped for coffee at Kyle of Lochalsh. The forecast was for rain but the garage attendant assured me that it may miss Glen Elchaig and apart from one heavy shower he was proved right. On this occasion I was greeted by highland cattle blocking the track soon after the tarmac road finished. However, Aonach Buidhe is a grand mountain, nearly 3,000ft and with views to familiar Munros north, south and east. Apart from letting my water bottle leak and destroy my phone, it was a great cycle and walk.

My Routes

AONACH BUIDHE
(with bike 5-6 hours)

I parked just before Killilan and cycled eight miles, initially down a tarmac road, then a well maintained track to Iron Lodge. From Iron Lodge I walked 300m along the north side of the stream, then took the right hand path across the An Crom-allt. After a further 150m I climbed steeply NNE up the south ridge of the mountain. At 1,500ft the route became less steep and I continued in the same direction to the summit.

Key Details

» Distance 21 miles (33km) including 16 miles cycling

» Height climbed 2,800ft

» O/S Landranger 25

» Parking at 941304.

SGUMAN COINNTICH AND FAOCHAIG (7-8 hours)

There is a parking area just under 1km before Killilan from where I walked into the hamlet. From Killilan I followed a path ENE ascending the north side of the Allt a' Choire Mhoir. After 2km the ascent ceased and I crossed the stream to climb the slopes to the south, turning east to the summit of Sguman Coinntich.

I followed the broad ridge east passing over Sron na Gaoithe. I turned NE then north to climb the final 700ft to Faochaig. I descended south picking up a stalkers path at the Allt Domhain which descended to Carnach. It was a long walk back from Carnach to Killilan.

Key Details

» Distance 14 miles (23km)

» Height climbed 4,100ft

» O/S Landranger 25

» Parking at 941304.

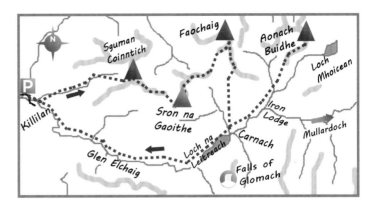

Looking south from Faochaig to Carnach. The coloured dots are tents of the Mountain Marathon visible at the bottom of the valley (2009).

LURG MHOR

Sheasgaich from Lurg Mhor *(Heather Thomas-Smith)*.

LURG MHOR (3,234ft)
BIDEIN A' CHOIRE
SHEASGAICH (3,100ft)
BEINN THARSUINN (2,831ft)
BEINN DRONAIG (2,615ft)

» A long day, Lurg Mhor and Bidein a' Choire Sheasgaich are two very remote Munros.

» Beinn Tharsuinn would normally be climbed on route to the Munros. Beinn Dronaig could be climbed if approaching the Munros from Loch Carron.

» Steep cliffs on the north side of Bidein a' Choire Sheasgaich made my route challenging.

» Alternatively, Lurg Mhor and Bidein a' Choire Sheasgaich can be climbed from Attadale using a bike.

Personal View (Jonathan)

Lurg Mhor epitomises what climbing in Scotland is all about. There is an air of mystery on the mountain, almost fear, due to its remoteness. Any Lurg Mhor ascent requires an overnight stop or a very long day. I still remember my first visit with Barry in 1993, one of the longest and hardest days I ever spent on the Scottish Munros.

We headed out from Craig and Barry persuaded me that Beinn Tharsuinn was on the route which is debatable. However, it was after Tharsuinn that we encountered problems. By now heavy rain and low cloud had set in and from the col between Tharsuinn and Sheasgaich we made a direct ascent of the cliffs ignoring SMC advice. I went up first and was soon in trouble on a cliff edge thirty feet above Barry. I called out for help, nothing from Barry or maybe a faint shout of straight on up. Somehow I managed to find a way up and he followed muttering that perhaps we should have looked at the guide book.

By the time we reached Lurg Mhor the rain was monsoon like so we missed the 'Top' and returned via the head of Loch Monar passing some wild ponies. It was then an endless trudge in atrocious conditions back to the Bealach Bhearnais. Fourteen years later I explored Lurg Mhor's southern flanks and found a fantastic campsite at Loch Calavie. It was the end of October and the deer were rutting. After pitching the tent I climbed the Lurg Mhor 'Top' then ticked Dronaig on the way back the following day.

My Routes

LURG MHOR, BIDEIN A' CHOIRE SHEASGAICH AND BEINN THARSUINN

(10-12 hours)

We climbed all three summits from Craig. We followed the path up the Allt a' Chonais, crossed the footbridge at 074467 and continued to the Bealach Bhearnais. After climbing Beinn Tharsuinn, we descended to the col between the summit and the west top, then descended to the 1,800ft Bealach an Sgoltaidh.

The ridge to Sheasgaich rose steeply ahead with rock bands. We climbed it direct but we should have traversed right before the rock bands. Using this route, a steep scramble is still needed to reach the near level ridge above.

From the summit of Sheasgaich we descended south then SE to a col at 2,400ft, then a broader ridge led to the summit of Lurg Mhor. From Lurg Mhor we descended north and crossed the valley west of the head of Loch Monar. We walked back up to the Bealach Bhearnais along the Allt Bealach Crudhain.

BEINN DRONAIG

(with bike 5-6 hours)

I started from Attadale Gardens (ref. 925387, O/S Landranger 25) and cycled to Bendronaig Lodge, only seven miles but it was hard work. The track rose to 1,000ft before dropping to 750ft at the Lodge and well kept bothy.

From the bothy, I climbed steadily to the broad summit ridge then walked east to the trig point. The return journey was 18 miles with 3,000ft of climbing. The bike reduced the time by two hours.

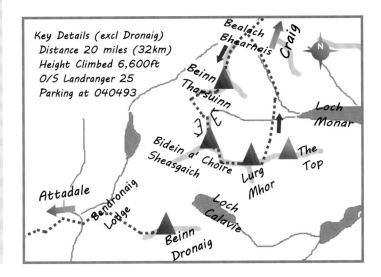

Key Details (excl Dronaig)
Distance 20 miles (32km)
Height Climbed 6,600ft
O/S Landranger 25
Parking at 040493

Lurg Mhor from Beinn Dronaig (2016).

ACHNASHEEN SUMMITS

FIONN BHEINN *(3,062ft)*
MORUISG *(3,045ft)*
SGURR NAN CEANNAICHEAN
(2,995ft)

» Sgurr nan Ceannaichean was promoted to Munro status in the 1981 tables but relegated again in 2009.

» Fionn Bheinn is an isolated Munro near Achnasheen.

My Routes

FIONN BHEINN *(4-5 hours)*

I started at a small car park in Achnasheen. The car park was off the main road just east of the bridge over the river. A helpful sign with the soles of two feet shows the way to the path. This goes up the east side of Allt Achadh na Sine. I climbed NW then north and after nearly 4km reached the jutting out spur of Creagan nan Laogh. From here I walked NW to the summit.

Key Details

» Distance 6 miles (10km)
» Height climbed 2,600ft
» O/S Landranger 25 and 20
» Parking at 162586.

MORUISG AND SGURR NAN CEANNAICHEAN *(4-5 hours)*

There was parking just over 1km west of the outflow of Loch Sgamhain. From here we crossed the river by a footbridge, then went under the railway line. We followed the footpath towards the Alltan na Feola, then went straight up Moruisg heading broadly SE. Gentle slopes initially became steeper. There were crags to the west and finally a moderate incline to the summit. We descended south from Moruisg then SW to the col at 2,400ft. From the col we climbed west and finally SW to the summit of Sgurr nan Ceannaichean.

Near the summit of Fionn Bheinn *(Chris Wood)*.

Personal View (Alistair)

I did not follow the described route up Moruisg because of new deer fences but struck straight for the top. At first it was a gentle incline then a steep pull to the left of crags and up a slope to reach the summit. Down and back up to Ceannaichean, debatable value as now only a Corbett but Barry was hoping for some good photographs. I was relieved that the rain in Torridon missed me.

On the day I climbed Fionn Bheinn (travelling back from Torridon) the weather was glorious with clouds clearing from the summit. Fionn Bheinn is not the most exciting hill but the initial walk beside the twinkling, tumbling mountain stream was great in early morning sunshine. I reached the benign south ridge which I followed to the top with the last 200ft in cloud. There were superb views south on the descent.

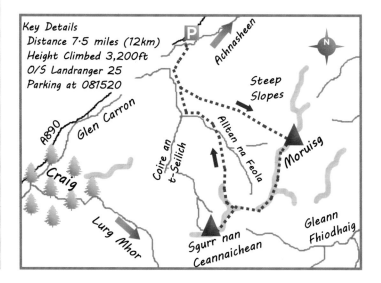

Key Details
Distance 7.5 miles (12km)
Height Climbed 3,200ft
O/S Landranger 25
Parking at 081520

LUNNDAIDH THREE

SGURR A' CHAORACHAIN
(3,455ft)
MAOILE LUNNDAIDH
(3,304ft)
SGURR NA FEARTAIG
(2,828ft)

» Sgurr Choinnich (3,278ft),
a Munro, is also climbed.

My Route (9-11 hours)

Marcus joined us for our 1998 Scottish tour. It was to be his only Munro trip as he emigrated to New Zealand soon afterwards. We started at Craig and walked 10km along the track leaving it just after Glenuaig Lodge. A bike would be useful for this section.

We crossed the An Crom-allt, then climbed steeply up the SSE ridge of Carn nam Fiaclan and crossed the plateau to Maoile Lunndaidh.

We returned to Carn nam Fiaclan and continued west for just over 1km. A descent SW took us to a col with two small lochs where we had lunch. After lunch we climbed SW up 1,200ft to reach the col between Bidean an Eoin Deirg and Sgurr a' Chaorachain. We continued along the ridge going west over Sgurr a' Chaorachain and Sgurr Choinnich to the Bealach Bhearnais.

From the Bealach it is a short 900ft climb to the summit of Sgurr na Feartaig but Corbetts were not on our agenda. So I returned to Craig in 2014 taking the now bulldozed track for 4km to where a stalkers' path branched off west. I followed the path most of the way to Sgurr na Feartaig, going south to the summit after passing two lochans.

Personal View (Alistair)

I traversed the 'Lunndaidh three' on a cold November day. Daylight was limited so I took a bike. Starting at Craig, it was a cycle and walk up the track continuing until it split near the Bealach Bhearnais, one branch continuing to Lurg Mhor (eventually!), the other circling round and climbing to the top of Choinnich. With ice on the ground and clouds swirling round the summits I continued quickly.

I made a route finding error at the col between Choinnich and Chaorachain, annoying but recovered quickly. After the summit of Chaorachain, I went down and up the opposite shoulder then a long flat trudge across a snow field took me to the summit of Maoile Lunndaidh. Just a long walk and cycle back now, but when I thought I had surely completed the quickest and maybe only round of the month I was caught by another guy also on a bike. He said he had started 20 minutes behind me, not even the quickest round of the day!

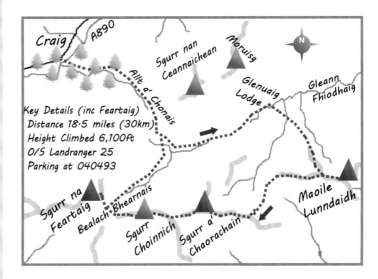

Key Details (inc Feartaig)
Distance 18·5 miles (30km)
Height Climbed 6,100ft
O/S Landranger 25
Parking at 040493

Progress comes to a halt on the way to Maoile Lunndaidh in 1998.

STRATHFARRAR

SGURR A' CHOIRE GHLAIS
(3,554ft)
SGURR NA RUAIDHE
(3,258ft)
BEINN A' BHA' ACH ARD
(2,827ft)

» The walk goes over four Munros. Beinn a' Bha'ach Ard is normally climbed separately.

» The additional Munros are Sgurr Fhuar-thuill (3,442ft) and Carn nan Gobhar (3,255ft).

» There are restrictions on taking cars down the Glen (currently closed on Tuesday).

Strathfarrar Munros from the north.

My Routes

STRATHFARRAR MUNROS
(6-8 hours road to road)
We had two cars so we left one at the bottom of the Allt Coire Mhuillidh. We carried on down the road parking the other car at the Allt Toll a' Mhuic. The stalkers' path climbed past Loch Toll a' Mhuic to the col between Sgurr na Fearstaig and Sgurr Fhuar-thuill, the first Munro. After this we followed the summit ridge over Sgurr a' Choire Ghlais and Carn nan Gobhar.

We descended SSE to a col at 2,600ft before ascending ESE to the final Munro, Sgurr na Ruaidhe. Another descent SW took us to the Allt Coire Mhuillidh which led south back to the Strathfarrar road.

BEINN A' BHA' ACH ARD
(4-5 hours)
I parked at the power station (ref 379404, O/S Landranger 26) 2km west of the gate into Glen Strathfarrar. A good track went west for 2km. I turned right up the hillside just after it came out of the woods and headed NNW aiming for the prominent surveyor marker. The route continued north to reach the summit returning the same way.

9 miles, 2,600ft of climbing.

Personal View

I climbed the four Munros north of Strathfarrar in 1994. After break-fast in Blair Atholl I met Jonathan and JP in Dalwhinnie at 9 a.m. We had coffee at the Struy Inn then drove to the entrance to Strathfarrar where the gatekeeper took our names. He confirmed that the gates closed at 7 p.m. We left a car at the finish of the walk and drove to the start at the Allt Toll a' Mhuic.

There was wind and showers which turned into cloud and rain as we headed up Sgurr a' Choire Ghlais. However, the weather improved and off the last Munro JP managed a 300ft standing snow glissade even though it was June.

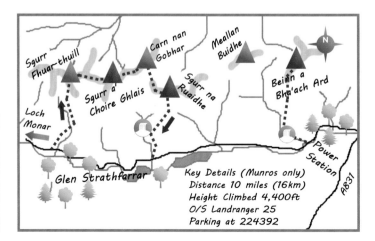

Key Details (Munros only)
Distance 10 miles (16km)
Height Climbed 4,400ft
O/S Landranger 25
Parking at 224392

GLEN STRATHCONAN

SGURR A' MHUILINN
(2,883ft)
MEALLAN NAN UAN (2,749ft)

» Two Corbetts on the north side of Glen Strathconan, a glen that is not visited by Munroists but is one of the most beautiful in Scotland.

» This is a good half day circuit with the climbing starting straight from the road.

My Route (4-5 hours)

I drove over ten miles down Glen Strathconan on a single track road. There was parking just south of Strathanmore and information on deer stalking. From there I climbed west up grassy slopes then SW to the top of Creag Ruadh.

From Creag Ruadh I followed an attractive ridge NW for 1.5km, then a final steep climb of 400ft led to the summit of Meallan nan Uan. From the summit I descended NW for 1km to a col at 2,100ft overlooking Loch Coire a' Mhuilinn. From the col I climbed NE up Sgurr a' Mhuilinn then descended steeply SE to make a direct return to the car.

POINTS OF INTEREST

Prior to the highland clearances in the 1840s, Glen Strathconan was the most populated glen in the highlands. At Strathanmore there is a Telford church, 1km before the car parking spot.

PLACES TO STAY/DRINK

There are hotels and guest houses in Beauly, Muir of Ord and Strathpeffer but no pubs or cafes in Glen Strathconan.

Personal View

After a late lunch at Strathpeffer I drove down Glen Strathconan for the first time and completed this circuit on a late June afternoon in clear and at times sunny weather.

The drive down Strathconan to the start was over ten miles on a single track road but it was worth the journey. The route quickly climbed to the ridge at Creag Ruadh and from there I enjoyed the walk with good views all around. I could have added the two summits north west of Sgurr a' Mhuilinn but decided against it, preferring to reach the Ferry Boat Inn at Ullapool before it stopped serving bar snacks.

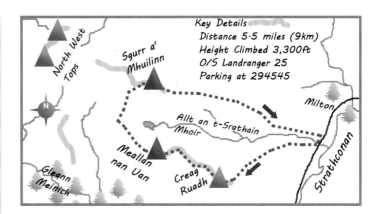

Key Details
Distance 5·5 miles (9km)
Height Climbed 3,300ft
O/S Landranger 25
Parking at 294545

Looking down to Loch Coire a' Mhuilinn between the two Corbetts (2012).

NORTH OF LOCH MONAR

BAC AN EICH *(2,787ft)*
AN SIDHEAN *(2,671ft)*

» Two Corbetts situated to the north of Loch Monar.

My Routes

BAC AN EICH (3-4 hours)

I turned off the single track road up Glen Strathconan at Inverchoran and after 200m parked near a bridge. I crossed the bridge, walked past Inverchoran farm and followed the track SW as it headed up Gleann Chorainn. Once past the woods on the right the track deteriorated into a path. I carried on for a few hundred metres, crossed a stream then made a rising traverse towards the shoulder of Bac an Eich. After some steep climbing I reached the summit ridge and walked NW to the summit over some peat hags.

Key Details

» Distance 6 miles (10km)
» Height climbed 2,300ft
» O/S Landranger 25
» Parking at 260507.

AN SIDHEAN (5-6 hours)

It was Monday lunchtime in August and the road down Strathfarrar was open until 8 p.m. This gave plenty of time even though it was a 30 minute drive from the gate to the dam. I parked and walked past the lodge joining the stalkers' path which ran along the shore of Loch Monar.

After 3km I crossed a bridge and followed another path which branched off right up the hillside. At 1,650ft I left the path and headed north up the hillside and across a plateau to the summit.

Key Details

» Distance 9.5 miles (15km)
» Height climbed 2,000ft
» O/S Landranger 25
» Parking at 203394.

Deer crossing the route near Inverchoran (2013).

Personal View

Loch Monar is surrounded by Munro giants such as Lurg Mhor, Maoile Lunndaidh and Sgurr na Lapaich, all familiar names to Munroists. However, when I climbed An Sidhean it was the first time I had walked along its shores. After two weeks of heavy rain I was relieved that the stalkers' path was 'Rolls Royce' standard and kept my feet dry as it crossed the hillside above Loch Monar. An Sidhean turned out to be a near neighbour of Maoile Lunndaidh and had a large summit plateau. It was a lengthy walk across the plateau but I was back in Beauly in time for late afternoon tea.

The previous year I had climbed Bac an Eich after a long drive up from Loughborough, stopping at Tebay Services for breakfast and Pitlochry for coffee. Walking past Inverchoran farm I came across large numbers of deer and noisy dogs. Thereafter the walk was peaceful and the summit was a lovely place to be on a late summer afternoon.

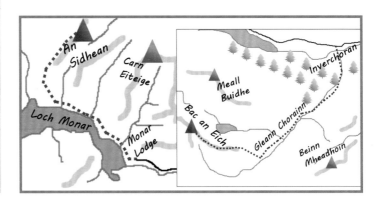

Beinn Dearg from Liathach.

SCOTLAND: NORTH HIGHLANDS

The North Highlands cover the area from Glen Carron in the south to Ullapool in the north.

There are 52 Top 500 Summits divided into 20 walks:

WALKS 1 TO 10

	Walk	Feet	Pg.
1	Sgorr Ruadh	3,156	256
	Beinn Liath Mhor	3,036	
	Fuar Tholl	2,976	
2	Maol Chean-dearg	3,060	258
	An Ruadh-stac	2,926	
3	Beinn Damh	2,959	259
	Sgorr nan Lochan Uaine	2,857	
	Sgurr Dubh	2,566	
4	Beinn Bhan	2,938	260
	Sgurr a' Chaorachain	2,598	
5	Sgurr Mhor	3,235	262
	Tom na Gruagaich	3,025	
6	Ruadh-stac Beag	2,940	263
	Meall a' Ghiubhais	2,910	
7	Ruadh-stac Mor	3,313	264
	Spidean Coire nan Clach	3,258	
8	Spidean a' Choire Leith	3,460	266
	Mullach an Rathain	3,356	
9	Beinn Dearg	2,998	268
	Baosbheinn	2,871	
	Beinn an Eoin	2,805	
10	Mullach Coire Mhic Fhearchair	3,343	270
	Sgurr Ban	3,245	
	Slioch	3,217	
	A' Mhaighdean	3,173	
	Beinn Tarsuinn	3,075	
	Ruadh Stac Mor	3,012	
	Beinn a' Chlaidheimh	2,998	
	Beinn Lair	2,821	

The North Highlands cover the area between Inverness and Applecross in the south and Ullapool in the north. Most of the mountains lie to the west of the A835, the road which runs from Inverness to Ullapool.

This area includes many of the greatest mountains in the British Isles including An Teallach, arguably the greatest of them all. Further south lies Torridon and its magnificent south facing wall of mountains, Beinn Eighe, Liathach and Beinn Alligin. Between Torridon and An Teallach lies the Fisherfield Forest, one of the last great British wildernesses. The round of the six Munros of the Fisherfield Forest is a tough undertaking and includes A' Mhaighdean, probably the most remote Munro of them all.

To the east of the A835, the mountains are more rounded but some are a long way from any road, in particular Seana Bhraigh and Carn Ban. Directly north of Inverness lies Ben Wyvis, dominating the landscape for many miles around.

There are many great places to stay in the area. My favourites include Lochcarron, Torridon, Gairloch and Ullapool, all superb locations next to the sea.

WALKS 11 TO 20

	Walk	Feet	Pg.
11	Beinn a' Chaisgein Mor	2,812	272
	Beinn Airigh Charr	2,595	
12	Beinn Dearg Mor	2,985	273
	Beinn Dearg Bheag	2,690	
13	Bidein a' Ghlas Thuill	3,484	274
14	Sgurr Breac	3,281	276
	A' Chailleach	3,270	
15	Sgurr Mor	3,642	277
	Sgurr nan Clach Geala	3,586	
	Beinn Liath Mhor a' Ghiubhais Li	2,513	
16	Ben Wyvis	3,433	278
	Little Wyvis	2,507	
	Carn Chuinneag	2,750	
17	Beinn Dearg	3,556	280
	Cona Mheall	3,208	
	Am Faochagach	3,130	
	Eididh nan Clach Geala	3,045	
	Beinn Enaiglair	2,915	
18	Creag Rainich	2,647	282
	Sail Mhor	2,516	
19	Carn Ban	2,772	283
	Beinn a' Chaisteil	2,582	
20	Seana Bhraigh	3,040	284

Looking down the NW ridge of Slioch *(Heather Thomas-Smith).*

COIRE LAIR

Beinn Liath Mhor from above Coire Lair (2014).

SGORR RUADH *(3,156ft)*
BEINN LIATH MHOR *(3,036ft)*
FUAR THOLL *(2,976ft)*

» Three fine rocky mountains just
north of Craig on the road from
Achnasheen to Lochcarron.

» Fuar Tholl is a fantastic
mountain and one of the
best Corbetts.

» The round of two Munros and
one Corbett can be completed
in one day but most walkers
miss out Fuar Tholl as it is
not a Munro.

Personal View

These three magnificent mountains lie just north of Craig in the Coulin Forest. Fuar Tholl, in my view the finest of the three, falls below
the magic 3,000ft mark and is often omitted by those focussing
on the Munros. This is a shame particularly as Fuar Tholl can be
climbed by making a short detour and a 1,000 foot climb from the
track which leads from Coire Lair to Sgorr Ruadh.

My first visit to Coire Lair was in July 1998 in poor weather with
cloud down to 1,500ft. Alistair and Marcus went off to climb Beinn
Eighe and Jonathan and I decided to climb Beinn Liath Mhor and
Sgorr Ruadh. Progress over Beinn Liath Mhor was slow in thick mist
and drizzle and slowed further when I left my camera on the east
summit and had to go back for it. We staggered over Sgorr Ruadh
but did not climb Fuar Tholl.

We returned in 2014 joined by Alistair and made our way to the col
between Fuar Tholl and Sgorr Ruadh at which point I branched off
for Fuar Tholl whilst my brothers continued to Sgorr Ruadh. As I
descended from Fuar Tholl the clouds parted and at last the magnificent Mainreachan Buttress was revealed.

COIRE LAIR continued

My Routes

BEINN LIATH MHOR AND SGORR RUADH (6-7 hours)

We parked next to the A890 at the end of the private road leading to Achnashellach station and walked to the station. After walking SW for 100m there was a gate and a path leading up to Coire Lair.

At 1,200ft, when the Coire opened out, the paths split. We carried on NNW then climbed NW to the east top of Beinn Liath Mhor at 2,875ft. We continued WNW for 2km over another top to the summit of Beinn Liath Mhor. The descent SW was down difficult terrain to a lochan, then over a top (2,520ft) and then past another lochan. From there we ascended the NW ridge of Sgorr Ruadh and returned, leaving Fuar Tholl for another day.

FUAR THOLL (4-5 hours)

When I returned sixteen years later we followed the same route to the junction of the paths at 1,200ft in Coire Lair. This time we turned left crossing the River Lair with difficulty (Jonathan fell in). We continued until the path crossed a small stream directly north of Coire Mainreachean.

From there I climbed south into the Coire. With the Mainreachean Buttress on my right I followed a path steeply up grass then scree. This led to the small col between the summit of Fuar Tholl and the summit above Mainreachean Buttress. I visited both summits before returning.

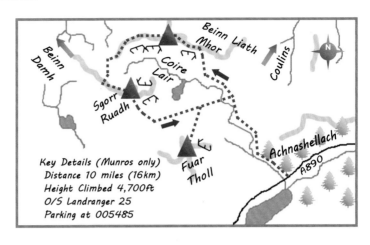

Key Details (Munros only)
Distance 10 miles (16km)
Height Climbed 4,700ft
O/S Landranger 25
Parking at 005485

POINTS OF INTEREST

Fuar Tholl has acquired the nickname 'Wellington's Nose' because the summit ridge is similar in profile to an upturned face, in this case a supposed likeness to the first Duke of Wellington.

On the ridge of Beinn Liath Mhor *(Chris Wood)*.

COULAGS

MAOL CHEAN-DEARG
(3,060ft)
AN RUADH-STAC *(2,926ft)*

» Maol Chean-Dearg and An Ruadh-Stac are stunning mountains surrounding a triple bealach. They lie near Lochcarron.

Looking down from the NE ridge of An Ruadh-Stac to the triple bealach and lochs.

My Routes (6-8 hours for both summits)

It would be possible to climb Maol Chean-Dearg and An Ruadh-Stac on the same day ascending both from the triple bealach. However, I climbed them separately.

On each occasion I parked next to the road at Coulags bridge four miles east of Lochcarron. I followed the path north. After 2.5km I crossed to the west side of the stream and continued for another 2km past a bothy and the Stone of Fingal's Dogs. From there I climbed west up a good path to the triple bealach between Maol Chean-dearg, An Ruadh-Stac and Meall nan Ceapairean.

To ascend Maol Chean-Dearg, Alistair and I climbed NW from the col up a broad ridge to the summit and then returned to the col.

To climb An Ruadh-stac, I walked south then SW to circumvent some small lochs and reach the rocky NE ridge of An Ruadh-Stac. I climbed the ridge, at times scrambling, to the summit then returned by the same route.

POINTS OF INTEREST

Clach nan Con-fionn (Stone of Fingal's dogs) is reached 4km from the start. The legendary Fingal is meant to have tied his hunting dogs here.

Personal View

I climbed Maol Chean-dearg with Alistair in 2002 but the weather was atrocious and my recollections of the climb are almost non existent.

In June 2015 the weather was dry but the path from Coulags Bridge was under water after two months of rain. I passed a bothy (which was open and looked clean and dry) then the Stone of Fingal's Dogs which stood out on the moorland. Climbing to the triple bealach the sun came out and the magnificent NE ridge of An Ruadh-Stac appeared in front of me. I scrambled up the rocky ridge relieved that there was a break in the weather to appreciate this magnificent peak.

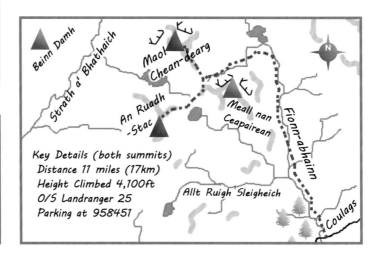

Key Details (both summits)
Distance 11 miles (17km)
Height Climbed 4,100ft
O/S Landranger 25
Parking at 958451

SOUTH OF TORRIDON

BEINN DAMH *(2,959ft)*
**SGORR NAN LOCHAN
UAINE** *(2,857ft)*
SGURR DUBH *(2,566ft)*

» Beinn Damh is one of the highest Corbetts and is conveniently climbed from the Torridon Inn.

» The other two Corbetts lie in the Coulin Forest and make a good circular walk.

My Routes

BEINN DAMH (4-5 hours)

At the Torridon Inn we found signs to Beinn Damh. The path crossed the A896 just west of the river and we continued SW through Rhododendrons bushes. At the top the path forked. We took the right fork and continued SW into the corrie of Toll Ban. In worsening weather we climbed to the col between Beinn Damh and Sgurr na Bana-Mhoraire, then from the col a path went SE missing the subsidiary tops on the west side. A final climb took us to the summit.

SGORR NAN LOCHAN UAINE AND SGURR DUBH (5-6 hours)

There is a car park at the foot of Coire Dubh on the A896. I walked east for 100m across a bridge then followed a path south past the Ling Hut. After continuing for 3km until due west of Sgorr nan Lochan Uaine, I climbed ESE turning ENE at 1,800ft to the NW shoulder of the Corbett. It was straightforward to follow this ridge to the summit of Sgorr nan Lochan Uaine.

I descended NNE to a col at 1,700ft and continued up the barren slopes to the summit of Sgurr Dubh, turning NE past a minor summit at 2,100ft. I returned to the car by descending north off the summit. However, a better route off Sgurr Dubh is shown on the map.

Personal View

Jonathan and I climbed Beinn Damh on a Saturday in July 2013 when the rest of Britain was basking in warm sunshine. The day started dry but steadily got worse. When we reached 1,700ft the cloud came down and rain drove in from the west. On the top we huddled in a shelter by the cairn and ate some butterscotch before a miserable walk down. In fact the weather conditions that day were so bad that only 11 out of 150 competitors in the Celtman (a very tough triathlon challenge) were allowed to go up Beinn Eighe on safety grounds.

Earlier in the week I had climbed Sgorr nan Lochain Uaine and Sgurr Dubh on a day of strong winds and 'heavy showers merging'. Fortunately the mist stayed above 2,500ft or I would probably have become lost on the confusing traverse between the mountains. On the final descent to the road I went north off the summit of Sgurr Dubh trying to stay sheltered from the strong SW winds, not a recommended route but it was possible with care. My mobile phone got drenched but revived in front of the log fire at the Torridon Hotel.

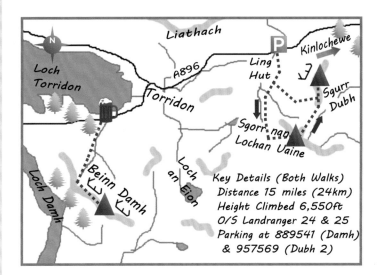

Key Details (Both Walks)
Distance 15 miles (24km)
Height Climbed 6,550ft
O/S Landranger 24 & 25
Parking at 889541 (Damh)
& 957569 (Dubh 2)

Beinn Damh from the east *(Heather Thomas-Smith)*.

APPLECROSS SUMMITS

Looking east from the summit of Beinn Bhan, I took this photo ten years after Jonathan's visit to this spectacular spot.

BEINN BHAN *(2,938ft)*
SGURR A' CHAORACHAIN *(2,598ft)*

» Beinn Bhan is a high and imposing summit usually photographed from the east from where its corries look spectacular.

» Sgurr a' Chaorachain is an easy ascent from the Bealach na Ba.

» Both Corbetts can be climbed from the Bealach na Ba where the road climbs to over 2,000ft. However, to appreciate the true glories of these mountains it is better to climb them from the east.

Personal View (Jonathan)

My house is called 'Applecross', such is my love for this forgotten corner of the Scottish coast with two Corbetts guarding its secret. We hired a cottage for the May Bank Holiday on Applecross Bay, a wonderfully remote spot, accessed by the spectacular Bealach na Ba.

As we were in Applecross the entire family including three year old daughter and arthritic border collie (Bracken) had to climb the two Corbetts, or at least one of them. We trooped up the easy slopes of Sgurr a' Chaorachain and enjoyed a picnic at the summit cairn. However, the job was only half done and as soon as I returned the family to the path back to the Bealach na Ba, I headed up the more demanding slopes of Beinn Bhan.

The summit of Beinn Bhan was in cloud when I arrived so I could not see the spectacular eastern corries. Thus I did not linger and legged it back to the Bealach to find the rest of the family (dog excluded) reading their books and unconcerned as to my return. Perhaps I should have taken my time and hoped for a clearance on Beinn Bhan but my biggest regret is not tackling these magnificent peaks from the east.

APPLECROSS SUMMITS continued

My Route (5-6 hours)

I followed the same route as Jonathan to climb these two Corbetts. Starting from the car park at the top of the Bealach na Ba I followed the access track towards the radio mast for 400m. From here I went right traversing SE to a col between the two tops (776m and 792m) of Sgurr a' Chaorachain. The route continued east over a sandstone tower to the summit.

I returned to the col then headed north past the radio mast. After a further 2.5km over heather and boulders the col separating Beinn Bhan from Sgurr a' Chaorachain appeared. I turned ENE to the Bealach nan Arr, then climbed east and finally ENE to the summit of Beinn Bhan. I returned by the same route turning west before reaching the radio mast.

Key Details
Distance 8·5 miles (14km)
Height Climbed 2,200ft
O/S Landranger 24
Parking at 775425

POINTS OF INTEREST

The Bealach na Ba is an historic pass through the mountains of the Applecross Peninsula. The road has a number of very tight hairpin bends and has the greatest ascent of any road climb in Britain going from sea level to 2,053ft.

PLACES TO STAY/DRINK

I had lunch at the Applecross House cafe and restaurant. In addition, there is the Applecross Inn and a campsite with a cafe and restaurant attached.

Jonathan's family having a picnic on the summit of Sgurr a' Chaorachain.

BEINN ALLIGIN

SGURR MHOR *(3,235ft)*
TOM NA GRUAGAICH
(3,025ft)

» Beinn Alligin is the third of the great Torridonian giants with fine views overlooking the sea.

» Tom na Gruagaich became a Munro in the 1997 listing.

My Route (5-6 hours)

On the previous day we had cycled from Inverness to the Torridon Youth Hostel. The following morning we cycled from the Youth Hostel to the Coire Mhic Nobuil car park. On the north side of the road a path went north then west into Coire nan Laoigh. From there we raced up to the top of Tom na Gruagaich.

We descended north to a col at 2,500ft then climbed Sgurr Mhor, the highest point of Beinn Alligin. Just below the summit we passed the sheer sided gash, Leum na Caillich. To create a circular route and see the best of the mountain we went over the Horns of Alligin. From the third and last Horn the path descended SE.

PLACES TO STAY/DRINK

The start point is two miles west of Torridon Village which has a campsite, youth hostel and shop. There are also guest houses and the Torridon Hotel and Inn is just around the bay.

POINTS OF INTEREST

A great cleft, Leum na Caillich, cuts into the ridge south of the summit. This is the scar of the most spectacular rock avalanche in Britain, which took place around 3,750 years ago.

Beinn Alligin on a fine morning in 1977.

Personal View

I climbed this mountain with a friend from Newcastle during a cycling tour from Inverness in August 1977. It was the start of a sunny spell of weather in Scotland. We climbed quickly up Tom na Gruagaich (being younger and fitter in those days!) before a more leisurely traverse over Sgurr Mhor and the Horns of Alligin. A superb day with great views means I have had always had good memories of Beinn Alligin.

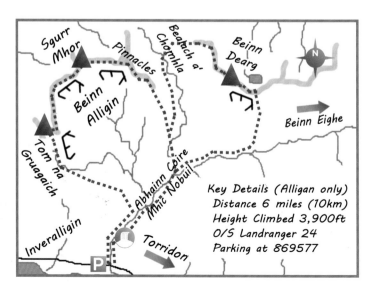

Key Details (Alligan only)
Distance 6 miles (10km)
Height Climbed 3,900ft
O/S Landranger 24
Parking at 869577

WEST OF LOCH MAREE

RUADH-STAC BEAG *(2,940ft)*
MEALL A' GHIUBHAIS
(2,910ft)

» Two large and steep sided Corbetts in a magnificent location between the Torridon mountains and Loch Maree.

» The access to the mountains is via the Beinn Eighe mountain trail and you can complete most of this as part of the walk.

My Route (6-7 hours)

After a short two mile drive north from Kinlochewe I found the car park at the start of the mountain trail. I walked under the road from the car park and took the left fork to ascend south then SW along the trail path. A large cairn denoted the top of the trail at 1,800ft.

The walk continued SW for 2km descending 300ft and reached the Allt Toll a' Ghiubhais. I followed this upwards to the south end of Ruadh-stac Beag. A rocky spur climbed north to the summit plateau. The cairn was at the south end of the plateau. I returned from the summit by a shortcut down the steep scree slopes east of the rocky spur.

From the bottom of the scree slope I descended beside the stream to 1,500ft, then headed across the plateau to reach the bottom of the steep grassy slopes up Meall a' Ghiubhais. It was a steep climb NW up these slopes to the summit which is at the SW end of the ridge.

POINTS OF INTEREST

The start and finish of this walk follow a mountain trail. The trail is 6.5km long and rises to 1,800ft illustrating the wildlife, scenery and geology of the area.

Personal View

I climbed these two fine Corbetts on a hot summer day in 2013, the last day of our Torridon tour and the day after we climbed Liathach. As the sun came up I drove to the car park by the side of Loch Maree. An excellent mountain trail took me up to 1,800ft as the heat increased. From there I climbed Ruadh-Stac Beag by the steep rocky ridge on its south side.

There was some enjoyable scree running on the way down Ruadh-Stac Beag then a strenuous pull up steep grassy slopes led to Ghiubhais. It was now stiflingly hot but fortunately the mountain water was plentiful and I drank three litres. Finally I descended by the mountain trail and had a wash in the cold waters of Loch Maree to cool off.

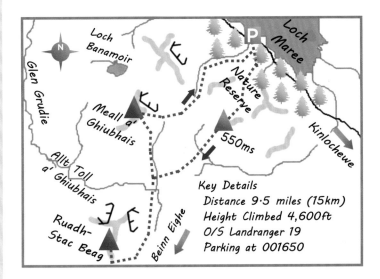

Key Details
Distance 9·5 miles (15km)
Height Climbed 4,600ft
O/S Landranger 19
Parking at 001650

Ruadh-stac Beag from the summit of Meall a' Ghiubhais (2013).

BEINN EIGHE

Beinn Eighe from the south *(Heather Thomas-Smith)*.

RUADH-STAC MOR *(3,313ft)*
SPIDEAN COIRE NAN CLACH *(3,258ft)*

» Beinn Eighe is the most easterly of the three Torridon giants. It is a complex mountain with two Munros and four Munro Tops.

» The full ridge from Sail Mhor to Creag Dubh descending to Kinlochewe is an excellent traverse.

» Spidean Coire nan Clach was promoted to Munro status in the 1997 tables.

Personal View (Jonathan)

On the drive from Kinlochewe to Torridon, two great quartzite mountains appear on the right blocking the view north, the first one is Beinn Eighe, the second, Liathach. Whilst Liathach is often considered the greatest of the Torridonian giants, Beinn Eighe is also a great and complex mountain which takes time to explore.

Barry, JP and myself had endured a dreadful day on Beinn Eighe in 1994 with horizontal rain leading to a fast ticking of Ruadh-stac Mor, and a failed attempt to reach the top of Sail Mhor. Barry was soaked and shivering with inadequate clothing.

Four years later JP and myself returned for an assault on the whole ridge taking in the new Munro, Spidean Coire nan Clach. The weather was better although there was some cloud on the ridge. The crossing to Sail Mhor was a challenge with some tricky scrambling. Thereafter the three mile ridge was straightforward except for one nasty step near Sgurr nan Fhir Duibhe. The best moment of the walk came at the end as we started the long descent to Kinlochewe. Miraculously the clouds parted, the sun came out and the mountains to the east were shown in all their glory. We took a seat on the hillside before the prospect of beer at Kinlochewe drew us down.

My Route

RUADH-STAC MOR
(5-6 hours)

There is a car park on the A896 road west of the Allt a' Choire Dhuibh Mhoir. We followed the footpath up the west side of the stream to the top of the pass between Beinn Eighe and Liathach. A path went off to the right round the prow of Sail Mhor and led to Loch Coire Mhic Fhearchair.

We walked round the east side of the loch and ascended to the col linking Ruadh-stac Mor with the main ridge. After walking north for 1km we arrived at the summit of Ruadh-stac Mor.

It would have been possible to add Spidean Coire nan Clach by returning to the col and ascending to the main ridge east of Coinneach Mhor. The ridge could then be followed to Spidean Coire nan Clach. However, Spidean Coire nan Clach was not a Munro at that time, so I returned later to climb it directly from the road.

PLACES TO STAY/DRINK

The start point for climbing Beinn Eighe is equidistant from Kinlochewe and Torridon and both offer food, drink and accommodation. I prefer Torridon because of its superb location by the sea. There is a youth hostel and campsite at Torridon Village with food and drink at the Torridon Hotel and Inn.

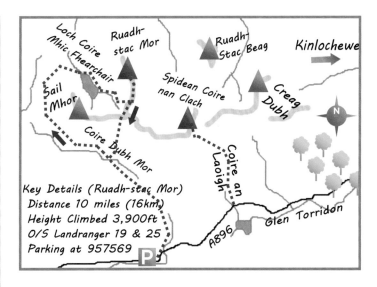

Key Details (Ruadh-stac Mor)
Distance 10 miles (16km)
Height Climbed 3,900ft
O/S Landranger 19 & 25
Parking at 957569

POINTS OF INTEREST

One of the best known features of Beinn Eighe is Coire Mhic Fhearchair, known as the Triple Buttress Corrie after its three large rock features. There are many rock climbs on the buttresses and in 1951 a converted Lancaster crashed near the top of it.

Ruadh-Stac Mor from the summit of Ruadh-Stac Beag.

LIATHACH

Looking west from the summit of Spidean a' Choire Leith to Mullach an Rathain (2013).

**SPIDEAN A' CHOIRE LEITH
(3,460ft)
MULLACH AN RATHAIN
(3,356ft)**

» Liathach comprises two Munros, Spidean a' Choire Leith and Mullach an Rathain.

» Liathach is deservedly regarded as one of the best mountains in Britain and is the central and highest of the 'Torridonian giants'.

» Mullach an Rathain was promoted to Munro status in the 1980 tables.

» The 'drop' between Spidean a' Choire Leith and Mullach an Rathain is 500ft, the smallest 'drop' on the top 500 list.

Personal View

Liathach is one of the great Scottish mountains rising straight from Glen Torridon as a rock wall 3,000ft high. It is in my top five mountains in Britain because of its magnificent south facing wall and great summit ridge which is a joy to traverse on a Summer day.

I have climbed Liathach twice, in 1977 and 2013, a gap of 36 years. My diary of the 1977 ascent is brief, 'steep climb up the Mullach, cloud remaining on the tops as we traversed the ridge, managed to hitch a lift back to the Torridon Youth Hostel at the end'.

In 2013 I traversed the ridge with Alistair and Jonathan on a glorious July day. We traversed the ridge east to west going over Spidean a' Choire Leith first and then on to the Mullach. The descent from the Mullach was long and steep and Alistair fell badly bruising his leg. A dozen operations on his knees make descents hard work. We returned to the Torridon Inn to watch Andy Murray win Wimbledon for the first time, and talk to some of the competitors who had taken part in the Ironman Triathlon in atrocious weather the previous day.

LIATHACH continued

My Route (5-6 hours)

We parked by the side of the A896 road just west of the Allt an Doire Ghairbh. There is a car park marked on the 2.5 inch map. Fifty metres to the west of the stream a cairn signalled the start of a path which we followed all the way to the ridge. On reaching the ridge we headed west going over a Munro Top, Stob a' Choire Liath Mhor, before the ascent to the summit of Spidean a' Choire Leith.

From the summit we descended south and then SW to a col. After this we followed the path around the south side of the Am Fasarinen Pinnacles (I have never attempted to go over the Pinnacles). The path then climbed in a WNW direction to the summit of Mullach an Rathain.

From the summit of the Mullach we descended south into a corrie and then followed a stream, the Allt an Tuill Bhain, to the road 2km east of the start.

POINTS OF INTEREST

As the drop between Spidean a' Choire Leith and Mullach an Rathain is recorded at both 152m and 153m (around 500ft) we took an Altimeter. According to our reading the drop is just over 500ft so Mullach an Rathain is included in the Top 500 list.

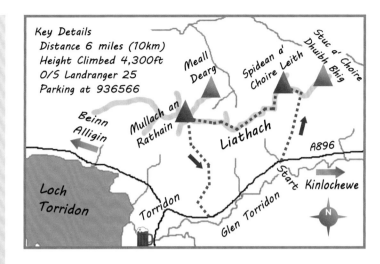

Key Details
Distance 6 miles (10km)
Height Climbed 4,300ft
O/S Landranger 25
Parking at 936566

Meall Dearg

Spidean a' Choire Leith

Stuc a' Choire Dhuibh Bhig

Beinn Alligin

Mullach an Rathain

Liathach

A896

Start

Kinlochewe

Loch Torridon

Torridon

Glen Torridon

N

Ascending Liathach (2013).

FLOWERDALE PEAKS

Beinn an Eoin and Baosbheinn from Gairloch.

BEINN DEARG *(2,998ft)*
BAOSBHEINN *(2,871ft)*
BEINN AN EOIN *(2,805ft)*

» Beinn Dearg was the highest
Corbett until the recent Munro
demotions. Two more feet and
it would be a popular Munro.

» The other two Flowerdale
Corbetts are spectacular
mountains with great views.

» The traverse of all three
Corbetts is a long day,
24 miles and 7,000ft
of climbing.

Personal View

Beinn an Eoin and Baosbheinn are two fine Corbetts standing in
the Flowerdale Forest just north of the Torridon giants, Beinn Eighe,
Liathach and Beinn Alligin. I climbed them on a trip up to Torridon
with Jo and Kyle in June 2011.

We were also thinking of climbing Beinn Dearg which would have
made for a very long day. However, this plan was scuppered when
we locked the car keys in one of the rooms. As it was 6 a.m. in the
morning it took over an hour to find somebody to open the door, so
we were delayed setting out and did not have time to climb Beinn
Dearg. The highlight of the walk was Baosbheinn, a big and spectacular mountain with five separate peaks to traverse. The weather
cleared at the summit and there were superb panoramic views.

I had always thought Beinn Dearg would be a great mountain to
traverse but it wasn't until July 2013 that Jonathan and I climbed it.
Following a steep ascent of 1,500ft we reached the ridge near Stuc
Loch na Cabhaig. Although the day was cloudy and windy, the ridge
to the summit and the east ridge were both magnificent.

My Routes

BAOSBHEINN AND BEINN AN EOIN (8-10 hours)

There is a small car park next to a green shed off the A832 Kinlochewe to Gairloch road. The track led SE over a footbridge and continued 5km, turning south to reach the ridge up Beinn an Eoin. We climbed the ridge bypassing the NW buttress then continued SSE passing over three minor tops. On the final summit climb the ridge narrowed. From the summit we descended south down the ridge for 400m, then dropped down steeply west to the Poca Buidhe bothy.

From the bothy we walked SW then west to the bottom of the ridge leading to Baosbheinn. From here we climbed NW over two tops, pt 707m and pt 806m and finally to the summit of Baosbheinn. From there the ridge continued over three minor tops. We descended from a col before reaching Creag an Fhithich.

BEINN DEARG (5-6 hours)

From the Coire Mhic Nobuil car park (as for Beinn Alligin) we followed the path NE up the corrie. Shortly after crossing the river at a bridge we took the left fork to the Bealach a' Chomhla. On reaching the bealach, we climbed steeply east to Stuc Loch na Cabhaig. The ridge dropped 200ft, then climbed to the summit of Beinn Dearg. From the summit we descended SE then east to a col and up a narrow ridge. A descent over two rock steps gave some scrambling. We carried on along the ridge and descended before the next rise at a cairn.

Key Details

» Distance 8 miles (13km)
» Height climbed 3,300ft
» O/S Landranger 19 and 24
» Parking at 869577.

For reference, see Beinn Alligin for map of Beinn Dearg.

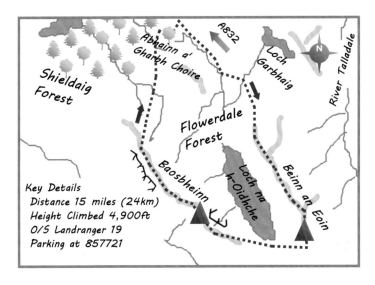

Key Details
Distance 15 miles (24km)
Height Climbed 4,900ft
O/S Landranger 19
Parking at 857721

Looking south along the summits of Baosbheinn, Beinn an Eoin behind (2011).

FISHERFIELD FOREST

The Causeway between Dubh Loch and Fionn Loch, Beinn Lair in the background *(Heather Thomas-Smith)*.

**MULLACH COIRE MHIC
FHEARCHAIR *(3,343ft)*
SGURR BAN *(3,245ft)*
SLIOCH *(3,217ft)*
A'MHAIGHDEAN *(3,173ft)*
BEINN TARSUINN *(3,075ft)*
RUADH STAC MOR *(3,012ft)*
BEINN A' CHLAIDHEIMH
(2,998ft)
BEINN LAIR *(2,821ft)*

» This classic two day walk from
Kinlochewe to Dundonnell goes
over eight Top 500 Summits
including six Munros and two
Corbetts.

» These are some of the most
remote mountains in Scotland
with A' Mhaighdean arguably
the most remote of them all.

» Beinn A' Chlaidheimh was
recently remeasured and
demoted from Munro to
Corbett status.

Personal View

The Fisherfield Forest contains some of the most remote mountains in Scotland. A' Mhaighdean competes for the title of the most remote Munro with Lurg Mhor and Carn an Fhidhleir, all three are brutal distances from the road over difficult terrain. The route outlined below took us two days requiring over thirty miles of walking and more than 11,000ft of climbing. We completed it in June 1991. The weather was generally good with most of the summits clear but we had snow showers on the second day.

I regard it as the finest walk that we completed when climbing the Munros. We intended to stay in the bothy at Carnmore but it was locked (I believe it is now kept open). Fortunately it was a lovely evening and sleeping outside was not a problem.

On the second day it took us over thirteen hours to walk from Carnmore to Dundonnell over the 'Fisherfield Big Six'. Coming off Beinn Tarsuinn after six hours of walking I took the rare step of demanding that we stop for lunch. Jonathan started on the brew as the snow started to fall. The end result was a lukewarm colourless liquid to which we added chocolate, shortbread and a bun. Hardly a healthy mix but it seemed to do the trick and kept us going over the next three Munros. Towards the end we were starting to feel weak and the landrover track back to Corrie Hallie seemed never ending. Almost certainly we were suffering from a lack of food so it was great that Reg was there to transport us to the Fish and Chip shop at Ullapool.

FISHERFIELD FOREST continued

My Route (two days, 23-26 hours walking)

We parked by the side of the road at Incheril near Kinlochewe and followed the path to the south end of Loch Maree. After crossing a bridge we turned right and followed a path up Gleann Bianasdail. After 2km we reached a stream, the Tuill Bhain, and followed a path to the summit of Slioch.

From the summit of Slioch we descended to the west end of Loch Garbhaig. We climbed NW up Beinn Lair, a very remote Corbett, and then walked WNW to the Bealach Mheinnidh. From the bealach a path led NNE past Dubh Loch to Carnmore where we stayed the night.

We made an early start the following morning following paths in an easterly direction, turning right to the north end of Fuar Loch Mor. The route continued SE to the col between Ruadh Stac Mor and A'Mhaighdean. We climbed Ruadh Stac Mor first, then returned to the col and climbed A'Mhaighdean.

We descended the SE ridge, then climbed Beinn Tarsuinn, an impressive mountain with a good ridge. Again we descended SE, then started walking north over the rough summits of Mullach Coire Mhic Fhearchair and Sgurr Ban. The traverse to Beinn a' Chlaidheimh was long and tiring. From the summit we descended north for 1km, then east down grassy slopes to reach the track to Corrie Hallie.

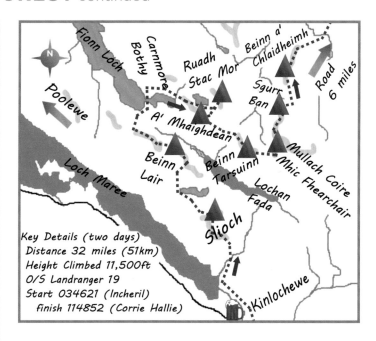

Key Details (two days)
Distance 32 miles (51km)
Height Climbed 11,500ft
O/S Landranger 19
Start 034621 (Incheril)
finish 114852 (Corrie Hallie)

PLACES TO STAY/DRINK

I understand that the Carnmore Bothy is now left open but the accommodation is basic. There are hotels and guest houses at Kinlochewe. There is a hotel and camping at Dundonnell.

Summit of Beinn Lair (1991).

FISHERFIELD CORBETTS

BEINN A' CHAISGEIN MOR
(2,812ft)
BEINN AIRIGH CHARR
(2,595ft)

» Two remote Corbetts in the Fisherfield Forest.

My Routes

BEINN A' CHAISGEIN MOR
(with bike 7-8 hours)
There is roadside parking where the A832 crosses the Gruinard River. It was a rough cycle south splashing through streams for 7km to the Allt Loch Ghiubhsachain, where I abandoned the bike. The route continued south to Loch Ghiubhsachain and I made my way past the loch on the west side.

After passing the loch I walked a few hundred metres further south, then climbed steep hillside to Lochan na Bearta. I traversed part of the way round the south side of the lochan, then easy slopes led SW to the summit of Beinn a' Chaisgein Mor. The descent took me due north over point 682m, magnificent walking. After descending north from point 682m I made my way directly back to where I had left the bike.

BEINN AIRIGH CHARR
(6-7 hours)
I drove to Poolewe, turned off the main road and found a car park just off the minor road to Inveran and Kernsary. The walking was easy down a tarmac single track road but I wished I had a bike. After passing Loch an Doire Ghairbh, I followed a path, at times faint, across the moorland SE for 1km to join the track from Kernsary to Ardlair.

1km after joining this track, an old sheep fold can be spotted about 100m to the left of the track. I turned left here and followed a path which climbed to the col between Spidean nan Clach and Meall Chnaimhean. Finally I traversed round a large bowl to the summit of Beinn Airigh Charr.

Looking north from point 682m on Beinn a' Chaisgein Mor (2016).

Personal View

Beinn a' Chaisgein Mor and Beinn Airigh Charr are two remote Corbetts in the Fisherfield Forest. It would be possible to climb both in the same walk but this would be a very long undertaking probably requiring an overnight stop at Carnmore. Beinn a' Chaisgein Mor is a contender for the most remote Corbett, whilst Beinn Airigh Charr has excellent views over Loch Maree.

I wanted to find a clear day to climb Beinn a' Chaisgein Mor, one of the great Corbetts of the far north west, remote, brooding, and rarely visited. The forecast was good as I set out from next to the Gruinard River in May 2016. A rough cycle ride was followed by some pathless walking to reach Lochan na Bearta, a beautiful loch nestling high in the hills. However, the real rewards came as I descended north down Chaisgein's summit slopes, the sun glistening over the sea and nearby lochs. This was my second last Corbett and not one I will forget.

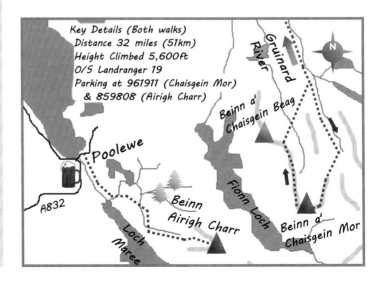

Key Details (Both walks)
Distance 32 miles (51km)
Height Climbed 5,600ft
O/S Landranger 19
Parking at 961911 (Chaisgein Mor)
& 859808 (Airigh Charr)

SHENAVALL CORBETTS

BEINN DEARG MOR *(2,985ft)*
BEINN DEARG BHEAG
(2,690ft)

» These two classic Corbetts are usually completed by a circuit from Shenavall Bothy.

» The Corbetts could be combined with An Teallach in a two day expedition staying at Shenavall.

» Beinn Dearg Mor is a stunning mountain.

Personal View

Beinn Dearg Mor is a fine mountain and one of the best Scottish Corbetts. It is remote and climbing it from Corrie Hallie with its near neighbour Beinn Dearg Bheag would make for a very long day. Therefore we decided to walk to Shenavall Bothy the previous evening, stay the night, and climb both Corbetts the following day.

Thus Alistair, Jonathan, JP and I met at Shenavall Bothy at 9 p.m. early in July 2006. In the morning Alistair set off for Ruadh Stac Mor and A' Mhaighdean in the Fisherfield Forest, whilst we struggled up the steep slopes of Beinn Dearg Mor. Once on the summit of Beinn Dearg Mor the day became easier and we were able to get back to Ullapool in time for a bar snack at the Ferry Boat Inn.

My Route (return to Corrie Hallie, 10-12 hrs)

I left the A832 at Corrie Hallie and followed the track south for 3km. At the highest point a path went right to Shenavall Bothy where we stayed the night.

The following morning we crossed the Abhainn Srath na Sealga and continued WSW to Larachantivore (this may not be possible in very wet weather). We walked south for a short distance, then made a steep rising traverse SW then NW up a steep corrie. Finally we turned north to the summit of Beinn Dearg Mor.

From the summit the route went SW initially but soon turned NW to descend the ridge to the col before Beinn Dearg Bheag. From the col we climbed NW up the ridge to the summit of Beinn Dearg Bheag. We returned to the col and descended NE past Loch Toll an Lochan. A wet crossing round the head of Loch na Sealga led back to Shenavall Bothy and the long walk to Corrie Hallie.

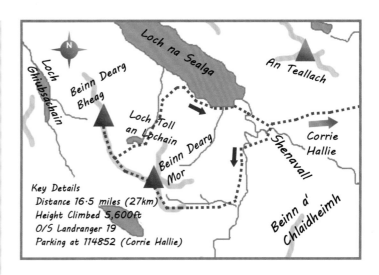

Key Details
Distance 16·5 miles (27km)
Height Climbed 5,600ft
O/S Landranger 19
Parking at 114852 (Corrie Hallie)

Beinn Dearg Bheag from the south.

AN TEALLACH

An Teallach in early morning mist *(Heather Thomas-Smith)*.

BIDEIN A' GHLAS THUILL
(3,484ft)

» **Sgurr Fiona (3,478ft) is the second Munro on the ridge.**

» **An Teallach is arguably the most magnificent mountain in Britain.**

» **There are spectacular views of An Teallach on the approach from Ullapool along 'Destitution Road'.**

» **The ridge walk gives excellent scrambling over the crest of Corrag Bhuidhe but the difficulties can be avoided by following the path on the SW side.**

Personal View (JP)

An Teallach is a cracking mountain, arguably the greatest mountain in the British Isles, a colossus. The ridge with its two Munros makes an excellent day walk but can be completed by ordinary mortals without too much difficulty. With Alistair and Jonathan I turned right off the Shenavall track and mounted broad backed Sail Liath in 1996. The pinnacled ridge was brilliant and if you are wary of heights, like Barry who claims gale force winds in 78, there is a path on the western side. Fine views over Fisherfield and Lord Berkeley's Seat is an airy must. Once over the summits it is a long descent to Dundonnell by the stalkers' path.

Talking about Dundonnell, I was at the O2 watching U2 recently and the Scottish girl next to me was amazed that I had been to Dundonnell, maybe it was she who served me in the Pub. "18 years in London and you are the first person I have met who knows my village" she said.

Another time I horseshoed Mheall Liath and came off Mheall Mor, rough over the flats then hazardous route finding through the crags. Steer clear of that way, stick to the classic route, because that is what it is.

My Route (6-7 hours)

I climbed An Teallach back in 1978 with Donald and Chris Storey in a strong SW wind. We started at Dundonnell and finished at Corrie Hallie car park, having arranged transport back from Corrie Hallie to save the two mile road walk.

The track from Dundonnell left the A832 500m SE of the Hotel. The path led WSW over Meall Garbh until it was due north of Bidein a' Ghlas Thuill. From here we walked south over a small top to its summit. We continued to Sgurr Fiona by descending 450ft to a col, then climbed a steep and rocky ridge to its summit. During this ascent we were blown ten feet at a time by gale force winds. Squally showers passed over but in the gaps between them the scenery was spectacular.

Having completed Sgurr Fiona, the second Munro, it was possible to go back the same way. However, we continued SSE using the footpath on the west side as the wind was too strong to follow the crest of the ridge. After climbing Sail Liath we descended SE to the path leading back from Shenavall to Corrie Hallie.

PLACES TO STAY/DRINK

The Dundonnell Hotel is close to the start and finish of the walk and provides food and accommodation.

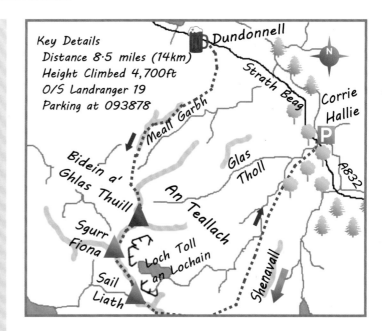

Key Details
Distance 8·5 miles (14km)
Height Climbed 4,700ft
O/S Landranger 19
Parking at 093878

POINTS OF INTEREST

An Teallach is a complex mountain with ten distinct summits or 'Tops' over 3,000ft. The most spectacular ridge walking is the traverse of the Corrag Bhuidhe pinnacles and Lord Berkeley's Seat, an overhanging pinnacle.

Approach to An Teallach from Dundonnell *(Heather Thomas-Smith)*.

WESTERN FANNICHS

SGURR BREAC *(3,281ft)*
A' CHAILLEACH *(3,270ft)*

» These two Munros lie west of the main Fannich ridge.

» The Munros are normally climbed separately from the main Fannich ridge.

» There is a connecting col to the main Fannich ridge at 1,800ft so it is possible to climb all the Fannichs in one day.

Relaxing at the summit of Sgurr Breac in 1991.

My Route (6-7 hours)

We started from the A832 where the private road runs south to Loch a' Bhraoin. We followed the private road south to the east end of the loch. A stalkers' path led south towards the 1,800ft col between Sgurr nan Clach Geala and Sgurr Breac. After walking nearly 3km along the stalkers' path, we climbed SW to reach the summit of Sgurr Breac.

From the summit the ridge went west over the Top of Toman Coinnich, then descended to 2,700ft before the final climb west to A' Chailleach. We descended NNE to Sron na Goibhre, then east towards the stream descending from Loch Toll an Lochain. We followed the stream down, then headed NE to Loch a' Bhraoin and the start point.

POINTS OF INTEREST

During the 1980s there were plans to dam Loch a' Bhraoin and pipe the water to a turbine house further down the Glen. However, these plans were resisted and the loch remains intact.

Personal View

We climbed these two Munros in 1991 after our two day trip through the Fisherfield Forest so we were tired with sore feet. We made a shortcut by heading straight up Sgurr Breac before we reached the top of the pass. It was a tough ascent so we regretted the deviation from the suggested route.

I had forgotten that ridge walking in the Fannichs is very pleasant, the underfoot conditions are good, the views superb and the undulations not too demanding. It was a shame that my right boot was giving so much pain particularly going downhill. We returned to a cafe in Ullapool for Haggis with Tea and Apple Juice after the walk.

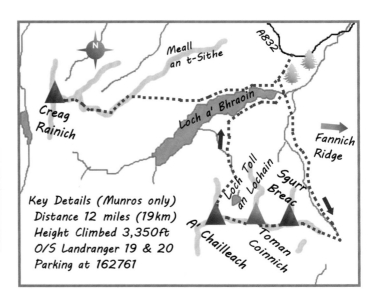

Key Details (Munros only)
Distance 12 miles (19km)
Height Climbed 3,350ft
O/S Landranger 19 & 20
Parking at 162761

CENTRAL FANNICHS

SGURR MOR *(3,642ft)*
SGURR NAN CLACH GEALA
(3,586ft)
BEINN LIATH MHOR A'
GHIUBHAIS LI *(2,513ft)*

» The main ridge of the Fannichs contains seven Munros, the other five are An Coileachan (3,028ft), Meall Gorm (3,114ft), Beinn Liath Mhor Fannaich (3,130ft), Meall a' Chrasgaidh (3,064ft), Sgurr nan Each (3,028ft).

» The traverse of the full ridge needs transport at both ends.

My Routes

It took me three walks to complete the Fannich Munros and the solitary Corbett which lies near the ridge.

CENTRAL RIDGE (6-7 hours)
In 1986 I started from the A832 road near Loch a' Bhraoin and followed the private road to the east end of the loch. I continued south on the stalkers' path for 5km to the top of the pass. A climb east up the hillside led to the main Fannich ridge. I climbed south to the top of Sgurr nan Each then north over Sgurr nan Clach Geala and Meall a' Chrasgaidh.

SGURR MHOR AND EAST RIDGE (8-9 hours)
Many years later I climbed Sgurr Mor and the three other Munros on the main Fannich ridge. From An Coileachan, the last Munro, it was a long walk back to the road.

BEINN LIATH MHOR A' GHIUBHAIS (2-3 hours)
Finally in 2006 I climbed the Corbett, Beinn Liath Mhor a' Ghiubhais LI. This was a straightforward walk starting and finishing on the A835 road near the NW end of Loch Glascarnoch.

Personal View (JP)

Rucksack, bag, stove and tent onto my back, off into the hills again. Took the bus to Aultguish Inn on a balmy Summer day. Due west to the Fannichs was the aim, first to Loch Gorm, not good underfoot, a trudge through ex forestry ditches and peat hags. I kept to the higher ground with only skylarks for company and was glad to reach the steeper slopes. Sweaty business but the summit of An Coileachan was a great viewpoint of rolling hillsides and lochs.

Fast going up to Meall Gorm and a steep pull to Sgurr Mor landed me at the highest point of the trip. Mars Bar consumed and round the horseshoe taking in the three western Munros. Plenty of snow in Geala's NE corries but the clouds were now building overhead. Coming off Sgurr nan Each I was wary of the fast approaching front so took off south to the lochside to camp. I found a dilapidated barn, cooked my rice and settled satisfactorily as the rain pounded what was left of the roof. It had been a good day, 20km from my start point with six Munros ticked.

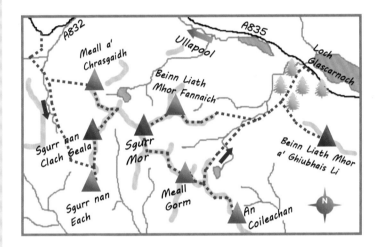

Rainbow on the Fannichs *(Chris Wood)*.

EASTER ROSS

Ben Wyvis and Little Wyvis from Beinn a' Chaisteil.

BEN WYVIS *(3,433ft)*
LITTLE WYVIS *(2,507ft)*
CARN CHUINNEAG *(2,750ft)*

» One Munro and two Corbetts situated in Easter Ross, not far north of Inverness.

» Ben Wyvis is the best known of these mountains. In the 1970s there were plans to build a ski area on the mountain and a funicular railway up from Strathpeffer.

» Carn Chuinneag is normally climbed separately and gives an excellent excuse to explore the area west of Bonar Bridge.

Personal View (JP)

Garbat leaves me stone cold. Having motored past it many times on the way to Ullapool I cannot bring myself to go through the plantations to glorious Ben Wyvis to the east. So one June day I attacked Wyvis from the lodge inland of coastal Evanton. Yes, this left a trudge up a forested track but it is a lonely one spitting me out at Loch Glass. A mile later I turned left up rough slopes. Above the rock line at 2,500ft a good walk transpired around the whole horseshoe of the mountain.

A broad easy ridge led to the first top, Tom a' Choinnich and then to the summit of Ben Wyvis. This whole upper circuit would be great to ride, cycle or run round with snow in the eastern corries for a good part of the summer. Detouring south to An Cabar, I rounded the head of a small grassy corrie to hit the ridge back east. An easy descent led to a long but lovely wild trudge down the glen with plunge pools and plenty of flora. A longer but better route to Ben Wyvis than through the forest from Garbat.

Not far to the north of Ben Wyvis Lodge lies Carn Chuinneag which Barry climbed after driving in from Bonar Bridge. He visited Croick Church then cycled up a private track to the foot of the mountain, it sounded like an easy day in the hills!

POINTS OF INTEREST
Croick Church (see opposite) was built in 1827 and can be visited when climbing Carn Chuinneag. It has messages scratched on its east window with stories of those who lost their homes in the Highland clearances.

My Routes

BEN WYVIS AND LITTLE WYVIS (combined 5-6 hours)

These two summits can be combined but I climbed them separately. On both walks I parked 500m south of Garbat where there is a car park just off the A835 near the start point.

A good path led through the trees on the north bank of the Allt a' Bhealaich Mhoir. After 2km I came out of the trees. I climbed Ben Wyvis by continuing in an easterly direction following a good path up An Caber. From there it was 3km to the summit of Ben Wyvis walking NE along a broad ridge.

I climbed Little Wyvis by branching right in a southerly direction at the end of the trees. I climbed the hillside to the col between Tom na Caillich and Little Wyvis, then followed a good path along the broad ridge to the summit.

CARN CHUINNEAG (with bike 4-5 hours)

I drove up Strathcarron turning left one mile before Croick Church. There is parking on the opposite site of the road from Glencalvie Lodge. A 5km cycle south took me down Glen Calvie. Shortly after a track went off to Diebidale Lodge a stalkers' track climbed up the hillside. This headed towards the west top of Carn Chuinneag. I turned left to go east passing below the west summit. Finally a detour from the path took me NE to the main summit. I descended NNW to the private road and my bike.

Key Details

» **Distance 11 miles (18km)**
» **Height climbed 2,500ft**
» **O/S Landranger 20**
» **Parking at 464891.**

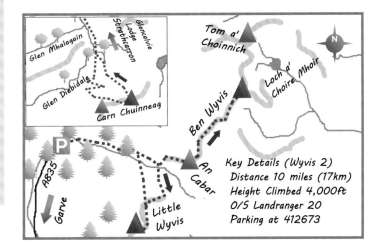

Croick Church (2013).

BEINN DEARG GROUP

Looking NW from the col between Beinn Dearg, Cona Mheall and Meall nan Ceapraichean (2012).

BEINN DEARG *(3,556ft)*
CONA MHEALL *(3,208ft)*
AM FAOCHAGACH *(3,130ft)*
EIDIDH NAN CLACH GEALA
(3,045ft)
BEINN ENAIGLAIR *(2,915ft)*

» There is a fifth Munro, Meall nan Ceapraichean (3,206ft).

» All five Munros can be completed in one day but Beinn Enaiglair will normally be climbed separately.

» Beinn Dearg is the most northerly mountain in Britain over 3,500ft.

Personal View

Beinn Dearg is one of a handful of Munros that I have climbed three times. It has a magnificent summit and on my first climb back in 1975 we could see both the Atlantic and the North Sea. On numerous other occasions I have admired it across Loch Broom from the bar of the Ferry Boat Inn. Next to it and to its right as viewed from the Ferry Boat Inn stands Beinn Enaiglair.

We climbed both mountains in 1975 starting from the nearest point on the A835. This was the first Corbett and Munro we climbed without being in a guided party. Donald took a rock home from the summit.

Twice I have climbed Beinn Dearg and the three Munros nearby but missed out Beinn Enaiglair. On the first of these walks we started south of Braemore Junction so we could also traverse Am Faochagach to give five Munros for the day. Jonathan suffered from a migraine for most of the day so he had a thoroughly miserable walk and kept apologising for his slow pace. Finally we took Alistair on the round of four Munros from Inverlael which I have outlined under 'My Route'.

My Routes

BEINN DEARG, CONA MHE-ALL AND EIDIDH NAN CLACH GEALA (8-10 hours)

At Inverlael there is a car park just off the A835 south of Ullapool. We followed a private road 3km through the forest, then continued on a stalkers' path up the glen past a small lochan to the col to the north of Beinn Dearg. We walked past another lochan to a dry stone wall. This climbed south to the summit plateau of Beinn Dearg. We walked SSW across the plateau to the cairn.

From the summit we returned NNE to the gap in the dry stone wall. We followed the west side of the wall down to the col. This is the centre point for three Munros, Beinn Dearg, Cona Mheall and Meall nan Ceapraichean. First, we went east to the top of Cona Mheall, a climb of 600ft, then returned to the col. The climb to Meall nan Ceapraichean was just under 450ft.

We continued NE from Meall nan Ceapraichean over a top, then descended NE taking care to stay on the compass bearing as there was thick mist and tricky ground to negotiate. Finally we turned NW up grassy slopes to Eididh nan Clach Geala.

BEINN ENAIGLAIR (3-4 hours without Beinn Dearg)

In 1975 we climbed Beinn Enaiglair directly from the A835. We carried on over Iorguill to the summit of Ben Dearg, a magnificent walk.

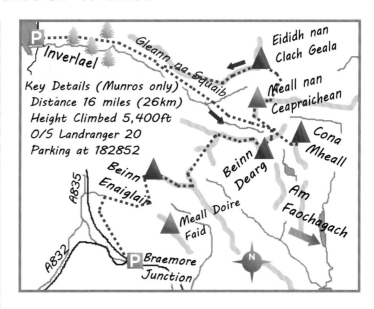

Key Details (Munros only)
Distance 16 miles (26km)
Height Climbed 5,400ft
O/S Landranger 20
Parking at 182852

Ascending Beinn Dearg (2012).

DESTITUTION ROAD

CREAG RAINICH *(2,647ft)*
SAIL MHOR *(2,516ft)*

» Both Corbetts are climbed from the A832 road to Gairloch known as 'Destitution Road'.

My Routes

CREAG RAINICH *(5-6 hours)*
I started from the A832 four miles NE of Braemore junction where a private road branched off to Loch a' Bhraoin. After walking along the private road to the boathouse, I followed the track along the north side of Loch a' Bhraoin. Just over halfway along the loch, I left the track and climbed up the hillside on the right to the broad ridge. It was an easy walk past point 749m to reach the summit.

For reference, see map with West Fannichs on page 276.

SAIL MHOR *(3-4 hours)*
I parked by the road at Ard-essie and followed a path up the east side of the water-falls. When the path levelled out, I crossed the stream and walked west to the bottom of the steep south ridge. I climbed north, then followed the ridge to the summit.

Key Details

» Distance 10 miles (17km) (Creag Rainich) and 5 miles (8km) (Sail Mhor)

» Height climbed 2,000ft (Creag Rainich) and 2,500ft (Sail Mhor)

» O/S Landranger 19 and 20

» Parking at 162761 (Creag Rainich) and 052896 (Sail Mhor).

POINTS OF INTEREST
The name 'Destitution Road' arose because the road was built during the Highland Potato Famine of 1846/7 to provide employment to crofters.

Looking east from Creag Rainich down Loch a' Bhraoin (2011).

Personal View

CREAG RAINICH
Creag Rainich is an isolated Corbett which does not fit easily with the Fisherfield or Fannich Munros although it has good views over both. I started at the same point as for the central Fannich Munros. It was an uneventful walk apart from wading through the loch to avoid some highland cattle.

Evening on the summit of Sail Mhor (2014).

SAIL MHOR
Sail Mhor lies further down Destitution Road past Dundonnell. It is like a forgotten child of An Teallach lying round the back of that great mountain. Its summit on a September evening was a beautiful place. To the west Desolation Road seemed to lead directly to the sea and the Summer Isles. The inland view was dominated by An Teallach, but as my eyes moved right the legendary Corbetts of Beinn Dearg Mor and Beinn Dearg Bheag appeared and finally, behind them, the great peaks of the Fisherfield Forest.

CARN BAN

CARN BAN *(2,772ft)*
BEINN A' CHAISTEIL
(2,582ft)

» Carn Ban is one of the most
remote Corbetts and is best
climbed by cycling ten miles
up the track from Black Bridge.

» Climbing Beinn a' Chaisteil
with Carn Ban adds two hours
to the day.

My Route (with bike 9-12 hours)

There is a small car park just
off the A835 near Black Bridge.
I parked and cycled north to
the track which runs along the
east side of Loch Vaich.

I continued north on the bike
past Loch Vaich and Meall a'
Chaorainn (a Graham) then
turned west. I stopped due
south of Carn Ban next to a
bridge and followed the stalkers' path west then north.
Soon I was on open hillside
and a long walk north over
undulating tops led me to Carn
Ban.

On the return journey I left the
bike at the high point of the
track NW of Beinn a' Chaisteil
and climbed SE to the summit.

Personal View

Carn Ban is a very remote Corbett which I thought could be combined with Beinn a' Chaisteil but only by using a bike. It was a long
cycle from Black Bridge and I found it difficult to average more than
six miles per hour on the rough track. I had not expected to see anyone all day but met a man from Dundee when parking the bike and
one from Derby near the summit of Carn Ban. The latter had only
twenty Corbetts to complete his round and had camped beneath
Carn Ban, having walked in over Beinn a' Chaisteil the previous day.

I was doubtful if I would have the energy to climb Beinn a' Chaisteil
on the way back but, from the highest point on the track to Carn
Ban it was a short climb with 1,300ft of ascent. Much relieved at
having climbed two remote Corbetts I cycled slowly back to Black
Bridge and then drove to the Aultguish Inn.

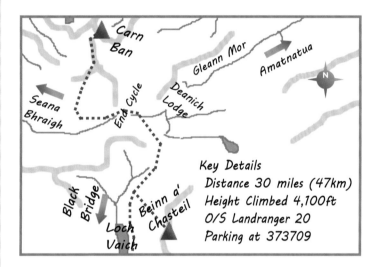

Key Details
Distance 30 miles (47km)
Height Climbed 4,100ft
O/S Landranger 20
Parking at 373709

Looking NW from Carn Ban (2013).

Summit of Beinn a' Chaisteil (2013).

SEANA BHRAIGH

SEANA BHRAIGH (3,040ft)

» Seana Bhraigh is one of the most remote and impressive Munros in Northern Scotland.

» There are three separate routes to Seana Bhraigh, from the A835 at Inverlael, by bike down Glen Achall (my route), and by bike from the north down Strath Mulzie.

Seana Bhraigh from the north (*Chris Wood*).

My Route (from Ullapool with bike 8-10 hours)

We ascended Seana Bhraigh from the NW by cycling down Glen Achall from Ullapool. Without bikes the route from Inverlael appears to be the shortest. The walk could be combined with one or more of the Munros near Beinn Dearg. However, there are long distances to be covered and plenty of time should be allowed for any ascent from Inverlael.

From 2km north of Ullapool we cycled east down a private track, tarmac until Rhidorroch House. We continued on the bikes to East Rhidorroch Lodge, then walked south down a stalkers' path to the River Douchary. From here we climbed SE to the col between point 592m and the summit of Seana Bhraigh, then climbed SE to the summit.

We descended due north from the summit crossing the Allt a' Choire Bhuidhe, then went NW beside the Allt nan Caorach to Glen Achall. From there we made our way by a cross country route back to the bikes. On the map there is a good track along the north side of Glen Achall which may have been an easier route back to the bikes.

Personal View (JP)

Filthy day, I had spent the night in the bothy by Loch a' Choire Mhoir. Thundering rain announced a late and dismal dawn, light struggling through dense cloud that tore across the landscape on the teeth of a howling westerly.

This made me appreciate the Mountain Bothy Association, I had a decent fire and was nice and snug, why move? But the hill called and I set off after breakfast. Visibility was ten metres and I was quickly soaked despite my excellent gear. Barry, Alistair and Jonathan have always claimed that I missed the summit of Seana Bhraigh, a place I gave little thought to, but it afforded momentary shelter for a Mars bar.

I trudged south downhill, cheeks stinging and boots sloshing, grassy slopes led to the peat hagged morass at the head of Glen Douchary. I had intended to summit Clach Geala but turning into the rain changed my mind. I swam down the stalkers' track above Inverlael Forest, fording ever more dangerous streams up to my thighs. Popping out of the cloud at 800ft I immediately entered the shelter of the forest. Somehow I hitched back to Ullapool and a hot shower as the Ferry Boat Inn beckoned.

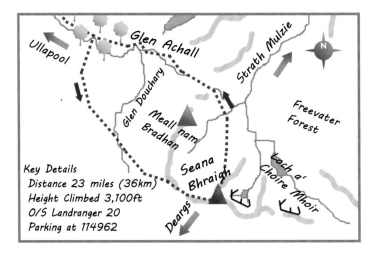

Key Details
Distance 23 miles (36km)
Height Climbed 3,100ft
O/S Landranger 20
Parking at 114962

Looking across Loch Shin to Beinn Leoid and Meallan an Chuail.

SCOTLAND: FAR NORTH

Far North Scotland covers the area from Ullapool in the south to the far north coast of the Scottish mainland.

There are 21 Top 500 Summits divided into 9 days walking:

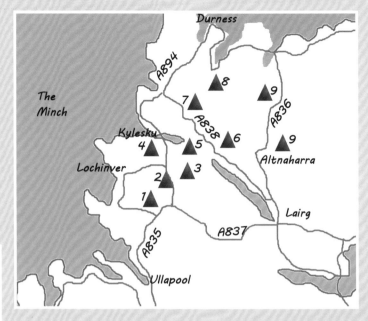

WALKS 1 TO 9

	Walk	Feet	Pg.
1	Cul Mor	2,787	288
	Cul Beag	2,523	
2	Canisp	2,775	290
	Breabag	2,670	
3	Ben More Assynt	3,273	291
4	Sail Gharbh	2,651	292
	Sail Gorm	2,546	
	Spidean Coinich	2,507	
5	Beinn Leoid	2,599	293
	Glas Bheinn	2,546	
6	Ben Hee	2,863	294
	Meallan Liath Coire Mhic Dhughaill	2,627	
	Carn an Tionail	2,490	
7	Foinaven	2,988	296
	Arkle	2,582	
	Meall Horn	2,548	
8	Cranstackie	2,625	298
	Beinn Spionnaidh	2,534	
	Ben Loyal	2,506	
9	Ben Klibreck	3,154	300
	Ben Hope	3,040	

To drive from Ullapool to the north coast of Scotland is to experience a wondrous and beautiful landscape, each turn in the road revealing new peaks jutting out from a wild landscape dotted with lochans. Ben More Coigach appears first followed by Cul Beag and Stac Pollaidh, Canisp, Ben More Assynt and Quinag.

After passing Quinag the new bridge at Kylesku is crossed and the landscape changes again, small lochans appearing reminiscent of the Hebrides and then ahead is the magnificent grey quartzite wall of Foinaven. Finally Cranstackie is passed and the north coast is reached at Durness.

Inland from the Ullapool to Durness road lies a number of additional mountains which include Ben Hope, the most northerly Munro, Ben Hee, a large rounded Corbett and beautiful Ben Loyal, sometimes called the 'Queen of Scottish mountains'.

The Top 500 Summits in the Far North include 3 Munros, 17 Corbetts and 1 Graham. They are all enjoyable mountains to climb.

Furthest north. Cranstackie from the west.

CUL MOR AND CUL BEAG

Stac Pollaidh from Lochan Dearg a' Chuil Mhoir (2012).

CUL MOR *(2,787ft)*
CUL BEAG *(2,523ft)*

» Cul Mor and Cul Beag are two of the great peaks of the far north lying just north of Ullapool. Both are Corbetts and Top 500 Summits.

» They can be climbed separately but combining them gives a complex and interesting crossing past lochs, islands and rivers.

» Two cars are required to avoid a long return walk.

Personal View

Cul Mor and Cul Beag are the first two Corbetts that appear when driving north from Ullapool. They can be climbed separately but combining these two great Corbetts gives an interesting and complex route. Going north to south, as we did, the final ascent of Cul Beag is hard and steep finishing directly on its sharp summit.

Jonathan and I completed the walk in June 2012. We left a car close to Cul Beag and started on the A835 just north of Knockan Crag. It was a quick ascent to the top of Cul Mor but the crossing was slow and the route finding complex.

We descended south from Cul Mor then a descending traverse took us to Lochan Dearg a' Chuil Mhoir, a remote and lonely lochan with a beach at one end. Now turning south again, another descending traverse took us to the shores of Lochan Dearg and the lowest point of the traverse, a paltry 200ft above sea level. From here we were finally able to make a direct and steep ascent to the summit of Cul Beag.

My Route (6-8 hours)

From Ullapool we drove north along the A835 and left a car just off the single track road to Lochinver, 250 yards past the east end of Loch Lurgainn. After driving back to the A835, we continued north and found a car park and path leading up Cul Mor.

We followed the path north and, after 2km, climbed WNW directly towards Cul Mor along a broad ridge. On reaching Meallan Diomhain we turned NNW to a small lochan, then climbed a steeper ridge SW to the summit.

From Cul Mor one option is to return by the same route, drive round to Loch Lurgainn and climb Cul Beag from there. This may be quicker and easier than doing the traverse but an excellent Scottish walk would be missed.

From the top of Cul Mor we descended SW to a col, then went east before descending SW to Lochan Dearg a' Chuil Mhoir. This required careful route finding. From here we walked south to Lochan Dearg. After skirting the west side of this loch, we climbed steeply west to a small col on the north ridge of Cul Beag.

This fine ridge took us to the summit of Cul Beag. We descended south until clear of the rocky buffs, then SSW down steeper ground to the car at Loch Lurgainn.

POINTS OF INTEREST

Knockan Crag lies close to the start point for Cul Mor. This tourist site shows how the earth evolved 500 million years ago.

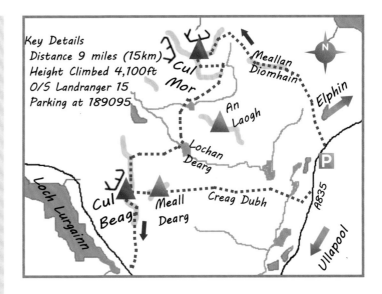

Key Details
Distance 9 miles (15km)
Height Climbed 4,100ft
O/S Landranger 15
Parking at 189095

Ascending Cul Beag (2012).

BREABAG AND CANISP

CANISP *(2,775ft)*
BREABAG *(2,670ft)*

» The route to Breabag passes prominent caves used by people in prehistoric times.

» Canisp is a fine Corbett with great views.

My Routes

CANISP (3-4 hours)

We started three miles north of Ledmore Junction at the north end of Loch Awe where there was space to park. A good path led west from the road crossing the River Loanan just north of Loch Awe. We followed the path (which disappeared at times) WNW towards the northern of two ridges coming off the east side of Canisp. We reached the northern ridge and went west turning NW for 800m to the summit with its circular shelter.

BREABAG (3-4 hours)

I started five miles north of Ledmore Junction where there is a salmon hatchery and car park. There were a few cars but most people were walking to the caves rather than the summit of Breabag. A good path led up the valley in an easterly direction. After 2km the caves appeared on the hillside to the right. The valley then split, I took the left fork and after a few hundred metres there was a steep section. At the top of this I climbed east up slopes which led to the broad summit ridge. At 2,000ft I turned south and walked 1km to reach the summit.

Key Details (both summits)

» Distance 13 miles (20km)

» Height climbed 4,900ft

» O/S Landranger 15

» Parking at 250159 (Canisp) and 252179 (Breabag).

The old caves on the way up Braebag (2011).

Personal View

Breabag would be a fine Corbett in clear conditions. Unfortunately the cloud was down at 1,800ft when I climbed it, so the views were poor and I trudged up the final 500ft in damp and misty conditions. The caves were interesting though, it is remarkable to think that prehistoric men lived in these caves thousands of years ago before even the pyramids in Egypt were built. The caves are 8,000 years old and amongst the remains of many species are human, reindeer, bear, wolf, lynx and arctic fox.

Jonathan and I climbed Canisp in June 2012 after a morning in the local coffee shop at Ullapool. It was windy on the summit and there were no views but the weather cleared on the descent. It would be possible to carry on from Canisp to Suilven eventually finishing in Lochinver. This would be a fabulous crossing but requires transport at both ends.

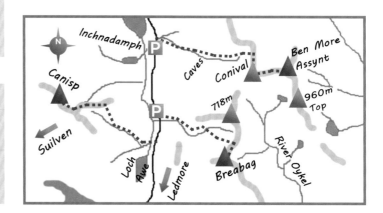

BEN MORE ASSYNT

BEN MORE ASSYNT *(3,273ft)*

» Conival (3,238ft), a second Munro, is climbed with Ben More Assynt.

» There are good summit ridges particularly if the Munro Top south of Ben More Assynt is visited.

» A detour can be made to see the Traligill caves.

My Route (6-7 hours)

In 1986 I started at the Inchnadamph Hotel leaving the A837 north of the hotel. Initially I followed a farm track on the north side of the River Traligill. The track crossed the river to go to the Traligill caves. However, I continued on the north side of the river and headed up the SW face of Beinn An Fhurain. I kept below the line of crags to reach the col between Conival and Beinn an Fhurain.

From the col I went south over the summit of Conival then east to traverse to Ben More Assynt. The underfoot terrain was poor on the crossing from Conival to Ben More Assynt. My notes from 1986 describe the ridge as narrow and airy but, for those who carry on to the south top of Ben More Assynt, the ridge becomes even narrower.

It would be possible to include Breabeg on a long circuit commencing from the Inchnadamph Hotel.

For reference, see map on the page opposite.

Key Details

» Distance 11 miles (17km)
» Height climbed 3,400ft
» O/S Landranger 15
» Parking at 251218.

Personal View (Jonathan)

Ben More Assynt and Conival lie twenty-five miles north of Ullapool and are the only Munros amongst the spectacular Corbetts in the area. I abandoned my pregnant wife in a cottage near Lochinver at 5.30 a.m. and headed off to climb them. Within an hour the rain had started and by the time I arrived at the summit of Conival it was simply foul.

The crossing from Conival to Ben More Assynt was not too bad but I was keen to tick off the Munro Top south of Ben More Assynt. I scrambled along an unpleasant wet ridge to a cairn which was surely the Top. Enough was enough and I took a near direct descent to the loch below. With zero visibility and incessant rain the descent was very difficult. At one point I had to lower myself down a waterfall in full spate, a fall could have been fatal. However, thirty minutes later the sun came out and I was strolling back to Inchnadamph.

Ben More Assynt seen across Loch Shin.

QUINAG

SAIL GHARBH *(2,651ft)*
SAIL GORM *(2,546ft)*
SPIDEAN COINICH *(2,507ft)*

» Three excellent Corbetts with a high start at 750ft.

» Spectacular views, interesting walking.

My Route (6-7 hours)

I started from the car park two miles north of Skiag Bridge. A path led west up Spidean Coinich and the rock bands can be ascended without difficulty. The traverse from Spidean Coinich to Sail Gorm took me over two tops at 713m and 745m. The 745m summit is the centre point of Quinag. After this summit I descended to a col, then climbed north to the summit of Sail Gorm.

From the summit of Sail Gorm I returned towards point 745m, traversing past it on the north side to the ridge leading east to the summit of Sail Gharbh. I returned along the Sail Gharbh ridge past point 745m to the low col. It was possible to descend from the col and return to the start along a good stalkers' path.

POINTS OF INTEREST

Kylesku Bridge lying north of Quinag was opened by the Queen in 1984. Previously the only way north was to use the Kylesku Ferry.

PLACES TO STAY/DRINK

Jonathan always suggests a visit to the Kylesku hotel when in this area. This hotel with its fine views is only four miles north of the start point for Quinag.

Quinag from Glas Bheinn.

Personal View (Jonathan)

Munros complete, what next? Although I was keen to complete the Munro Tops a holiday in Ullapool offered a more interesting alternative, Sutherland. Away from the Scottish islands Sutherland has some of the most spectacular landscape in Britain. Here lies a unique wilderness of lochs, sea, and rough moorland with mountains that climb precipitously from the wilderness. The underfoot terrain is hard but once high the walking improves and the views are wonderful.

JP and I set off for the Quinag where three Corbetts lie. Parking near Loch na Gainmhich we set off on a decent path to climb to the obvious Bealach. We climbed Spidean Coinich to the south then Sail Gorm to the north. Finally we summited Sail Gharbh and returned directly to the car and a two mile drive to Kylesku to enjoy one of the finest views from any pub in Britain. My abiding memory was how quickly we completed three Corbetts, are these the three easiest Corbetts in Scotland?

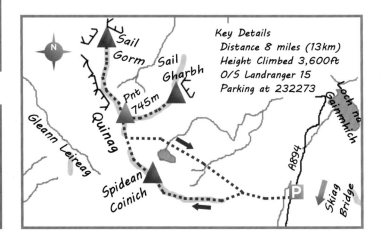

Key Details
Distance 8 miles (13km)
Height Climbed 3,600ft
O/S Landranger 15
Parking at 232273

CENTRAL CORBETTS

BEINN LEOID *(2,599ft)*
GLAS BHEINN *(2,546ft)*

» Beinn Leoid is best approached from the east.

» Glas Bheinn is a relatively short climb from the top of the A894 south of Unapool.

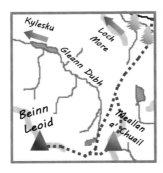

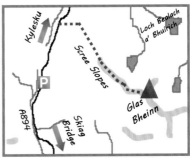

My Routes

BEINN LEOID *(4-5 hours)*

I started from the A838 2km SE of Loch More. A good stalkers' path climbed south and then SW to a broad saddle north of Meallan a' Chuail. From the saddle I traversed SSW to another stalkers' path, which climbed south to the col between Beinn Leoid and Meallan a' Chuail. I climbed WNW up a wide ridge to the summit of Beinn Leoid. I returned over Meallan a' Chuail. At 2,461ft, this summit only just misses the Top 500 list.

GLAS BHEINN *(2-3 hours)*

I started from the A894 just north of its highest point. A path went east for a short distance, then turned SE to a grassy gully which led to the NW ridge of the hill. I followed the ridge to the summit which was set back 200m south of the edge of the ridge.

Personal View

By March 2016 I only had six more mountains in the Top 500 to climb including two fine summits in the far north of Scotland, Beinn Leoid and Ben Loyal. It was a bright spring morning as I drove to Leoid from Bonar Bridge. A well built stalkers' path took me up to 1,600ft, then I enjoyed ascending Leoid followed by Meallan a' Chuail, its rocky neighbour. Beinn Leoid lies in the centre of the mountains of the far north of Scotland. From its summit I could make out all the peaks in the far north except Cul Beag.

Glas Bheinn sits across the A894 from Quinag. It is regarded as a fine viewpoint but this does not do it justice. In 2014 I found it an enjoyable climb with a steep pull leading to its gentle NW ridge.

Beinn Leoid from the slopes of Meallan a' Chuail (2016).

Key Details

» Distances 8.5 miles (14km) (Beinn Leoid) and 4 miles (6km) (Glas Bheinn)

» Height climbed 2,500ft (Beinn Leoid) and 1,800ft (Glas Bheinn)

» O/S Landranger 15

» Parking at 357333 (Beinn Leoid) and 238284 (Glas Bheinn).

PLACES TO STAY/DRINK
I saw a coffee sign at the Oak Lodge bed and breakfast at Overscaig next to Loch Shin. The coffee and cakes were very welcome.

REAY FOREST

Meallan Liath Coire Mhic Dhughaill from Carn an Tionail (2014).

BEN HEE *(2,863ft)*
**MEALLAN LIATH COIRE
MHIC DHUGHAILL** *(2,627ft)*
CARN AN TIONAIL *(2,490ft)*

» Three mountains in the Reay
Forest which lie just south of
their more popular neighbours,
Foinaven and Arkle.

» They could all be climbed on
one long day although I left
Ben Hee for a separate day.

» Meallan Liath Coire Mhic
Dhughaill is a complex
mountain with a number
of tops.

Personal View

These three mountains, two Corbetts and one Graham look north
to the 'High Priests' of the far north, Foinaven and Ben Hope. Ben
Hee is more eastern in character with high rolling slopes whilst Carn
an Tionail and Meallan Liath Coire Mhic Dhughaill have steeper
slopes plunging to lochans. They lie off the road from Lairg to Laxford Bridge, a passing place road where there are few cars. The
mountains tend to be the preserve of those climbing Corbetts and
Grahams but they are great summits.

I climbed them on successive days in 2014. On the first day I was
walking with Jonathan along the grand highway which is the summit
ridge of Carn an Tionail when we were surprised by deer appearing
no more than fifty yards in front of us. They had made a steep
climb up the east side of the ridge. There were twenty of them in
single file, the back markers appearing to be tired after the climb
up the steep hillside. After watching them pass we carried on to the
summit then followed a winding ridge to Meallan Liath Coire Mhic
Dhughaill.

The following day I climbed Ben Hee. It was a straightforward ascent
and as I arrived at the summit, suddenly all the peaks between Ben
Hee and the Atlantic Ocean to the north, including Ben Hope and
Ben Loyal, stood in front of me.

REAY FOREST continued

My Routes

CARN AN TIONAIL AND MEALLAN LIATH COIRE MHIC DHUGHAILL
(7-8 hours with two cars)

Having driven up from Ullapool, we parked at West Merkland. We had left Jonathan's car near Kinloch at the SE end of Loch More to avoid an additional three miles of road walking at the end of the day. I decided to leave Ben Hee until the next day so we followed the private road up the glen for 2km. After leaving the road we climbed north up the hillside to the long summit ridge of Carn an Tionail.

We followed the ridge for 3km to the summit, then descended steeply NW to the north end of Lochan a' Bhealaich. The route continued round the top of the loch, then ascended the NE ridge of Carn Dearg. A long winding ridge led to the summit of Meallan Liath Coire Mhic Dhughaill. From the summit we descended to the house at Aultanrynie where we had left Jonathan's car.

BEN HEE (4-5 hours)

The following day I climbed Ben Hee. Again I started at West Merkland and followed the same private road up the glen. After 1.5km I turned right and followed a stalkers' path east. The path ran next to a stream and climbed towards the summit. Finally I climbed NE to the trig point.

POINTS OF INTEREST

These mountains are situated in the Reay Forest. The estate is owned by the Duke of Westminster. One of the distinctive black telephone boxes can be seen at Achfary.

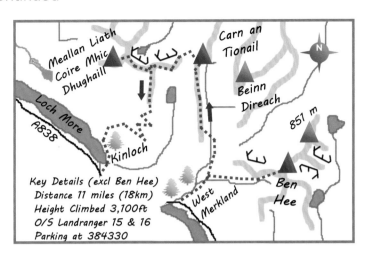

Key Details (excl Ben Hee)
Distance 11 miles (18km)
Height Climbed 3,100ft
O/S Landranger 15 & 16
Parking at 384330

Looking north from Ben Hee summit (2014).

FOINAVEN AND ARKLE

Arkle across Loch Stack (2013).

FOINAVEN *(2,988ft)*
ARKLE *(2,582ft)*
MEALL HORN *(2,548ft)*

» Three Corbetts in the far north of Scotland.

» Foinaven and Arkle are magnificent quartzite peaks in the far north.

» Foinaven was recently in the news as a possible new Munro but failed by twelve feet.

» Anyone attempting all three peaks in one day, a long undertaking, will need transport at both ends.

Personal View

Foinaven and Arkle are two of the great mountains of the far north with a unique appearance because of their grey quartzite slopes. Two famous racehorses have been named after them, Foinavon winning the Grand National in 1967. They can be climbed together (adding Meall Horn) in one long day but it took me two walks to complete them.

Jonathan and I climbed Foinaven in 2006. It was an uneventful climb with the cloud level just below the summit so the views were restricted. I returned seven years later to climb Arkle and Meall Horn. I had brought the bike for my week long trip and was determined to use it for every climb so I cycled to just past Lorne. From there I climbed to point 758m after which an interesting ridge ran for 1km to Arkle's summit. Fortunately the weather was clear and I had magnificent views of Foinaven.

Meall Horn turned out to be the poor neighbour of Foinaven and Arkle. A grassy climb of 1,200 foot from the stalkers' track took me to the summit just as a heavy shower arrived. I returned to the excellent stalkers' track and jogged down to pick up the bike at Lorne.

My Routes

ARKLE AND MEALL HORN (7-8 hours)

After driving up the A894 north from Ullapool I turned right at Laxford Bridge and followed the A838 for six miles. There was parking 100m up the private road and a short cycle ride took me to Lorne. I left the bike and took the left hand track which soon started winding its way up the mountain.

I left this track at ref 321432 and climbed north, passing the west side of Meall Aonghais, to point 758m. I descended 300ft as the ridge went west, then ascended north to the summit. After returning to point 758m I went over Meall Aonghais before heading east to Meall Horn. After crossing the stalkers' path at 1,300ft grassy slopes led to the summit of Meall Horn.

FOINAVEN (5-6 hours)

A few years before my ascent of Arkle and Meall Horn Jonathan and I had climbed Foinaven from the A838. We parked 4km NE of Rhiconich, then headed SSE to reach the summit by the most direct route.

All three mountains could be combined in a classic walk starting near Loch Stack. Arkle would be climbed first then, after a detour to Meall Horn, a long traverse would be required to reach Foinaven. The descent from Foinaven to the A838 north of Rhiconich is straightforward but a second car or willing driver would be needed for the pick up.

Key Details (Foinaven)

» **Distance 7 miles (11km)**
» **Height climbed 3,000ft**
» **O/S Landranger 9**
» **Parking at 275540.**

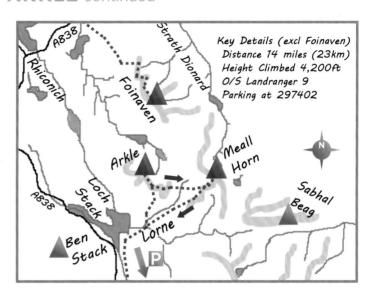

Key Details (excl Foinaven)
Distance 14 miles (23km)
Height Climbed 4,200ft
O/S Landranger 9
Parking at 297402

Foinaven from Arkle (2013).

FAR NORTH CORBETTS

Beinn Spionnaidh from Cranstackie; the sea off the far north of the Scottish mainland is seen beyond Beinn Spionnaidh (2013).

CRANSTACKIE *(2,625ft)*
BEINN SPIONNAIDH *(2,534ft)*
BEN LOYAL *(2,506ft)*

» Three Corbetts occupying the most northerly ground over 2,000ft in Britain.

» Beinn Spionnaidh is the most northerly Top 500 Summit.

» Cranstackie and Beinn Spionnaidh are little known peaks but give some of the most enjoyable walking in Britain.

» Ben Loyal is sometimes known as the 'Queen of Scottish Mountains' and is a very distinctive mountain lying near Tongue.

Personal View

Cranstackie and Beinn Spionnaidh are the most northerly summits in the Top 500 listing. They are both fine summits in their own right but it is their situation that makes them special. They overlook the sea north of Durness where the Atlantic Ocean merges into the North Sea. This was one of my favourite Corbett days which I hope to repeat soon.

I climbed Cranstackie and Beinn Spionnaidh in 2013. On the way up Cranstackie I met a group of six men, all Munroists. In total we calculated we had eight rounds between the seven of us! Cranstackie is a magnificent mountain and I was lucky enough to have clear and at times sunny weather. Then I walked north ascending Beinn Spionnaidh with its summit plateau overlooking the sea. The rain started on the way down Beinn Spionnaidh, so I headed quickly for a coffee shop in Durness where I learnt that a race to Cape Wrath was taking place at the weekend.

Tongue sits proudly on the north coast of Scotland with its own mountain, Ben Loyal, behind it. To reach Tongue I had driven up from Altnaharra in the 'rush hour' but had not seen a single car for fifteen miles. I love the peace and tranquillity of the far north. Ben Loyal is a grand mountain with a ridge that would be fun to complete end to end on a summer's day. To the east I could see Ben Hope and to the north the Orkney Islands.

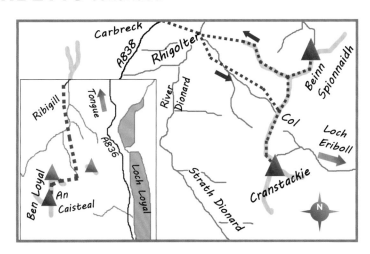

My Routes

CRANSTACKIE AND BEINN SPIONNAIDH (5-6 hours)

I parked near Carbreck on the A838 and cycled SSE to the farm at Rhigolter. From here I walked to Calbhach Coire and climbed to the col between Cranstackie and Beinn Spionnaidh.

I climbed SW up the ridge to the summit of Cranstackie, the quartzite near the summit making the walking awkward. After returning to the col I climbed north up Beinn Spionnaidh. The trig point was at the NE end of the summit ridge. I returned along the summit ridge, then descended NW down a grassy ridge to reach Rhigolter Farm.

Key Details

» Distance 8 miles (13km)
» Height climbed 3,200ft
» O/S Landranger 9
» Parking at 332592.

BEN LOYAL (4-5 hours)

I drove a short distance south from Tongue parking at a cattle grid before Ribigill Farm. The private road south turned into a track after it passed the farm. I continued south crossing a river, then followed a path up the hillside to the Bealach Clais nan Ceap. An ascent west up steep hillside led to the ridge just south of Sgor Chaonasaid. I followed the broad ridge south ascending An Caisteal (the summit) from the west side.

Key Details

» Distance 9 miles (14km)
» Height climbed 2,500ft
» O/S Landranger 10
» Parking at 584546.

PLACES TO STAY/DRINK

Durness is an excellent place to stay and has a variety of accommodation and eating places as well as craft shops. Tongue is also a great place to stay set in an inlet on the north coast. There are two hotels, the Tongue Hotel and the Ben Loyal Hotel, and a youth hostel.

Approaching Ben Loyal from the north (2016).

FAR NORTH MUNROS

BEN KLIBRECK *(3,154ft)*
BEN HOPE *(3,040ft)*

» Ben Hope is the most northerly Munro.

» These Munros are climbed separately but they can be completed in one day.

My Routes

BEN KLIBRECK *(4-5 hours)*

There was a car park off the A836 almost due west of Ben Klibreck. We crossed the river and aimed for the south end of Loch na Glas-choille. We continued to the north end of Loch nan Uan, then climbed SE up grassy hillside to a col at 688m. From here we followed the ridge north then east to the summit.

Key Details

» Distance 7 miles (11km)
» Height climbed 2,600ft
» O/S Landranger 16
» Parking at 545303.

BEN HOPE *(3-4 hours)*

After climbing Ben Klibreck we drove north, turning left off the A836 at Altnaharra, onto a minor road that passed the west side of Ben Hope. We parked 2km north of Alltnacaillich near a sheep shed. From here a path climbed beside a stream and through a break in the cliffs. Finally we walked north following the cliff edge to the summit.

Key Details

» Distance 4 miles (6km)
» Height climbed 3,000ft
» O/S Landranger 9
» Parking at 462476.

POINTS OF INTEREST

Rumour has it that it if you camp on the top of Ben Hope on a midsummer night, you can see the midnight sun (assuming it is not raining!).

Barry, not looking like a professional hill walker, on the ascent of Ben Hope (2004).

Personal View (Alistair)

A long evening in the Ferry Boat Inn at Ullapool had taken its toll; I woke up in the campsite with my head pounding, maybe a substantial breakfast would remedy the situation. We were late setting off and the drive to the car park near Ben Klibreck was long and the road twisted and turned, not good. We parked in a small car park just off the A836. Barry set off towards the hill.

That day Klibreck felt like an unrelenting slog across rough moorland then up steep slopes, at one stage we seemed to be caught on a craggy rock face but I put that down to Barry's poor route finding. Back the same way and I was now looking forward to a drink at the local hostelry and perhaps an afternoon swim off the coast at Durness. But it was not to be, Barry insisted on climbing Ben Hope as he had only five Munros to go.

Fortunately the weather was good now and I enjoyed the climb up Ben Hope, fine waterfalls easing the pain of the ascent and then we were there at the summit of this, the most northerly Munro. As a viewpoint the top is hard to beat and we spent twenty minutes there enjoying the sunshine before heading back. On the way back we stopped for a drink and a bar snack at the Crask Inn and at 11 p.m. I crawled back into my tent at Ullapool, tired but chuffed by the day.

Skye Cuillin from Elgol
(*Heather Thomas-Smith*).

SCOTLAND: SCOTTISH ISLANDS

The Scottish Islands covers the area from the Isle of Harris in the north to the Isle of Arran in the south.

There are 18 Top 500 Summits divided into 9 walks:

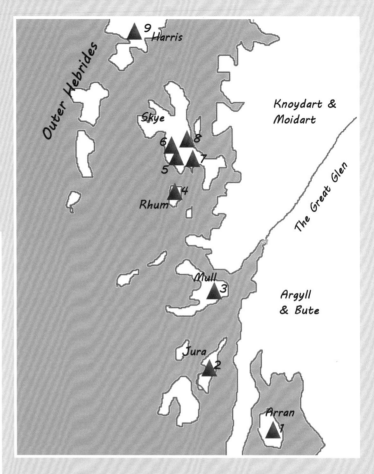

WALKS 1 TO 9

Walk		Feet	Pg.
1	Goat Fell	2,868	304
	Caisteal Abhail	2,817	
	Beinn Tarsuinn	2,710	
	Cir Mhor	2,620	
2	Beinn an Oir	2,576	306
	Beinn Shiantaidh	2,485	
3	Ben More	3,170	308
	Dun da Gaoithe	2,512	
	Beinn Talaidh	2,497	
4	Askival	2,663	310
	Ainshval	2,562	
5	Sgurr Alasdair	3,257	312
	Inaccessible Pinnacle	3,234	
6	Sgurr nan Gillean	3,167	314
7	Blaven	3,046	316
8	Garbh-bheinn	2,650	317
	Glamaig	2,542	
9	Clisham	2,622	318

The most mountainous island in the British Isles is the Isle of Skye with 11 Munros on its black Cuillin ridge. The Cuillin ridge is the best ridge in the British Isles and requires a good head for heights. Even reaching the ridge can be difficult. In total there are 6 Top 500 Summits on the Isle of Skye.

The other Scottish Islands with Top 500 Summits are the Isles of Arran (4 Summits), Jura (2 Summits), Mull (3 Summits), Rum (2 Summits), and Harris (1 Summit).

There is fine ridge walking over connected summits on the Islands of Arran and Rum whilst the Paps of Jura give excellent rough walking. The Islands of Mull and Harris with their various peaks are great places to visit.

Tobormory, Isle of Mull.

ARRAN CORBETTS

Caisteal Abhail from the summit of Goatfell (2015).

GOAT FELL *(2,868ft)*
CAISTEAL ABHAIL *(2,817ft)*
BEINN TARSUINN *(2,710ft)*
CIR MHOR *(2,620ft)*

» The Isle of Arran is an easy ferry trip, just under one hour, from the west coast of Scotland near Ayr.

» The walk described in our route is a classic walk over four Corbetts. Parts of the ridges are rocky and exposed but most of the difficulties can be avoided.

» The area is owned by the Scottish National Trust and the paths are excellent.

» The route starts two miles from Brodick Pier where passengers disembark from the Ferry. This means that there is no need to take a car across to Arran to climb these hills.

Personal View (Mist, Jonathan's dog)

I am a five year old Border Collie called Mist who has been antici-pating this day for months. Jonathan, my slow walking human friend and owner (not my choice) had promised for months to take me to the magical Island of Arran for a really good walk. His brother, Barry, wants to climb the four Corbetts on the island so I have been invited along to ensure they don't get lost.

7.00 a.m. found four of us (now including Jo, Barry's climbing friend) ascending alongside Glenrosa Water with overcast skies. We squelched through the bog towards the rocky tors of Beinn Nuis and the flat iron tower. Humans really are hopelessly slow but thank-fully I was allowed to run back and forth looking for sheep. I also prefer to be out front, sniffing for human smells on the trail, but the overwhelming deer musk frequently interrupted my concentration causing Barry and Jo to keep bumping into me. At the top they stopped briefly for a chocolate snack, telling me I wouldn't like it and it would be bad for me, Grrrummph!

Near the second top deer spoor, a flash of red above the path, and a sharp musky smell pulled me off the trail, only to be shouted back by Jonathan. I am not supposed to harass sheep but the rules on deer are less clear and they would be fun to chase, giving me some proper exercise. While Barry and Jo carried on to the third Corbett, Jonathan and I tackled the cliff face descent to the Saddle together. When I say together, I really mean on my own. Back legs first and facing into the hill may be an option for a human but for me it was head first, brace four legs across the groove and move one leg at a time, no helping hand from my 'owner'. My heart raced as my paws scratched the rough granite but eventually I slithered to the bottom. Now we ascended the granite tors of Goat Fell, the highest peak on Arran. I could see the Mull of Kintyre, the Paps of Jura; I felt like a dog in a million.

My Route (9-11 hours)

We drove from the hotel to the Glen Rosa road end where there was limited space to park. After walking 2.5km along a good path up Glen Rosa we turned west and followed a path up the hillside. This turned NW to the summit of Beinn Nuis. This summit is the start of a ridge which runs over three Corbetts and finishes above North Sannox Bridge.

The path dropped 250ft then climbed back up to Beinn Tarsuinn. We descended from the summit to where the path split, the right hand branch went over A' Chir and the left hand one went below the ridge missing the difficulties. As it was windy we followed the left hand path joining the ridge again below Cir Mhor. A steep climb led to the summit of magnificent Cir Mhor, then we descended to the col before Caisteal Abhail.

We ascended Caisteal Abhail and decided not to go on past the Witches Step to Glen Sannox. Thus, to climb Goat Fell, we returned over Cir Mhor and descended to the Saddle. The drop down from Cir Mhor to the Saddle required some scrambling as we lowered ourselves down the rocks. A good ridge climbed to North Goatfell and eventually to the summit of Goat Fell, with its trig point and circular viewfinder.

From the summit we descended east down a good path. At 2,000ft we turned south and followed a path which finished on the road just south of Brodick Castle.

PLACES TO STAY/DRINK

There are hotels, guest houses, restaurants and pubs in Brodick. We enjoyed dinner at the Brodick Bar.

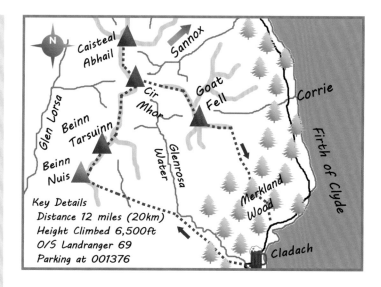

Key Details
Distance 12 miles (20km)
Height Climbed 6,500ft
O/S Landranger 69
Parking at 001376

POINTS OF INTEREST

Arran has been populated since prehistoric times but the population is now under 5,000. The main industry today is tourism with the attractions including Brodick Castle, Machrie Moor Stone Circle and Holy Isle.

Goatfell from Brodick Pier.

PAPS OF JURA

Beinn An Oir (right) and Beinn a' Chaolais from Beinn Shiantaidh *(Cornell Griffith)*.

BEINN AN OIR *(2,576ft)*
BEINN SHIANTAIDH *(2,485ft)*

» The Paps of Jura includes one additional Graham, Beinn a' Chaolais (2,407ft).

» The Paps of Jura is one of the classic Scottish walks with great views.

» The normal route to Jura requires two ferry crossings, first a ferry from the mainland to Islay then a short onward ferry from Islay to Jura.

» The difficult terrain means that the traverse of the Paps of Jura takes longer than expected.

Personal View

The Paps of Jura are iconic out of all proportion to their size. They rise up spectacularly in the centre of the remote Isle of Jura. They can be seen clearly from the Mull of Kintyre and far away places such as the Isle of Arran and the Arrochar Alps. The Paps of Jura are a place of dreams and should not be missed even though the island is hard to reach. Starting at Tarbert on the Mull of Kintyre it requires two ferries and a drive across Islay to reach the Isle of Jura.

In the 1980s I stayed on the Mull of Kintyre and watched the Paps of Jura turn red as the sun went down in the west. Finally I went over to Jura in June 2008 with my brothers, JP and his wife, Ella. In the sunshine it is a fantastic place. At Craighouse we sat outside in the evenings with a drink (or more) overlooking the sea.

We climbed Beinn an Oir and Beinn Shiantaidh in a superb round from the bridge over the Corran River. In retrospect it would have been good to add Beinn a' Chaolais but at least this failure gives an excuse for a second visit. If I was younger the fell race over the Paps would definitely be on my schedule, particularly as there are rumours that a bottle of Jura Whisky is given to every finisher.

My Route (6-7 hours)

There was parking off the A846 near the bridge over the Corran River. From the Corran River we climbed NW over a low shoulder to reach the east end of Loch an t-Siob. We walked west along the south side of the loch, then climbed to the col between Beinn An Oir and Beinn Shiantaidh. From here there was a path up the NE ridge of Beinn an Oir to its summit.

After returning to the col we ascended east to the summit of Beinn Shiantaidh. The descent SE was down bouldery and steep slopes. These led to the north side of Loch an t-Siob from where the path took us back to the start.

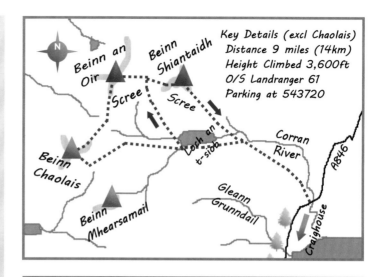

Key Details (excl Chaolais)
Distance 9 miles (14km)
Height Climbed 3,600ft
O/S Landranger 61
Parking at 543720

POINTS OF INTEREST

Over two hundred runners compete in the annual fell race over the Paps of Jura. The distance is 18 miles with over 7,500ft of climbing. The race is sponsored by the Jura distillery in Craighouse which produces Isle of Jura malt whisky.

Craighouse with Beinn Shiantaidh behind *(Cornell Griffith)*.

PLACES TO STAY/DRINK

Craighouse has a hotel and space for camping. The hotel provides bar snacks.

ISLE OF MULL

Alistair completes the Munros, summit of Ben More (2016).

BEN MORE *(3,170ft).*
DUN DA GAOITHE *(2,512ft)*
BEINN TALAIDH *(2,497ft)*

» Ben More is the only Munro on the Scottish Islands outside of Skye.

» Ben More was Jonathan's first and Alistair's last Munro.

» Beinn Talaidh used to be classified as a Corbett but was demoted and is now one of the highest Grahams.

» The Isle of Mull is normally reached by ferry from Oban to Craignure. This runs regularly.

Personal View (Alistair)

On Saturday, 28 May 2016, at 5.15 a.m., I opened the curtains at our bed and breakfast and looked out over Tobermory Bay. It was a glorious morning and my final Munro day on Ben More, Mull's highest peak and only Munro. There were seven of us climbing, my two brothers, Donald, my oldest son, Dan, and two canoeing friends, Pete and Ian. Finally supervising the climb the two dogs, Mist and Bronte, and on the shoreline, my wife Helen.

We kept it simple, straight up and down from the shores of Loch na Keal near Dhiseig on a well trodden path. Unusually it was warm, verging on hot at times as we meandered to the summit enjoying fantastic views. At 2,500ft a swarm of midges interrupted us, particularly unpleasant for those wearing shorts. Soon the summit shelter came into view, clouds now rising up the north facing slopes. At the summit we all had champagne then descended meeting Helen lower down with our other dog, Martha, and another bottle of champagne.

It was a long night in Tobermory as I recalled tales of the last forty years, yes forty. My first Munro was Stob Ban in the Mamores in 1976 at the age of seventeen, a lifetime of hillwalking! Thank you to all those who were there and the many others who supported me over the years.

My Routes

BEN MORE (4-5 hours)

We started from the shore of Loch na Keal at a car park on the B8035 near Dhiseig. A path ran SE up the mountain on the north side of the Abhainn Dhiseig passing the house at Dhiseig. The mountain turned rocky when we reached the zigzags of the summit scree slopes.

The return distance was just over five miles with 3,200ft of climbing.

James descending Ben More (2000).

DUN DA GAOITHE (3-4 hours)

I started at Scallastle Farm, parking just off the A849, and walked up the road to the farm, passing between the farmhouse and the coachworks. A track continued for 500m keeping west of the river then crossed a Ford.

From here I walked west then SW up the hillside to the east ridge and followed this to the summit. I varied the return route by going north from the summit and back over Beinn Chreagach.

BEINN TALAIDH (2-3 hours)

It was possible to park next to a bridge at reference 643329 just off the A849. I followed a good track NW for 100m then took a path which went left past a seat. It continued through open woodland reaching a stream as it came out of the woodland. I climbed NW beside the stream to the Mam Bhradhadail, then NNW to the broad south ridge which led to the summit.

PLACES TO STAY/DRINK

Tobermory is a beautiful place to stay when on the Isle of Mull.

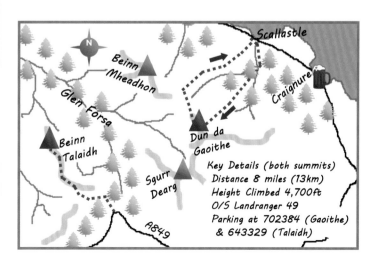

Key Details (both summits)
Distance 8 miles (13km)
Height Climbed 4,700ft
O/S Landranger 49
Parking at 702384 (Gaoithe)
& 643329 (Talaidh)

RUM CORBETTS

View of Ainshval and Trallval from Askival (2010).

ASKIVAL *(2,663ft)*
AINSHVAL *(2,562ft)*

» **The full five peaks traverse on Rum includes two Corbetts and one Graham, Trallval (2,303ft). It is a superb day walk.**

» **The Isle of Rum is a great island to visit not only for its classic ridge walking but also to see wildlife.**

» **There are regular ferries from Mallaig.**

Personal View

The Isle of Rum lies just south of the Isle of Skye. It is dominated by a ridge of mountains known as the Cuillin of Rum. This gives a fine traverse that can be completed by walkers in one day. We went over to Rum in June 2010 taking the ferry from Mallaig and stayed at Kinloch Castle where there is a bar and accommodation. We arrived in the afternoon and in the evening climbed an isolated Marilyn, while Alistair enjoyed some canoeing round the bay.

The following day we had great weather on the traverse of the 'five peaks' ridge of the Cuillin of Rum. It was an interesting route with plenty of ascent and descent. The climb over Trallval (a Graham) was the hardest section. The walk back from Sgurr nan Gillean was long but we completed it in time to catch a late afternoon ferry back to Mallaig. On the ferry I recall watching England's first match in their disappointing 2010 World Cup campaign when they failed to beat USA.

RUM CORBETTS continued

My Route (8-9 hours)

We started at Kinloch Castle and followed a signposted route SSW up Coire Dubh. At the head of the corrie the path went up gravelly slopes to the Bealach Bairc-mheall.

We followed a path around the west side of Hallival (although this could be climbed) then climbed south up Askival. We traversed to the east side of Askival to avoid the pinnacle, and climbed steep but easy rocky slopes to the summit. From the summit we descended the west ridge of Askival to the Bealach an Oir (1,500ft).

From here we went over Trallval. It was a steep ascent of 800ft to the summit and then 600ft of descent to the next Bealach. Trallval could be missed but the ascent is worthwhile and Trallval qualifies as a Graham. At 2,303ft it is not high enough to be a Top 500 Summit.

It was a steep climb up Ainshval. We avoided the lower rock buttress by traversing to the west side of the ridge. We continued along the ridge to Sgurr nan Gillean, a magnificent spot overlooking the sea, then descended east to Dibidil Bothy. From here a coastal path went east then north back to Kinloch.

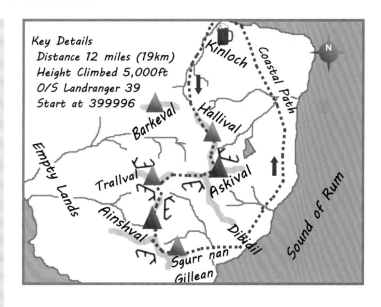

Key Details
Distance 12 miles (19km)
Height Climbed 5,000ft
O/S Landranger 39
Start at 399996

POINTS OF INTEREST

The Island of Rum is a national nature reserve run by Scottish National Heritage. It is famous for its wildlife which includes eagles, shearwaters, deer and Rum ponies. The website *www.isleofrum.com* is worth viewing before going over to the Island.

Jonathan at the top of Sgurr nan Gillean, the last peak on our traverse of the Rum Cuillin (2010).

PLACES TO STAY/DRINK

There is hostel accommodation at Kinloch House and a guest house. Camping was allowed along the shore. There is a tea shop, bar and food at Kinloch Castle.

SGURR ALASDAIR

On the way to Coire Lagan, Sgurr Alasdair is the centre peak.

SGURR ALASDAIR (3,257ft)
INACCESSIBLE PINNACLE (3,234ft)

» Sgurr Alasdair is the highest peak on the Isle of Skye and the highest 'Island' peak in the British Isles.

» The round of Coire Lagan includes an additional Munro, Sgurr Mhic Choinnich (3,110ft).

» A guide is necessary as the Inaccessible Pinnacle is a rock climb requiring ropes.

» This is a fantastic walk for those who enjoy ridge walking and scrambling.

Personal View

The Inaccessible Pinnacle is a rock climb requiring ropes so we hired a guide to help us to climb it in 1989. I recall that the second pitch up the East Ridge to the summit of the 'Inn Pin' was very exposed, a false move unroped would mean disaster. Then I was on the top of the Inn Pin, technically the hardest of the Munros. Our guide tied the rope to the boulder stone near the summit and lowered us off the west side. I counted thirty people on Sgurr Dearg, a few climbing the Pinnacle, the remainder either watching or eating lunch in the beautiful sunshine.

The ascent of the Pinnacle was the highlight of a memorable day. We scrambled to the summit of magnificent Sgurr Mhic Choinnich with the plaque commemorating John Robertson (died 1958) and then went on to Sgurr Alasdair, Skye's highest point, before returning down the Stone Shute. Sgurr Alasdair remains one of my favourite mountains. On my previous ascent we had climbed the two Munros at the south end of the ridge, Sgurr nan Eag and Sgurr Dubh Mor, before making a big diversion to avoid the Thearlaich Dubh Gap and climb to the summit of Sgurr Alasdair.

SGURR ALASDAIR continued

My Route (7-9 hours)

We followed the path from Glenbrittle House as far as Loch an Fhir-bhallaich, then climbed the west shoulder of Sgurr Dearg. We continued east and finally NE to the summit.

Our guide then roped us up to climb the Inaccessible Pinnacle by the East Ridge route. This is a Moderate rock climb but very exposed. It should not be climbed without a professional guide. Once we had climbed the east ridge, our guide arranged the ropes and helped us to abseil down the more difficult west side (picture opposite).

After climbing the Inaccessible Pinnacle we went SE past An Stac. An airy and exposed ridge was then followed to Sgurr Mhic Choinnich, a Munro. We continued over Sgurr Thearlaich to Sgurr Alasdair, my third ascent of this Munro, the highest point on the Isle of Skye. We descended to Coire Lagan by the Alasdair Stone Shute.

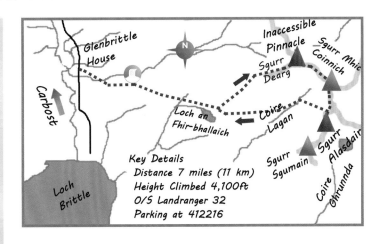

Key Details
Distance 7 miles (11 km)
Height Climbed 4,100ft
O/S Landranger 32
Parking at 412216

Abseiling off the Inaccessible Pinnacle in 1989.

PLACES TO STAY/DRINK

At Glenbrittle there is camping available and a youth hostel where I stayed in 1976.

POINTS OF INTEREST

One of the great mountain challenges in Britain is the completion of the Cuillin ridge in one day. Although only seven miles in length, the ridge requires rock climbing and normally takes at least fifteen hours with a guide.

SGURR NAN GILLEAN

Climbing over the 3rd Pinnacle on Sgurr nan Gillean *(Mark Pyman)*.

SGURR NAN GILLEAN (3,167ft)

» Sgurr nan Gillean is one of the best mountains in Britain, a magnificent peak with three great ridges.

» Sgurr nan Gillean is best climbed from Sligachan. Two additional Munros Am Basteir (3,066ft) and Bruach na Frithe (3,143ft) can be added.

» The West Ridge, which needs to be traversed to reach Am Basteir from the summit of Sgurr nan Gillean, is a difficult scramble.

Personal View

Before my first visit to Skye, my uncle David said 'Give my love to Sgurr nan Gillean'. Such is the capacity of this mountain to inspire generations of walkers and climbers. However, our first attempt on Sgurr nan Gillean in 1975 was a miserable failure. With mist at 1,500ft and map reading which was non existent, we ended up on a deserted part of the ridge south of Bruach na Frithe! After failing again the following day, Donald and I were successful on our third attempt three years later.

In 1989 Jonathan, JP and I were making our way along the Cuillin Ridge from Bruach na Frithe. After reaching the summit of Am Basteir our enthusiasm was high and we could not resist an attempt on the west ridge of Sgurr nan Gillean. Halfway up we tried to regain the crest from the north side of the ridge and encountered the bad step. JP struggled up it and noted the crest was very narrow at the top. The rest of us followed with difficulty (the Gendarme had fallen off the previous year). However, at 5.00 p.m. we sat on the summit in glorious sunshine, the Cuillin at its best. My third and final ascent to date was in 2009 when we hired a guide to help us over the Pinnacle Ridge. This was followed by an unusual route down the west ridge along an exposed ledge (not advised) then we ascended Am Basteir and the Basteir Tooth.

My Routes

(1989 ascent, 7-8 hours)

Following two failures, my first successful ascent of Sgurr nan Gillean started at the car park 200m SW of the Sligachan Hotel. There was a footpath on the south side of the road which soon crossed the Allt Dearg Mor.

After heading SSW for 2km the path crossed the Allt Dearg Beag at a footbridge. We followed the path south past Coire Riabhach ignoring a path to the right which leads to the Pinnacle ridge. Eventually we saw a band of rocks with a scree gully and ascended by a path which led to the SE ridge of Sgurr nan Gillean. We followed the ridge to the summit returning by the same route.

On my second ascent in 1989 we climbed Bruach na Frithe, then worked our way around the north side of Am Basteir to the Bealach a' Basteir. From here we climbed Am Basteir, then scrambled up the west ridge of Sgurr nan Gillean. This route is shown on the map.

Most recently in 2009 we climbed Sgurr nan Gillean by the Pinnacle ridge (with a guide). We descended the west ridge before climbing Am Basteir and the Basteir Tooth. The ascent of the Basteir Tooth enabled Jonathan to complete the Munro Tops.

PLACES TO STAY/DRINK

The route starts and finishes at the Sligachan Hotel where there is food, drink, accommodation and a camp site.

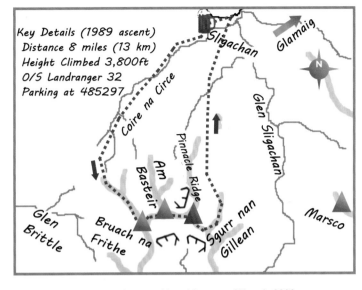

Key Details (1989 ascent)
Distance 8 miles (13 km)
Height Climbed 3,800ft
O/S Landranger 32
Parking at 485297

Alistair on our route down the west ridge of Sgurr nan Gillean in 2009. This route should be avoided, one slip could be disastrous.

BLAVEN

BLAVEN *(3,046ft)*

» Blaven is a magnificent Munro on the Isle of Skye climbed from sea level at Loch Slapin.

» There are fantastic views over the Black Cuillin ridge.

» Blaven is thought to mean 'Blue Mountain'.

My Route (4-5 hours)

We started from the B8083. There was a car park near the bridge over the Allt na Duna-iche on the west side of Loch Slapin. The path went up the other side of the stream from the car park.

We followed the path up the north side of the stream. After 1.5km it crossed two streams and continued SW up Coire Uaigneich. On reaching the grassy bowl of Fionna-choire, it zigzagged up steep slopes. At 2,000ft the grass became scree and the path continued to a shoulder at 2,600ft. We climbed west and there was some scrambling to the main ridge of Blaven and the summit.

PLACES TO STAY/DRINK

In 1976 we stayed in the youth hostel at Broadford. There are also hotels, guest houses and a campsite at Broadford.

POINTS OF INTEREST

Blaven stands in the Strathaird Estate, owned by the John Muir Trust. This is a charitable trust dedicated to protecting some of the wild landscape in the UK.

Blaven across Loch Slapin *(Heather Thomas-Smith)*.

Personal View

During the summer of 1976 I spent a month travelling round Scotland. After spending a couple of nights at the youth hostel in Kintail, Alistair and I managed to hitch a lift to Kyle of Lochalsh, then we boarded the ferry to Kyleakin (there was no bridge in those days) before walking the eight miles from Kyleakin to the Broadford Bar where we met two university friends.

After an evening in the Broadford Bar they gave us a lift to the foot of Blaven the following morning. Despite our lack of experience on the Isle of Skye we managed to climb to the summit by the 'normal' route from Loch Slapin. I have no idea how we managed to get back to Broadford!

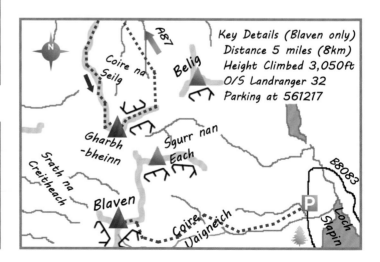

Key Details (Blaven only)
Distance 5 miles (8km)
Height Climbed 3,050ft
O/S Landranger 32
Parking at 561217

SKYE CORBETTS

GARBH-BHEINN *(2,650ft)*
GLAMAIG *(2,542ft)*

My Routes

GARBH-BHEINN (3-4 hours)
It was possible to park just off the A87 at the SW end of Loch Ainort. We crossed the bridge and a path led SSW up the Druim Eadar Da Choire. At the top we turned SE and descended to a col before climbing south up a rocky ridge to the summit.

We descended ENE down a narrow ridge then steep scree slopes to the Bealach na Beiste. The weather was poor so we returned direct to the road.

For reference, see map of Garbh-bheinn opposite.

Key Details
» Distance 5 miles (8km)
» Height climbed 2,600ft
» O/S Landranger 32
» Parking at 534267.

GLAMAIG (3-4 hours)
From the Sligachan Hotel I walked 400m down the road towards Broadford, then headed onto the hillside in an easterly direction. The route became steeper and rockier as I neared the summit. As time was short, I returned the same way.

Key Details
» Distance 4 miles (6km)
» Height climbed 2,500ft
» O/S Landranger 32
» Parking at 486299.

Personal View
Glamaig and Garbh-bheinn are the only Corbetts on the Isle of Skye. However, there are a number of peaks over 2,000ft including The Storr, a magnificent peak north of Portree. Glamaig is close to the Sligachan Hotel and is well known for its hill race (see points of interest) and Garbh-bheinn gives a magnificent round from Loch Ainort particularly if Belig, a Graham, is added.

I climbed Glamaig on a beautiful evening in June leaving the Sligachan at 5 p.m. Despite climbing the mountain as fast as possible it took 1 hour 25 mins just for the ascent so I gave up the idea of ever competing in the hill race. Unfortunately the weather was poor when we climbed Garbh-bheinn with strong winds and low cloud.

POINTS OF INTEREST
The Glamaig hill race was started more than a hundred years ago when a Ghurka ran barefoot to the summit and back in under an hour. Today the record is under 45 minutes and some 200 runners take part in the annual race in July.

Moonrise over Glamaig *(Heather Thomas-Smith)*.

CLISHAM

CLISHAM *(2,622ft)*

» Clisham is the only mountain over 2,500ft in the Outer Hebrides.

» It is a short climb but a long journey to reach the mountain.

My Route (2-3 hours)

I caught the ferry from Ullapool to Stornoway on the Isle of Lewis, then drove south on the A859. There is parking beside the bridge crossing the Abhainn Mharaig.

I followed a path NW along the north side of the stream continuing NW to the wide SE ridge of the mountain. This was followed to the large walled summit cairn.

Key Details

» **Distance 4 miles (6km)**

» **Height climbed 2,000ft**

» **O/S Landranger 14**

» **Parking at 173058.**

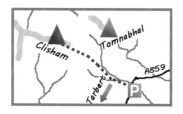

PLACES TO STAY/DRINK

Stornoway (Isle of Lewis) is the best place to stay if crossing from Ullapool on the ferry. Tarbert (Isle of Harris) is the best place to stay if crossing from the Isle of Skye on the ferry.

POINTS OF INTEREST

The Callanish Standing Stones, opposite, date back to 2700 BC and are well worth the detour from the A859.

Callanish standing stones on the Isle of Lewis (2014).

Personal View

Wow, what an amazing place!

The ferry arrived at Stornoway at 12.30 p.m. and I had until 8 p.m. before returning to Ullapool, enough time to climb Clisham and fit in something else; in the end I chose to visit the Standing Stones at Callanish. These are enthralling, what must it have been like living here next to the sea 5,000 years ago?

After coffee and lunch in the Visitors' Centre at Callanish, I continued to mountainous Harris, completely different in character to Lewis. At the start point for Clisham a couple were debating what to do next. When I told them they were a 'short' climb from the highest point in the Outer Hebrides, they were sold and I saw them later near Clisham's summit. Returning to Stornoway I had an hour to spare so played a few holes on Stornoway's very welcoming golf course. The ferry returned me to Ullapool on time at 11.30 p.m.

View from the slopes of Clisham (2014).

Near the summit of the
Basteir Tooth.

TOP 500 SUMMITS

	Name	Height (ft)	Height (m)	Chapter
1	Ben Nevis	4,411	1,345	Central Highlands
2	Ben MacDui	4,296	1,309	East Highlands
3	Braeriach	4,252	1,296	East Highlands
4	Cairn Toul	4,236	1,291	East Highlands
5	Aonach Beag	4,049	1,234	Central Highlands
6	Carn Mor Dearg	4,002	1,220	Central Highlands
7	Ben Lawers	3,984	1,214	South Highlands
8	Beinn a' Bhuird	3,927	1,197	East Highlands
9	Carn Eighe	3,880	1,183	North West Glens
10	Beinn Mheadhoin	3,878	1,182	East Highlands
11	Stob Choire Claurigh	3,862	1,177	Central Highlands
12	Ben More	3,852	1,174	South Highlands
13	Ben Avon	3,843	1,171	East Highlands
14	Stob Binnein	3,821	1,165	South Highlands
15	Beinn Bhrotain	3,795	1,157	East Highlands
16	Lochnagar	3,790	1,155	East Highlands
17	Sgurr nan Ceathreamhnan	3,776	1,151	North West Glens
18	Sgurr na Lapaich	3,774	1,150	North West Glens
19	Bidean nam Bian	3,773	1,150	Rannoch to Glencoe
20	Ben Alder	3,765	1,148	Central Highlands
21	Geal Charn	3,714	1,132	Central Highlands
22	Ben Lui	3,708	1,130	South Highlands
23	Creag Meagaidh	3,707	1,130	Central Highlands
24	Binnein Mor	3,706	1,130	Central Highlands
25	An Riabhachan	3,704	1,129	North West Glens
26	Beinn a' Ghlo – Carn nan Gabhar	3,704	1,129	East Highlands
27	Ben Cruachan	3,695	1,126	Rannoch to Glencoe
28	A' Chralaig	3,673	1,120	North West Glens
29	Meall Garbh	3,668	1,118	South Highlands

TOP 500 SUMMITS continued

	Name	Height (ft)	Height (m)	Chapter
30	Sgor Gaoith	3,668	1,118	East Highlands
31	Stob Coire Easain	3,660	1,115	Central Highlands
32	Sgurr Mor	3,642	1,110	North Highlands
33	Sgurr nan Conbhairean	3,639	1,109	North West Glens
34	Meall a' Bhuiridh	3,636	1,108	Rannoch to Glencoe
35	Mullach Fraoch-choire	3,614	1,102	North West Glens
36	Creise	3,609	1,100	Rannoch to Glencoe
37	Sgurr a' Mhaim	3,606	1,099	Central Highlands
38	Sgurr Choinnich Mor	3,592	1,095	Central Highlands
39	Sgurr nan Clach Geala	3,586	1,093	North Highlands
40	Bynack More	3,575	1,090	East Highlands
41	Stob Ghabhar	3,575	1,090	Rannoch to Glencoe
42	Beinn a' Chlachair	3,566	1,087	Central Highlands
43	Snowdon	3,560	1,085	Wales
44	Beinn Dearg	3,556	1,084	North Highlands
45	Schiehallion	3,554	1,083	Rannoch to Glencoe
46	Sgurr a' Choire Ghlais	3,554	1,083	North West Glens
47	Beinn a' Chaorainn	3,550	1,082	East Highlands
48	Beinn a' Chreachain	3,547	1,081	Rannoch to Glencoe
49	Ben Starav	3,538	1,078	Rannoch to Glencoe
50	Beinn Heasgarnich	3,536	1,078	South Highlands
51	Beinn Dorain	3,530	1,076	Rannoch to Glencoe
52	Braigh Coire Chruinn-bhalgain	3,510	1,070	East Highlands
53	An Socach	3,508	1,069	North West Glens
54	Meall Corranaich	3,507	1,069	South Highlands
55	Sgurr Fhuaran	3,505	1,068	North West Glens
56	Glas Maol	3,504	1,068	East Highlands
57	Carnedd Llewelyn	3,490	1,064	Wales
58	An Teallach – Bidein a'Ghlas Thuill	3,484	1,062	North Highlands

	Name	Height (ft)	Height (m)	Chapter
59	Liathach – Spidean a'Choire Leith	3,460	1,055	North Highlands
60	Toll Creagach	3,458	1,054	North West Glens
61	Sgurr a' Chaorachain	3,455	1,053	North West Glens
62	Glas Tulaichean	3,449	1,051	East Highlands
63	Beinn a' Chaorainn	3,445	1,050	Central Highlands
64	Geal Charn	3,443	1,049	Central Highlands
65	Chno Dearg	3,435	1,047	Central Highlands
66	Creag Mhor	3,435	1,047	South Highlands
67	Ben Wyvis	3,433	1,046	North Highlands
68	Cruach Ardrain	3,432	1,046	South Highlands
69	Beinn Iutharn Mhor	3,427	1,045	East Highlands
70	Meall nan Tarmachan	3,425	1,044	South Highlands
71	Stob Coir'an Albannaich	3,425	1,044	Rannoch to Glencoe
72	Carn Mairg	3,419	1,042	Rannoch to Glencoe
73	Carrauntoohil	3,414	1,041	Ireland
74	Sgurr na Ciche	3,412	1,040	Far West Highlands
75	Meall Ghaordaidh	3,410	1,039	South Highlands
76	Beinn Achaladair	3,404	1,038	Rannoch to Glencoe
77	Carn a' Mhaim	3,402	1,037	East Highlands
78	Sgurr a' Bhealaich Dheirg	3,399	1,036	North West Glens
79	Gleouraich	3,394	1,035	Far West Highlands
80	Carn Dearg	3,391	1,034	Central Highlands
81	Beinn Fhada	3,385	1,032	North West Glens
82	Carn an Righ	3,377	1,029	East Highlands
83	Carn Gorm	3,377	1,029	Rannoch to Glencoe
84	Ben Oss	3,376	1,029	South Highlands
85	Sgurr na Ciste Dubh	3,370	1,027	North West Glens
86	Sgurr a' Mhaoraich	3,369	1,027	Far West Highlands
87	Ben Challum	3,363	1,025	South Highlands

TOP 500 SUMMITS continued

	Name	Height (ft)	Height (m)	Chapter
88	Beinn a' Bheithir – Sgorr Dhearg	3,361	1,024	Rannoch to Glencoe
89	Liathach – Mullach an Rathain	3,356	1,023	North Highlands
90	Buachaille Etive Mor – Stob Dearg	3,353	1,022	Rannoch to Glencoe
91	Aonach air Chrith	3,350	1,021	North West Glens
92	Ladhar Bheinn	3,345	1,020	Far West Highlands
93	Beinn Bheoil	3,343	1,019	Central Highlands
94	Mullach Coire Mhic Fhearchair	3,343	1,019	North Highlands
95	Garbh Chioch Mhor	3,323	1,013	Far West Highlands
96	Beinn Ime	3,318	1,011	South Highlands
97	Beinn Udlamain	3,314	1,010	Central Highlands
98	Sgurr an Doire Leathain	3,314	1,010	North West Glens
99	The Saddle	3,314	1,010	North West Glens
100	Beinn Eighe – Ruadh-stac Mor	3,313	1,010	North Highlands
101	Sgurr Eilde Mor	3,313	1,010	Central Highlands
102	Beinn Dearg	3,307	1,008	East Highlands
103	Maoile Lunndaidh	3,304	1,007	North West Glens
104	An Sgarsoch	3,300	1,006	East Highlands
105	Beinn Fhionnlaidh	3,298	1,005	North West Glens
106	Beinn an Dothaidh	3,294	1,004	Rannoch to Glencoe
107	Sgurr Mor	3,290	1,003	Far West Highlands
108	Aonach Meadhoin	3,284	1,001	North West Glens
109	Beinn a' Bheithir – Sgorr Dhonuill	3,284	1,001	Rannoch to Glencoe
110	Meall Greigh	3,284	1,001	South Highlands
111	Sgurr Breac	3,281	1,000	North Highlands
112	Glyder Fawr	3,279	999	Wales
113	Stob Ban	3,278	999	Central Highlands
114	Ben More Assynt	3,273	998	Far North Scotland
115	Glas Bheinn Mhor	3,271	997	Rannoch to Glencoe
116	A' Chailleach	3,270	997	North Highlands

TOP 500 SUMMITS continued

	Name	Height (ft)	Height (m)	Chapter
117	Spidean Mialach	3,268	996	Far West Highlands
118	An Caisteal	3,264	995	South Highlands
119	Carn an Fhidhleir	3,261	994	East Highlands
120	Sgor na h-Ulaidh	3,260	994	Rannoch to Glencoe
121	Beinn Eighe – Spidean Coire nan Clach	3,258	993	North Highlands
122	Sgurr na Ruaidhe	3,258	993	North West Glens
123	Sgurr Alasdair	3,257	993	Scottish Islands
124	Carn nan Gobhar	3,255	992	North West Glens
125	Sgairneach Mhor	3,251	991	Central Highlands
126	Beinn Eunaich	3,245	989	Rannoch to Glencoe
127	Sgurr Ban	3,245	989	North Highlands
128	Cnoc na Peiste	3,240	988	Ireland
129	Gulvain	3,238	987	Far West Highlands
130	Beinn Alligin – Sgurr Mhor	3,235	986	North Highlands
131	Lurg Mhor	3,234	986	North West Glens
132	Sgurr Dearg – Inaccessible Pinnacle	3,234	986	Scottish Islands
133	Ben Vorlich	3,231	985	South Highlands
134	Slioch	3,217	981	North Highlands
135	Beinn a' Chochuill	3,215	980	Rannoch to Glencoe
136	Ciste Dhubh	3,211	979	North West Glens
137	Scafell Pike	3,210	978	England
138	Beinn Dubhchraig	3,209	978	South Highlands
139	Cona Mheall	3,208	978	North Highlands
140	Stob Ban	3,205	977	Central Highlands
141	Carn Liath	3,200	975	East Highlands
142	Stuc a' Chroin	3,199	975	South Highlands
143	Carn a' Gheoidh	3,198	975	East Highlands
144	Beinn Sgritheall	3,194	974	Far West Highlands
145	Ben Lomond	3,194	974	South Highlands

TOP 500 SUMMITS continued

	Name	Height (ft)	Height (m)	Chapter
146	A' Mhaighdean	3,173	967	North Highlands
147	Aonach Eagach – Sgorr nam Fiannaidh	3,173	967	Rannoch to Glencoe
148	Ben More (Mull)	3,170	966	Scottish Islands
149	Sgurr nan Gillean	3,167	965	Scottish Islands
150	Sgurr Thuilm	3,160	963	Far West Highlands
151	Carn a' Chlamain	3,159	963	East Highlands
152	Sgorr Ruadh	3,156	962	North Highlands
153	Ben Klibreck	3,154	961	Far North Scotland
154	Beinn nan Aighenan	3,150	960	Rannoch to Glencoe
155	Stuchd an Lochain	3,150	960	Rannoch to Glencoe
156	Beinn Fhionnlaidh	3,145	959	Rannoch to Glencoe
157	Meall Glas	3,145	959	South Highlands
158	Buachaille Etive Beag – Stob Dubh	3,143	958	Rannoch to Glencoe
159	Sgurr nan Coireachan	3,136	956	Far West Highlands
160	Stob Gaibhre	3,133	955	Central Highlands
161	Am Faochagach	3,130	954	North Highlands
162	Brandon Mountain	3,127	953	Ireland
163	Beinn Mhanach	3,125	953	Rannoch to Glencoe
164	Sgurr nan Coireachan	3,125	953	Far West Highlands
165	Meall Chuaich	3,120	951	East Highlands
166	Helvellyn	3,116	950	England
167	Beinn Bhuidhe	3,111	948	South Highlands
168	Y Garn	3,107	947	Wales
169	Meall Buidhe	3,105	946	Far West Highlands
170	Carn Bhac	3,104	946	East Highlands
171	Sgurr na Sgine	3,104	946	North West Glens
172	Bidean a' Choire Sheasgaich	3,100	945	North West Glens
173	Carn Dearg (Monadh Liath)	3,100	945	Central Highlands
174	Stob a' Choire Odhair	3,100	945	Rannoch to Glencoe

TOP 500 SUMMITS continued

Name	Height (ft)	Height (m)	Chapter
175 An Socach	3,097	944	East Highlands
176 Ben Vorlich	3,093	943	South Highlands
177 Binnein Beag	3,093	943	Central Highlands
178 Carn na Caim	3,087	941	East Highlands
179 Carn Dearg	3,087	941	Central Highlands
180 Luinne Bheinn	3,082	939	Far West Highlands
181 Mount Keen	3,080	939	East Highlands
182 Beinn Tarsuinn	3,075	937	North Highlands
183 Beinn na Lap	3,074	937	Central Highlands
184 Beinn Sgulaird	3,074	937	Rannoch to Glencoe
185 Sron a' Choire Ghairbh	3,074	937	Far West Highlands
186 Fionn Bheinn	3,062	933	North West Glens
187 Beinn Chabhair	3,061	933	South Highlands
188 Maol Chean-dearg	3,060	933	North Highlands
189 Meall Buidhe	3,057	932	Rannoch to Glencoe
190 Ben Chonzie	3,054	931	South Highlands
191 Skiddaw	3,054	931	England
192 Blaven	3,046	928	Scottish Islands
193 Eididh nan Clach Geala	3,045	928	North Highlands
194 Meall nan Eun	3,045	928	Rannoch to Glencoe
195 Moruisg	3,045	928	North West Glens
196 Ben Hope	3,040	927	Far North Scotland
197 Seana Bhraigh	3,040	927	North Highlands
198 Lugnaquilla	3,039	927	Ireland
199 Beinn Narnain	3,038	926	South Highlands
200 Beinn Liath Mhor	3,036	926	North Highlands
201 Buachaille Etive Beag – Stob Coire Raineach	3,035	925	Rannoch to Glencoe
202 Elidir Fawr	3,029	923	Wales
203 Beinn Alligin – Tom na Gruagaich	3,025	922	North Highlands

TOP 500 SUMMITS continued

	Name	Height (ft)	Height (m)	Chapter
204	Sgiath Chuil	3,021	921	South Highlands
205	Galtymore	3,018	920	Ireland
206	Gairich	3,015	919	Far West Highlands
207	A' Ghlas-bheinn	3,012	918	North West Glens
208	Creag nan Damh	3,012	918	North West Glens
209	Ruadh Stac Mor	3,012	918	North Highlands
210	Geal Charn	3,008	917	Central Highlands
211	Meall na Teanga	3,008	917	Far West Highlands
212	Ben Vane	3,004	915	South Highlands
213	Tryfan	3,002	915	Wales
214	Beinn Teallach	3,002	915	Central Highlands
215	Beinn a' Chlaidheimh	2,998	914	North Highlands
216	Beinn Dearg (Torridon)	2,998	914	North Highlands
217	Sgurr nan Ceannaichean	2,995	913	North West Glens
218	Sgurr a' Choire-bheithe	2,994	913	Far West Highlands
219	Beinn Bhreac	2,992	912	East Highlands
220	Leathad an Taobhain	2,991	912	East Highlands
221	The Fara	2,989	911	Central Highlands
222	Foinaven	2,988	911	Far North Scotland
223	Beinn Dearg Mor	2,985	910	North Highlands
224	Meall Buidhe	2,985	910	Rannoch to Glencoe
225	Beinn nan Oighreag	2,982	909	South Highlands
226	Streap	2,982	909	Far West Highlands
227	Fuar Tholl	2,976	907	North Highlands
228	Beinn Maol Chaluim	2,975	907	Rannoch to Glencoe
229	Leum Uilleim	2,972	906	Central Highlands
230	Aran Fawddwy	2,970	905	Wales
231	Ben Vuirich	2,962	903	East Highlands
232	Beinn Damh	2,959	902	North Highlands

TOP 500 SUMMITS continued

Name	Height (ft)	Height (m)	Chapter
233 Ben Tee	2,957	901	Far West Scotland
234 Beinn an Lochain	2,956	901	South Highlands
235 Beinn Mheadhonach	2,956	901	East Highlands
236 Sgurr an Fhuarain	2,956	901	Far West Highlands
237 Beinn Odhar	2,955	901	Rannoch to Glencoe
238 Culardoch	2,953	900	East Highlands
239 Aonach Buidhe	2,949	899	North West Glens
240 Great Gable	2,949	899	England
241 Y Lliwedd	2,946	898	Wales
242 Sgurr nan Eugallt	2,946	898	Far West Highlands
243 Beinn a' Bhuiridh	2,942	897	Rannoch to Glencoe
244 Ben Tirran	2,941	896	East Highlands
245 Gairbeinn	2,940	896	Central Highlands
246 Ruadh-stac Beag	2,940	896	North Highlands
247 Beinn Bhan	2,938	896	North Highlands
248 Creag Mhor	2,936	895	East Highlands
249 Cross Fell	2,930	893	England
250 Cadair Idris	2,929	893	Wales
251 Pillar	2,927	892	England
252 An Ruadh-stac	2,926	892	North Highlands
253 Beinn a' Chuallaich	2,926	892	Rannoch to Glencoe
254 Aonach Shasuinn	2,917	889	North West Glens
255 Beinn Enaiglair	2,915	889	North Highlands
256 Sgurr Dhomhnuill	2,914	888	Far West Highlands
257 Creagan na Beinne	2,913	888	South Highlands
258 Ben Aden	2,910	887	Far West Highlands
259 Meall a' Ghiubhais	2,910	887	North Highlands
260 Beinn a' Chaisteil	2,907	886	Rannoch to Glencoe
261 Pen y Fan	2,906	886	Wales

TOP 500 SUMMITS continued

	Name	Height (ft)	Height (m)	Chapter
262	Buidhe Bheinn	2,904	885	North West Glens
263	Garbh Bheinn	2,903	885	Far West Highlands
264	Cam Chreag	2,900	884	Rannoch to Glencoe
265	The Cobbler	2,899	884	South Highlands
266	Stob Dubh	2,897	883	Rannoch to Glencoe
267	Beinn Odhar Bheag	2,895	882	Far West Highlands
268	Rois-Bheinn	2,895	882	Far West Highlands
269	Beinn Chuirn	2,887	880	South Highlands
270	Sgurr Mhurlagain	2,886	880	Far West Highlands
271	Ben Ledi	2,883	879	South Highlands
272	Creag Uchdag	2,883	879	South Highlands
273	Fraochaidh	2,883	879	Rannoch to Glencoe
274	Sguman Coinntich	2,883	879	North West Glens
275	Sgurr a' Mhuilinn	2,883	879	North West Glens
276	Carn an Fhreiceadain	2,879	878	Central Highlands
277	Creag an Loch	2,874	876	East Highlands
278	Baosbheinn	2,871	875	North Highlands
279	Goat Fell	2,868	874	Scottish Islands
280	Sgurr na Ba Glaise	2,867	874	Far West Highlands
281	Ben Hee	2,863	873	Far North Scotland
282	Fairfield	2,863	873	England
283	Moel Siabod	2,861	872	Wales
284	Morven	2,861	872	East Highlands
285	Sgorr nan Lochan Uaine	2,857	871	North Highlands
286	Stob a' Choin	2,850	869	South Highlands
287	Meall na Meoig	2,848	868	Central Highlands
288	Blencathra	2,847	868	England
289	Faochaig	2,847	868	North West Glens
290	Garbh Bheinn	2,844	867	Central Highlands

TOP 500 SUMMITS continued

	Name	Height (ft)	Height (m)	Chapter
291	Bidean a' Chabhair	2,844	867	Far West Highlands
292	Conachcraig	2,838	865	East Highlands
293	Carn a' Choire Ghairbh	2,837	865	North West Glens
294	Beinn Mhic Chasgaig	2,835	864	Rannoch to Glencoe
295	Beinn Tharsuinn	2,831	863	North West Glens
296	Carn Liath	2,829	862	East Highlands
297	Cam Chreag	2,828	862	Rannoch to Glencoe
298	Meall na h-Aisre	2,828	862	Central Highlands
299	Sgurr na Feartaig	2,828	862	North West Glens
300	Beinn a' Bha'ach Ard	2,827	862	North West Glens
301	Beinn Lair	2,821	860	North Highlands
302	Morrone	2,819	859	East Highlands
303	Caisteal Abhail	2,817	859	Scottish Islands
304	Beinn Luibhean	2,815	858	South Highlands
305	Fraoch Bheinn	2,815	858	Far West Highlands
306	Carn Dearg Mor	2,813	857	East Highlands
307	Beinn a' Chaisgein Mor	2,812	857	North Highlands
308	Cruach Innse	2,812	857	Central Highlands
309	Beinn a' Chrulaiste	2,811	857	Rannoch to Glencoe
310	Beinn an Eoin	2,805	855	North Highlands
311	Beinn Bhuidhe	2,805	855	Far West Highlands
312	Stob an Aonaich Mhoir	2,805	855	Central Highlands
313	Arenig Fawr	2,801	854	Wales
314	Creach Bheinn	2,798	853	Far West Highlands
315	Slieve Donard	2,796	852	Ireland
316	Grasmoor	2,795	852	England
317	Meall an t-Seallaidh	2,794	852	South Highlands
318	Baurtregaum	2,792	851	Ireland
319	Mullaghcleevaun	2,788	850	Ireland

TOP 500 SUMMITS continued

	Name	Height (ft)	Height (m)	Chapter
320	Bac an Eich	2,787	849	North West Glens
321	Cul Mor	2,787	849	Far North Scotland
322	Beinn nan Imirean	2,785	849	South Highlands
323	Sgurr Ghiubhsachain	2,784	849	Far West Highlands
324	Ben Donich	2,778	847	South Highlands
325	Canisp	2,775	846	Far North Scotland
326	Beinn Resipol	2,772	845	Far West Highlands
327	Carn Ban	2,772	845	North Highlands
328	The Merrick	2,766	843	Southern Uplands
329	Mangerton Mountain	2,766	843	Ireland
330	St Sunday Crag	2,760	841	England
331	Beinn Mholach	2,759	841	Central Highlands
332	Ben Vrackie	2,759	841	East Highlands
333	Sgurr an Airgid	2,759	841	North West Glens
334	Brandon Peak	2,756	840	Ireland
335	Ben Rinnes	2,756	840	East Highlands
336	Broad Law	2,756	840	Southern Uplands
337	Beinn Trilleachan	2,755	840	Rannoch to Glencoe
338	Beinn Udlaidh	2,755	840	Rannoch to Glencoe
339	Sgurr Gaorsaic	2,752	839	North West Glens
340	Carn Chuinneag	2,750	838	North Highlands
341	Meallan nan Uan	2,749	838	North West Glens
342	Meall na h-Eilde	2,749	838	Far West Highlands
343	Sron a' Choire Chnapanich	2,746	837	Rannoch to Glencoe
344	Sgurr Cos na Breachd-laoidh	2,739	835	Far West Highlands
345	Purple Mountain	2,739	835	Ireland
346	Carn Dearg	2,736	834	Central Highlands
347	Creag nan Gabhar	2,736	834	East Highlands
348	Beinn Dearg	2,723	830	Rannoch to Glencoe

TOP 500 SUMMITS continued

	Name	Height (ft)	Height (m)	Chapter
349	Cadair Berwyn	2,723	830	Wales
350	Brown Cow Hill	2,721	829	East Highlands
351	Carn Mor	2,719	829	Far West Highlands
352	High Street	2,718	828	England
353	An Dun	2,713	827	East Highlands
354	Beenoskee	2,710	826	Ireland
355	Beinn Tarsuinn	2,710	826	Scottish Islands
356	Geal-charn Mor	2,703	824	Central Highlands
357	White Coomb	2,694	821	Southern Uplands
358	Benvane	2,694	822	South Highlands
359	Geal Charn	2,692	821	East Highlands
360	Beinn Dearg Bheag	2,690	820	North Highlands
361	Beinn Chaorach	2,685	818	Rannoch to Glencoe
362	Carn na Drochaide	2,685	818	East Highlands
363	Sgurr na Diollaid	2,684	818	North West Glens
364	Tonelagee	2,680	817	Ireland
365	Stob Coire Creagach	2,680	817	South Highlands
366	Carn Dearg	2,680	817	Central Highlands
367	Carn a' Chuilinn	2,677	816	Central Highlands
368	The Cheviot	2,674	815	England
369	Mweelrea	2,671	814	Ireland
370	An Sidhean	2,671	814	North West Glens
371	An Stac	2,671	814	Far West Highlands
372	Breabag	2,670	814	Far North Scotland
373	Corserine	2,669	814	Southern Uplands
374	Beinn Each	2,667	813	South Highlands
375	Sgor Mor	2,667	813	East Highlands
376	Askival	2,663	812	Scottish Islands
377	Carn na Saobhaidhe	2,660	811	Central Highlands

TOP 500 SUMMITS continued

Name	Height (ft)	Height (m)	Chapter
378 Waun Fach	2,660	811	Wales
379 Meall a' Bhuachaille	2,657	810	East Highlands
380 Creach Bheinn	2,656	810	Rannoch to Glencoe
381 Creag Mac Ranaich	2,654	809	South Highlands
382 Meall na Fearna	2,654	809	South Highlands
383 Sgurr Innse	2,654	809	Central Highlands
384 Hart Fell	2,651	808	Southern Uplands
385 Quinag – Sail Gharbh	2,651	808	Far North Scotland
386 Garbh-bheinn	2,650	808	Scottish Islands
387 High Stile	2,648	807	England
388 Monamenach	2,648	807	East Highlands
389 Creag Rainich	2,647	807	North Highlands
390 Nephin	2,646	806	Ireland
391 Beinn nam Fuaran	2,645	806	Rannoch to Glencoe
392 Ben Gulabin	2,645	806	East Highlands
393 Meall nan Subh	2,645	806	South Highlands
394 Beinn na h-Eaglaise	2,641	805	Far West Highlands
395 Carn Mor	2,639	804	East Highlands
396 Geal Charn	2,638	804	Far West Highlands
397 Coniston Old Man	2,635	803	England
398 The Sow of Atholl	2,634	803	Central Highlands
399 Ben Lugmore	2,634	803	Ireland
400 Beinn Bhreac-liath	2,633	803	Rannoch to Glencoe
401 Greenane	2,631	802	Ireland
402 Kirk Fell	2,631	802	England
403 Fan Brycheiniog	2,630	802	Wales
404 Meallan Liath Coire Mhic Dhughaill	2,627	801	Far North Scotland
405 Beinn Iaruinn	2,625	800	Central Highlands
406 Cranstackie	2,625	800	Far North Scotland

TOP 500 SUMMITS continued

	Name	Height (ft)	Height (m)	Chapter
407	Clisham	2,622	799	Scottish Islands
408	Pen Llithrig y Wrach	2,622	799	Wales
409	Cir Mhor	2,620	799	Scottish Islands
410	Am Bathach	2,618	798	North West Glens
411	Beinn Dronaig	2,615	797	North West Glens
412	Cairnsmore of Carsphairn	2,614	797	Southern Uplands
413	Beinn Bhan	2,612	796	Far West Highlands
414	Sgurr Coire Choinnichean	2,612	796	Far West Highlands
415	Mam na Gualainn	2,611	796	Central Highlands
416	Beinn Mhic-Mhonaidh	2,610	796	Rannoch to Glencoe
417	Sgurr an Utha	2,610	796	Far West Highlands
418	Mount Leinster	2,610	796	Ireland
419	Knockmealdown	2,605	794	Ireland
420	Carn Ealasaid	2,600	792	East Highlands
421	Beinn Leoid	2,599	792	Far North Scotland
422	Sgurr a' Chaorachain	2,598	792	North Highlands
423	Glas Bheinn	2,597	792	Central Highlands
424	Fauscoum	2,597	792	Ireland
425	Beinn Airigh Charr	2,595	791	North Highlands
426	Grisedale Pike	2,595	791	England
427	Druim nan Cnamh	2,592	790	North West Glens
428	Auchnafree Hill	2,589	789	South Highlands
429	Meall Dubh	2,585	788	North West Glens
430	Mickle Fell	2,585	788	England
431	Arkle	2,582	787	Far North Scotland
432	Beinn a' Chaisteil	2,582	787	North Highlands
433	Meall Tairneachan	2,582	787	South Highlands
434	The Brack	2,582	787	South Highlands
435	Carn na Nathrach	2,579	786	Far West Highlands

	Name	Height (ft)	Height (m)	Chapter
436	Beinn an Oir	2,576	785	Scottish Islands
437	Temple Hill	2,575	785	Ireland
438	Beinn na Caillich	2,575	785	Far West Highlands
439	Stumpa Duloigh	2,572	784	Ireland
440	Beinn Mhic Cedidh	2,569	783	Far West Highlands
441	Farragon Hill	2,569	783	South Highlands
442	Moel Hebog	2,566	782	Wales
443	Sgurr Dubh	2,566	782	North Highlands
444	Ainshval	2,562	781	Scottish Islands
445	Corryhabbie Hill	2,561	781	East Highlands
446	Sgurr Mhic Bharraich	2,561	781	North West Glens
447	Meall nam Maigheach	2,558	780	South Highlands
448	Glasgwm	2,557	779	Wales
449	Beinn Bheula	2,556	779	South Highlands
450	Mount Battock	2,554	778	East Highlands
451	Meall Horn	2,548	777	Far North Scotland
452	Red Screes	2,547	776	England
453	Glas Bheinn	2,546	776	Far North Scotland
454	Quinag – Sail Gorm	2,546	776	Far North Scotland
455	Meall na Leitreach	2,544	775	Central Highlands
456	Sgorr Craobh a' Chaorainn	2,543	775	Far West Highlands
457	Shalloch on Minnoch	2,543	775	Southern Uplands
458	Glamaig	2,542	775	Scottish Islands
459	Meall a' Phubuill	2,540	774	Far West Highlands
460	Beinn nan Caorach	2,539	774	Far West Highlands
461	Mullaghanattin	2,539	774	Ireland
462	Beinn Spionnaidh	2,534	772	Far North Scotland
463	Meall Lighiche	2,533	772	Rannoch to Glencoe
464	Coomacarrea	2,533	772	Ireland

	Name	Height (ft)	Height (m)	Chapter
465	Sheeffry Hills	2,533	772	Ireland
466	Beinn Stacath	2,531	771	South Highlands
467	Stob Coire a' Chearcaill	2,528	770	Far West Highlands
468	Moelwyn Mawr	2,527	770	Wales
469	Beinn a' Choin	2,525	770	South Highlands
470	Druim Tarsuinn	2,525	770	Far West Highlands
471	Cul Beag	2,523	769	Far North Scotland
472	Waun Rydd	2,523	769	Wales
473	Meallach Mhor	2,522	769	East Highlands
474	Carn Dearg	2,520	768	Central Highlands
475	Sail Mhor	2,516	767	North Highlands
476	Slieve Commedagh	2,516	767	Ireland
477	Beinn Liath Mhor a' Ghiubhais Li	2,513	766	North Highlands
478	Dun da Gaoithe	2,512	766	Scottish Islands
479	Fuar Bheinn	2,512	766	Far West Highlands
480	Braigh nan Uamhachan	2,510	765	Far West Highlands
481	Meall an Fhudair	2,508	764	South Highlands
482	Croagh Patrick	2,507	764	Ireland
483	Little Wyvis	2,507	764	North Highlands
484	Quinag – Spidean Coinich	2,507	764	Far North Scotland
485	Ben Loyal – An Caisteal	2,506	764	Far North Scotland
486	Stony Cove Pike	2,502	763	England
487	High Raise	2,500	762	England
488	Beinn na h-Uamha	2,500	762	Far West Highlands
489	Sgurr a' Chaorainn	2,497	761	Far West Highlands
490	Beinn Talaidh	2,497	761	Scottish Islands
491	Cnoc Coinnich	2,497	761	South Highlands
492	Beinn a' Chapuill	2,490	759	Far West Highlands
493	Carn an Tionail	2,490	759	Far North Scotland

LISTING

336

MUNROS NOT QUALIFYING FOR 500 LIST

Name	Height (ft)	Height (m)	Chapter
494 Shee of Ardtalnaig	2,490	759	South Highlands
495 Beinn Shiantaidh	2,485	757	Scottish Islands
496 Kippure	2,484	757	Ireland
497 Y Llethr	2,480	756	Wales
498 Cook's Cairn	2,479	756	East Highlands
499 Creag Dhubh	2,479	756	Central Highlands
500 Knockanaffrin	2,477	755	Ireland

THE NEXT TEN (JUST MISSED OUT!)

Name	Height (ft)	Height (m)	Chapter
501 Dale Head	2,470	753	England
502 The Stob	2,470	753	South Highlands
503 Beann	2,467	752	Ireland
504 Plynlimon	2,467	752	Wales
505 Moel Llyfnant	2,464	751	Wales
506 Errigal Mountain	2,464	751	Ireland
507 Meallan a' Chuail	2,461	750	Far North Scotland
508 Groban	2,457	749	North Highlands
509 Sgurr Choinich	2,457	749	Far West Highlands
510 Mona Gowan	2,456	749	East Highlands

MUNROS NOT QUALIFYING FOR 500 LIST

	Name	Height (ft)	Height (m)	Chapter
1	Sgor an Lochain Uaine (Angel's Peak)	4,127	1,258	East Highlands
2	Cairngorm	4,084	1,245	East Highlands
3	Aonach Mor	4,006	1,221	Central Highlands
4	Mam Sodhail	3,875	1,181	North West Glens
5	Derry Cairngorm	3,790	1,155	East Highlands
6	Carn a' Coire Boidheach	3,668	1,118	East Highlands
7	An Stuc	3,668	1,118	South Highlands
8	Stob Coire an Laoigh	3,662	1,116	Central Highlands
9	Aonach Beag	3,662	1,116	Central Highlands
9	Monadh Mor	3,652	1,113	East Highlands
11	Tom a' Choinich	3,649	1,112	North West Glens
12	Stob a' Choire Mheadhoin	3,626	1,105	Central Highlands
13	Beinn Ghlas	3,619	1,103	South Highlands
14	Beinn Eibhinn	3,616	1,102	Central Highlands
15	Stob Coire Sgreamhach	3,517	1,072	Rannoch to Glencoe
16	Cairn of Claise	3,491	1,064	East Highlands
17	An Teallach – Sgurr Fiona	3,478	1,060	North Highlands
18	Na Gruagaichean	3,465	1,056	Central Highlands
19	Stob Poite Coire Ardair	3,458	1,054	Central Highlands
20	Sgurr Fhuar-thuill	3,442	1,049	North West Glens
21	Carn an t-Sagairt Mor	3,435	1,047	East Highlands
22	Am Bodach* (Marilyn as drop is over 150m)	3,386	1,032	Central Highlands
23	Mullach Clach a' Blair	3,345	1,019	East Highlands
24	Carn an Tuirc	3,343	1,019	East Highlands
25	Cairn Bannoch	3,320	1,012	East Highlands
26	Carn Liath (Creag Meagaidh)	3,301	1,006	Central Highlands
27	The Devil's Point	3,294	1,004	East Highlands
28	Sgurr an Lochain	3,294	1,004	North West Glens
29	Sgurr na Carnach	3,288	1,002	North West Glens

	Name	Height (ft)	Height (m)	Chapter
30	Sail Chaorainn	3,288	1,002	North West Glens
31	Sgurr Choinnich	3,278	999	North West Glens
32	Stob Diamh	3,274	998	Rannoch to Glencoe
33	Broad Cairn	3,274	998	East Highlands
34	Carn nan Gobhar, Strathfarrar	3,255	992	North West Glens
35	Creag Leacach	3,240	987	East Highlands
36	Druim Shionnach	3,239	987	North West Glens
37	Conival	3,238	987	Far North Scotland
38	Mullach na Dheiragain	3,224	982	North West Glens
39	An Gearanach* (Marilyn as drop is over 150m)	3,222	982	Central Highlands
40	Creag Mhor	3,220	981	Rannoch to Glencoe
41	Stob Coire a' Chairn	3,219	981	Central Highlands
42	Maol Chinn-dearg	3,218	981	North West Glens
43	Stob Coire Sgriodain	3,213	979	Central Highlands
44	Meall nan Ceapraichean	3,206	977	North Highlands
45	A' Mharconaich	3,200	975	Central Highlands
46	Sgurr a' Ghreadaidh	3,192	973	Scottish Islands
47	Meall Garbh	3,176	968	Rannoch to Glencoe
48	Sgurr na Banachdich	3,166	965	Scottish Islands
49	Bruach na Frithe	3,143	958	Scottish Islands
50	Tolmount	3,143	958	East Highlands
51	Carn Ghluasaid	3,140	957	North West Glens
52	Tom Buidhe	3,140	957	East Highlands
53	Saileag	3,137	956	North West Glens
54	Buachaille Etive Mor – Stob na Broige	3,136	956	Rannoch to Glencoe
55	Beinn Liath Mhor Fannaich	3,130	954	North Highlands
56	Aonach Eagach – Meall Dearg	3,128	953	Rannoch to Glencoe
57	Meall Gorm	3,114	949	North Highlands

MUNROS NOT QUALIFYING FOR 500 LIST continued

	Name	Height (ft)	Height (m)	Chapter
58	Sgurr Mhic Choinnich	3,110	948	Scottish Islands
59	Creag a' Mhaim	3,107	947	North West Glens
60	Dreish	3,107	947	East Highlands
61	Beinn Tulaichean	3,104	946	South Highlands
62	Sgurr Dubh Mor	3,097	944	Scottish Islands
63	Beinn a' Chroin	3,085	940	South Highlands
64	Mullach nan Coirean	3,080	939	Central Highlands
65	A' Bhuidheanach Bheag	3,071	936	East Highlands
66	Am Basteir	3,066	934	Scottish Islands
67	Meall a' Chrasgaidh	3,064	934	North Highlands
68	The Cairnwell	3,061	933	East Highlands
69	Beinn Bhreac	3,055	931	East Highlands
70	A' Chailleach	3,051	930	Central Highlands
71	Mayar	3,045	928	East Highlands
72	Geal Charn	3,038	926	Central Highlands
73	Meall a' Choire Leith* (Marilyn as drop is over 150m)	3,038	926	South Highlands
74	Creag Pitridh	3,032	924	Central Highlands
75	Sgurr nan Eag	3,031	924	Scottish Islands
76	An Coileachan	3,028	923	North Highlands
77	Sgurr nan Each	3,028	923	North Highlands
78	An Socach (Glen Affric)	3,022	921	North West Glens
79	Carn Sgulain	3,018	920	Central Highlands
80	Sgurr a' Mhadaidh	3,012	918	Scottish Islands
81	Carn Aosda	3,009	917	East Highlands
82	Beinn a' Chleibh	3,005	916	South Highlands

INDEX OF MOUNTAIN COMPANIONS/PHOTOGRAPHERS

Bailey, Donald 58, 64, 65, 91, 161, 182, 237, 275, 280, 308
Bradwell, Jo 14, 24, 25, 26, 27, 46, 68, 268, 304
Cox, John 84, 85
Dadds, Marcus 249, 256
Dalton, Dave   143
Delamere, John   68
Dentith, Wayne   16
Dobson, Peter   97
Franks, Chris   97
Griffith, Ceryse 67, 71
Griffith, Cornell 67, 71, 306, 307
Holland, Yvonne   117
Hopkin, Nick   171
Jackson, Peter   308
Kachhela, Trusha 52, 67, 71, 97, 168
Keighley, John   24
Maddison, Stuart 84, 85
Mead, Graham   68
Miller, Alistair   14
Miller, Angie   14
Pattinson, Kyle 38, 268
Paton, David   314
Pyman, Ella 68, 112, 114, 115, 126, 208, 306
Pyman, Elspeth   126
Pyman, Mark   314
Pyman, Mike   126
Richardson, Neville 26, 27
Russell, Sean 48, 132
Shields, Colin 90, 100, 104, 108, 115, 122
Simon, Ian   308
Smith, Alex 6, 176
Smith, Charlotte   261
Smith, Daniel   308
Smith, Douglas   131
Smith, Helen   308
Smith, Helen E.   261
Smith, James 6, 36, 176, 309
Smith, Julian 131, 133
Smith, Lucy   261
Smith, Tom 4, 126
Sondhi, Kiran   144
Storey, Chris   275
Thomas-Smith, Heather 29, 32, 79, 88, 91, 93, 105, 112, 118, 119, 147, 149, 151, 155,
                                         185, 219, 226, 231, 240, 243, 246, 255, 259, 264, 270, 274, 275,
                                         301, 316, 317
Waugh, Reg 170, 191, 270
Wilkinson, Keith   101
Wood, Chris 96, 98, 106, 115, 133, 160, 169, 173, 197, 227, 233, 234, 238,
                                         248, 257, 277, 284

Dogs: Bracken, Bronte, Corrie, Kizzy, Mist.

BIBLIOGRAPHY

Hamish Brown, *A Mountain Walk*
Alan Dawson, *Relative Hills of Britain*
Mark Jackson, *More Relative Hills of Britain*
ED Clements, *The Hewitts and Marilyns of Ireland*
The Scottish Mountaineering Club Guide – *The Munros*
The Scottish Mountaineering Club Guide – *The Corbetts*
The Scottish Mountaineering Club Guide – *The Grahams and the Donalds*
Andrew Dempster, *The Grahams*
Paddy Dillon, *The Mountains of Ireland – A Guide to Walking the Summits*
A Wainwright, *A Pictorial Guide to the Lakeland Fells, Books 1 to 7*
Ken Wilson/Richard Gilbert, *The Big Walks*